Narrating War and Peace in Africa

Rochester Studies in African History and the Diaspora

Toyin Falola, Senior Editor
The Frances Higginbotham Nalle Centennial Professor in History
University of Texas at Austin

(ISSN: 1092-5228)

A complete list of titles in the Rochester Studies in African History and the Diaspora, in order of publication, may be found at the end of this book.

Narrating War and Peace in Africa

Edited by Toyin Falola and
Hetty ter Haar

UNIVERSITY OF ROCHESTER PRESS

Copyright © 2010 by the Editors and Contributors

All Rights Reserved. Except as permitted under current legislation, no part of this work may be photocopied, stored in a retrieval system, published, performed in public, adapted, broadcast, transmitted, recorded, or reproduced in any form or by any means, without the prior permission of the copyright owner.

First published 2010
Transferred to digital printing and reprinted in paperback 2017

University of Rochester Press
668 Mt. Hope Avenue, Rochester, NY 14620, USA
www.urpress.com
and Boydell & Brewer Limited
PO Box 9, Woodbridge, Suffolk IP12 3DF, UK
www.boydellandbrewer.com

ISSN: 1092-5228
hardcover ISBN-13: 978-1-58046-330-0
paperback ISBN-13: 978-1-58046-913-5

Library of Congress Cataloging-in-Publication Data

Africa Conference (Tex.) (2008 : University of Texas at Austin)
 Narrating war and peace in Africa / edited by Toyin Falola and Hetty ter Haar.
  p. cm. — (Rochester studies in African history and the diaspora, ISSN 1092-5228 ; v. 47)
 Papers presented at the Africa Conference held March 28–30, 2008, at the University of Texas at Austin.
 Includes bibliographical references and index.
 ISBN 978-1-58046-330-0 (hardcover : alk. paper) 1. War in mass media—Congresses. 2. War in literature—Congresses. 3. Peace in literature—Congresses. 4. Mass media and war—Africa, Sub-Saharan—Congresses. 5. War—Press coverage—Africa, Sub-Saharan—Congresses. 6. Mass media and peace—Africa, Sub-Saharan—Congresses. 7. Peace—Press coverage—Africa, Sub-Saharan—Congresses. 8. Stereotypes (Social psychology) in mass media—Africa, Sub-Saharan—Congresses. 9. Africa, Sub-Saharan—In mass media—Congresses. I. Falola, Toyin. II. Haar, Hetty ter. III. Title.
 P96.W352A34 2008
 070.4'49967—dc22

2010016236

Cover art: Aderonke Adesanya, *Hack Down the Enemy*. Acrylic and charcoal on paper, 12" x 8 1/2", 2009.

To the memory of Nelly ter Haar-Meulenkamp and Margaret Kumbuka

Contents

Preface ix

Introduction: Narrating War and Peace in Africa 1
Toyin Falola and Hetty ter Haar

Part One: Struggles for Independence

1 Wars of Words: Enlisting Colonial Languages in the Fight for Independence in Africa 21
Ann Albuyeh

2 Alternative Representations of War in Africa: *New Times and Ethiopia News* Coverage of the 1935–41 Italian-Ethiopian War 44
Metasebia Woldemariam

3 All's Well in the Colony: Newspaper Coverage of the Mau Mau Movement, 1952–56 56
Melissa Tully

Part Two: Ungendering Conflicts, Engendering Peace

4 Pedagogies of Pain: Teaching "Women, War, and Militarism in Africa" 79
Alicia C. Decker

5 Women and War: A Kenyan Experience 98
Pamela Wadende

6 Mass Rape as a Weapon of War in the Eastern DRC 113
Jonathan Zilberg

7 Mozambique: The Gendered Impact of Warfare 141
Zermarie Deacon

Part Three: Narrative Strategies and Visions of Peace

8 Acting as Heroic: Creativity and Political Violence in Tuareg Theater in Northern Mali — 155
   Susan Rasmussen

9 Representations of War and Peace in Selected Works of Ben Okri — 180
   Kayode Omoniyi Ogunfolabi

10 Visions of War, Testaments of Peace: The "Burden" of Sierra Leone — 195
   Cheryl Sterling

Part Four: The Duty to Remember

11 (Re)Writing the Massacre of Thiaroye — 231
   Sabrina Parent

12 In Search of Lost Kabyles in Mehdi Lallaoui's *La colline aux oliviers* — 241
   Aména Moïnfar

13 "Lament for the Casualties": The Nigerian War of 1967–70 and the Poetry of John Pepper Clark-Bekederemo — 271
   Michael Sharp

Bibliography — 281

List of Contributors — 309

Index — 313

Preface

The chapters in *Narrating War and Peace in Africa* emerged from the eighth international Africa Conference held at the University of Texas at Austin, March 28–30, 2008. The conference—convened by Toyin Falola and coordinated by Roy Doron—had the theme "Wars and Conflicts in Africa." In the conference program, Toyin Falola notes that although human conflict is universal, wars and conflicts in Africa "seem at times to engulf the entire continent." While the postcolonial state and global politics determine the ways in which wars are fought and conflicts resolved in Africa, Africa's past, geography, and people need to be taken into account as well.

The emphasis in *Narrating War and Peace in Africa* is specifically on representations of war and peace in Africa, and the volume aims to undo the negative stereotypes that abound in relation to Africa in general and to its wars and conflicts in particular. As the contributors come from various academic and scholarly backgrounds, the volume is multi- and interdisciplinary in scope. The disciplines and fields of study include history, women's studies, linguistics, communication and media studies, journalism, (comparative) literature, African and African diaspora studies, anthropology, human relations, and adult education. The bibliography following the chapters will guide readers to many books, articles, DVDs, and websites relevant to the theme of representing war and peace in Africa.

The editors would like to thank the anonymous readers and Jessica Achberger for reviewing the chapters and for their insightful and invaluable comments as this volume was being prepared.

Introduction

Narrating War and Peace in Africa

Toyin Falola and Hetty ter Haar

This volume examines war and peace in Africa—mainly in the twentieth century and up to the present time—with an emphasis on the manner of their representation. Such an approach is justified and called for, as too many Western representations tend to reduce Africa and its inhabitants to negative generalized stereotypes. These stereotypes are found everywhere: from philosophy to historiography and popular culture. According to Hegel (1770–1831), Africa "is no historical part of the World,"[1] while Hugh Trevor-Roper in 1963 did not hesitate to write about the African past as the "unrewarding gyrations of barbarous tribes in picturesque but irrelevant corners of the globe."[2] These days, postcolonial imagery of the Third World is presented as a spectacle:[3] "Next to Bacardi-rum beaches, images of suffering, starvation and bloodshed circulate through the media networks of the world's electronic Colosseum."[4] If, therefore, general representations of Africa are problematic, representations of wars and conflicts in Africa are even more so.

Although wars and conflicts appear to typify the African continent in the second half of the twentieth century, we have to remember that "the whole of human history includes wars, massacres, and every kind of torture and cruelty."[5] However, in postindependence Africa, there have been, and still are, numerous wars and violent conflicts, for example, in Nigeria, Rwanda, Burundi, Zaire/the Democratic Republic of Congo (DRC), Somalia, Sierra Leone, Uganda, Mozambique, South Africa, and Chad,[6] and more recently in Sudan, Zimbabwe, and Kenya. Many of these conflicts culminate(d) in civil wars, and so it is that, with a few exceptions, "the history of the gains of independence now appears distant."[7] These gains appear to be distant because "the nation-state has proved a burden, capitalism a failure, and liberal democracy elusive."[8] As there are no credible alternatives to these Western legacies, the question is,

How can the various ethnic groups accept the notion of the nation-state? If an ethnic group operates like a mini-nation within a modern country, how can the clashes between mini-states be prevented? A mini-nation continues to use its collective history, identity, language, and other aspects of culture to strengthen ethnicity and compete with other groups within the new country.[9]

Therefore, in the postindependence era, "the pain is what a new generation knows, the agony is what the intellectuals talk about, and the crisis is what Afro-pessimists and the Western media are happy to report."[10] James Campbell aptly describes Western reporters as follows:

> As Africa's agonies multiplied, a legion of journalists descended on the continent. Though they carried satellite phones and fax machines rather than maxim guns and Bibles, these reporters were the lineal descendants of the explorers and missionaries of the nineteenth century, the latest participants in the long tradition of Western writing about Africa. Like their pith-helmeted predecessors, they sought out the continent's most harrowing corners, creating through their daily dispatches a new Dark Continent narrative to edify and horrify readers in their comfortable homes in Europe and the United States.[11]

However, in order to reach a balanced representation, it is necessary to distinguish between anticolonial violence and postindependence violence—the former being considered to possess a greater degree of legitimacy.[12] Indeed, Fanon's dictum, that "At the level of individuals, violence is a cleansing force," seems hardly to be applicable in the context of Rwanda in 1994: anticolonial violence at the national level did not result "in the liquidation of regionalism and of tribalism."[13] Ali Mazrui elaborates on the point, noting that "the seeds of the postcolonial wars themselves lie in the sociological mess which colonialism created in Africa by destroying old methods of conflict-resolution without creating effective [substitutes] in their place."[14] The worst postcolonial conflicts are ethnic, and, Mazrui adds, "so-called 'tribal.'"[15]

Jonathan Glover, referring to hostilities in the Middle East, Cyprus, Ireland, Lebanon, and elsewhere, explains that

> we call these hostilities tribal, sometimes thinking of this as metaphorical. The common view is that real tribes are in Africa, where the same tribal hatreds have been fought out in battles since the Stone Age. Calling the conflict in Northern Ireland tribal is a kind of rebuke: you are behaving like primitive tribes in Africa. But this picture is wrong. These other conflicts are tribal in more than metaphor: in Ireland, Yugoslavia and elsewhere they are as literal enactments of tribal hostility as those in Africa. The picture of Africa is wrong too. Some of the tribal divisions are recent creations. The origins of African tribal war and massacre are more complex than the "ancient hatred" accounts allow.[16]

While Jonathan Glover, in his discussion of particular conflicts outside Africa, makes the point that these outside conflicts are tribal in nature and identical to many violent conflicts and civil wars in Africa, we do not endorse the use of the terms "tribe" and "tribal." Expressions derived from the adjective "ethnic" are preferred, as these encompass common national, racial, religious, linguistic, cultural, or indeed so-called tribal backgrounds or origins.[17] This preference is not a matter of political correctness: the term "tribe" is simply too limited in scope and constitutes a misrepresentation in itself.[18]

Therefore, representations of wars in Africa, viewed from the perspective of primitive tribes—and therefore deemed savage and barbaric—result in more stereotypical representations, that is, in more *negative* stereotypical representations. The Cairo speech of President Obama is instructive here: on June 5, 2009, he said, "I consider it part of my responsibility as president of the United States to fight against negative stereotypes of Islam wherever they appear."[19] Scholars and academics have a similar responsibility regarding the fight against negative stereotypes of Africa. Such negative stereotyping would be reinforced if the focus of the present volume were solely on postindependence conflicts. However, the volume achieves a representational balance by examining wars and conflicts during the colonial era as well.

Considering the representational challenges vis-à-vis Africa in general and its wars and conflicts in particular, it should come as no surprise that representations of African women in times of war and conflict are especially problematic. Too often, African women fall victim to such stereotypical representations—whether put forward by Western scholars or feminists or by male African writers. As Nkiru Nzegwu contends, "Prevailing definitions of gender in African studies have come from disciplines located within the Western body of knowledge."[20] It may be useful to remember Carole Boyce Davies, writing in 1986 that African male writers did not necessarily get the representation of women right, any more than Westerners did. Boyce Davies argues that

> [they] sought to present the truth of their cultures as a direct rebuttal to the distortions perpetuated by white/colonial missionaries, anthropologists and sociologists. In their writing, the image of women was in some ways and to an extent rehabilitated, but in many cases, new sexist stereotypes were created and older African ones went unchallenged.[21]

Such misrepresentations are also present in the historiography. Gloria Chuku, for example, notes that

> the distortion and/or omission of the indispensable contribution of women to the African nationalist movements may result from data that have been almost

exclusively provided by males, whether Europeans or Africans. These sources have created the false idea that nationalist movements and politics in Africa were mainly male concerns.[22]

It is, of course, a positive development that the role of women during struggles for independence is now receiving more attention, as evidenced by Chuku's remarks. It is also probable that women and children are as vulnerable now in situations of war and violent conflict as they have always been. The chapters on gender in part 2 are unequivocal in demonstrating the vulnerability of women in times of war. However, they also examine the strategies women adopt in order to cope in war situations, and, equally important, to recover once the war is over. Rebuilding their lives is especially difficult for those women who have been victims of rape as a weapon of war. Here another important point relating to women as victims of war presents itself, namely, that too often representations are made on behalf of victims rather than the victims, men and women, being allowed to speak for themselves, as Cheryl Sterling argues in chapter 10. Moreover, there is always the danger that Western programs designed to help victims do so by using culturally inappropriate means—a point made by Zermarie Deacon in chapter 7.

While parts 1 and 2 of this volume concentrate on the factual, the focus of parts 3 and 4 is on fictional and creative representations of war and peace in Africa, although the chapters in parts 3 and 4 also provide the historical context of the conflicts they discuss. The chapters here are thus illustrative of the Yoruba god Ogun, who symbolizes the creative-destructive principle.[23] Wars in Africa, as elsewhere, are not only destructive but result in creative expressions as well. Thus, the chapters in parts 3 and 4, like the other chapters, contribute to the reversal of any stereotypical notions of war and peace in Africa and, most important of all, will make sure these wars and their victims are not forgotten, long after the news reports have been.

Part 1: Struggles for Independence

The focus of part 1 is on struggles for independence—in general and in relation to the Italian-Ethiopian War and the Mau Mau movement. In chapter 1, "Wars of Words: Enlisting Colonial Languages in the Fight for Independence in Africa," Ann Albuyeh explores the link between language and identity and reaches a somewhat unexpected conclusion. Here the role of language is set in the context of the anticolonial struggles in Africa, with particular reference to the French and English languages. To Ngugi wa Thiong'o, the imposition of the colonizers' languages "was crucial to the domination of the mental universe of the colonised."[24] He abandoned writing in English and reverted to his mother tongue, Gikuyu, in 1986. Ngugi believes that Gikuyu, "a Kenyan language, an African language, is part and parcel of the anti-imperialist struggles of Kenyan and African peoples."[25] He is referring to the impact of colonialism on languages and cultural identities in Africa, or to what Anthony Appiah calls "the search for authenticity."[26] Albuyeh contends that, while the debate over whether European languages are adequate to express African cultures, values, and perspectives continues, European colonizers did not anticipate the subversive potential of the purportedly superior education they brought to Africa.

Albuyeh traces the trajectory of linguistic communities from precolonial times to the era of independence, making the point that the use of European languages by the educated elite during the anticolonial struggles made the relationship between language and identity less straightforward than the research on linguistic communities suggests. The new Western-educated middle class envisioned its role in a modern state, in contrast to the earlier opponents of colonialism who advocated a return to older traditions. In the struggle for independence, emerging leaders such as Kwame Nkrumah used European languages. As Nkrumah interacted with other Africans who were to take on leadership roles in the anticolonial struggle, European languages became lingua francas.[27] Albuyeh explains how these languages were used to establish national newspapers, youth movements, political parties, Pan-African conferences, and the Organization of African Unity. Thus, "the elite became not just the consumer of culture, but the creator of new ones."[28] At the time, this use of European languages was not seen as contradictory or unsuitable: on the contrary, European languages were wielded as a weapon—the English language was ultimately used as a weapon to conquer the British Empire.

Continuing the exploration of anticolonial resistance and colonial aggression, the chapters by Metasebia Woldemariam and Melissa Tully examine two specific violent conflicts, namely, the 1935–41 Italian-Ethiopian War and the 1952–56 Mau Mau uprising in Kenya. These two chapters complement one another and contrast two forms of representation, that is, mainstream news reporting on the Mau Mau and alternative media reporting on the Italian-Ethiopian War. The Italian invasion of Ethiopia was all the more poignant as the country had until then managed to remain independent, which "became a source of pride and hope for millions of Africans all over the world."[29] Once Ethiopia was invaded by Italy, neither European countries nor the League of Nations adopted a forceful stance, which brought into relief the dangers of imperialism and of fascism.[30] The participants in the Mau Mau revolt consisted mainly of landless Kikuyu peasants, but beyond its primary aim of land recovery, the movement adopted a broader nationalist, anticolonial stance.[31] The colonial authorities, failing to appreciate the extent of the insurgents' discontent, denounced the movement "as evil and barbaric."[32]

6 *Introduction*

In chapter 2, "Alternative Representations of War in Africa: *New Times and Ethiopia News* Coverage of the 1935–41 Italian-Ethiopian War" by Metasebia Woldemariam, the theme of anti-imperialism is important, as it was in chapter 1. Woldemariam examines the manner in which the *New Times and Ethiopia News* (*NT&EN*)—an independent weekly newspaper largely dedicated to the Ethiopian cause—covered the 1935–41 Italian-Ethiopian War. She also explains the dilemma faced by the mainstream Euro-American media on how to reconcile Western support for Ethiopia—Italy's invasion of a member state of the League of Nations could not be condoned—with Europe's colonialism and America's racial segregation.

The *New Times and Ethiopian News* was first published by Sylvia Pankhurst, the British suffragist, in 1936, when she realized that the letters she was writing to newspapers did little to keep Ethiopia in the news. While mainstream reporting was confronted with the representational dilemma as indicated earlier on, the *New Times and Ethiopian News* came out in support of Ethiopia and adopted a firm antifascist stance. It may appear that *NT&EN*'s anti-imperialist and Pan-African position was merely an example of unconventional news reporting, but, as Woldemariam argues, *NT&EN* should be viewed as an alternative media outlet. Drawing on the critical work on alternative media by Nina Eliasoph, Robert McChesney, Chris Atton, John Downing, and James Hamilton, Woldemariam establishes the reasons why *NT&EN* should be seen as an alternative newspaper. As "alternative media are defined by their content as well as by their mode of production," readers will also "act as writers, editors, and distributors." Although the *NT&EN* contributors might take up differing ideological positions, for example, as suffragists and Pan-Africanists and so forth, they all adopted "a pro-League, pro-Ethiopia, or antifascist stance." The chapter pays particular attention to *NT&EN*'s role in the Pan-African movement: to Pan-Africanists, the Italian invasion was not only an act of aggression against Ethiopia but an act of aggression against everyone of African origin.

In chapter 3, "All's Well in the Colony: Newspaper Coverage of the Mau Mau Movement, 1952–56," Melissa Tully sets out to give a systematic analysis of news coverage of the Mau Mau. She examines this news coverage in relation to the social and cultural climate in America, Great Britain, and Kenya during a critical period for the Mau Mau movement. The author concentrates on an analysis of the *Times* of London and the *New York Times* because of these two newspapers' different relationships to Kenya. She conducted a content analysis of 342 stories from the two newspapers over the period 1952 to 1956.

After providing a historical overview of the emergence of Mau Mau, the chapter examines the official British response, which focused on long-held fears of Africans and prejudices about them. The Mau Mau was represented as a savage and barbaric movement, based on primitive religion, while political motivations were ignored. Coverage of the Mau Mau disregarded the political motivations of the movement, instead focusing primarily on violence. The *New York Times* represented the Mau Mau as a movement of terrorists, dismissing political motivations, which suggests "that the coverage lacked key information necessary for understanding the Kenyan situation." Although the *Times* reports were more accurate than those of the *New York Times*, they too did not get beyond Mau Mau's violence and the official response. Not much appears to have changed since that time, as James Campbell points out: "The African stories that captivated Western readers in the 1990s, were, almost without exception, violent—military coups, civil war, ethnic cleansing."[33] Finally, Tully makes the point that coverage of Mau Mau needs to be seen in the context of decolonization and the demise of the British Empire: a context in which "the government needed to reassure its citizens that all was well in the colony to keep them committed to the colonial cause." The reassurance offered by the British government turned out to be empty: Kenya gained independence in 1963.

Part 2: Ungendering Conflicts, Engendering Peace

In part 2, we move to representations of women in relation to war and peace in Africa. It is too easy to represent women only as victims of war, which is why it is crucial to pay attention to their coping strategies as well. However, it is equally important to move beyond war to the stage of peace building and reconstruction, as the chapters that follow indicate. While women remain especially vulnerable in times of war as demonstrated in part 2, the ratification of the Protocol on the Rights of Women in Africa in 2008 by twenty-three countries is promising.[34] According to Catharine MacKinnon, the protocol "rejects violence against women in 'private or public life in peacetime and during situations of armed conflicts or of war.'"[35] MacKinnon notes that the African protocol is "far from being paralyzed by cultural differences or intimidated by cultural relativism. . . . It puts Africa on a par with Latin America on the question of violence against women and *in the lead on women's equality in world law.*"[36] Whereas Simone de Beauvoir observed that "representation of the world, like the world itself, is the work of men," in the protocol, women represent themselves.[37]

Chapter 4, "Pedagogies of Pain: Teaching 'Women, War, and Militarism in Africa,'" could be said to present the overall theme of this volume, bringing into sharp relief the representational dilemmas concerning war and peace in Africa. Alicia C. Decker addresses the questions, "How does one teach about the brutal realities of war without contributing to the so-called pornography of violence? . . . Are there constructive ways to educate students about war and violence without completely demoralizing them in the process?" The author examines some of the ethical and pedagogical challenges that she faced in the context of teaching about war and militarism in a women's studies classroom at a small liberal arts college in the southeastern United States. This is indeed a challenge, considering that "America's awareness of Africa focuses overwhelmingly on the victims"[38] and that "Americans tend to think of Africa's wars as remote from [their] history and irrelevant to [their] interests."[39] The author not only presents a reflection on her experience of teaching such a course (in 2007) but offers a variety of relevant pedagogical strategies as well. Ultimately, the author hopes that her discussion will result in "a broader dialogue about the politics of representing violence in the classroom."

Decker observes that the students lacked basic knowledge about Africa. Here too there was the danger posed by negative stereotypes of Africans as being essentially "savage" or "brutal." The students, therefore, had to familiarize themselves with the geography of the African continent, and, through films, novels, and memoirs, with its cultural diversity. When Decker realized that the texts and films were having a profound effect on the students, she wondered if she had completely immobilized students "by overwhelming them with graphic depictions of violence day after day." Decker even considers the possibility that she might have reinforced the stereotypical representations instead of dispelling them as she had set out to do. The students were also required to follow news reports on conflict-related issues in Africa. The author suspects that "if the assignment had focused specifically on global peace-building initiatives (versus peace and conflict more generally), students would not have felt so overwhelmed by violence." These reflections are followed by a description of the course itself, with particular reference to women, children, and feminism, while the course material is usefully provided in the appendices.

In chapter 5, "Women and War: A Kenyan Experience," Pamela Wadende discusses the role of women in Kenya during the Mau Mau rebellion, during cattle-raiding conflicts, and during the conflict following the 2007 presidential election. This last conflict unequivocally demonstrates that "tribal" conflicts are emphatically not a matter of ancient hatreds. Wadende argues that Kenyan women have played important roles in these three violent conflicts and that a proper representation of women's roles is important in order not to underestimate their contributions to Kenyan society. The chapter adopts a "womanist" rather than a feminist perspective and highlights women's traditional and nontraditional roles during wars and violent conflicts. According to Wadende, the more traditional roles of women as carers remain crucial to the well-being of society in general but are especially important in times of violent conflict. This means that the discussion does not focus only on the active involvement of women in the anticolonial struggle—looking after a family in times of violent conflict is in itself a heroic feat, but one that is not often acknowledged.

As the author employs a narratological approach, the emphasis is specifically on the stories of individual women as told by the women themselves: for example, the story told by Wambui Otieno, which covers her role in the Mau Mau movement but also her role as a mother and carer. Wadende always places these stories in the broader context of the specific conflicts in which the women were involved. Given the author's focus on women's coping strategies in times of conflict, her discussion of the role of *chama*—Swahili for "association" or "society"—in both Kenya and the Kenyan diaspora is especially relevant. The chapter concludes with the observation that while women now head some of the country's ministries, which would have been impossible less than ten years ago, "their role as mothers and carers remains just as crucial as it has always been."

In chapter 6, "Mass Rape as a Weapon of War in the Eastern DRC," Jonathan Zilberg demonstrates that many women have to cope with mass rape as a weapon of war, as well as with the physical and mental consequences of that rape. Zilberg writes specifically with the Africanist academic community in mind, to encourage active engagement within universities. The Internet and other media outlets play a huge role in garnering support for the various campaigns that aim to end the use of rape as a weapon of war in the Democratic Republic of Congo. Another aim of these campaigns is to alleviate the suffering—mental and physical—of the victims. Some of the initiatives Zilberg mentions are the Congo Global Action Project, the ENOUGH and STAND campaigns, Friends of the Congo, the Harvard Humanitarian Initiative, and the HEAL Africa campaign.

Zilberg finds in these campaigns a parallel with the Congo Reform Association of nearly a hundred years ago and notes that "the public sphere appears to be far in advance of the academy in awareness and engagement." On the other hand, as Zilberg notes, the social sciences are extremely valuable when it comes to comprehending the background and the nature of the violence. Drawing on reports by, for example, the *Guardian*, the *New York Times*, Human Rights Watch, the Integrated Regional Information Network (IRIN), the International Crisis Group (ICG), and the United Nations, Zilberg sees no reason for optimism about the situation in the DRC. The incidence of rape has become endemic, having spread from armies to militias into the civilian population, that is, into nonmartial contexts.

Zermarie Deacon begins chapter 7, "Mozambique: The Gendered Impact of Warfare," with the observation that "there is still a tendency to overlook women's experiences of warfare in favor of a male-centered paradigm that governs responses to survivors of armed conflict." Deacon sets out to address the gap between social science and practice. To this end, she carried out a qualitative investigation of factors that helped Mozambican women to recover once the recent war was over. She gathered data through semistructured interviews with forty-seven women from northern Mozambique who had lived through the war. Apart from providing a better understanding of these factors as they relate to the women of the area, the analysis may also be useful with regard to the recovery of women in other developing nations emerging from warfare.

Deacon discusses the gendered impact of war, and then specifically the war in Mozambique (1976–92) between the FRELIMO government and the South African–supported RENAMO. After the war, women were found to be suffering from psychological, physical, and sociocultural symptoms of trauma. The forty-seven women who were interviewed considered themselves to have recovered from the war, after which they had found support at all levels of the social system. Deacon emphasizes the importance of the availability of culturally appropriate resources and indigenous interpretations of distress and well-being, which turned out to be particularly pertinent to the postwar recovery process for both individual women and their communities. In her conclusion, the author discusses the implications of her findings for future policies and practice. In order to empower women, it is essential to strengthen their access to economic resources and to support their postwar access to the rights they have now formally gained. Moreover, it is crucial to listen to what the women themselves have to say about their experiences. In addition, their reintegration into the community is critical, especially for those women who have been raped by enemy soldiers during the war.

Part 3: Narrative Strategies and Visions of Peace

The works analyzed in part 3 demonstrate the link between aesthetics and war, conflict, and peace, whether in literary texts, film, photography, or theater. The three chapters in part 3 examine creative expressions in Mali and Nigeria and in relation to the civil war in Sierra Leone. Chapter 10 is also a critique of the way Hollywood tends to fetishize Africa and its wars and conflicts, thus continuing the tradition of negative stereotypes.

In chapter 8, "Acting as Heroic: Creativity and Political Violence in Tuareg Theater in Northern Mali," Susan Rasmussen makes reference to the oral, but also scripted, culture of Tamajaq-speaking Tuareg communities of northern Mali. The chapter is based on the author's 2006 project on theatrical performance, modernity, and memory, and it focuses on performance in the town of Kidal. Rasmussen examines plays called *des sketches* and actors called *ibaraden*, a Tamajaq term for "courageous (brave) people" or "notables." Adopting an interdisciplinary approach involving anthropology, history, and aesthetics/performance, Rasmussen addresses the question of why the term *ibaraden* should have the meanings referred to above, and how these are "historically, socially, and culturally constructed." She examines the manner in which the actors' experience of violence shapes their artistic creativity, observing that while aesthetics may be therapeutic they may also be appropriated by the central state and NGOs.

Rasmussen provides historical and ethnographic background on the Tuareg, with particular reference to the town of Kidal and its cultural heritage, and the effects that outbreaks of armed conflict—between the national army of Mali and Tuareg rebels—have on the inhabitants in general and on actors in particular. In her detailed discussion of actors, performance, and verbal art in Tuareg society, the author makes the point that Tuareg actors and acting have to be approached "from the more general verbal art performance heritage." If the analysis contributes to anthropological theories of performance, memory, and narrative in a wider context, these performances contest, but also reproduce, cultural ideologies of power. The "narratives of nationhood" offered, for example, by the actors and the plays "also encode resistance to the state and other bureaucracies." Many performances, therefore, display a "merging of aesthetics with sociopolitical concerns." Rasmussen argues that the sketches and plays "narrate, but also critique, nationhood," just as the "'courageous notables' critique and assert alternative identities and 'scripts' in their creativity."

In chapter 9, "Representations of War and Peace in Selected Works of Ben Okri," Kayode Omoniyi Ogunfolabi examines Ben Okri's short story "Laughter beneath the Bridge" from *Incidents at the Shrine* (1986) and Okri's novella *Astonishing the Gods* (1995). The short story narrates the experience of a ten-year-old boy during the Nigerian civil war (1967–70). *Astonishing the Gods* is not a war narrative as such, but it does offer a vision of peace. In both texts, language plays an important role, but while in "Laughter beneath the Bridge" language serves as the instrument used to determine the speaker's ethnic background, in the novella all linguistic differentiation has disappeared. Ogunfolabi first sketches the historical background to the Nigerian civil war and gives a brief overview of some of the literary works that have the war as their theme. In his discussion of "Laughter beneath the Bridge," Ogunfolabi follows Okri by concentrating on the divisive effects that language may have in relation to ethnic profiling. The term "Yamarin" in the story illustrates the point: "Yamarin," according to Ogunfolabi, is a derogatory expression used to refer to Igbo people but also to ethnic minorities in eastern Nigeria. In *Astonishing the Gods*, ethnic designations no longer play a role: the protagonist communicates with others in a manner that is "beyond words," and thus the limitations imposed by language disappear. In order to appreciate the novella, it is necessary to be aware that this is a narrative that fits into the tradition of utopian writing, while it also significantly deviates from this tradition.

Ogunfolabi, while acknowledging the fictional nature of Okri's solution to the problems posed by ethnicity in Africa, discusses the concept of ethnicity in relation to identity and notes that, following Amartya Sen, ethnicity is only one aspect of a person's identity. Rather than erasing the existence of ethnicity in the real world, it might be possible, as Patrick Chabal and Jean-Pascal Daloz discuss in *Africa Works,* to adopt ethnicity as the foundation myth for Africa. If ethnicity were no longer to play the role it does now, this would obviously be a positive development for everyone, but especially for women. "Laughter beneath the Bridge" and the chapters on gender in part 2 of this volume demonstrate the extent to which being a woman is critical in wars and conflicts—but let us not forget that being a woman can be just as critical in noncombat, "everyday" life.

In chapter 10, "Visions of War, Testaments of Peace: The 'Burden' of Sierra Leone," Cheryl Sterling examines the "ethos of Empire" as reflected in postcolonial representations—visual and textual—of the civil war in Sierra Leone. The analysis focuses on examples from three different media: the films *Blood Diamond* (2006) and *Ezra* (2006); the text *A Long Way Gone* (2007) by Ishmael Beah; and the e-book *Don't Let Me Die* (2005) by Adisa Andwele (ÁJA). The chapter sets out to critique "the paternalistic, problematic vision of Africa inherited through the discourse of the white man's burden, reflected in the film *Blood Diamond,* by debunking its representational myths about the continent." These "representational myths" are similar to James Campbell's "inherited discourses" regarding Africa;[40] to Pieterse's discussion of Western hegemony; and to the concept of stereotypes—defined as oversimplified mental images—and the representation of "otherness."[41] Sterling argues that Hollywood fetishizes Africa and African conflicts, thus subjecting the viewer to yet another ethnographic spectacle, while at the same time perpetuating the "ethos of Empire," as exemplified by the film *Blood Diamond.*

Western human rights narratives, as in the stance adopted by *Blood Diamond,* establish "a problematic pattern of having the privileged speak *for* rather than *with* the oppressed." Black filmmakers, as in the case of the maker of *Ezra,* may be considered to be "rewriting their own narratives." The detailed and insightful analysis of the films, the text, and the e-book is placed in a broader context by the explication of numerous views from other thinkers and critics, such as Stuart Hall, Ania Loomba, and Achille Mbembe. The chapter concludes that the narratives of *Ezra, A Long Way Gone,* and *Don't Let Me Die* demand that "we face ourselves and our responses, whether they generate concrete action or more passivity, not just in reaction to the texts or the images, but in reaction to the realness of the world."

Part 4: The Duty to Remember

The chapters in part 4 concentrate in various ways on memory, remembrance, and reconciliation, but also on the rewriting of history. Niyi Osundare, the Nigerian poet, makes some apt observations regarding writers and memory: first, memory is a complex phenomenon that varies in degree and intensity from writer to writer.[42] Second, Osundare distinguishes between

> passive memory which is basically a reservoir of impressions, mostly residual, mostly dormant, retained by the individual or community, and active memory, which is those impressions in dynamic recall.[43]

However, Osundare maintains that human memory is not perfect, and that "many obstacles litter the road between memory and remembering," which is how he arrives at the issues of memory manipulation and selective remembrance.[44] Literature, nevertheless, possesses a humanistic potential because of

> its ability to create alternative realities, to push further the frontiers of quotidian actuality through a relentless thrust of fresh imagination, its ability to create new answers for old questions, . . . its concern for beauty, for the harmonious elevation of the human spirit, and, therefore, its capacity for "seducing" us from ugliness, for healing rifts and stifling fragmentations.[45]

Memory, remembrance, and the rewriting of history are especially relevant in representations of war and peace in Africa, as the chapters here demonstrate, and may play a role in "healing rifts and stifling fragmentations."

In chapter 11, "(Re)Writing the Massacre of Thiaroye," Sabrina Parent focuses on Senegalese literary representations of the massacre of Thiaroye, that is, the 1944 mutiny of African soldiers that was so brutally suppressed by the French army. Parent argues that while French cultural discourse remains silent on the massacre of Thiaroye, West African artists continue to interpret its meaning. The author gives a detailed historical account of the massacre, an overview of the artistic works with the massacre as their subject, and then an analysis of three selected texts. These are a poem by Léopold Sédar Senghor, "Tyaroye" (1948); a play by Boubacar Boris Diop, *Thiaroye terre rouge* (1981); and a play by Cheikh Faty Faye, *Aube de sang* (2005). The chapter, with its focus on "the multiple literary (re)writings of a historical event," argues that the interpretations of Thiaroye are not univocal: "they depend on each author's critical intentions and sociopolitical agenda." The three selected works are from different eras: Senghor's poem belongs to the preindependence era; Diop's play to the so-called postcolonial period; and Faye's play to the global era. The chapter examines the main stylistic, textual, and rhetorical strategies in relation to the historical perspective from which each author represents the massacre.

The "textual (generic) and stylistic strategies" in Senghor's poem "transform the *tirailleurs* of Thiaroye into victims and Thiaroye itself into the prototype of a sacrifice." Diop's play denounces the French colonizer more openly than the poem by Senghor. Although the play may at first appear to represent the massacre in Manichean terms, it addresses "the complexity and the paradoxes of the (neo)colonial situation" as well, thus transforming the play's apparent Manicheism. Faye's play, takes "abstract historical forces [as] shaping the destiny of particular continents or countries" and deconstructs the binary pair of colonizer/colonized. Sabrina Parent concludes that the massacre of Thiaroye is in Senegalese literature "a site of memory," that is to say, "an event that writers revisit and engage with from the perspective and vantage point of their own historical situation."

The concept of "sites of memory" again plays an important role in chapter 12, "In Search of Lost Kabyles in Mehdi Lallaoui's *La colline aux oliviers*." In this chapter, Aména Moïnfar's concern is with the recovery of the memory of the insurrection of 1871, during which Arab and Kabyle leaders in Algeria collaborated in resistance to the French confiscation of their lands. The French, having crushed the insurrection, deported its leaders to penal colonies in New Caledonia. Mehdi Lallaoui, a French writer of Kabyle origin, has devoted two works to the 1871 insurrection and its aftermath, *Kabyles du Pacifique* (1994) and *La colline aux oliviers* (The Olive Grove; 1998). Moïnfar explains why Lallaoui occupies "a distinctive place" in Beur literature, that is, literature by French writers of North African origin. In *La colline aux oliviers*, Kamel, a fictional character of Algerian descent, tries to discover the truth about his great-uncle, who was involved in the insurrection of 1871 and was subsequently deported by the French authorities. The chapter argues for the relevance of Pierre Nora's concept of *lieux de mémoire* (memory sites) as an analytical category in understanding Lallaoui's novel, which takes the form of a detective story. Central to the main argument is the manner in which collective memory operates and the way this concept may be applied to *La colline aux oliviers*, that is to say, how an oppressed community "cultivates, protects, and preserves memory." Apart from memory sites, *le devoir de mémoire* (the duty to remember) also appears to be crucial in *La colline aux oliviers*. The olive grove represents not only the memory of the Kabyles but also the very reason "why they fought to keep this memory free and alive." In short, "land is memory, land is roots," but the main protagonist, Kamel, does not see this, and he has to learn to read the olive grove as a site of memory. Moïnfar concludes that Lallaoui's message of reconciliation asks "France to admit, acknowledge, and accept its colonial past." Lalloui achieves this message of reconciliation "by deconstructing simplistic dichotomies and by valorizing intricate complexities." Bearing in mind the fact that the novel is no longer in print, the chapter itself becomes an important site of memory.

In chapter 13, "'Lament for the Casualties': The Nigerian War of 1967–70 and the Poetry of John Pepper Clark-Bekederemo," Michael Sharp examines John Pepper Clark-Bekederemo's collection of poems, *Casualties* (1970). The theme of the collection is the war between federal Nigeria and secessionist Biafra. The poems in *Casualties* reflect on "battle, fratricide, disease, ethnic division, and the West African tradition of *ars moriendi*." Sharp notes that Bekederemo's war poetry has not received the critical attention it deserves, and he sees here a parallel with the scholarly criticism of the World War I poets, which has tended to focus on poetry by soldiers rather than on poetry by concerned civilians.

Chapter 13 concentrates first on the chronological beginning of the war: for example, the third poem in the sequence, "Vulture's Choice," examines the coup leaders' dilemma over how to govern Nigeria. The following poems present "the federation's gradual descent into civil war." The first twenty-one poems of *Casualties* mirror images of death and destruction that appeared in the news media around the world. The section "Poems about Friends" focuses on the consequences of the war suffered at a personal level as it brought with it "both the death of friends and the cooling of friendships." "Death of a Weaverbird"—a praise poem for the poet Christopher Okigbo—is, according to Sharp, "one of the elegiac masterpieces of Nigerian poetry." In the poem "The Casualties," Clark-Bekederemo attacks the novelist Chinua Achebe as the latter tried to gather international support for Biafra to conclude that "everyone is a casualty of the Nigerian war." In the poem "Night Song," which completes *Casualties,* Clark-Bekederemo reflects on the loss of his friends and on Okigbo's sacrifice, which may have "some consolatory effect on the outcome of the war." However, as a twenty-ninth poem, "Epilogue to *Casualties*"—dedicated to the poet Michael Echeruo and added to the sequence a few years later—indicates, the poet finds much devastation but little consolation in erstwhile Biafra, as Nigeria and Biafra are "still in conflict."

Conclusion

Not only are inaccurate representations detrimental to Africa from the point of view of knowledge, but they may also affect the continent negatively in a concrete manner, as proposed by William Gumede and Louise Mushikiwabo. Gumede writes in his article, "Africa Remains Shrouded in Myth," that "'Africa' is still often . . . in the news only because of war, as a development 'burden' or as a humanitarian crisis."[46] To the Western media, "the whole continent of Africa [is] one country rife with corruption, 'tribal' conflicts, natural and humanitarian disasters." Africa, then, "is a place of exotic, bizarre and unexplainable goings-on."[47] Referring to the 2008 crisis in the Democratic Republic of Congo, Gumede notes that the conflict tends to be represented in terms of "tribal wars," while the media fail to address the role Western companies play in the conflict. Gumede argues that, because of this incorrect representation, Western governments are unable to respond with appropriate policies on Africa.[48]

Louise Mushikiwabo, the foreign minister of Rwanda, also notes the concrete consequences of inaccurate and incorrect reporting on Africa; she is referring to a story that appeared in the media before Christmas 2009, saying that "the Rwandan government was about to follow a neighboring country in criminalizing homosexuality."[49] The story found its way onto the Internet, although it was emphatically untrue. Eventually the Rwandan justice minister made it absolutely clear that the government did not intend to introduce legislation on homosexuality, as sexual orientation was considered to be a private matter. Mushikiwabo wonders why it is that the *Independent* newspaper proceeded to repeat the story, whose truth could have so easily been checked by contacting government officials.[50]

Mushikiwabo observes that such stories are published carelessly, without taking into account the damage they may cause in developing countries, where "irresponsible and/or inaccurate reporting . . . has the potential to reaffirm inaccurate stereotypes which, in turn, affects the region's ability to attract support and investment."[51] Gumede argues along similar lines, that "looking for solutions [in Africa] through prejudiced Western eyes . . . reinforces stereotypical views . . . and encourages the belief that Africa's problems are so exotic they are beyond resolving, or deserve simplistic solutions."[52] However, the chapters in *Narrating War and Peace in Africa* achieve—through their geographical, historical, and cultural scope and diversity—the (necessary) move away from stereotypical to balanced narrations of war and peace in Africa.

Notes

1. Georg Wilhelm Friedrich Hegel, *The Philosophy of History*, trans. J. Sibree (Amherst, NY: Prometheus Books, 1991), 99.

2. Hugh Trevor-Roper, quoted in Osarhieme Benson Osadolor, "Contested History in Colonial Historiography," in *The Foundations of Nigeria: Essays in Honor of Toyin Falola*, ed. Adebayo Oyebade (Trenton, NJ: Africa World Press, 2003), 58.

3. Jan Nederveen Pieterse, *White on Black: Images of Africa and Blacks in Western Popular Culture*, trans. Jan Nederveen Pieterse (reprint paperback edition, New Haven, CT: Yale University Press, 1998; originally published in Dutch, 1990), 235.

4. Ibid.

5. Jonathan Glover, *Humanity: A Moral History of the Twentieth Century* (London: Pimlico, 2001; originally published 1999), 3.

6. See Toyin Falola, *Nationalism and African Intellectuals* (Rochester, NY: University of Rochester Press, 2004; originally published 2001).

7. Ibid., 109.
8. Ibid., 117
9. Ibid.
10. Ibid., 109.

11. James T. Campbell, *Middle Passages: African American Journeys to Africa, 1787–2005* (New York: Penguin Books, 2006), 367.

12. See Kwasi Wiredu, ed., *A Companion to African Philosophy* (Oxford: Blackwell, 2006), 19.

13. Frantz Fanon, *The Wretched of the Earth*, trans. Constance Farrington (London: Penguin Books, 2001), 74.

14. Ali A. Mazrui, "Nationalism, Ethnicity, and Violence," in Wiredu, *A Companion to African Philosophy*, 480.

15. Ibid.

16. Glover, *Humanity: A Moral History of the Twentieth Century*, 119.

17. *Merriam-Webster's Collegiate Dictionary*, 11th ed. (Springfield, MA: Merriam-Webster, 2005), 429, s.v. "Ethnic."

18. A tribe is "a social group comprising numerous families, clans, or generations together with slaves, dependents, or adopted strangers." Ibid., s.v. "Tribe."

19. Barack Obama, "Remarks by the President on a New Beginning." The White House: Office of the Press Secretary (Cairo, Egypt), June 4, 2009, http://www.whitehouse.gov/the_press_office/Remarks-by-the-President-at-Cairo-University-6-04-09/.

20. Nkiru Nzegwu, "Feminism and Africa: Impact and Limits of the Metaphysics of Gender," in Wiredu, *A Companion to African Philosophy*, 560.

21. Carole Boyce Davies, "Motherhood in the Works of Male and Female Igbo Writers: Achebe, Emecheta, Nwapa and Nzekwu," in *Ngambika: Studies of Women in African Literature*, ed. Carole Boyce Davies and Anne Adams Graves (Trenton, NJ: Africa World Press, 1990; originally published 1986), 242.

22. Gloria I. Chuku, "Women and Nationalist Movements" in Falola, *Africa*, vol. 4, *The End of Colonial Rule: Nationalism and Decolonization*, 110.

23. Wole Soyinka, *Myth, Literature and the African World* (reprint paperback edition, Cambridge: Cambridge University Press/Canto, 1999; originally published 1976), 28.

24. Ngugi wa Thiong'o, *Decolonising the Mind: The Politics of Language in African Literature* (Nairobi: Heinemann, 1988; originally published 1986), 16.

25. Ibid., 28.

26. Kwame Anthony Appiah, "African Philosophy and African Literature," in Wiredu, *A Companion to African Philosophy*, 539.

27. Falola, *Nationalism*, 57.

28. Ibid.

29. J. I. Dibua, "Pan-Africanism," in Falola, *Africa*, vol. 4, *The End of Colonial Rule*, 33.

30. Ibid., 34.

31. Adebayo Oyebade, "Radical Nationalism and Wars of Liberation," in Falola, *Africa*, vol. 4, *The End of Colonial Rule*, 72.

32. Ibid., 73.

33. Campbell, *Middle Passages*, 380.

34. Catharine A. MacKinnon, *Are Women Human? And Other International Dialogues* (Cambridge, MA: Belknap Press of Harvard University Press, 2006), 8–9. As of February 26, 2008, the twenty-three countries that had ratified the protocol were Angola, Benin, Burkina Faso, Cape Verde, the Comoros, Djibouti, The Gambia, Ghana,

Lesotho, Libya, Malawi, Mali, Mauritania, Mozambique, Namibia, Nigeria, Rwanda, Senegal, Seychelles, South Africa, Tanzania, Togo, and Zambia. See Protocol on the Rights of Women in Africa, http://www.equalitynow.org/english/campaigns/african-protocol_en.html. Kenya and the Democratic Republic of Congo did not ratify the protocol.

35. MacKinnon, *Are Women Human?* 9.
36. Ibid. Emphasis added.
37. Simone de Beauvoir, *The Second Sex*, trans. and ed. H. M. Parshley (Harmondsworth, England: Penguin Books, 1979), 175.
38. Bill Berkeley, *The Graves Are Not Yet Full: Race, Tribe and Power in the Heart of Africa* (New York: Basic Books, 2001), 7.
39. Ibid., 17.
40. Campbell, *Middle Passages*, 384.
41. Pieterse, *White on Black*, 224–25.
42. Niyi Osundare, *Thread in the Loom: Essays on African Literature and Culture* (Trenton, NJ: Africa World Press, 2002), 14.
43. Ibid.
44. Ibid., 15.
45. Ibid.
46. William Gumede, "Africa Remains Shrouded in Myth," *Guardian* (London), January 16, 2010, http://www.guardian.co.uk/commentisfree/2010/jan/16/africa-western-view.
47. Ibid.
48. Ibid.
49. Louise Mushikiwabo, "Africa Needs Responsible Reporting," *Guardian* (London), January 24, 2010, http://www.guardian.co.uk/commentisfree/2010/jan/24/africa-media-rwanda-homosexuality.
50. Ibid.
51. Ibid.
52. Gumede, "Africa Remains Shrouded in Myth."

Part One
Struggles for Independence

1

Wars of Words

Enlisting Colonial Languages in the Fight for Independence in Africa

Ann Albuyeh

> *Depart white man....*
> Do not ignore, dismiss,
> Pretending we are foolish ....
> We know your language.
>
> Edwin Thumboo, from "May 1954" (1979)

Introduction

When Africans fought European colonialism, it was perhaps fitting that armed struggle was most often required against the Portuguese, those Europeans who, first in, seemed determined to be last out.[1] However, throughout the world, local patriots in the colonies of Europe relied on words as well as guns in their fight to liberate themselves from the shackles of empire. As in Singapore in 1954, where a young Edwin Thumboo fresh from the bloody riots sweeping the colony made "We know your language" an anticolonial battle cry,[2] throughout the far-flung European imperial possessions, European languages were often used to reject their native speakers and everything they stood for.

This chapter examines ex-colonial languages in the context of the current controversies surrounding their use by Africans. It explores the issue of language and identity and examines it from a precolonial African perspective. The chapter, then, considers the introduction of European languages to Africa, focusing on colonial policies, the philosophies they reflected, and the contradictions inherent in each. Examining the changing relationship of language and identity in Africa during the colonial period, the chapter analyzes the use of colonial languages in the fight for independence, leading to a discussion of Kwame Nkrumah as an exemplary case. The discussion concludes with an examination of the unique relationship between language and identity epitomized by this "Greatest Generation" of African patriots, a unique speech community indeed, who successfully waged wars of words against the foreign governments they sought to drive out.

Ex-colonial Languages in the Context of the Current Debate

Even before the colonial period had ended, Africans from the educated elite were formally considering the issue of the use of European languages. The Second Congress of Negro Writers and Artists, convened in Rome in 1959, drafted a resolution stating

> (1) that free and liberated black Africa should not adopt any European or other language as a national tongue;
>
> (2) that one African language should be chosen . . . [and] that all Africans would learn this national language besides their own regional language.[3]

Capping this decades-long debate, Ngugi wa Thiong'o's famous 1986 "farewell to English" reflected this concern over the connection between language and identity,[4] or rather the lack of identity, when African writers express themselves using European languages. That the debate is still ongoing is evident from the 2000 declaration of the international conference of writers and scholars in Asmara, Eritrea, called "Against All Odds: African Languages and Literatures into the 21st Century," which voiced concern over the "profound incongruity in colonial languages speaking for the continent." The goals spelled out in the declaration focus on the strengthening of African vernaculars in opposition to ex-colonial lingua francas, calling for Africans to take an Ngugi-like stance: "Africa must firmly reject this incongruity and affirm a new beginning by returning to its languages and heritage."[5]

Implicit in the wording of this declaration is the idea that the spread of one language threatens others, that the adoption of one language undermines another. Mirroring this view are the titles of recent linguistics books, such as *Languages in Competition, Languages in Conflict,* and the pistol-packing *Duelling Languages.*[6] However, the picture conjured up by this perspective can hinder efforts to learn more about the interaction of languages within complex societies, which is a gap worth filling. As the Nigerian African studies scholar Moradewun Adejunmobi states in her 2004 book, *Vernacular Palaver,* in acknowledging imposition of colonial languages as a historical fact we have not yet begun to address appropriation of colonial languages as an on-going reality and to probe the motivations underlying such acts of appropriation.[7]

Language and Identity

The 1985 publication of Robert Le Page and Andrée Tabouret-Keller's groundbreaking book, *Acts of Identity: Creole-based Approaches to Language and Ethnicity*, caused linguists to focus renewed attention on the ways in which language choice and linguistic evolution reflect identification with a community of speakers. The central concept of Le Page and Tabouret-Keller's book is that "linguistic behaviour [is] a series of *acts of identity* in which people reveal both their personal identity and their search for social roles."[8]

Le Page and Tabouret-Keller were, in particular, seeking to provide a model for the speech variety found among Afro-Creole communities in the Caribbean and among Caribbean immigrants in Britain, many of whom function within "a multidimensional sociolinguistic space in order to accommodate to different encounters and different topics of conversation."[9] In the words of Le Page and Tabouret-Keller,

> The individual creates for himself the patterns of his linguistic behaviour so as to resemble those of the group or groups with which from time to time he wishes to be identified, or so as to be unlike those from whom he wishes to be distinguished.[10]

However, as the battle cry "We know your language" makes clear, the relationship between language and identity in the war against colonialism includes factors rarely considered either in traditional views or in the ongoing linguistic research that considers models of *acts of identity*.[11] Moreover, the use of a language such as English by the educated elite in multilingual colonies throughout the empire challenges both traditional and recent discussion of what constitutes a linguistic community. As linguists Roxy Harris and Ben Rampton point out,

> historically a speech community has been conceptualized as an empirically identifiable "real" thing, a body of people who interact regularly, who have attitudes and/or pragmatic rules in common, and who constitute the largest unit that one can generalize about in any given study (cf. Gumperz 1968; Labov 1989). That view is, however, now breaking down.[12]

Language and Identity in Precolonial Africa

It was obvious to Le Page and Tabouret-Keller that even the tiny Caribbean island of St. Lucia is fraught with ethnic complexity reflected in the diverse linguistic codes that coexist there (English in various dialects is spoken alongside the French-based Creole),[13] as is that most English of cities, London, where, a 1999 census claims, some three hundred languages are spoken by its schoolchildren.[14] Yet if complex situations with regard to ethnicity and language can be found worldwide, surely the countries within the continent of Africa, especially those south of the Sahara with the greatest density of local languages, top any linguist's list.[15] As Kenyan scholars Ali A. and Alamin M. Mazrui have pointed out,

> It is generally acknowledged that the African continent constitutes the most complex multilingual area in the world. The complexity results from the high numbers of languages, the way they are distributed, the relatively low numbers of speakers per language and the intensive language contact in many areas of the continent resulting in widespread multilingualism.[16]

Across Africa, literally thousands of languages, dialects, and pidgins and creoles have gained and lost speakers throughout the centuries in patterns that reflect shifts of allegiance on the part of speakers responding to the complex factors that make up the identity of some of the most multilingual people in the world.[17]

The Languages Carried by Conquest

As Nicholas Ostler's 2005 *Empires of the Word* illustrates, the spread of languages has been linked to imperial expansion throughout history. On the African continent, African languages have been transplanted and carried to new speakers through conquest: for example, the Mande languages were carried to new populations by Manding warriors during the period of the Mali Empire (thirteenth–fifteenth centuries).[18] Moreover, Arabic was carried with spectacular success through military conquest and religious conversion to vast areas in North Africa and the northern reaches of sub-Saharan Africa. Although Europeans arrived much later on the scene, their linguistic impact, while in many respects significantly different from the cases just mentioned, has been no less important or long lasting.

Trade and notably the trans-Atlantic slave trade brought the Portuguese and successive groups of European nationals to African shores from the late fifteenth century onward. Yet while this contact was to have a significant linguistic impact on the development of Afro-European pidgins and creoles both on the continent and ultimately on the plantations of what the Europeans designated the New World, it was the so-called Scramble for Africa that arguably would have an even greater linguistic impact. From the late 1870s until the beginning of World War I, European powers carved up the continent, until, in historian Thomas Pakenham's words, "thirty new colonies and protectorates, 10 million square miles of new territory and 110 million dazed new subjects" were in British, French, Portuguese, German, Belgian, Italian, or Spanish hands.[19] In addition, although imperial maps, like the one shown in figure 1.1, do not show a Dutch presence, the Dutch settlers in South Africa also had a significant and long-lasting linguistic impact as the continuing use of the dialect Afrikaans attests.[20] The Scramble and the European colonial governments it established had the effect of altering the balance of languages used from Algeria to Namibia, from Cameroon to Kenya.

As the word "scramble" suggests, the Europeans were in both a race and a competition, and those who came out ahead were to dominate linguistically as well as politically. Just as prowess at sea had earlier enabled the Portuguese to raise the first European flag over an African trading fort,[21] this technological advantage was decisive in the Scramble, where the world's leading sea power, the self-proclaimed *Great* Britain, added vast tracts of the continent to its world empire. In this pursuit, the French were a close second, with the weakened Portuguese still strongly present in Africa. The conflicts among the European powers in Europe were reflected in their colonies. On the eve of independence, the outcomes of the two world wars in Europe had affected both those who controlled what in Africa and which language was used to do so (see fig. 1.2). By 1950, all of the German colonies (post–World War I) and most of the Italian colonies (post–World War II) had been ceded, especially to Britain and France's gain.

Imperial Languages: Two Views

However, when it came to the establishment of imperial languages in their colonies in Africa, Britain and France came from notably diverging traditions. In fact, it is hardly surprising that the French language would be transplanted to Africa as a result of France's colonial reach. French imperialists had centuries-old linguistic ambitions that were alien to the English. Even before 1634, when Cardinal Richelieu first suggested the formation of an official Académie française, members of the French elite had been interested not only in purifying their language but in equipping it to replace Latin, as Latin had replaced Greek, as an imperial language of high culture and power.[22] In contrast, the British considered but rejected the establishment of such an academy (Samuel Johnson called it "un-English"),[23] beginning a tradition of ambivalence with regard not to only "language purity" but

Figure 1.1. Colonial Africa 1914. Reproduced by permission from Toyin Falola, ed., *Africa*, vol. 3, *Colonial Africa, 1885–1939* (Durham, NC: Carolina Academic Press, 2002), 4.

also to the spread of the English language abroad. Illustrating that tradition is the late-twentieth-century complaint of a British member of the House of Lords that "A major cause of deterioration in the use of the English language is very simply the enormous increase in the number of people who are using it."[24]

Mazrui and Mazrui characterize this difference as a contest between cultural arrogance on the part of the Latin colonial powers (France, Portugal, French-speaking Belgium, Italy, and Spain) and the racial arrogance of the Germanic colonial powers (Britain, Germany, Flemish-speaking Belgium, and Dutch-speaking Afrikaner South Africa).[25] While cultural arrogance promotes the spreading of your language, racial arrogance promotes the keeping of it to yourself.

Figure 1.2. Colonial Africa Post–World War II. Map by Sam Saverance.

Philosophical Underpinnings; Linguistic Consequences

The Anglican clergyman, historian, and political philosopher J. N. Figgis wrote in 1855 that

> if ideas in politics more than elsewhere are the children of practical needs, none the less is it true, that the actual world is the result of men's thought. The existing arrangement of political forces is dependent at least as much upon ideas, as it is upon men's perceptions of their interests.[26]

Despite a universal focus on convenience and expediency and, most of all, in today's parlance, "the bottom line," colonial policy throughout the

European empires also reflected shifting philosophical viewpoints that had important linguistic consequences.

Partly due to the European discovery and translation of classic texts in languages such as Sanskrit and Arabic by English and French scholars such as Sir William Jones,[27] a renewed awareness of the "Orient"[28] captured the European imagination in the eighteenth century. This offshoot of the romantic movement's challenge to the rationalism of the Enlightenment produced Orientalist philologists, ethnologists, anthropologists, and men and even women of science and adventure. As Edward Said has extensively argued, the British and French Orientalists in particular were critical in aiding European expansion and administration, in which they favored the use of indigenous languages in the colonies.[29] A case in point is the British East India Company, which required British administrators to learn classical languages and vernaculars of the areas they governed, leading to the teaching of those languages in company schools and British universities. Thus, for example, Jones, who became the high court judge in Calcutta, added Sanskrit, Persian, Hindi, and many other languages to those European languages that he had learned before he joined the East India Company.[30]

The contradictions inherent in the Orientalist amalgam of admiration and arrogance can be seen in the nineteenth-century British imperialist, Sir Richard Burton. An adventurer and British spy, Burton was a polyglot racist admirer of African languages. Pointing out difficulties such as tonal distinctions that "the stranger's ear unless acute, will fail to detect," he nonetheless exhorted his fellow Europeans to learn languages such as Mpingwe:[31]

> Liquid and eminently harmonious, concise and capable of contraction, the Mpingwe language does not deserve to die out. . . . The people have never invented any form of alphabet, yet the abundance of tale, legend, and proverb which their dialect contains might repay the trouble of acquiring it.[32]

However, arrogance would win out over admiration. Orientalist thinking came under attack by a reinvigorated rationalism on the one hand and Christianity on the other, as the sense of Western superiority, fueled by imperial successes, continued to grow even among the Orientalists themselves. In the British Empire, the result was an uneasy truce between the victors in the guise of Utilitarians and Evangelicals.[33]

Orientalist administrators had tended to suppress meddling by missionaries; it upset the status quo and was, therefore, bad for business. However, the improving bent of the Utilitarian administrators allowed the missionaries much greater freedom. Nonetheless, as much as the Utilitarian administrators and Christian missionaries believed in the superiority of their own beliefs, they sought different linguistic means to those ends. From the mid-nineteenth century on, governing bodies tended to favor conducting business in European languages; missionaries chose to exploit local vernaculars.[34]

Because the Scramble occurred late in the nineteenth century, European interest in local languages and willingness to learn them had waned, whether among the concessionary companies or later the European governments,[35] leaving the missionaries as a significant source of support for indigenous languages within the colonies. Bible translation, which often introduced a writing system, and education in the local languages played an important role in missionary efforts to convert Africans to Christianity. In contrast, nineteenth-century Anglicists began voicing French-style ambitions for the imperial spread of English culture and the English language. Edwin Guest proclaimed that English is "becoming the great medium of civilization, the language of law and literature to the Hindoo, of commerce to the African, of religion to the scattered islands of the Pacific."[36]

Language Policy and Education

In 1885, the Berlin Conference divided up African lands among the European powers, resulting in colonial languages officially becoming the sole languages of administration, education, and written transactions within the European colonies.[37] However, although as might be expected, administration of the colonies was, therefore, ultimately conducted in the mother tongues of the respective Europeans involved, language policies on the ground were not uniform, and the tactics of the Christian missionaries were not the only cause of this.

In contrast with the system of direct rule established in many of the other colonies, notably those of France, the British system of indirect rule relied on intermediary traditional African leaders. This gave the British a reason to support at least some of the African languages in local contexts. As a result, in the educational reforms that preceded the modern independence movements, the colonial powers pursued different language policies with regard to African education, such as it was. The French required the teaching of the French language, even in the missionary schools. The British settled for a compromise. The education that would be provided would involve different languages at different stages: basic education in select local vernaculars, higher education in English.[38]

Language and Identity under Colonialism

Although shared ancestry in terms of clan, lineage, and even extended family as well as membership in age sets, village communities, secret societies, and the like have been important sources of identity in Africa, the Ghanaian scholar, Kwame Anthony Appiah, argues that these began to lose their power in the European colonies.[39] The European obsession with the "tribe" caused the colonizers to highlight ethnic identity, and the subsequent policies this inspired resulted in the privileging of certain ethnic groups over others. This had social as well as linguistic consequences, as people sometimes found it expedient to assume an influential ethnic identity and language. Appiah claims that this happened in late-nineteenth-century coastal East Africa, where many adopted a Swahili identity, and in contemporary Ghana and Togo, where many people have assumed an Ewe identity.[40]

Political scientist David Laitin has even argued that colonialism had the effect of increasing linguistic differences in at least one case.[41] Laitin claims that there is evidence that during the precolonial period of Asante dominance there was reasonable mutual intelligibility among speakers of various Akan languages. However, missionary and colonial policies through World War II effectively encouraged an emphasis on linguistic differences. Because educational and administrative benefits were based on supposed tribal boundaries, this produced incentives for local chiefs to emphasize linguistic and ethnic separateness. Whether Laitin's claim that "By 1950, Akan speakers were more differentiated linguistically than they had been 100 years earlier" can withstand careful scrutiny, it is true that the mixed language policy of the colonial governments, especially under British indirect rule, for example, as applied to the Gold Coast, privileged certain languages and groups.[42]

Moreover, the fact that national identity and language tend to have no one-to-one correspondence in these multilingual areas increases the complexity of the picture. Discussing the weak linguistic nationalism of the most multilingual areas of the continent, Mazrui and Mazrui assert that Africans south of the Sahara are

> nationalistic about their race, and often about their land; and of course many are nationalistic about their particular "tribe." But nationalism about African languages is relatively weak as compared with India, the Middle East or France.[43]

Besides the linguistic diversity within and across national borders, and the fact that many sub-Saharan African languages have relatively few speakers, Mazrui and Mazrui, as mentioned above, point to the issue of oral versus written tradition as inhibiting linguistic nationalism. The fact that the majority of sub-Saharan languages lacked a written tradition pre-Scramble certainly provided a vacuum for European languages to fill in the service of first the colonial and later the national administration and the educational systems designed to supply these administrations.

Mazrui and Mazrui have created a continuum analyzing the languages that invaded Africa with regard to how strongly language use implies belonging to a community.[44] At one extreme, they place Arabic, stating that Arabs are those who speak Arabic no matter where they live. Midway on this continuum lies French, due to an assimilationist colonial policy that tended to accord French rights to subjects who absorbed French culture. While it is weaker than the connection between Arabic and being Arab, to some extent the idea that you're French if you speak French characterizes this relationship between language and identity.[45] Finally, at the other extreme is English, because in no sense did a person become English by speaking the language.[46]

Western Education and the Fight for African Independence

Efforts to placate unhappy colonial subjects and hold off the demands of radical nationalists led to educational reforms from the beginning of World War II. These reforms expanded after the war ended, culminating in the rapid establishment of a number of universities in 1948, such as the University College of East Africa at Makerere (Uganda), the University College of Ibadan (Nigeria), and the University College of the Gold Coast at Legon (Ghana).[47] However, by increasing the number of people with access to European education and languages, countries such as Britain and France threw not water but fuel on the flames of resistance. It added insult to injury that, as Nigerian historian Apollos Nwauwa stresses, the educational institutions were African in location only and revealed a hidden agenda:

> European curricula were imposed without reference to African conditions. . . . It was a calculated effort on the part of Europeans to position themselves well for a neo-colonial role should the post-war winds of change sweep them out of power in Africa, placing Africans in charge.[48]

Despite the different philosophies and aims of European imperialists as noted earlier, their educational policies shared an important linguistic and social consequence: they tended to create a local educated elite whose members grew, simultaneously, comfortable in the language of the colonizer and dissatisfied with the limitations imposed on them by racist and paternalistic European rule. The size and breadth of the British Empire makes its case exemplary, creating a special linguistic community indeed. From Singapore to India to the Gold Coast, and with the support of fellow activists in North America and the Caribbean, the elite group shared the inherent contradictions within their Western education (a slave-owning Thomas Jefferson pens the words: "All men are created equal"); the raised then dashed expectations they experienced under a colonial "glass ceiling";[49] and the linguistic wherewithal to fight back: "We know your language."

The contradictions and the danger to the colonial administration did not go unnoticed, especially as nationalist pressure was reaching a crescendo. In his 1955 essay, "Social Changes and Social Problems in Negro Africa," anthropologist and sociologist Georges Balandier describes the dilemma: "The colonizing power has created a situation involving profound social changes, but the control which it exercises imposes an upper limit to these processes."[50]

This was especially galling to the expectations of the new Western-educated middle class, whose hopes for the future were pinned on their role in a modern state. Whereas earlier opponents of colonial rule had looked to a restoration of the traditions of the past, later nationalists saw independence as the establishment of a new order.[51] Kofi A. Busia, a professor at the University College of the Gold Coast who would become a postindependence prime minister of Ghana, outlined the goals of the nationalists in his 1951 essay, "The Present Situation and Aspirations of Elites in the Gold Coast":

> The conflict between the new literate elite and the European group is a bid by the former to oust the latter . . . as wielders of political power [and] as a standard-setting group in the social sphere.[52]

The Western-educated elite's demands for the Africanization of colonial rule and increased responsibilities for the few Africans in the civil service were, of course, unsuccessful. Recognizing that they were to have no future in the colonial civil service, those who had had the greatest educational opportunity turned to other professions. Unfortunately, for the colonial powers, a number of the educated Africans thus spurned turned to journalism.

Although newspapers such as *Akede Eko* in Yoruba and *Al-Liwa* in Arabic used widely spoken lingua francas to spread nationalist ideas to the larger population, many others voiced their opposition in the languages of the colonizers, even in a few missionary newspapers. Early newspapers produced in English included the *Accra Herald* (founded 1857), the *Sierra Leone Weekly* (1884), the *Lagos Weekly Record* (1890), and the *Gold Coast Independent* (1895). French newspapers, from colonies with stricter censorship, appeared later: *Le Guide de Dahomey* (1920), *L'Eclaireur de la Côte d'Ivoire* (1935), and *Réveil* (1944). Outside Africa, the call was taken up by publications such as *Race Nègre*, the *Negro World*, the *African Times*, and the *Orient Review*.[53]

A number of future presidents of African nations founded newspapers. In the 1930s, Léopold Sédar Senghor, who would become president of Senegal in 1960, founded *L'Etudiant Noir* with fellow writer Aimé Césaire of Martinique, as well as a new political and cultural movement known as Négritude. The newspaper and the movement opposed colonialism and white racism.

Nominated for the Nobel Prize on more than one occasion for his verse in French, and as a member of the French Academy, Senghor expressed the "identity crisis of the Westernized African":[54]

> Car je suis les deux battants de la porte, rythme binarie de l'espace, et
> Le troisième temps
> Car je suis le movement du tamtam, force de l'Afrique future.
> [For I am both sides of a double door, the binary rhythm of space
> And the third beat, I am the movement of drums
> The strength of future Africa.][55]

Perhaps the best-known African leader of this period is Kwame Nkrumah. The English-language newspaper he founded, *The Accra Evening News* (1948), was the official organ of Nkrumah's Convention People's Party. Expressing Nkrumah's and the party's condemnation of colonial government and their demand for rapid self-rule, an editorial proclaimed:

> As long as we remain under an imperialist government we shall continue to be poor, unemployed, ill-fed, ill-clad and continually oppressed, enslaved and exploited. Therefore to ameliorate our condition we can do nothing but ask for Self-Government.[56]

A 1955 issue of the *Gold Coast Weekly Review* quotes Nkrumah's ambitions for his country:

> This country must progress politically—indeed political self-determination is the means of further realization of our social, economic and cultural potentialities. It is political freedom that dictates the pace of economic and social progress.[57]

Kwame Nkrumah: A Case in Point

Kwame Nkrumah was born in 1909 in Nkroful, in the southwestern part of the Gold Coast, present-day Ghana. His mother tongue was Nzima (Nzema), an Akan language spoken by only some three hundred thousand people, residing mostly in Ghana but also in the neighboring Côte d'Ivoire.[58] It goes without saying that Ghana is both multicultural and multilingual, and Nzima is one of over a hundred languages and dialects spoken there.

Nkrumah was the only child of his mother, who took him to the nearby town of Half Assini to join his father's compound. There Nkrumah grew up in a traditional family composed of his father, his father's other wives, and his half-siblings. Neither Nkrumah's father, a goldsmith, nor his mother, a retail market trader, could read or write. His mother insisted that he be educated, and he was sent to a one-room Roman Catholic mission school where he was taught religion, English, arithmetic, and geography by Europeans.[59]

After graduating near the top of his class, Nkrumah became a pupil-instructor in one of the Half Assini primary schools, where he attracted the attention of British administrators, who recommended that he continue his studies at the Accra Government Training College. Nkrumah came under the influence of an African teacher at the school, Dr. Kwegyir Aggrey, who had studied in the United States—a man who wore European clothes but spoke out against the colonial education system and its neglect of relevant African subject matter.

In 1928, the school was transferred to Achimota, where it became part of the Prince of Wales College, and Nkrumah studied Latin and higher mathematics in order to keep up with his new classmates, who had finished secondary school and were from privileged backgrounds with fathers who were both chiefs and colonial clerks. After graduating from the college and working as an educator, Nkrumah went to Lincoln University in Pennsylvania. The oldest African American institution of higher education in the United States, it was also the alma mater of the future first president of Nigeria, Benjamin Nnamdi Azikiwe, who had influenced Nkrumah through his editorship of the Gold Coast's anticolonialist paper, the *African Morning Post*.[60] After receiving his BA in economics and sociology (1939), Nkrumah continued his studies at the University of Pennsylvania, another alma mater of Azikiwe's, where he studied philosophy and education, and earned another BA, in theology, and an MA in education (1942). Having almost completed his PhD and while lecturing part-time,[61] Nkrumah decided to move to Britain in 1945 to study law at the London School of Economics.

While pursuing his university studies in the United States and Britain, Nkrumah was exposed to the views of the most important thinkers of his time: from the Pan-Africanism of the American W. E. B. DuBois and the Jamaican/American leader Marcus Garvey to the Satyagraha philosophy, embracing civil disobedience, of Indian nationalist Mohandas Gandhi. Moreover, English translations introduced him to the socialism of the German political philosopher Karl Marx and the Russian Communist V. I. Lenin.[62]

From his student days to his presidency, Nkrumah interacted with and was influenced by other Africans destined for leadership roles in the movements to oust the Europeans, men such as Azikiwe, mentioned above, president of Nigeria; Jomo Kenyatta, president of Kenya; Patrice Lumumba, prime minister of the Democratic Republic of the Congo; and Kamuzu Banda, prime minister of Malawi. These men used the European languages in their arsenal to establish not only nationalist newspapers but everything from African youth movements, national political parties, and Pan-African conferences to the Organization of African Unity.

As many nationalists understood it, Adejunmobi points out, successful resistance involved a commitment to modernity, "which in turn required the forging of new political structures and new alliances, cutting if need be across existing ethno-linguistic lines."[63] As the Nigerian author Chinua Achebe wrote in 1990,

> We chose English, not because the English desired it, but because having tacitly accepted the nationalities into which colonialism had grouped us, we needed its language to transact our business, including the business of overthrowing colonialism itself.[64]

Achebe made these remarks within the context of current criticism regarding the use of ex-colonial languages such as is reflected in the concerns of the 2000 Eritrean conference referred to above. In fact, current preoccupations with language choice, especially the use of English, can be found worldwide.[65] It is, therefore, all the more striking that numerous accounts of Nkrumah's life treat his use of English as so normal as to be unremarkable.

This is made all the more noteworthy by the fact that criticism and controversy are such a part of Nkrumah's story, and as with many of his contemporaries, these reflect his shifting allegiances within local and global spheres. A Roman Catholic (with the given name of Francis) who is said to have once considered the Jesuit priesthood, Nkrumah became so linked to Communist thought in both the West and Africa that this would inspire Ali Mazrui's infamous 1966 essay, paradoxically titled "Nkrumah: The Leninist Czar." Moreover, the shifting politics and fortunes of Nkrumah's presidency led some to revile him as a despot, even as others revered him as the "Father of African Independence"[66] (see fig. 1.3). Thus, it seems significant that another title, Nkrumah's oft-used bilingual honorific title, "Osagyefo" (that is, paramount chief or warrior in Akan[67]) followed by the English "Doctor," best epitomizes the acceptance of the cultural contradiction under which the nationalists of his generation lived. Nkrumah wrote in 1943 that "The problem now is how to educate and then initiate the African into modern life without uprooting him from his home and tribal life."[68]

Conclusion

In his 1855 book, *English Past and Present*, Anglican Archbishop Richard Chenevix Trench saw war as a force that mobilized attempts at social unification:

> It is one of the compensations, indeed the greatest of all, for the wastefulness, the woe, the cruel losses of war, that it causes a people to know itself as a people; and leads each one to esteem and prize most that which he has

Figure 1.3. Statue of Kwame Nkrumah, Accra, Ghana. Photograph by author.

in common with his countrymen, and not now any longer these things which separate and divide him from them. And the love of our own language, what is it in fact, but the love of our country expressing itself in one particular direction?[69]

Mirroring Trench's view of the positive role of war in solidifying national identity and the importance of language, Mazrui and Mazrui argue that

> one of Africa's post-colonial tragedies continues to be, paradoxically, that there have been no external wars for which to plan and calculate, for which to invoke a sense of national purpose.... Having lacked the impetus of external conflict, statewide nationalism in Africa is made more difficult by the weakness of loyalty to indigenous languages.[70]

The unifying nature of struggle as envisioned by Trench and Mazrui and Mazrui is set on its head by the African nationalists' uniting around European languages. At the beginning, they may have been engaging in acts of identity that fit the thrust of Le Page and Tabouret-Keller's model. When the African elite of this period first set out to learn these foreign tongues, they may have wished to be, as modern persons of a new age, identified at least to a certain extent with fellow speakers in the European colonial powers. However, clearly, anticolonialists such as Nkrumah and his colleagues defined a new model for linguistic acts of identity when their desire to distinguish themselves from the Europeans did not cause them to abandon European languages but instead to wield them as weapons and to become joined together, through these languages, as members of the international speech communities epitomized by this confrontational stance.

Growing up in the United States after World War II, I have often heard my father's peers referred to as "The Greatest Generation," because of their sacrifice in war and their ultimate triumph. Surely, in the modern African context, Nkrumah and his fellow nationalists Azikiwe, Kenyatta, Senghor, Lumumba, Banda, and many others can be seen as members of an equally great generation, for their sacrifice and the success of their war to liberate a continent. Citing the instability of identity, the sociolinguist Norma Mendoza-Denton points to the fact that "Constant transformation is an essential feature of the political structures and social circumstances that bring identities into existence."[71] As the political structures and social circumstances that formed the complex identities of the nationalist leaders have changed, and as language choice in Africa has come to be viewed through new eyes, Nkrumah and his fellow patriots' unique embodiment of the juncture of language and identity may never occur again.

When people talk about "linguistic betrayal" nowadays, they most often mean the use of someone else's language in ways that acknowledge the power of that language and its speakers over you. Yet the linguistic betrayal of the anticolonialists worldwide was quite the opposite of this. The nineteenth-century English poet (and product of the British Empire), Samuel Taylor Coleridge wrote:

> For language is the armory of the human mind;
> and at once contains the trophies of its past
> and the weapons of its future conquests.[72]

Coleridge certainly could not have foreseen the wars of words to be fought throughout Africa and the colonial world, nor could he have anticipated the possibility that the English language itself would be the weapon that would conquer the British Empire.

Notes

I would like to thank my colleagues at the University of Puerto Rico, Drs. Dannabang Kuwabong and Michael Sharp, from Ghana and England respectively, for their discussion of some of the issues presented in this chapter.

1. Armed struggle against the Portuguese was required in Angola, Mozambique, and Guinea Bissau; against the British in Kenya and Southern Rhodesia (Zimbabwe), where a white settler government was critical; against the French in Algeria; and against the white settler South African government in Namibia. The Portuguese gained the first European toehold in Africa in the late fifteenth century. Although South Africa was the first African colony to become independent of Europe when Britain renounced its sovereign authority in 1910, independence and self-determination for the black population did not arrive until 1994, making South Africa the last African colony to achieve majority rule.

2. Alastair Pennycook, *The Cultural Politics of English as an International Language* (London: Longman, 1994), 279–80.

3. Alamin M. Mazrui, *English in Africa: After the Cold War* (Clevedon, England: Multilingual Matters, 2004), 91.

4. Ngugi wa Thiong'o, "A Statement," in Ngugi wa Thiong'o, *Decolonising the Mind: The Politics of Language in African Literature* (London: James Currey, 1988; originally published 1986), xiv.

5. Alamin Mazrui, *English in Africa*, 129–30.

6. Ronald Wardhaugh, *Languages in Competition: Dominance, Diversity, and Decline* (London: Blackwell, 1987); Paul Schach, ed., *Languages in Conflict* (Lincoln: University of Nebraska Press, 1981); Carol Myers-Scotton, *Duelling Languages: Grammatical Structures in Codeswitching* (Oxford: Clarendon, 1993).

7. Moradewun Adejunmobi, *Vernacular Palaver: Imaginations of the Local and Nonnative Languages in West Africa* (Clevedon, England: Multilingual Matters, 2004), 53.

8. Robert Le Page and Andrée Tabouret-Keller, *Acts of Identity: Creole-based Approaches to Language and Ethnicity* (Cambridge: Cambridge University Press, 1985), 14

9. Ibid.

10. Robert Le Page and Andrée Tabouret-Keller, *Acts of Identity: Creole-based Approaches to Language and Ethnicity*, 2nd ed. with additional comments (Fernelmont, Belgium: InterCommunications & EME, 2006), 181.

11. Harris and Rampton state: "Within the linguistics academy, there are a number of ways in which the study of creole languages has actually been quite radical. Both Sebba (1997) and Mühläusler (1992) talk about it as a 'theory-buster' . . . and there can be no doubt that in some quarters, it has involved a very profound rethinking of the basis of linguistics—Le Page and Tabouret-Keller (1985), for example." Roxy Harris and Ben Rampton, "Creole Metaphors in Cultural Analysis," in *Deconstructing Creole*, ed. Umberto Ansaldo, Stephen Matthews, and Lisa Lim (Amsterdam: John Benjamins, 2007), 270.

12. Harris and Rampton, "Creole Metaphors in Cultural Analysis," 271.

13. Definitions of *pidgin* and *creole* vary, and there are many controversies surrounding both. A *pidgin* (e.g., Nigerian Pidgin English) is usually seen as the result of contact between speakers of different languages. It is an invented means of communication, which is made up of parts from a number of source languages and has simpler grammar, vocabulary, and so forth, than a full language. Pidgins are spoken in addition to one's native language, that is, they are no one's mother tongue. A *creole* (e.g., Krio in Sierra Leone, Creole in Haiti) is usually seen as a complete language, which may be a mother tongue and may have developed as a result of the expansion of a previous pidgin.

14. Philip Baker and John Eversley, eds., *Multilingual Capital: The Languages of London's Schoolchildren and Their Relevance to Economic, Social, and Educational Policies* (London: Battlebridge, 2002).

15. See map of African languages, *Ethnologue: Languages of the World*, http://www.ethnologue.com/.

16. Ali A. Mazrui and Alamin M. Mazrui, *The Power of Babel: Language and Governance in the African Experience* (Oxford: James Currey, 1998), 17.

17. The question of what might constitute African identity will be further discussed below.

18. G. Tucker Childs, *An Introduction to African Languages* (Amsterdam: John Benjamins, 2003), 195–203.

19. Thomas Pakenham, *The Scramble for Africa: White Man's Conquest of the Dark Continent from 1876 to 1912* (New York: Avon Books, 1991), xxi.

20. Note that, since the days of the slave trade, Denmark had also had a presence in West Africa but, along with Holland, sold its bases there to the British at the end of the nineteenth century. Toyin Falola, *Key Events in African History: A Reference Guide* (Westport, CT: Greenwood, 2002), 178.

21. The Portuguese built a trading post and castle on the largest island in Arguin Bay (Mauritania), completed in 1461. Important for early Portuguese dominance was the fact that the Treaty of Tordesillas, brokered by Pope Alexander VI in 1493, divided the New World into Portuguese and Spanish spheres of influence; the Portuguese half included Africa.

22. See, for instance, Robert L. Cooper, *Language Planning and Social Change* (Cambridge: Cambridge University Press, 1989); and Wardhaugh, *Languages in Competition*. These authors report that the Ordinance of Villers-Cotterêts of 1539, which forbade the use of languages other than French in all official functions within the territories of France, applied outside France as well.

23. Cooper, *Language Planning and Social Change*, 11.

24. Robert McCrum, William Cran, and Robert MacNeil, *The Story of English*, 2nd ed. (New York: Penguin Books, 1992), 339.

25. Mazrui and Mazrui, *The Power of Babel*.

26. Roland N. Stromberg, *European Intellectual History since 1789* (Englewood Cliffs, NJ: Simon and Schuster, 1990), 1.

27. Jones was a British judge and multilingual scholar in India in the latter part of the eighteenth century whose work led to the understanding of the genetic relationship among the languages from India to Europe that we now know as the Indo-European language family.

28. Note that the "Orient" in this context is broadly defined as anything non-European.

29. Edward Said, *Orientalism: Western Conceptions of the Orient* (New York: Vintage, 1979; originally published 1978).

30. Garland Cannon, *The Life and Mind of Oriental Jones: Sir William Jones, the Father of Modern Linguistics* (Cambridge: Cambridge University Press, 1991).

31. Edward Rice, *Captain Sir Richard Francis Burton* (New York: Charles Scribner's Sons, 1990). Rice, Burton's biographer, includes this quotation in a section on Burton's three years in West Africa, but it is difficult to identify the language that is referred to. Since Burton also traveled through East Africa, it is possible that he encountered the language referred to there. Although we know that he abandoned his goal of reaching Lake Nyasa (Lake Malawi), it is possible that, since "Mpingwe" appears in later maps as the name of a populated area in the former Nyasaland (now the Republic of Malawi), he might have learned a language spoken in this area and it might be this language he is referring to here.

32. Rice, *Captain Sir Richard Francis Burton*, 376.

33. Richard D. Altick, *Victorian People and Ideas* (New York: Norton, 1973).

34. Mazrui and Mazrui, *The Power of Babel*.

35. At various periods, the concessionary companies that had characterized the European presence in Africa since the era of the slave trade gave way to direct European control. The British tended to make this change early, for example, revoking the charter of the Royal Africa Company in 1898 and assuming formal control over Nigeria in 1900. In contrast, the Portuguese government would not assume formal control over Mozambique until 1942. See Sean Stilwell, "The Imposition of Colonial Rule," in Falola, *Africa*, vol. 3, *Colonial Africa, 1885–1939*, 12.

36. E. Guest, *A History of English Rhythms* (London: George Bell, 1838/1882), 703, as reported in Pennycook, *The Cultural Politics of English as an International Language*, 99.

37. Roland J.-L. Breton, "Sub-Saharan Africa," in *Languages in a Globalising World*, ed. Jacques Maurais and Michael A. Morris (Cambridge: Cambridge University Press, 2003), 206.

38. Apollos O. Nwauwa, "Educational Policies and Reforms," in Falola, *Africa*, vol. 4, *The End of Colonial Rule: Nationalism and Decolonization*, 167–83.

39. Kwame Anthony Appiah, "Ethnicity and Identity in Africa: An Interpretation," in Appiah and Gates, *Africana*, 703–5.

40. Ibid., 705.

41. David D. Laitin, "The Tower of Babel as a Coordination Game: Political Linguistics in Ghana," *American Political Science Review* 88, no. 3 (1994): 622–34.

42. Ibid., 623.

43. Mazrui and Mazrui, *The Power of Babel*, 5.

44. Ibid., 20.

45. Mazrui and Mazrui speculate that the crucial difference between the two may be that the French empire did not remain in power for as long as that of the Arabs.

46. It could be that the size and success of Britain's mother tongue English-speaking ex-colonies have also weakened any perceived connection between speaking English and being English. For example, I am a North American native English speaker, but despite having some English ancestry, I have never thought of myself as in any way "English." Although the United States' break from Britain was hundreds of years earlier, the trend in other such ex-colonies, for example, Australia, seems also to be to emphasize an identity separate from Englishness. See McCrum, *The Story of English*, for a wide-ranging survey of global varieties of English and the attitudes of some of the speakers of these varieties. As cited in Mazrui and Mazrui, *The Power of Babel*, 210, George Bernard Shaw, himself an Irishman, famously quipped that the Americans and the British were a people divided by the same language.

47. Nwauwa, "Educational Policies and Reforms," 176.

48. Ibid., 177.

49. Thomas Hodgkin, "The African Middle Class," *Corona: The Journal of Her Majesty's Overseas Service*, March 1956, 88, as reported in Martin L Kilson Jr., "Nationalism and Social Classes in British West Africa," *Journal of Politics* 20, no. 2 (1958): 379. Kilson states that "nationalism, in one of its aspects, clearly expresses the dissatisfaction of an emerging African middle class with a situation in which many of the recognized functions and rewards of a middle class—in the commercial, professional, administrative and ecclesiastical fields—are in the hands of 'strangers.' . . . The demand for African control of the State power is in part a demand for unrestricted access to these functions." Kilson, "Nationalism and Social Classes in British West Africa," 379.

50. Georges Balandier, "Social Changes and Social Problems in Negro Africa," in *Africa in the Modern World*, ed. Calvin W. Stillman (Chicago: University of Chicago Press, 1955), 63.

51. See Funso Afolayan, "African Nationalism, 1914–1939," in Falola, *Africa*, vol. 3, *Colonial Africa, 1885–1939*, 285. As Afolayan points out, one of their grievances was the way in which indirect rule excluded them from any meaningful participation in the administration of the colonies, favoring traditional leaders instead. Afolayan quotes the *Gold Coast Leader*'s 1927 criticism of the unprecedented powers that chiefs enjoyed under indirect rule: "The time is coming when a chief once installed will sit firmly on the neck of the people, like the old man of the sea, and rule them in his own way without any means of getting rid of him." This situation was exacerbated by the fact that where preexisting traditional chiefs were not available, the colonial powers created them.

52. Kilson, "Nationalism and Social Classes in British West Africa," 378.

53. Afolayan, "African Nationalism, 1914–1939," 299–300.

54. David P. Johnson Jr., "Léopold Sédar Senghor," in Appiah and Gates, *Africana*, 1691.

55. Léopold Sédar Senghor, *Ethiopiques: Poèmes* (Paris: Seuil, 1964); trans. Melvin Dixon as *The Collected Poetry* (Charlottesville: University of Virginia Press, 1991).

56. Kilson, "Nationalism and Social Classes in British West Africa," 386.

57. Ibid., 380.

58. Raymond G. Gordon, ed., *Ethnologue: Languages of the World*, 15th ed. (Dallas, TX: SIL International, 2005; online version. http://www.ethnologue.com).

59. See, for example, Kwame Nkrumah, *Ghana: The Autobiography of Kwame Nkrumah* (Edinburgh: Thomas Nelson, 1957); Yuri Smertin, *Kwame Nkrumah* (New York: International Publishers, 1987); June Milne, *Kwame Nkrumah: A Biography* (London: Panaf, 1999). However, there is some doubt about the details of Nkrumah's early life, and it is not clear what language the subjects aside from English were taught in, although I assume it to have been Nzima.

60. Azikiwe went on to establish a chain of newspapers, including the *West African Pilot*. Appiah, "Benjamin Nnamdi Azikiwe," in Appiah and Gates, *Africana*, 154. It is also noteworthy that six members of the cabinet in Namibia's first independence government were also graduates of Lincoln. Lisa Clayton Robinson, "Lincoln University (Pennsylvania)," in Appiah and Gates, *Africana*, 1168–69; and the Lincoln University website, http://www.lincoln.edu.com.

61. In addition, Nkrumah held numerous jobs during the time he was a student, including summer jobs on seagoing vessels.

62. Nkrumah, *Ghana: The Autobiography of Kwame Nkrumah*; Michael W. Williams, "Nkrumahism as an Ideological Embodiment of Leftist Thought within the African World," *Journal of Black Studies* 15, no. 1 (1984): 117–34; Smertin, *Kwame Nkrumah*; Bill Sutherland and Matt Meyer, *Guns and Gandhi in Africa: Pan-African Insights on Nonviolence, Armed Struggle and Liberation in Africa* (Trenton, NJ: Africa World Press, 2000).

63. Adejunmobi, *Vernacular Palaver*, 24.

64. Chinua Achebe, "New Songs of Ourselves," *New Statesman and Society*, February 9, 1990, 32.

65. For example, this debate is a part of daily life in the Spanish-speaking U.S. territory, Puerto Rico, where I live and teach.

66. See, for example, T. Peter Omari, *Kwame Nkrumah: The Anatomy of an African Dictatorship* (New York: Africana, 1972); and Henry L. Bretton, *The Rise and Fall of Kwame Nkrumah: A Study of Personal Rule in Africa*. (London: Pall Mall, 1966). Nkrumah has had other similar titles, such as the "Father of African Nationalism," the title of David Birmingham's book, which also discusses his rise and fall: *Kwame Nkrumah: The Father of African Nationalism*, rev. ed. (Athens: Ohio University Press, 1998). Moreover, people still voice these opposing opinions of Nkrumah. For example, a 2005 BBC *Africa Live* story, called "Rebels Who Became Leaders," invited comments via the Internet (the story and discussion are still available online at http://news.bbc.co.uk/2/hi/africa/4176844.stm). "From the action of the three leaders: Kabila, Meles, and Nkrumah, it is crystal clear that they all had good intentions at the very beginning but after tasting power, they themselves became like their predecessors," commented reader Omorodion Osula, Boston, United States. Reason Wafawarove, Zimbabwe, replied that "Kwame Nkrumah is the Father of African Independence and a legendary leader, period." As the first comment indicates, Nkrumah is not the only African leader to be both revered and reviled. For example, an almost direct

parallel is found in the caption to a photo of the 2000 interment of Haile Selassie's remains, which reads: "The late emperor is seen by some as a founding father of African independence, by others as a despot." See "Picture Gallery: Emperor Haile Selassie's Funeral," http://news.bbc.co.uk/2/hi/africa/1008721.stm.

67. Barbara S. Monfils, "A Multifaceted Image: Kwame Nkrumah's Extrinsic Rhetorical Strategies," *Journal of Black Studies* 7, no. 3 (1977): 318.

68. Smertin, *Kwame Nkrumah*, 16.

69. Richard Chenevix Trench, *English Past and Present*, ed. with emendations by A. Smythe Palmer (London: Routledge, 1905).

70. Mazrui and Mazrui, *The Power of Babel*, 4.

71. Norma Mendoza-Denton, "Language and Identity," in *The Handbook of Language Variation and Change*, ed. J. K. Chambers, Peter Trudgill, and Natalie Schilling-Estes (London: Blackwell, 2004), 491.

72. Samuel Taylor Coleridge, *Biographia Literaria XVI*, vol. 2, 22, in *Inquiring Spirit: A Coleridge Reader*, ed. Kathleen Coburn (London: Minerva, 1951).

2

Alternative Representations of War in Africa

New Times and Ethiopia News Coverage of the 1935–41 Italian-Ethiopian War

Metasebia Woldemariam

Introduction

On the very day in May 1935 that the first edition of *New Times and Ethiopia News* (*NT&EN*) went to press in Great Britain, the fascist Italian army entered Addis Ababa, Ethiopia's capital. *NT&EN* was designed as a weekly antifascist paper; the first edition's banner headline grimly set the tone for future editions, noting: "Remember: Everywhere, Always, Fascism Means War."[1] *NT&EN*'s bias in favor of the Ethiopian cause far outweighed what was found in mainstream European and American newspapers of the era. More importantly, their sympathy was not simply based on the fact that the Italian invasion violated the League of Nations Covenant; it was based on an anti-imperialist and Pan-African worldview. Given that *NT&EN* was published in the heart of the British Empire, one might consider the tone and content of this newspaper as providing rather remarkable alternative constructions. As will be demonstrated, while mainstream Euro-American newspapers sometimes faced the problem of supporting Ethiopian independence during the height of the colonial era, the alternative *NT&EN* flouted conventions to become a significant contributor to the anti-imperialist, Pan-African discourse. However, more in tune with recent scholarship on alternative media, it is useful to explore how production values and cultural positioning more accurately frame *NT&EN* as an alternative outlet.

As many scholars have noted, defining what makes media "alternative" can be tricky business considering the differing perspectives that come into play. Nina Eliasoph has documented her participant-observation experiences in a politically oppositional newsroom. What is significant is her finding that news content was influenced by the relationship between the reporters' and the owners' ideological positions on the one hand, and the ideology of both the reporters and the station in relation to "their social positions and involvement with the audience and the social movements and institutions that are the subject of news" on the other hand. This suggests that while the content might be alternative, the mode of production—in terms of relationships to owners and their ideologies—is not necessarily so.[2]

Robert McChesney says that independent (or alternative) content is generally considered too risky for mainstream media giants, although he notes ironically the current trend in which media conglomerates produce risky content that has proven marketable.[3] Going further, Chris Atton suggests that alternative media are not just defined by their content, which can indeed be reproduced in mainstream media: "It is not simply the attitude of a publication but crucially its *position* with respect to the relations of production that gives it its power and enables it to avoid recuperation by the mere duplication of its ideas in the mainstream."[4] He finds that alternative media in Scotland have encouraged readers to become writers, thereby influencing the means of production. As he notes, "Readers as writers; readers as editors, designers, publishers, printers and distributors: we see here a radical realignment of roles and responsibilities that is unique to alternative media."[5]

John Downing has written extensively on alternative/radical media, saying in 1984 that they are "dissonant in the sense that they have posed a genuine alternative to the media patterns of both West and East. These media have articulated and amplified popular challenges to power structures; they have enabled people fighting injustice to communicate with each other; they have empowered communities and classes and women and ethnic minorities."[6] Almost two decades later, he would criticize his own works as being too focused on binary oppositions. Given Cold War realities, it is not surprising that his earlier works focused on the analysis of East/West media systems.[7]

Similarly, James Hamilton and Chris Atton offer a useful critique of the scholarship on alternative media. Of particular relevance to this analysis is their assertion that, too often, studies "operate with a separatist agenda, celebrating the simple presence of newspapers, magazines, and other media produced by marginalized or dissenting groups."[8] At the same time, research has tended to focus on vanguard individuals connected to an alternative medium, as well as (usually) its alternative content.

Such studies additionally tend to adopt essentialist views about the social movements with which these media are linked. Essentialism often assumes that media production follows the creation of social movements, as though these are "fully formed" rather than in any sense transformative practices.[9] Consequently, alternative media are too often assumed to passively reflect social movements rather than, presumably, being conceptualized as sites of cultural production, of contestation, and of discourse.[10] The combined focus on vanguards and essentialist views of social movements creates a predicament, as studies almost exclusively focus on individuals, "their publications, and increasingly [on] the technologies they use.... As a result, even when attempting to be social histories 'from bottom up,' many studies of alternative media end up too often being decontextualized, elite narratives of movement leaders and their activities."[11]

Considering such critiques, this chapter will provide a brief overview of the historical circumstances that enabled the creation of *NT&EN*. It will discuss mainstream coverage of Ethiopia in the 1930s (a) to better situate *NT&EN* as an alternative paper and (b) to demonstrate how rather than passively reflecting antifascist movements, its distribution patterns and alternate values helped, in interesting and sometimes unanticipated ways, to invigorate Pan-African discourse in relation to the Italian invasion of Ethiopia.

Mainstream Coverage of the Ethiopian Crisis

By early 1935, the growing certainty that an Italian invasion of Ethiopia would occur was making headline news around the world. Interest was high because both Italy and Ethiopia were members of the League of Nations; article 16 of the League's Covenant specified that an act of war committed by one member nation against another would ipso facto be deemed an act of war against all of the members.[12] If the League's members were to react according to this article, it seemed that an Italian invasion would very possibly be the catalyst leading to another world war.

The foreign correspondents who flocked to Ethiopia's capital in the early months of 1935 were somewhat dismayed that the anticipated war did not start upon their arrival. Michael Salwen offers insight into the journalists' predicaments through his analysis of the novelist Evelyn Waugh's perceptions of Waugh's own (and other journalists') experiences in Ethiopia. Salwen's discussion demonstrates the dramatic license journalists often took as editors in Europe and the United States pressured them for stories at a time when there was not much to report. Journalists, therefore, filed stories about Ethiopia's history, local conditions, and other flowery exotic tales. Indeed, their presence was due more to the necessity of covering the war than to any sympathy for the Ethiopian cause.[13]

Representational Dilemma

At the time—with the notable exception of the black diaspora and its press—there was generally little knowledge of or interest in Ethiopia in

Europe and the United States. People were excited by the Italian aggression primarily because it went against the League of Nations' principles. Indeed, covering Ethiopia created a representational dilemma for most mainstream newspapers in the Euro-American context. On the one hand, the member states of the League of Nations were obliged by the Covenant to defend the victim nation. On the other hand, Ethiopia was one of only a handful of independent black nations during the heyday of twentieth-century European colonial enterprise and American racial segregationism. Patricia Romero notes that Ethiopia at this time was something of an anomaly for the British. While there was sympathy for the Ethiopian situation, in the 1930s Britain was also "the largest imperialist power in the world. Her African colonies arguably re-enforced an element of racism that had existed since slavery."[14]

The mainstream representational dilemma, therefore, largely resided in the challenge of supporting a League member while at the same time ensuring that such support would not compromise the dominant colonial/segregationist discourse and projects of the era. How could one justify support for an African nation's independence and yet still rationalize the subjugation of other colonized peoples around the world? Mainstream coverage partly resolved this dilemma in at least three, albeit simplistic, ways. First, and to inspire the idea that Ethiopia was a valuable ally, the country's image was romanticized. Scholars such as Levine, Sorenson, and Wubneh and Abate have examined various historical representations of Ethiopia conjured up by Europeans and other outsiders. Many of these visions served Europe's hegemonic aspirations, which Edward Said famously labeled Orientalism.[15]

Thus, first, Ethiopia was often, although not exclusively, defined as an ancient and isolated Christian kingdom. The Semitic heritage of the ruling elite, coupled with the legend that the Ethiopian emperor, Haile Selassie, was a direct descendant of the Queen of Sheba and King Solomon,[16] only added to the exotic otherness of an isolated people ready to fight for independence against the fascist Italian state. Such writings, says John Sorenson, "contributed to the development of an image of Ethiopia as a magnificent kingdom and a desirable ally."[17] From Sorenson's historical perspective, the perpetuation of these Orientalist images had at least one important consequence during the late nineteenth century: for Europeans, it made more palatable Ethiopia's 1896 victory over Italy during Italy's first colonial excursion in Ethiopia.[18] By recycling the legends and myths of Ethiopia's past, the mainstream media of the 1930s continued to garner sympathy for the exotic Ethiopians.

Second, while Ethiopians were generally depicted as quaint but backward, their emperor was represented as uncharacteristic of the "natives"; he was often portrayed as a remarkable figure who not only had European physical characteristics but also possessed a Europeanized, modernized perspective. One need only look at one of the most important mainstream magazines of the era, *Time* magazine, to see how this representation was reinforced. As 1935's "Man of the Year," Haile Selassie was described as the leader of "Noble Savages" who was the only barrier against another world war between civilized nations:

> In 1935 there was just one man who rose out of murky obscurity and carried his country with him up & up into brilliant focus before a pop-eyed world. But for the hidden astuteness of this man, there would not now be the possibility of another world war arising out of idealism generated around the League of Nations in behalf of Ethiopia. . . . If it ends in the fall of Mussolini and the collapse of Fascism, His Majesty can plume himself on one of the greatest feats ever credited to blackamoors.
>
> Above all, Haile Selassie has created a general, warm, and blind sympathy for uncivilized Ethiopia throughout civilized Christendom. In the wake of the world's grandiose Depression, with millions of white men uncertain as to the benefits of civilization, 1935 produced a peculiar Spirit of the Year in which it was felt to be a crying shame that the Machine Age seemed about to intrude upon Africa's last free, unscathed and simple people. They were ipso facto Noble Savages, and the noblest Ethiopian of them all naturally emerged as Man of the Year.[19]

A third strategy utilized by mainstream media was to focus more on the consequences of violating the League's Covenant and less on racial politics. This approach was very useful to the Ethiopians, as one major barrier they faced was overcoming the mainstream Euro-American assumptions of racial superiority. In line with this approach, pro-League mainstream coverage, based on abstract values, was often eventually transformed into pro-Ethiopia coverage.

With a few notable exceptions, most American papers, possibly in line with isolationist thinking, tended to support the League—and ultimately the Ethiopian cause—but in a manner more detached than that of the European papers. James Dugan and Laurence Lafore explain that, until September 1935, the *New York Times* coverage, while very detailed and on the whole factually accurate, leaned toward "empty double-talk" that seemed intent on keeping foreign affairs foreign.[20] However, it is important to note that in 1935, and as evidenced by its 1935 index, the *New York Times* covered the Ethiopian situation extensively. While the paper may have engaged in some double-talk, it did so in ways that supported the League of Nations' principles. In the *New York Times*, one can therefore readily find examples of all three representational strategies within its extensive coverage of the crisis.

Genesis of *NT&EN*

After the Italian invasion began in October 1935, the League labeled Italy as the aggressor,[21] but little else happened. There was no declaration of war against Italy; only minimal, ineffective sanctions were imposed on it. For instance, the sanctions did not mention petroleum, so vital to the Italian war effort. This suggests that the League was either ineffective or that its powerful members were more interested in maintaining cordial relations with Italy than in assisting Ethiopia. At the same time, the League declined to furnish Ethiopia with loans to buy necessary military equipment.[22] As the threat of another world war was averted, mainstream coverage of Ethiopia waned considerably.

It was against this political and social backdrop that the famous British suffragist Sylvia Pankhurst pursued an aggressive campaign, writing to newspapers and prominent individuals in support of the League's principles. She was fully aware that newspapers were turning to other stories; understanding the news cycle, she realized that her letter-writing campaign was inadequate to keep Ethiopia in the news. In 1936, she began publishing *NT&EN* to maintain an interest in Ethiopia and antifascism.[23] Pankhurst's reasons for rallying to Ethiopia's cause, therefore, seem to be grounded in the ideals of justice and antifascism, although *NT&EN* would sometimes, in its pro-Ethiopia propaganda, manipulate the very same romantic images that have been outlined above.

By the start of the 1930s, Sylvia Pankhurst was already a famous and quite scandalous figure in Europe. She first came to public attention as a militant suffragist and a committed socialist. By 1914, she began publishing the *Women's Dreadnought* (later renamed the *Worker's Dreadnought*), a weekly paper dedicated to class issues and the socialist cause that has been considered "one of the most important antiwar, nonsectarian socialist papers in Britain, achieving an influential position by opening its columns to all shades of opinion on the left."[24] Mary Davis believes that Pankhurst's commitment to the women's movement and social/class issues made her unusually sensitive to matters related to racism and imperialism. By 1928, she would gain additional notoriety as an over-forty single mother who publicized the birth of her "eugenic" child.[25]

NT&EN and Alternative Values

As discussed earlier, Atton posits that alternative media are defined by their content as well as by their mode of production. Thus, readers also act as writers, editors, and distributors. Atton expands on this idea in his exploration of social movement media and the Internet. Specifically, he focuses on the

Indymedia network, which came to public attention during the 1999 World Trade Organization Summit in Seattle when a small group was able to transmit its (and related antiglobalization) perspectives around the world. The Indymedia network is diffuse, with most of its content provided by partisan "amateur journalists" writing from within communities and from "insider" perspectives. As Atton points out, alternative media have "have throughout their history privileged amateur journalists who are writing from a position of engagement with the event or process that is their subject. . . . The reporters' active, lived presence within these events, whilst no guarantor of impartiality, enabled the production of news that told other stories from those reported in the mainstream."[26] This has allowed activists to function as journalists and yet remain within the "rank and file" of social movements. Referring specifically to the Indymedia network, Atton explains that there is space for elite narratives as well, especially where they provide in-depth discursive analyses of events such as 9/11.[27]

While Sylvia Pankhurst wrote numerous articles and an antifascist column in the paper, *NT&EN*'s other articles were mainly written by readers and activists. Although these writers had differing ideological positions (suffragists, Pan-Africanists, and so on), the common theme within in their writings was maintaining a pro-League, pro-Ethiopia, or antifascist stance. *NT&EN* "sought, in articles, photographs, and cartoons, to expose the inequity of the fascist invasion, and occupation, of Ethiopia."[28] Therefore, contributors included Italian refugees, British citizens who had served in the Red Cross in Ethiopia, Ethiopian refugees, anti-Nazi refugees from Central Europe, American academics, and even a Welsh schoolteacher. The Ethiopian minister in London, Dr. Warqenah Eshete (also known as Dr. Charles Martin) also regularly contributed articles.

Considering that *NT&EN* was financed through contributions rather than traditional advertising, it had an impressive record in terms of readership. During its first year, ten thousand copies per week were printed, and, at its peak, forty thousand weekly copies were sold.[29] *NT&EN* accepted opinion pieces from around the world, most often to demonstrate that its position had widespread international support. For instance, prominence was given to an article published on August 22, 1936, by a Chinese national named Hu Chow Yuan, who wrote, in what was titled "Chinese Opinion," that "Many books, pamphlets and periodicals have been published in China to record your [Ethiopia's] holy struggle. His Majesty Haile Selassie is honoured by our people as the greatest leader of oppressed nations." *NT&EN* also reprinted articles and cartoons from mainstream media that reflected its ideological position. Atton, noting that the Indymedia network also maintains links with and includes material from mainstream media, says that "Indymedia is not pursuing an ideological purity in the nature of its sources."[30] He explains that such mainstream content tends to reflect the ideological focus of the movement; alternatively, the content is posted so that readers may critique official narratives.[31]

This was certainly the case with *NT&EN*, which, in an amusing twist, reprinted an article written by Mussolini himself in the Italian newspaper *Popolo d'Italia*. In an effort to explain *NT&EN*'s antifascist and pro-Ethiopian bias, Mussolini's piece, "Sylvia e Tafari," suggested a romantic liaison existed between *NT&EN*'s editor and the Ethiopian emperor. In reprinting Mussolini's article on February 13, 1937, *NT&EN* advised, "In order that our readers may appreciate in full the exquisite delicacy of mind of the present ruler of Italy, we give it [the article] in full; permitting for once the sullying of our pages."

More seriously, *NT&EN* would present official narratives in its counter-propaganda efforts. For instance, to deflect attention from its disregard of the Geneva Protocol, Italy framed its use of poison gas as retaliation for Ethiopian atrocities against captured Italian soldiers. Often using dubious sources and means, Italian propaganda depicted the Ethiopian fighters as barbaric and in violation of international law in their treatment of prisoners of war. The Ethiopian forces were also portrayed as attacking the International Red Cross. Such stories were duly published in Italian and international newspapers. "Mussolini at first denied the use of gas, then justified it as retaliation for Ethiopian atrocities. Both the international and national [Italian] public accepted his explanation."[32]

To counter such propaganda, *NT&EN* focused on Italian atrocities. For instance, on July 15, 1936, barely two months after the paper was started, a photograph showing what is described as the feet of an Ethiopian soldier was printed. Supposedly taken on March 19, 1936, the photograph shows the hideous effects of gas on the soldier's feet. He is standing on a box stamped "CROIX-ROUGE DE NORVÈGE," implying that the Norwegian Red Cross was both treating the soldier and recording his victimization. The banner headline reads, "The Symbol of Fascist Civilisation." The July 25, 1936, edition includes two photographs showing wounded Ethiopian soldiers who did not receive medical attention because the "Red Cross unit was destroyed."

What is significant is that while such stories highlighted Italian racial ideology and abuses, many more restored agency to Ethiopians and to Ethiopian women in particular. *NT&EN* not only wrote of their victimization under the Italian occupation but also championed those who actively led troops into combat, under subheadings such as "Women Warriors" and "Two Brave Women" in the edition published on January 7, 1937. Particularly noteworthy is the fact that *NT&EN* continued to insist that the Italian occupation of Addis Ababa did not mean the war was over and that Italy had, in effect, won. *NT&EN* consistently challenged this view, which was commonly held in Europe and the United States. The July 4, 1936, edition of *NT&EN* would note that Ethiopia's geography "is not well indicated in our atlases.

Otherwise, one could see that though Addis Ababa is occupied, only *one-fifth* of Ethiopia is held by the Italians."

Pan-Africanism and the Italian Invasion

By the 1930s, Pan-Africanist discourse hovered between nationalism and racialism as a result of differing ideologies promulgated by various intellectuals in Africa and the African diaspora.[33] According to Kwame Anthony Appiah, the genesis of Pan-African discourse dates back to Alexander Crummell, an African American who published *The Future of Africa* in 1862. Crummell posited that black people had a common destiny based on their race and that Africa was the home of all black people. He moved to Liberia and became one of the first to speak "*as* a Negro in Africa."[34] As Appiah explains, early Pan-Africanists from the United States and the Caribbean had in common a shared African ancestry; the assumption that their solidarity was based on race was not a surprising development, as ethnocentric as it appears. African Americans were "raised in a segregated American society and exposed to the crudest form of discrimination, social intercourse with white people was painful and uneasy."[35] However, Appiah also notes that there existed "a black world on which the white American world impinged in ways that were culturally marginal even though politically overwhelming."[36]

The experience of Africans under colonial rule on the continent was somewhat different, and, further, people were impacted by colonialism in various different ways. Although the political institutions of colonialism favored the colonialists, even those Africans that were uprooted from their cultural milieu and thrust into colonial schools often had primary experiences in their own traditions.[37] As Appiah says, "most of us who were raised during and for some time after the colonial era are sharply aware of the ways in which the colonizers were never as fully in control as our elders allowed them to appear. We all experienced the persistent power of our cognitive and moral traditions."[38]

Pan-African discourse in Africa inherited the American assumption that race was *the* organizing principle. The 1900 Pan-African Conference, organized by Trinidadian Henry Sylvester Williams, was held in London and attended by African intellectuals and leaders and their counterparts from the Americas. Samuel Asante convincingly argues that the budding West African nationalists were greatly influenced by the American focus on race as the common identity marker of Africans and the members of its diaspora.[39] At the time of the 1935 Italian invasion of Ethiopia, a discourse of protest emerged among those engaged in the Pan-African debate. Ethiopia was romanticized and idealized; the Italian invasion was viewed not only as an act of aggression against Ethiopia but as an act against everyone of African origin. The International African Friends of Abyssinia group was founded by the likes of Jomo Kenyatta, future first president of independent Kenya,[40] and J. B. Danquah, the famous Ghanaian nationalist.[41] In the United States, several black newspapers denounced the aggression, one declaring that "Ethiopia has become the spiritual fatherland of Negroes throughout the world, and from Bahia to Birmingham, and from New York to Nigeria, peoples of African descent have been stirred to unparalleled unity of thought."[42] The Ethiopian crisis helped to unify black American politics. Michael West says the National Negro Congress was founded in 1936 partly as a result of the unity that the crisis created, while the Council on African Affairs was formed due to the awakened interest in Africa as a direct result of the Italian invasion of Ethiopia.[43]

It is not surprising, therefore, that *NT&EN* was widely distributed among such circles in the United States, Great Britain, English-speaking Africa, and the Caribbean islands. It was translated into Ethiopia's official language, Amharic, for illegal distribution within the country. As the rest of the world turned to other news, *NT&EN* could be relied upon to deliver news about Ethiopia, and it was consequently widely quoted in selected papers elsewhere. For instance, Leslie Rollins quotes *The African*, a 1930s student publication in the United States, as saying: "Recent reports in the *Voice of Ethiopia* and *New Times and Ethiopia News* give irrefutable proof of the unusual number of Italian dead and wounded as a result of intensified guerrilla warfare by the Ethiopian troops in their continued fight for the maintenance of Ethiopian independence."[44] In his account of Pan-African protest in West Africa, Asante writes that *NT&EN* achieved extensive sales in Africa. While he does not provide actual numbers of sales, he says a popular feature in *NT&EN* was "Africa for Africans."[45] According to Asante, many articles were reprinted in full in local West African papers such as the *West African Pilot*, founded by Nigeria's future first president Nnamdi Azikiwe. Significantly, while most West Africans were unable to read newspapers, many were aware of the Italian invasion due to widespread oral reports. *NT&EN* was considered influential enough in stirring up not only dramatic pro-Ethiopian sentiments but also independence movements that it was banned in Sierra Leone.[46]

Conclusion

NT&EN's contribution to the African cause was deemed noteworthy enough that when its editor died in 1960, the famous American scholar W. E. B. DuBois would say of her, "I realised ... that the great work of Sylvia Pankhurst was to introduce black Ethiopia to white England ... and to make the British people realise that black folks had more and more to be recognised as human beings with the rights of women and men."[47] Decades have passed since *NT&EN* ceased publication. Its function was to offer alternative and consistently antifascist and pro-Ethiopian coverage at a time when mainstream media were struggling with representational dilemmas. The alternative constructions of the war enabled by *NT&EN* were largely based on alternative values and production codes, which in turn helped invigorate the Pan-African discourse in relation to the Italian-Ethiopian war.

Notes

1. Richard Pankhurst, *Sylvia Pankhurst: Counsel for Ethiopia* (Hollywood, CA: Tsehai Publishers, 2003), 22.
2. Nina Eliasoph, "Routines and the Making of Oppositional News," *Critical Studies in Mass Communication* 5 (1988): 315.
3. Robert W. McChesney, *Rich Media, Poor Democracy: Communication Politics in Dubious Times* (Chicago: University of Illinois Press, 1999).
4. Chris Atton, "Alternative Media in Scotland: Problems, Positions and 'Product,'" *Critical Quarterly* 42, no. 4 (2003): 41.
5. Ibid., 42.
6. John D. H. Downing. *Radical Media: The Political Experience of Alternative Communication* (Boston: South End Press, 1984), 2.
7. John D. H. Downing, *Radical Media: Rebellious Communication and Social Movements* (Thousand Oaks, CA: Sage, 2001).
8. James Hamilton and Chris Atton, "Theorizing Anglo-American Alternative Media: Toward a Contextual History and Analysis of US and UK Scholarship," *Media History* 7, no. 2 (2001): 123.
9. Ibid., 124.
10. Ibid.
11. Ibid.
12. A. Lawrence Lowell, "Alternatives before the League," *Foreign Affairs* 15, no. 1 (1936): 102–11.
13. Michael B. Salwen, "Evelyn Waugh in Ethiopia: The Novelist as War Correspondent and Journalism Critic," *Journalism Studies* 2, no. 1 (2001): 5–25.
14. Patricia W. Romero, *E. Sylvia Pankhurst: Portrait of a Radical* (New Haven, CT: Yale University Press, 1987), 226.
15. Donald N. Levine, *Greater Ethiopia: The Evolution of a Multiethnic Society* (Chicago: University of Chicago Press, 1974); John Sorenson, *Imagining Ethiopia: Struggles for History and Identity in the Horn of Africa* (New Brunswick, NJ: Rutgers University Press, 1993); Mulatu Wubneh and Yohannis Abate, *Ethiopia: Transition and Development in the Horn of Africa* (Boulder, CO: Westview, 1988); Edward W. Said, *Orientalism: Western Conceptions of the Orient* (New York: Vintage, 1978).
16. Levine, *Greater Ethiopia*, 9.
17. Sorenson, *Imagining Ethiopia*, 24.
18. Ibid.
19. *Time*, "Man of the Year," January 6, 1936, 13.

20. James Dugan and Laurence Lafore, *Days of Emperor and Clown: The Italo-Ethiopian War 1935–1936* (Garden City, NJ: Doubleday, 1973), 147.

21. Pankhurst, *Sylvia Pankhurst*, 1.

22. Alberto Sbacchi, *Legacy of Bitterness: Ethiopia and Fascist Italy, 1935–1941* (Lawrenceville, NJ: Red Sea Press, 1997), 209–13.

23. Pankhurst, *Sylvia Pankhurst*, 21.

24. Mary Davis, "Sylvia Pankhurst Memorial Lecture: Race, Class and Gender," Sylvia Pankhurst Memorial Committee, 2003, http://sylviapankhurst.gn.apc.org/SPML%202003.pdf, 9–10.

25. Romero, *Portrait of a Radical*, 168.

26. Chris Atton, "Reshaping Social Movement Media for a New Millennium," *Social Movement Studies* 2, no. 1 (2003): 10.

27. Ibid., 8–12.

28. Pankhurst, *Sylvia Pankhurst*, 23.

29. Davis, "Memorial Lecture," 13.

30. Atton, "Reshaping Social Movement Media," 12.

31. Ibid., 12–14.

32. Sbacchi, *Legacy of Bitterness*, 74.

33. For instance, see Kwame Anthony Appiah, *In My Father's House: Africa in the Philosophy of Culture* (New York: Oxford University Press, 1992); Samuel Kingsley Botwe Asante, *Pan-African Protest: West Africa and the Italo-Ethiopian Crisis 1934–1941* (London: Longman, 1977); Winston James, *Holding Aloft the Banner of Ethiopia: Caribbean Radicalism in Early Twentieth-century America* (New York: Verso, 1998).

34. Appiah, *In My Father's House*, 5.

35. Ibid., 6.

36. Ibid., 9.

37. Ibid., 7.

38. Ibid.

39. Asante, *Pan-African Protest*, 17–21.

40. Indeed, Kenyatta became the honorary secretary of this society.

41. Asante, *Pan-African Protest*, 45–46.

42. Levine, *Greater Ethiopia*, 14.

43. Michael O. West, "Like a River: The Million Man March and the Black Nationalist Tradition in the United States," *Journal of Historical Sociology* 12, no. 1 (1999): 87.

44. Leslie Rollins, "Ethiopia, African Americans, and African-Consciousness: The Effect of Ethiopia and Africa-Consciousness in Twentieth-century America," *Journal of Religious Thought* 54/55, no. 2/1 (1998): 21.

45. Asante, *Pan-African Protest*, 52.

46. Ibid., 192.

47. Davis, "Memorial Lecture," 13.

3

All's Well in the Colony

Newspaper Coverage of the Mau Mau Movement, 1952–56

Melissa Tully

Introduction

The Western media have traditionally presented Africa as a place that is difficult to understand because of its "backward" nature.[1] People are unfamiliar with Africa and its complex history, and thus the incomplete and inaccurate images of Africa that permeate the media often influence the way people understand the continent.[2] Americans are generally presented with information that lacks social, cultural, historical, or political context, and this perpetuates the idea that Africa is confusing and unstable.[3] The coverage of Africa was particularly problematic during the era of colonialism, because the colonial powers primarily controlled foreign news about Africa. Although news agencies had correspondents in Africa, problems of language and cultural understanding often hindered reporting.[4] In addition, there were not enough reporters on the continent, and correspondents in one part of Africa were ill-equipped to cover other regions.[5] This pattern of coverage persists into contemporary reporting.[6]

Due to a lack of cultural, social, and historical knowledge, many events are not covered or are inaccurately portrayed; however, conflict tends to receive a lot of coverage.[7] One such conflict, the Mau Mau revolt, received widespread news coverage in the early 1950s. The Mau Mau rebellion was a political and militant revolt against the colonial state in Kenya. The revolt occurred during a time of widespread turmoil in Africa, as various colonies, including many in the British Empire, sought independence from European domination. Researchers have argued that the British government and press attempted to manipulate the unfamiliar, non-Western traditions of the Kikuyu and ignored the Mau Mau's political and nationalist initiatives, to delegitimize the movement and to create an image of the Mau Mau as savage and primitive.[8] This chapter seeks to systematically analyze news coverage of the rebellion to better understand how the revolt was covered in light of the criticisms of news coverage of Africa.

For this particular analysis, I examined newspaper coverage of the Mau Mau in relation to the social and cultural climate of America, Great Britain, and Kenya during the critical years of the Mau Mau movement, from September 1952 through 1956. The focus is on news stories, which are here defined as any stories that are not editorials or op-eds, columns, briefs, or indexes. I selected two newspapers for their different relationships to Kenya: the *Times* of London, published in the colonial country, and the *New York Times*, published in the less-involved United States of America. Because Great Britain was the colonial power ruling Kenya, it had an established political relationship with the territory and was the overseer of government. The United States had a far less substantial relationship with Kenya; however, two key factors made the Mau Mau enticing to the American press. First, the Mau Mau presented a conflict between Africans and British that had not previously been seen in British colonies with large settler populations. Second, the spread of Communism and Soviet influence was a major concern beginning in the late 1940s. America was concerned with the fate of African nations because of the fear that they would side with the Soviets.[9] With little background or contextual knowledge of Kenyan politics, the Mau Mau could have been construed as a Communist-influenced movement. By using these two news sources, I compare the coverage to establish the variations and interpretations that appeared.

The next two sections provide a brief history of the colonial period in Kenya leading up to the Mau Mau and the official government message regarding the rebellion. It is important to consider government propaganda, because government actors and sources were so prominent in news stories. It is interesting to note the similarities between the government texts and news coverage. The final two sections address newspaper coverage in the *New York Times* and the *Times* of London, the themes that emerged in these texts, and the ideology reflected in the discourse. The conclusion sets the coverage in greater historical context, arguing that the coverage of the Mau Mau represents a simplified version of the conflict by portraying the Mau Mau as terrorists, and reflects British concerns with decolonization and with maintaining the impression that the government was effectively dealing with the conflict.

The Emergence of the Mau Mau

The British colonial period in Kenya began in 1888 and lasted until 1963. The region provided beautiful weather and fertile land to entice British settlers. Persuaded by Colonial Governor Sir Charles Eliot, the first white settlers began arriving in 1902.[10] A considerable number of white settlers appropriated land from Africans and controlled the political structure of the territory. Similar to that in other settler colonies, the Kenyan society that was formed was racist; the white settlers considered themselves superior to the Africans, and this was reflected in the development of the colony. This racist ideology created African resentment toward British colonial rule. However, from 1902 to 1952, the white minority ruled the colony with little serious opposition.[11]

Although British land policies negatively affected various African groups living in Kenya, the Kikuyu typically were the most displaced.[12] Residing in the Central Province and the Highlands, the Kikuyu had lived in and farmed on the most fertile land in the colony. As the British settled in this region, Kikuyu farmers were forced into tenant farmer roles or had to move to the urban center of Nairobi to look for work. Land would become the major driving force behind Kenyan political movements, particularly the Mau Mau, because many Kenyans felt the British had stolen land that was rightfully theirs.[13] Culturally, the Kikuyu were a farming people, and landlessness was highly undesirable and detrimental to their way of life.[14] It is no surprise that the Mau Mau developed primarily as a movement of the Kikuyu because they saw land loss as the biggest issue in colonial Kenya.[15]

The Mau Mau did not arise suddenly; various failed political movements had paved the way. Prior to the Mau Mau, the 1940s saw the most explicit political struggles between Africans and the colonial government. As early as the 1920s, however, Kenyan political movements were demanding better representation in the colonial government through elected African officials.[16] By the 1930s, government representation and land issues dominated the Kenyan political arena. David Anderson notes that "For the Kikuyu especially, the land question had by the 1930s become *the* crucial political grievance."[17] Although the Kikuyu political movements' demands and desires varied—with some supporting the status quo, others demanding radical change, which included violent rebellion—land remained the driving force behind Kikuyu politics.[18]

Generally speaking, there were three political factions, each with at least one affiliated political party: conservatives, moderate nationalists, and militant nationalists. The conservatives were the chiefs and Christian elders who gained authority through associating with the colonial government, and they often supported the status quo. Conservative leaders "were the gatekeepers of the colonial state, and they became used to wielding patronage under its auspices."[19] The conservatives' relationship with the colonizer made them unpopular among the younger educated generations and among the unemployed, poor, landless Kikuyu. The Kikuyu Association (KA) was the first conservative political party and exerted the most power in the 1920s and

1930s. Eventually the KA disintegrated, and many former leaders joined more progressive political movements.

The moderate nationalist and militant nationalist groups developed in opposition to the conservatives.[20] Although the moderates claimed to have a different, more modern outlook than the conservatives, Anderson argues that "The moderates wanted to replace the conservatives in positions of political leadership, and although they frequently criticized the actions and motives of conservative chiefs, it is not at all clear that their own agenda of political leadership was really very different."[21] The moderates' wealth, land, and education gave them access to the political sphere; however, they did not address the real problems facing poor Kikuyu: land and wages. More militant, predominantly urban Kenyans formed the East African Association (EAA) in reaction to the KA. Evicted Kikuyu farmers, younger people, urban workers, and the unemployed strongly supported the militant nationalists. The EAA had a short life span, but militant ideas continued to bubble under the surface of Kenyan politics. On the surface, however, moderate nationalists controlled Kenyan politics.[22]

In 1924, the moderate Kikuyu Central Association (KCA) was formed. The KCA became the most prominent political party of the era and would represent the moderates for the next fifteen years. The British banned the KCA in 1941 because they feared that it was becoming too powerful.[23] In 1945, the Kenya African Union (KAU), a new moderate nationalist party, was formed, but by 1950 the KAU was struggling to garner support. By 1952, support for moderate policies was waning, and more militant ideas were coming to the fore. These militant policies ultimately led to the Mau Mau rebellion. According to Anderson, "When it inevitably came, the rebellion came slowly, as rebellions often do, in a myriad of local struggles over the years following the Second World War."[24] The Mau Mau movement developed because of unmet needs, particularly with regard to land, and continued exploitation at the hands of the government.[25]

On the morning of October 7, 1952, Mau Mau assassins murdered Chief Waruhiu wa Kungu, the government's paramount chief for Central Province.[26] As the representative of the Kiambu district and the senior African official under Kenya's colonial administration, Waruhiu's influence was directly felt in Kiambu. His ties to the district were much stronger than those of any European government official. Waruhiu knew that land was the major issue driving Kikuyu politics; however, he was a moderate and not sympathetic to tenant farmers—he even evicted some from his own farm. He was even less sympathetic to the Mau Mau, because of his relationship with the colonial government. Although other politically motivated murders had occurred, Waruhiu's assassination sparked a public outcry, even from white settlers.[27] Two weeks later, on October 20, 1952, Governor Evelyn Baring declared a state of emergency in Kenya.[28] The declaration of the emergency marks the unofficial beginning of the Mau Mau movement. Carolyn Martin Shaw argues that "The greatest immediate effect of the declaration of emergency in Kenya in October 1952 was to increase solidarity among the Kikuyu and in part to legitimize the Mau Mau."[29]

Within a day of the declaration of the emergency, the first British battalion, the Lancashire Fusiliers, arrived to support six battalions of the King's African Rifles based in Kenya, and Operation Jock Scott, the name given to the roundup of the Mau Mau, was in progress. Arguably, Operation Jock Scott paved the way for the more militant Mau Mau fighters to move into leadership positions, because the more moderate leaders were being detained.[30] Although Mau Mau suspects were continually arrested, and the British thought they had a handle on the situation, on October 22, 1952, Senior Chief Nderi, a firm denouncer of Mau Mau, was brutally murdered while trying to break up an oathing ceremony. Nderi's spontaneous murder coupled with Waruhiu's planned assassination suggested that the Mau Mau was a more organized group than it truly was in October 1952.[31] The final two months of 1952 saw more Mau Mau murders, including the first murders of white settlers. As a result, the British and colonial governments, the military, and the police stepped up their intervention.[32]

For the next three years, violence continued in Kenya. The Mau Mau offensive gained and lost momentum through the course of the conflict.[33] The British managed to arrest most of the Mau Mau leaders by early 1956. On October 21, 1956, Dedan Kimathi, the last free Mau Mau leader, was captured.[34] Kimathi's capture marks the unofficial end of the Mau Mau's military campaign, which mostly consisted of guerrilla warfare tactics and attacks from the forests of Kenya. The British managed to defeat the Mau Mau military offensive but were unable to silence the general uprising. By 1959, it was clear that the British had lost the battle to hold on to Kenya, and, in 1963, Kenya became independent.[35]

Mau Mau: The Official Line

The British government responded to the Mau Mau movement with an intense propaganda initiative. British discourse focused on long-held fears of Africans and prejudices about them to create a picture of the Mau Mau as a savage, barbaric movement based on primitive religious practices with no political motivation or basis.[36] Because the Mau Mau did not rely on the written word and had to maintain secrecy to achieve their goals, the British version heavily dominated the public discourse.[37] According to Wunyabari Maloba, "The major aim of the government propaganda offensive against the Mau Mau locally and internationally was to discredit African nationalism as being basically a criminal endeavor."[38] The British, and their discourse, exaggerated the barbarism and violence of the Mau Mau and downplayed the use of violence against the Mau Mau, which was always justified as being necessary in order to control the movement. It is unlikely that the average person in Kenya or abroad would read the propaganda disseminated directly by the government, but newspapers used these documents to construct their stories, and government sources were the major contributors to news stories.

The government's influence on the press during the state of emergency allowed the government to dictate the image of the Mau Mau. Press releases and pamphlets told the story of the Mau Mau from the colonial perspective. *The Mau Mau in Kenya*, published in 1954, is an official government pamphlet.[39] It has a foreword by Granville Roberts, public relations officer for Kenya. The forty-eight-page pamphlet is filled with detailed descriptions of Mau Mau "atrocities" and the government response to these. *The Mau Mau in Kenya* represents the Mau Mau as a perverse religious movement based on barbaric Kikuyu rituals.[40] The pamphlet focuses on the secrecy and brutality of the fighters and supporters, while praising the loyalty of other Kenyans, and it treats the Mau Mau as an isolated group of deranged killers who force and coerce people to join the movement through oathing rituals. It assures the reader, however, that the situation is under control because of dedicated British and Kenyan forces. Roberts states in his foreword that

> this publication is intended to throw light upon the Mau Mau secret society and the foul atrocities it has committed. The initiation rites of Mau Mau, especially in the "higher" degrees, are too obscene for publication. No description of them is possible which would not be equally objectionable.[41]

By highlighting the violent nature of the movement rather than addressing its political agenda, the pamphlet refuses the Mau Mau any political legitimacy.

The pamphlet also highlights the achievements of British colonialism in Kenya, noting improvements in agriculture, manufacturing and production, commerce, industry, and medicine.[42] The pamphlet promotes the modernizing mission in comparison to the "primitive savagery" of the Mau Mau: "It is perhaps best summed up in the words of the Parliamentary Delegation to Kenya which declared that: 'Mau Mau intentionally and deliberately seeks to lead the Africans of Kenya back to the bush and savagery and not forward into progress.'"[43] There is no mention of the destruction that settlers caused to the land or the fact that settlers took land from natives.

The promotion of African loyalty was a major component of the British agenda. The pamphlet ends by praising African loyalists: "Tragedy brings forth heroism, and in Kikuyuland brave men and women have not been deterred by the indescribable atrocities of Mau Mau ... from doing their duty."[44] The use of the idea of the noble and ignoble savage allowed the

British to degrade the Mau Mau while praising their colonial successes and rewarding faithful Africans for their support. The British wanted to retain the support of loyal Africans and persuade uncertain Africans to join their cause, because African support was necessary to end the rebellion.

Maloba argues that news coverage of the Mau Mau discredited the political motivations of the movement because the coverage focused primarily on violence:

> The foreign press characteristically concentrated on how the Mau Mau were rebelling not on why they were rebelling. Without discussing in detail the reasons behind the revolt and exposing the ruthless British response, the Mau Mau movement appeared to the world as a revolt without cause, except for the desire of Africans to kill, maim, and terrorize. The world, therefore, woke up one morning confronted with a murderous movement guided by voodooism and without cause or aim, "except to kill and disembowel as many whites, chiefs, headmen, and non-Mau Mau Kikuyu as possible." Portrayed thus, it was difficult for the Mau Mau to be liked or tolerated.[45]

The lack of explanatory background or contextual information helped perpetuate the image of the Mau Mau as apolitical. There was nothing in the foreign coverage to make the Mau Mau appear to be anything but a terrorist group.[46]

The next section looks at newspaper coverage to achieve a better understanding of the type of stories that were being told about the Mau Mau and the manner in which the British and American press were portraying Mau Mau and the British.

The Mau Mau: News Coverage

In order to examine the newspaper coverage of the Mau Mau, I conducted a content analysis of 25 percent of the news stories from the *New York Times* and the *Times* of London from September 1952 to December 1956, which resulted in a sample of 342 stories.[47] Content analysis allows for a systematic approach to the coverage and can be used to find trends and patterns.[48] The stories were coded into four categories: Topics, Actors, Sources, and Victims. Topics refer to what the story is about; Actors to the people acting or being acted upon; Sources to those to whom information is attributed; and Victims to the people injured or killed. The Victims category is important because many of the stories about the Mau Mau are about violence, involving injuries or deaths. Every story must have a subject; therefore, the content analysis resulted in 342 stories containing Topics; however, only 305 stories feature Actors, only 140 feature Victims, and only 214 stories have a

Source attribution.[49] The total items in each category in both papers were analyzed, and finally, the *New York Times* and the *Times* were compared for similarities and differences in the coverage of the four categories.

In addition to the content analysis, a discourse analysis was carried out in order to achieve an understanding of the themes of the stories. The overall theme of a story can be determined by considering the Topics, Actors, Victims, and Sources. The most prominent themes of news stories are often reflected in the stories' headlines and subheads, and generally, headlines and subheads help guide how people read the stories.[50] They tell the reader what is most important. All news stories are products of selections made by journalists and the emphasis they place on certain aspects of a situation while downplaying or ignoring other aspects. These choices are reflected in the language used and the selection and representation of various voices. These three factors are key components of news construction.[51] News writers and producers have to make choices regarding whose voice to present and whose voice to ignore or marginalize.[52]

I conducted a textual analysis to examine the discourse that developed around the Mau Mau. Textual analysis allows for an analysis of the ideology represented in the text.[53] Ideologies are often not stated outright but rather are implicit in the text, and analyzing texts for ideologies reveals what is often taken for granted.[54] It is important to analyze news discourse, because news helps shape perceptions of reality.[55] News stories are constructions of reality that present a particular version, out of a range of possible representations, of a situation.[56] Teun van Dijk describes the story presented in news as "an ideological construct, based on the definitions given by the accredited sources of journalists, such as the government or the union leaders. In other words, the media are not a neutral, commonsensed, or rational mediator of social events, but essentially help reproduce preformulated ideologies."[57] For example, in relationship to the Mau Mau, the news discourse helped reproduce stereotypes about Africans as savage through the denial of the political legitimacy of the movement. This will be discussed in more detail below.

The following sections examine the Topics, Actors, Sources, and Victims in the news coverage of Mau Mau; the themes that emerged in the texts; and the way these themes relate to the ideological discourse that was produced.

Analysis of the Categories

Topics

The analysis yields 784 topical occurrences, with seven Topics emerging as the most prominent, namely, Response; Killing; Arrests/Capture; Mau

Mau Trials; Loyalty to the British; Terrorism; and Criticism of Government. These seven Topics account for 64.3 percent of the total. It is not surprising that the Response topic ($n = 153$) occurs most frequently, accounting for 19.5 percent of the total and appearing in 44.7 percent of stories (see table 3.1). Response encompasses government, police, military, and community response and often refers to government plans or police and military actions against the Mau Mau. Arrests/Capture is similar to Response. It is coded separately, however, because it appears frequently as the sole topic, often with little contextual information, whereas Response usually contains a more detailed description of actions.

An example of each (Arrests/Capture and Response) will help illustrate this point. The following one-sentence article from the November 7, 1952, *New York Times* is coded as Arrests/Capture: "British troops and policemen backed by armored cars and artillery, rounded up more than 2,000 natives today in a continuing effort to stamp out Mau Mau terrorism." The following two excerpts, one from the *New York Times* and one from the *Times* are examples of content that are considered Responses:

> Nearly 400 policemen and soldiers blocked off eight square miles of the Kikuyu tribal reserve near here today and drove away 4,000 head of cattle and thousands of sheep and goats.
>
> The reason for "Operation Cowboy" was that the 6,000 natives had refused to give police any cooperation in their hunt for the murders of Senior Chief Nderi and two African constables two weeks ago.[58]

> The Government of Kenya is considering an immediate *ex gratia* payment for those who have suffered financial losses through the activities of gangs inspired by subversive organizations.
>
> This was announced yesterday by Mr. E. A. Vasey, the Finance Minister in the Legislative Council, the emergency session of which stands adjourned until Tuesday after three bills strengthening the laws against the secret organization Mau Mau had been approved.[59]

Considered together, Response and Arrests/Capture ($n = 211$) account for 34.7 percent of the total Topics, appearing in 79.5 percent of stories. This focus on response, arrests, and other forms of capture indicates that press coverage was concerned with the manner in which the government, the military, and the police were reacting to Mau Mau. From the coverage, it often appears as if the rebellion is under control, or at least that the British are doing all they can to end the revolt.

Killing is another major Topic requiring further explanation and analysis. Killing refers to the killing of anyone by anyone; therefore, considering the

Table 3.1. Number and Percentage of Topics in *Times* and *NYT* Stories

Topics	n	Percentage of Topics (n=784)	Percentage of Stories (n=342)
Response	153	19.5	44.7
Killing	119	15.2	34.8
Arrests/Capture	58	7.4	17.0
Mau Mau Trials	55	7.0	16.1
Loyalty to British	46	5.9	13.5
Terrorism	37	4.7	10.8
Criticism of Government	36	4.6	10.5

actors and victims is important for understanding the true nature of this Topic. For example, some articles that are coded as Killing discuss the Mau Mau murdering settlers or Africans, while other articles are about the police and military killing suspected Mau Mau members. Killing is coded as one Topic because the Victims and Actors codes reveal who is killing whom. Examining an article coded as Killing distinguishes the differences in the language used to describe Mau Mau killings and police or military killings. An article from the *New York Times*, "12 More Natives Slain in New Mau Mau Drive," contains examples of the different kinds of language used to describe the killings:

> A gang of Mau Mau terrorists killed at least twelve pro-British native Home Guards in a night attack on an African village near Nyeri, it was announced today. The killings followed the massacre of at least 120 loyal natives near Nairobi Thursday.
>
> Early reports from Nyeri, sixty miles south of Nairobi, said the gang of about 100 terrorists was armed with pistols and rifles. The attack was made in the Chinga location, in the south Nyeri reserve.
>
> Troop reinforcements are to be flown from Britain to aid the anti-Mau Mau campaign. There has been no announcement of the total number of troops, who will begin to arrive Tuesday.
>
> A thousand Kikuyu tribesmen have been taken into custody for screening since the Thursday massacre at Lari. Police and security forces have between 200 and 300 of them identified as having taken part. Six known terrorists have been killed.[60]

This article depicts the Mau Mau killings as terrorist acts and the police killings as a response to these acts. This article is interesting for what it does not include about the Lari killings, which constituted a major turning point in the Mau Mau offensive. The killings were planned, targeted attacks on chiefs and loyalists, and the Mau Mau killed or injured approximately 120 people. Following the killings, security forces responded by killing over 200 Africans without solid evidence that they had taken part in the massacre. The security force killings were more random than the Mau Mau attacks on loyalists; however, this article mentions only that six "known terrorists" were killed.

Throughout the coverage, the Mau Mau killings are presented as terrorist acts, with little or no purpose beyond the desire to kill whites and loyal Africans. Police killings are most often presented as justified responses to terrorist acts. There are a few exceptions: police brutality allegations and the unnecessary killing of suspects emerge as a Topic eleven times. Nevertheless, police killings are overwhelmingly presented as a necessary step in defeating the Mau Mau. The portrayal of Mau Mau killings as random, brutal acts, coupled with the portrayal of British acts as justified, contributes to the larger themes of the Mau Mau as apolitical terrorists and the British as controlling the situation.

Actors

The analysis yielded a total of 593 Actors in the 305 stories that featured Actors. The majority of Actors in the coverage are government officials ($n = 220$), accounting for 37.1 percent of the total in this category and appearing in 72.2 percent of stories containing Actors. The Police/Military are the second most frequent group of Actors ($n = 178$). The Police/Military account for 30 percent of total Actors and appear in 58.5 percent of stories with Actors. Taken together, the government, police, and military account for 67.1 percent of the total (see table 3.2). The frequency of occurrence of these Actors coincides with the occurrence of the Response topic: the more often the Response topic occurs, the more the government, police, and military will have acted. The focus on Response and official Actors also has to do with the source choices in each article.

Sources

Source attribution is an important element when examining the manner in which a story is constructed. A total of 214 stories contained 266 source attributions. The sources selected help dictate the presentation of a certain version of events and influence the content and slant of a news article.

Table 3.2. Number and Percentage of Actors in *Times* and *NYT* Stories

Actors	n	Percentage of Actors (n=593)	Percentage of Stories (n=305)
Government	220	37.1	72.2
Police/Military	178	30.0	58.4
Mau Mau	81	13.7	26.6
Africans	55	9.3	18.0

There are bound to be various perspectives on the same issue; however, journalists and editors must select which aspects to highlight and which to leave out.[61] In the case of the Mau Mau, the government (n = 130) accounts for the vast majority of Sources, namely, 48.9 percent of the total Sources, and is present in 60.7 percent of the stories in this category. The police and military are another prominent source, accounting for 17.3 percent of the total and appearing in 21.5 percent of the stories with sources (see table 3.3). Official reports are documents and statements that are not attributed to any particular group but are referred to as "official." For example, "An official announcement today said the 214 prisoners had been released."[62] Official sources (n = 21) make up another 7.9 percent of the total in this category.

Combining the sources allows them to be clustered in three prominent groups: Official, Unofficial, and Mau Mau. Official Sources consist of Government; Police/Military; Church; British Press; Lawyers; and Official Reports. Official Sources are cited 218 times, and account for 81 percent of the total Sources. Africans and Settlers can be considered Unofficial Sources and are cited 28 times, accounting for 10.5 percent of the total Sources. Mau Mau refers to members and documents associated with the Mau Mau and accounts for only 4.5 percent of the total in this category. It is clear that official sources dominated the press coverage. The abundant use of official sources, particularly government, police, and military sources, corresponds to the frequency of the occurrence of the Response topic. Government, police, and military sources are most likely to discuss the response to the Mau Mau, because they were active in response activities such as arrests of suspected Mau Mau fighters and supporters, run-ins with Mau Mau fighters, and ambushes of Mau Mau camps. It was the job of the government, police, and military to put an end to the Mau Mau rebellion and restore order to the colony.

Table 3.3. Number and Percentage of Sources in *Times* and *NYT* Stories

Sources	n	Percentage of Sources (n=266)	Percentage of Stories (n=214)
Government	130	48.9	60.7
Police/Military	46	17.3	21.5
Official Reports	21	7.9	9.8
Africans	19	7.1	8.9
Mau Mau	12	4.5	5.6

Victims

Reference to Victims occurs in 140 stories. The majority of Victims in the coverage were actual or alleged Mau Mau members ($n = 86$), accounting for 39.1 percent of Victims and appearing in 61.4 percent of the stories that featured Victims (see table 3.4). However, if non–Mau Mau Africans and settlers are considered together, they are mentioned 96 times as Victims, accounting for 43.6 percent of the total and appearing in 68.8 percent of stories with victims. In terms of the overall number of Victims of Mau Mau killings and violence, Africans and settlers appear slightly more frequently than Mau Mau victims. Police and military deaths usually resulted from planned attacks on the Mau Mau as fighters killed police during confrontations. Although the numerical difference between the number of Mau Mau killed and the number of settlers and Africans killed is not that large, the way the victims are presented varies considerably. These differences are evident in the coverage of the killings as discussed earlier.

Framing the Mau Mau: Differences in Coverage

In general, the *Times* of London provides thorough coverage of the Mau Mau during the analyzed period. The articles usually consist of many paragraphs and are often full columns or extend into two columns. The situation in Kenya was important to the British for a variety of reasons, including economic interests, the stability of the empire, and the safety of the settlers.[63] The colony was a critical British holding in East Africa, and it is therefore not surprising that the British were concerned with putting a stop to the

Table 3.4. Number and Percentage of Victims in *Times* and *NYT* Stories

Victims	n	Percentage of Victims ($n=220$)	Percentage of Stories ($n=140$)
Mau Mau	86	39.1	61.4
Africans	55	25.0	39.3
Settlers	41	18.6	29.3
Police/Military	21	9.5	15.0

Mau Mau—the coverage in the *Times* reflects these concerns. Because Britain had a significant stake in Kenya, it had to provide the necessary information on the situation to its citizens.

In the *Times*, Response is the dominant topic, appearing in 47.2 percent of the stories. The British version presented the Mau Mau as a problem that was being handled by the government with proper military action. The government and the military were active agents trying to stop the Mau Mau from gaining strength and succeeding in its mission. Because the government and the military were such key players in the Mau Mau revolt, their actions formed the center of attention and the subject of debate, scrutiny, and praise. Although the government's actions were often praised for slowing down the movement, or for capturing or killing suspected terrorists, they were also criticized in some cases, particularly for allegations of unnecessary brutality. Overall, the *Times* presents multiple perspectives on the government and military; however, official sources are by far the most frequently utilized. The coverage lacks information regarding the Mau Mau's political and nationalist agenda, representing the Mau Mau more as an object and less as an active subject. The Mau Mau was something for the government to act upon and to stop.

The *New York Times* tends to sensationalize the revolt, highlighting murders and destruction. In general, the *New York Times* coverage of the Mau Mau has a tendency to simplify the situation by not going into great detail. Many of the articles consist of only a couple of sentences or, at most, a few paragraphs. The *New York Times* provides very little contextual or background information on the Mau Mau or the situation of the British in Kenya, and the understanding of the Mau Mau in the *New York Times* is completely tied to terrorism and conflict. The day after the government declared the state of emergency, one journalist described the Mau Mau as a "secret organization whose campaign of terror to drive the British out of Kenya has been responsible for nearly forty murders and many more beatings and attempted killings among natives and Europeans alike."[64] Terrorism is far more prominent in the *New York Times*—appearing in 21.9 percent of the articles, third behind Response and Killing—than in the *Times* coverage. In the *New York Times*, the Mau Mau is presented as an apolitical movement with no driving ideology—it was simply an outbreak of terrorism by uncivilized people who had no other way of expressing their frustrations.

A Deeper Look: Mau Mau Themes

Two major themes emerge from the analysis of the coverage of the Mau Mau. The first theme relates to the response to the Mau Mau. The majority of the articles are concerned with responding to the revolt. The Response topic appears most frequently in the coverage, but this is not the only reason for the emergence of the response theme, which develops through discussions of arrests and capture, the killing of suspected Mau Mau members, the trials of suspected Mau Mau members, detention camps and prisons, African loyalty to the British, government finances, Mau Mau surrender, praise and criticism of the government's response to the Mau Mau, and even allegations of police brutality.

The British were concerned with restoring law and order in Kenya by ending the Mau Mau rebellion. The focus on their response to the rebellion shows that the government was taking an active role in the situation and was aimed at showing that the government had the situation under control. It was important for the government and the media to portray the revolt as an isolated event that was actively being put down, because of the wave of decolonization that was spreading throughout the colonized world. Britain had a large stake in Kenya and needed to show its citizens that it was doing all it could to return order to the colony. When the actions of the government, the police, and the military were questioned, the British were presented in a negative light. To combat the negative coverage, the British highlighted the positive steps they were taking to end the Mau Mau rebellion. Although the coverage reveals that criticism of the government, the police, and the military was present in the public domain as early as 1952, the government continued its campaign against the Mau Mau with little major opposition.

The second major theme in the coverage is terrorism. The *New York Times* coverage focuses heavily on the Mau Mau as a terrorist group. References to terrorism in the *New York Times* are frequent in headlines, subheads, and lead paragraphs, which tend to influence the way people read a text.[65] *New York Times* articles describe the Mau Mau as a terrorist group that wants to drive the British out of Kenya. Examples of references to terrorism in the *New York Times* include the following: "The secret Mau Mau terror organization",[66] "Mau Mau, a secret society of Kikuyu tribesmen sworn to curb white control";[67] and "The report described the Mau Mau organization as 'a conspiracy designed to dominate first the Kikuyu tribe and then all other Africans and finally to exterminate or drive out all other races and seize power in Kenya.'"[68]

The rebellion is never described as political, and reference to political motives is sparse. Even when political motives are described, they are often dismissed and pitted against the British "civilizing" mission:

> Furthermore, since the Kikuyu cannot wage war they have had to give up their nomadic existence and settle in the territories held by them when law and order were brought to Kenya by the British. This has brought about a general land shortage, for their holdings are constantly divided from fathers to sons. Small parcels of land, often separated by great distances, had led to bad farming and soil erosion.[69]

This passage contains false and simplified references. The first sentence is simply false: much of Kikuyu life was concerned with farming, not warfare. Of course, warriors were a major part of traditional Kikuyu life, but they were not the only part. The paragraph reminds the reader of the colonial mission and the idea that without the British, the Kikuyu would not have "law and order." Finally, land concerns are mentioned, but the description oversimplifies the matter and does not hold the British government or the settlers responsible for the land shortage. This article was printed at the beginning of the emergency, showing that the government and the press were aware of land concerns and the potential for violent revolt, but little had been done to prevent the outbreak.

Focusing primarily on the government and military response to a "terrorist" organization, the news coverage presents a picture of the Mau Mau situation that is overwhelmingly favorable to the British. Even when there is criticism of the government or the campaign, it is often countered with descriptions of Mau Mau crimes, used to justify the actions of the government and the military. The dominant story of the Mau Mau was that of a terrorist organization that the British were determined to stop. This version of Mau Mau dominated until after Kenyan independence, and it was not until 1963 that the first Mau Mau accounts began to emerge in the form of memoirs by fighters and supporters, including *"Mau Mau" Detainee* by Josiah Mwangi Kariuki, a leader of "hardcore detainees," and Waruhiu Itote's *"Mau Mau" General*.[70]

The portrayal of the Mau Mau as terrorists and the British as responsible for restoring law and order to the colony exemplifies a larger ideological discourse about Africans and colonialism that was prevalent during the era. The notion that Africans were primitive, backward people and that the European colonial endeavor was a civilizing mission was common in

America and Europe.[71] The news discourse reflects this ideology through its depictions of Mau Mau fighters as savage and the British government and the military as simply trying to maintain order. This type of discourse has permeated the Western press throughout the colonial period and into contemporary times and is arguably responsible for the misconceptions about Africa that remain today.[72]

Conclusion

When considering complex historical events like the Mau Mau rebellion, it is tempting to simplify the situation to make it more understandable, or to attempt to fit it into one's preexisting worldviews. Researchers have argued that the coverage of Africa oversimplifies events, inaccurately portrays issues, and leads people to believe that the continent may be beyond understanding.[73] How does the coverage of the Mau Mau fit into the overall scheme of African coverage? In the *New York Times*, the portrayal of the Mau Mau as terrorists, the dismissal of political motivations, and the focus on response suggest that the coverage lacked key information necessary for understanding the Kenyan situation. The *Times* coverage was more accurate than that of the *New York Times* but still remained focused on the Mau Mau's use of violence and the official response to the revolt. The version of the rebellion presented in the mainstream media represents the version that was most readily available to readers. Although I cannot say what effects, if any, this coverage of Mau Mau had on readers, it is clear that the texts perpetuated common ideas and misconceptions about Africa that were part of public consciousness.

Discourse, as the formation of knowledge through language, has the power to create a version of history that has real and lasting influences.[74] In the case of the Mau Mau movement, the dominant discourse during the time was that of the British, who had the power to influence international coverage because most information regarding colonial affairs was filtered through Britain. Although the Mau Mau had discourse about themselves among themselves, for the most part it did not reach the larger society. Because the British had colonial interests at stake and the Mau Mau posed a real threat to the colonial situation, they portrayed the Mau Mau as predominantly a terrorist organization and not a legitimate nationalist or political movement.

The high stakes also led to stories attempting to show that the situation was under control. By 1952, the British Empire was no longer secure. With the loss of India in 1947 and the spread of decolonization through Africa, the British Empire was beginning to come to an end. Kenya was a settler colony that was beloved by many Britons, and losing it would pose a real threat to the empire and to Britain's image. The government needed to reassure its citizens that all was well in the colony to keep them committed to the colonial cause. Colonialism was an expensive endeavor in many ways: time, money, and personnel were needed to keep the empire afloat. As long as the situation in Kenya was perceived as being under control, the government could justify its continued response and its commitment to retaining the colony. By 1959, the veil was lifted, and it was clear that the British would have to leave Kenya. The country remained under a state of emergency until 1960, and in 1963 the country received its independence.

Notes

1. Bosah Ebo, "American Media and African Culture," in Hawk, *Africa's Media Image*, 15–25; Beverly G. Hawk, "Introduction: Metaphors of African Coverage," in Hawk, *Africa's Media Image*, 3–14.

2. Michael McCarthy, *Dark Continent: Africa as Seen by Americans* (Westport, CT: Greenwood, 1983).

3. Hawk, "Introduction"; Beverly G. Hawk, "African Politics and American Reporting," in *Media and Democracy in Africa*, ed. Goran Hyden, Michael Leslie, and Folu F. Ogundimu (New Brunswick, NJ: Transaction Publishers, 2002), 157–76.

4. Ulf Himmelstrand, "The Problem of Cultural Translation in the Reporting of African Social Realities," in *Reporting Africa*, ed. Olav Stokke (New York: Africana, 1971), 117–33.

5. Ibid.

6. Melissa Wall, "The Rwanda Crisis: An Analysis of News Magazine Coverage," *International Communication Gazette* 59, no. 2 (1997): 121–34.

7. Jeff Charles, Larry Shore, and Rusty Todd, "The *New York Times* Coverage of Equatorial and Lower Africa," *Journal of Communication* 29, no. 2 (1979): 148–55.

8. Wunyabari O. Maloba, *Mau Mau and Kenya: An Analysis of a Peasant Revolt* (Bloomington: Indiana University Press, 1993); Wunyabari O. Maloba, "The Media and Mau Mau: Kenyan Nationalism and Colonial Propaganda," in Hawk, *Africa's Media Image*, 51–61; David Anderson, *Histories of the Hanged: The Dirty War in Kenya and the End of Empire* (New York: Norton, 2005).

9. Maloba, *Mau Mau and Kenya*.

10. Anderson, *Histories of the Hanged*.

11. Ibid.

12. Ibid. David Maughan-Brown, *Land, Freedom and Fiction: History and Ideology in Kenya* (London: Zed Books, 1985).

13. Anderson, *Histories of the Hanged*, 10.

14. Maloba, *Mau Mau in Kenya*, 26–28.

15. Ibid.

16. Anderson, *Histories of the Hanged*.

17. Ibid., 10, emphasis in the original.

18. Ibid., 9–13; Maughan-Brown, *Land, Freedom and Fiction*, 23.

19. Anderson, *Histories of the Hanged*, 11.

20. Ibid., 9–13.
21. Ibid., 11.
22. Ibid., 13–23.
23. Ibid., 388.
24. Ibid., 3–4.
25. Maughan-Brown, *Land, Freedom and Fiction*, 23.
26. Anderson, *Histories of the Hanged*, 55, 390.
27. Ibid., 55–57.
28. Maloba, *Mau Mau in Kenya*, 69
29. Carolyn Martin Shaw, *Colonial Inscriptions: Race, Sex, and Class in Kenya* (Minneapolis: University of Minnesota Press, 1995), 151.
30. Anderson, *Histories of the Hanged*, 62–63.
31. Ibid., 68.
32. Ibid., 68–76.
33. Ibid., 244.
34. Ibid., 288, 393.
35. Marshall S. Clough, *Mau Mau Memoirs: History, Memory, and Politics* (Boulder, CO: Lynne Rienner, 1998), 206–7.
36. Maloba, *Mau Mau and Kenya*.
37. The Mau Mau relied heavily on oaths and songs, and they spread their message by word of mouth. They did not have any official presence in the press, because the state of emergency denied Africans access to newspapers, and the Mau Mau fighters needed to remain hidden or else they would be arrested and, as often happened, be killed. For more information about Mau Mau oaths, songs, and other means of communication, see Maina wa Kinyatti, ed., *Thunder from the Mountains: Mau Mau Patriotic Songs* (London: Zed Books, 1980); and Benjamin C. Ray, *African Religions: Symbol, Ritual, and Community* (Englewood Cliffs, NJ: Prentice-Hall, 1976).
38. Maloba, *Mau Mau and Kenya*, 98.
39. *The Mau Mau in Kenya*, with foreword by Granville Roberts (London: Hutchinson, 1954).
40. Ibid.
41. Roberts, foreword to *The Mau Mau in Kenya*, 7.
42. *The Mau Mau in Kenya*.
43. Ibid., 8.
44. Ibid., 48.
45. Maloba, "The Media and Mau Mau," 58.
46. Ibid.
47. The actual sample is slightly under 25 percent, because stories that were not news stories were removed from the sample.
48. Robert Philip Weber, *Basic Content Analysis*, 2nd ed., Sage University Paper Series on Quantitative Applications in the Social Sciences (Newbury Park, CA: Sage, 1990).
49. See tables 3.1–3.4.
50. James W. Tankard, "The Empirical Approach to the Study of Media Framing," in *Framing Public Life*, ed. Stephen D. Reese, Oscar H. Gandy Jr., and August E. Grant (Mahwah, NJ: Lawrence Erlbaum Associates, 2001), 95–106.

51. Gaye Tuchman, *Making News: A Study in the Construction of Reality* (New York: Free Press, 1978).

52. Tankard, "The Empirical Approach to the Study of Media Framing."

53. Norman Fairclough, *Critical Discourse Analysis: The Critical Study of Language* (London: Longman, 1995); Sonja K. Foss, "Ideological Criticism," in *Rhetorical Criticism: Exploration and Practice*, ed. Sonja K. Foss (Long Grove, IL: Waveland, 2004), 243, 245–48.

54. Fairclough, *Critical Discourse Analysis*, 5–6.

55. Tuchman, *Making News*.

56. Ibid.

57. Teun van Dijk, *News as Discourse* (Hillsdale, NJ: Lawrence Erlbaum Associates, 1988).

58. *New York Times*, "Kikuyus' Herds Seized as Hostages in Murder," November 11, 1952.

59. *Times* (London), "Mau Mau Raid of Kenya Farms: Compensation Discussed," September 28, 1952.

60. *New York Times*, March 29, 1953.

61. Tuchman, *Making News*.

62. *New York Times*, "93 Mau Mau Recaptured," September 20, 1954.

63. Anderson, *Histories of the Hanged*, 5–6.

64. *New York Times*, "Briton to Survey Terror in Kenya," October 22, 1952.

65. Tankard, "The Empirical Approach to the Study of Media Framing."

66. *New York Times*, "Two Kenya Chiefs Threatened," October 14, 1952.

67. *New York Times*, "Kenya Zone Closed to Check Mau Mau," May 30, 1953.

68. *New York Times*, "Mau Mau Stronger, Parliament Told," February 24, 1954.

69. *New York Times*, "British Worried by Kenya Terror," October 22, 1952.

70. Josiah Mwangi Kariuki, *"Mau Mau" Detainee: The Account of a Kenyan African of His Experiences in Detention Camps, 1953–1960*, with foreword by Margery Perham (London: Oxford University Press, 1963); Waruhiu Itote, *"Mau Mau" General* (Nairobi, Kenya: East African Publishing House, 1967); Clough, *Mau Mau Memoirs*, 61–82.

71. Ebo, "American Media and African Culture"; Maloba, "The Media and Mau Mau"; McCarthy, *Dark Continent*.

72. Beverly G. Hawk, ed., *Africa's Media Image* (New York: Praeger, 1992); and Hawk, "African Politics and American Reporting."

73. Hawk, *Africa's Media Image*; Hawk, "African Politics and American Reporting."

74. Norman Fairclough, *Media Discourse* (New York: Hodder Arnold, 1995), 55.

Part Two

Ungendering Conflicts, Engendering Peace

4

Pedagogies of Pain

Teaching "Women, War, and Militarism in Africa"

Alicia C. Decker

Introduction

Teaching a course about war and militarism in Africa presents a number of ethical and pedagogical challenges. How does one teach about the brutal realities of war without contributing to the so-called pornography of violence?[1] Is it possible to "give an account of . . . shocking events without giving in to a desire to shock?"[2] Are there constructive ways to educate students about war and violence without completely demoralizing them in the process? These difficult questions are just a few of the many that I confronted when I designed and taught "Women, War, and Militarism in Africa," an upper-division women's studies course at Agnes Scott College. In this essay, I reflect upon my experiences in teaching students about violence in Africa. After briefly introducing readers to the classroom setting, I move into a detailed discussion of the course structure as a whole. Here I not only describe the various assignments, readings, and lectures but also what did and did not work best for the students. Although my primary goals in this chapter are pedagogical, I hope this discussion sparks a broader dialogue about the politics of representing violence in the classroom.

Teaching "Women, War, and Militarism in Africa"

Agnes Scott College is one of the last remaining women's colleges in the nation. In the bustling urban environs of Atlanta, Georgia, the school functions as an intellectual refuge for students and faculty alike. During my one-year fellowship as a visiting lecturer, I had the opportunity to engage with students from a wide variety of backgrounds. Many of the women on campus were nontraditional students, meaning that they were married, had children, or were over twenty-four years of age. A large number also came from underrepresented racial and ethnic groups or identified themselves as lesbian or queer.[3] The diversity on campus guaranteed that classroom discussions would be lively and engaging.

When I taught the course in the spring of 2007, the country was deeply embroiled in the "war on terror." Although the battlefields of Iraq and Afghanistan seemed far removed from this idyllic college campus, most of my students had been touched by the war in some way or another. With their friends and family members serving in the U.S. military overseas, I found it incredibly difficult to articulate many of my criticisms of the war. I wanted students to understand why feminist scholars have historically resisted military interventions, but at the same time, I did not want to come across as uncaring or disrespectful.[4] Indeed, I walked a delicate tightrope throughout the semester.

If war was on the "home front," Africa certainly was not.[5] Most of my students had very little knowledge of the continent, save for the violent images of "tribal warfare" that flooded the nightly news from time to time. My challenge was to teach the students about the realities of war without reinforcing negative stereotypes about Africans as essentially "savage" or "brutal." On the first day of class, I handed out blank maps and asked the students to fill in the countries. Although I was pretty sure that this assignment would present a challenge, I never expected to find Sumatra, Java, and Indonesia mapped onto central Africa. Even the two students who had visited The Gambia on a study tour could not locate more than five or six countries. If students were this unfamiliar with the basics of geography, how could I possibly expect them to understand the complexities of African conflicts? To solve the problem, I decided to highlight three new countries at the beginning of every class. After relating a number of interesting facts about each place, I pointed out where the countries were located on the map. Throughout the discussion, I regularly returned to these specific countries so that they would become more familiar to my students. Every few weeks I gave cumulative map quizzes that counted toward their participation grade. By the end of the semester, nearly every student was able to fill in a blank map of the continent. I strongly believe that because African conflicts are so intimately linked to geographical borders, students must understand where countries are located.

Teaching about Africa also involves getting students to recognize the continent's tremendous diversity. Films, novels, and memoirs are excellent tools for enlivening classroom discussion.[6] When we engage students on a visceral level, they are more likely to think critically about the material.

One of the problems that I discovered with regard to this class, however, was how deeply these texts affected the students. Tears were a regular part of our classroom experience, and, at times, I worried that I had given the students more than they could handle. Some of them expressed feelings of great despair because they did not know what to do about the wars, violence, and suffering. My initial response was to tell them that they should be angry, sad, and confused. After all, it was these feelings that facilitated social activism. However, had I caused a deeper harm? Had I completely immobilized the students by overwhelming them with graphic depictions of violence day after day? Even worse, had I simply reinforced the very stereotypes about Africans and violence that I had been hoping to dispel?

One of my initial goals in the course was to make Africa seem relevant to the students' daily lives. Toward this end, I encouraged the students to keep abreast of current affairs, particularly as they related to the continent. Discussions of the news were an important part of our daily classroom ritual. I think the students were generally surprised by how difficult it was to find "good" news out of Africa. They wanted to know why most of the coverage focused on death and devastation. Was Africa really just about wars and violence? We spent a lot of time talking about how we "know" what we "know" about Africa.[7] In resistance to the Fox News Empire, I introduced the students to alternative media outlets, such as the Voice of America, the BBC World Service, and AllAfrica.com. They responded enthusiastically by flooding my in-box with Internet stories from all across the continent.

As a way of capitalizing on the students' interest in current affairs, I required them to keep a weekly journal tracking conflict-related issues in Africa. In addition to outlining the major facts of the story, the students discussed the way in which the conflict had been represented and what this ultimately suggested about the author's standpoint. They analyzed the news items for content, but also for what was left unsaid. For example, who were the twenty-five "civilians" that were massacred in Darfur? What did the author mean when she said that the "victims" included "women and children"? Is a massacre qualitatively more severe if women and children are targeted? Why or why not? It is interesting to note that very few of the students' entries concerned peace or reconstruction. Was this because there were fewer instances of peacekeeping than of war-making or because peacemaking was simply less noteworthy (read: sexy)? In retrospect, I suspect that if the assignment had focused specifically on global peace-building initiatives (versus peace and conflict in general), the students would not have felt so overwhelmed by violence. In addition to the journals, they completed an annotated bibliography and a twelve- to fifteen-page research paper on a topic of their choice. I did not require exams because I wanted students to engage in meaningful research projects that would allow them to explore items they were curious about. I did, however, ask them to submit one-page analytical responses to every unit. These write-ups not only ensured that the students completed the reading but also facilitated better discussions. Each of these assignments is described in greater detail in the course syllabus, which has been included as appendix A.

In order to expose the students to an array of theoretical and empirical perspectives, I organized the course into five major units. During the first few weeks of class, we grappled with a number of important feminist questions. For example, if women are "natural" peacemakers, why is the image of the Amazonian warrior so powerful?[8] Or, if military participation has the potential to emancipate women, why are so many female soldiers raped?[9] By discussing these types of issues, the students learned that there is no such thing as a feminist standpoint on war and militarism. Instead, there is a wide variety of debates, all of which are nuanced according to the individual's epistemic positioning. By reading the work of feminist scholars such as Cynthia Cockburn, Francine D'Amico, Cynthia Enloe, and Sara Ruddick, the students learned to identify some of the key arenas of contestation.

The second unit examined African women as warriors, focusing specifically on their involvement in national liberation struggles. I began by asking students to name the imperial powers that participated in the colonization of Africa. As they shouted out names, I listed them on the left-hand side of the chalkboard. On the right-hand side, we listed the countries that had been colonized.[10] After several minutes, the students were able to see the tremendous disparity between those who had power and those who did not. We also talked about the justifications for colonialism, paying particular attention to those who actually benefited most from colonial "development."[11] Why, for instance, did all the major roads and railways lead from the interior to the coast? What was the function of these colonial arteries? Whose labor actually built them?[12] I wanted students to recognize that colonial development was not as beneficial as their history books may have led them to believe. Moreover, in order to further illustrate why the "civilizing mission" was inherently racist, classist, and, in many ways, sexist, we read Rudyard Kipling's poem "The White Man's Burden" (1899).

Not surprisingly, gender was central to our discussion of colonialism. Not only did we consider how colonialism affected women and men in different ways, but also how gender influenced anticolonial resistance. For this section, I selected case studies from two different parts of Africa—Zimbabwe and Eritrea. Although women were active participants in both liberation struggles, the nature of their involvement was very different.[13] In Zimbabwe, women played an instrumental role in facilitating guerrilla warfare, serving most frequently as spies, messengers, and food providers. In Eritrea, on the other hand, they were much more actively engaged in frontline combat. What both groups of women shared, however, was the realization that their victories in war had not liberated them from inequitable gender relations.

In both contexts, patriarchy remained firmly entrenched. Much of our classroom discussion focused on why this has consistently been the case throughout Africa, and indeed, most of the world.

For the first case study, the students read an article by Tanya Lyons examining the various roles of women in the Zimbabwean anticolonial struggle.[14] I also had them read a beautiful novel by J. Nozipo Maraire called *Zenzele: A Letter for My Daughter*.[15] This book works particularly well in the classroom because it tells an engaging story while teaching students about a complex political history. I paired the novel with *Flame*, an excellent feature film about the wartime experiences of two young Zimbabwean girls.[16] The students were interested to learn that the Zimbabwean National Liberation War Veterans Association tried to ban the film because of its "subversive" content.[17] After watching the movie, I asked them to consider why the association may have perceived the film as threatening. We were then able to have a stimulating discussion about the politics of representation and the ways in which histories are remembered, as well as forgotten or silenced.

The second case study focused on Eritrea, a country with a very different political history. Unlike Zimbabwe, which was colonized by Europeans, Eritrea's chief antagonists were other Africans, namely, Ethiopians.[18] To help my students understand the nature of Eritrean women's participation in the protracted guerrilla struggle, I assigned *The Challenge Road* by Amrit Wilson.[19] Although this is a scholarly text, the students enjoyed the book because of the author's liberal use of rich oral interviews. We also watched a documentary about the lives of women in postwar Eritrea called *The Dream Becomes a Reality*.[20] The film introduces students to a number of women who participated in the liberation struggle in the 1980s, analyzing their roles in the war and reflecting upon the consequences of their involvement. Although the students were saddened that women's equality on the battlefield did not translate into permanent changes in gender relations, they were excited, nonetheless, to learn about the strength and courage of the Eritrean women.

The third unit was perhaps the most difficult to cover. Here, we examined gender-based violence in war zones across Africa. In our first case study, we read *The War within the War*, an investigative report by Human Rights Watch about the rape of women in the Democratic Republic of Congo.[21] I paired this reading with a film about the strategic use of rape in Sierra Leone. *Operation Fine Girl* vividly portrays the savagery unleashed upon women in the violent struggle for the nation's diamonds.[22] The second case study focused on the Sudan. In Audrey Macklin's powerful article, "Like Oil and Water, with a Match," the students learned how the militarization of commerce has contributed to displacement and to increased violence against women.[23] They also watched a feature-length documentary called *All about Darfur*, which examines different aspects of the crisis through the lens of a female Sudanese filmmaker.[24] In the final case study, we considered Burundian women's efforts to resist sexual and domestic violence within Tanzanian refugee camps.[25] We discussed the role of the international community—especially the United Nations High Commissioner for Refugees and various humanitarian aid agencies—in safeguarding the rights of the displaced.[26] Students also learned about the legal protections (theoretically) enshrined in international humanitarian and human rights law.[27] They were frustrated, however, that these conventions and treaties consistently failed to protect those who were the most vulnerable.

Unfortunately, the next set of readings only compounded their feelings of despair. In this unit, we examined children's gendered experiences of war. We began by reading Alcinda Honwana's *Child Soldiers in Africa*, a comparative case study of Mozambique and Angola.[28] Through an important discussion of tactical and strategic agency, Honwana considers ethical questions about children's culpability in war. She also pays careful attention to the wartime experiences of girls, a topic that is frequently ignored in the literature.[29] Although this book worked well in the classroom, other texts might be equally effective. P. W. Singer's *Children at War*, for instance, provides an excellent overview of child soldiering and would work well as an introductory text.[30] I would also recommend Ishmael Beah's touching memoir, *A Long Way Gone: Memoirs of a Boy Soldier*, or Ahmadou Kourouma's engaging novel, *Allah Is Not Obliged*.[31] Both poignantly illustrate the ways in which hypermasculinity is linked to the display of violence in situations of warfare. To help students better understand these painful realities, I included two short films. The first, *On the Frontlines*, is a fifteen-minute documentary about child soldiering in the DRC.[32] The second is entitled *Going Home*, and it follows the postwar demobilization and repatriation of a young Sierra Leonean boy soldier.[33]

This unit also considered child abductions during armed conflicts. Students read *Aboke Girls*, a moving narrative by Els De Temmerman about the 1996 abduction of 139 schoolgirls in northern Uganda by the Lord's Resistance Army.[34] They also read a variety of research reports about the "night commuters," those Ugandan children who walked substantial distances into towns every evening in search of a safe place to sleep.[35] I paired these readings with a popular documentary, *Invisible Children*, which vividly portrays the plight of these young migrants.[36] This film is particularly useful because it demonstrates how ordinary college students can transform their feelings of anger and powerlessness into positive social action. After watching the film, some of my students joined the Invisible Children Movement and participated in its National Night Out to raise awareness of the conflict.

The final unit examined women's peace and reconciliation efforts. The primary text for this section was *Liberian Women Peacemakers*, by the African Women and Peace Support Group.[37] Although the book is quite short, it does a good job of demonstrating how ordinary Liberian women resisted war through various peace-building activities. Students also read a number of chapters from *Women, War, and Peace*, by Elisabeth Rehn and Ellen Johnson Sirleaf.[38] In addition, to illustrate how far Liberians have come in such a short period of time, we examined the gripping documentary titled *Liberia: An Uncivil War*.[39] Although the students were shocked by the extreme levels of violence during the war, they were equally amazed by the tremendous transformation that had taken place in the brief postwar period. Liberia gave them hope. In retrospect, I believe that if I had discussed peace and conflict resolution throughout the course instead of saving it until the end, the students would not have felt so demoralized and helpless. They would have been able to recognize that even the darkest conflicts could be resolved through creativity, collaboration, and persistence.

Conclusion

Over the last year, I have continued to think about the overall structure of the course, as well as about the ethics of teaching about violence. I have come to recognize that although these types of classes are fraught with challenges, it is important to teach them. They expose students to an array of global issues, while at the same time helping them learn strategies that promote peace and conflict resolution. I am currently teaching a modified version of the class at the graduate level at Purdue University. Instead of focusing specifically on women's experiences of war and militarism, we are looking at gender issues more generally. By reinterpreting the course as "Gender, War, and Militarism," we are concentrating our attention on gender as a relational category of analysis (versus the category "women" as an essential or static category). In addition, I have broadened the scope to include other world areas. This was a strategic decision, in part to attract additional students but also to allow us to explore transnational connections and discontinuities. Although it is still early in the semester, the course is off to a great start. Because the students are engaged but not demoralized, I am looking forward to many enriching discussions in the months ahead.

Appendix A

Syllabus for Women, War, and Militarism in Africa Women's Studies/ Africana Studies 376

Course Description

Using a variety of academic texts, novels, and films, this interdisciplinary course examines the ways in which war and militarism are deeply gendered.

86 *Ungendering Conflicts, Engendering Peace*

After introducing students to key theoretical and historical issues, we will consider African women's participation in various anticolonial liberation struggles as well as their experiences within postcolonial conflicts. As part of this discussion, we will be looking at how women's bodies have been strategically utilized as weapons of war and symbols of peace. We will also consider the gendered ways in which children have been impacted by armed conflict. Prior experience in women's studies or African studies is useful but not mandatory to success in the course.

Required Texts

- Maraire, J. Nozipo (1996). *Zenzele: A Letter for My Daughter*
- Wilson, Amrit (1991). *The Challenge Road: Women and the Eritrean Revolution*
- African Women and Peace Support Group (2004). *Liberian Women Peacemakers*
- Honwana, Alcinda (2006). *Child Soldiers in Africa*
- De Temmerman, Els (2001). *Aboke Girls: Children Abducted in Northern Uganda*
- Course Reader

Optional Texts (available for free downloading or for purchase at the bookstore)

- Human Rights Watch (2002). *The War within the War: Sexual Violence against Women and Girls in Eastern Congo* (www.hrw.org)
- Human Rights Watch (2000). *Seeking Protection: Addressing Sexual and Domestic Violence in Tanzania's Refugee Camps* (www.hrw.org)
- Rehn, Elisabeth, and Ellen Johnson Sirleaf (2002). *Women, War and Peace* (www.womenwarpeace.org)

Websites

- Sites on Conflict and Displacement
    www.womenwarpeace.org
    www.internal-displacement.org
- Africa News Sites
    http://allafrica.com/
    http://news.bbc.co.uk/1/hi/world/africa//default.stm
    http://www.cnn.com/WORLD/africa/archive/

http://www.voanews.com/english/Africa/index.cfm
http://www.afrol.com/

Course Requirements

- *Peace and Conflict Journal:* Students will be required to keep a weekly journal that tracks key issues concerning peace and conflict in Africa. Each weekly entry should be at least one page and should be an analysis of major conflict-related issues on the continent. Students may choose to track a particular conflict over time or report on various different conflicts. A good source of information is www.allafrica.com. Click on "Topics" and scroll down to various categories that contain related news stories (e.g., Arms and Military Affairs, Civil War, Conflict, Human Rights, Peacekeeping, Postconflict, or Refugees). There is no required number of sources per entry, though please read enough articles to offer a thoughtful analysis. Journals will be collected every four weeks and should contain at least four new entries. These will count as 25 percent of the final grade, attendance as 20 percent.
- *Annotated Bibliography:* Using a minimum of ten sources, students must create an annotated bibliography that will be used for a final research paper. For each source, students must provide: a full citation of the book or article; a paragraph summarizing the author's main points and thesis statement; and an analytical assessment of the material. A brief three-page paper, evaluating the findings of your preliminary research, must accompany the completed bibliography. This will count toward 25 percent of the final grade.
- *Final Research Paper:* For this assignment students will write a twelve- to fifteen-page research paper on a related topic of your choice. Papers will count as 30 percent of the final grade.

Course Calendar/Readings

Feminist Theories of Women, War, and Militarism

- Rehn and Johnson Sirleaf, *Women, War and Peace* (1–60)
- Cockburn, "The Continuum of Violence: A Gender Perspective on War and Peace"
- Etchart and Baksh, "Applying a Gender Lens to Armed Conflict, Violence and Conflict Transformation"
- Film: *Women and War*
- D'Amico, "Feminist Perspectives on Women Warriors"

88 *Ungendering Conflicts, Engendering Peace*

- Ruddick, "'Woman of Peace': A Feminist Construction"
- Enloe, "Preface," and "How Do They Militarize a Can of Soup?"[40]
- Burke, "Women and Militarism"
- Enloe, "Feminism and Militarism"[41]

Women's Engagement in Armed Conflict

- Lyons, "Guerilla Girls and Women in the Zimbabwean National Liberation Struggle"
- Maraire, *Zenzele* (1–80)
- Maraire, *Zenzele* (81–194)
- Wilson, *The Challenge Road: Women and the Eritrean Revolution* (1–86)
- Wilson, *The Challenge Road: Women and the Eritrean Revolution* (87–154)
- Film: *The Dream Becomes a Reality*

Armed Conflict and Gender-based Violence

- Puechguirbal, "Women and War in the Democratic Republic of Congo"
- Human Rights Watch, *The War within the War* (1–22)
- Human Rights Watch, *The War within the War* (23–97)
- Film: *Operation Fine Girl*
- Halim, "Attack with a Friendly Weapon"
- Jok, "Militarization and Gender Violence in South Sudan"
- Special Evening Showing of *All about Darfur*
- Macklin, "Like Oil and Water, with a Match"
- Human Rights Watch, *Seeking Protection* (1–38)
- Film: *In the Wake of War*
- Human Rights Watch, *Seeking Protection* (39–81)

Children in War Zones

- Brett, "Girl Soldiers"
- Honwana, *Child Soldiers in Africa* (1–48)
- Film: *On the Frontlines: Child Soldiers in the DRC*
- Honwana, *Child Soldiers in Africa* (49–103)
- Film: *Going Home* (31 min.)
- Honwana, *Child Soldiers in Africa* (104–64)
- Nordstrom, "Girls and War Zones: Troubling Questions"
- De Temmerman, *Aboke Girls* (1–80)

- Human Rights Watch, *Stolen Children: Abduction and Recruitment in Northern Uganda*
- De Temmerman, *Aboke Girls* (81–160)
- Women's Commission for Refugee Women and Children, *No Safe Place to Call Home: Children and Adolescent Night Commuters in Northern Uganda*
- Patrick, "Surrounded: Women and Girls in Northern Uganda"
- Film: *Invisible Children*

Women, Peace, and Reconstruction

- Rehn and Johnson Sirleaf, *Women, War and Peace* (chapters 5–9)
- United Nations Economic Commission for Africa, "*Post-conflict Reconstruction in Africa: A Gender Perspective*"
- African Women and Peace Support Group, *Liberian Women Peacemakers* (1–38)
- Rehn and Johnson Sirleaf, *Women, War and Peace* (chapter 10)
- Special Evening Showing of *Liberia: An Uncivil War*
- African Women and Peace Support Group, *Liberian Women Peacemakers* (39–94)

Appendix B

Films about Women and War in Africa

All about Darfur (82 min.) [2005]

Abstract: "Up until now the perilous situation in Sudan has been seen only from outside the country. *All about Darfur* offers an opportunity to hear it explained by eloquent, diverse, even contradictory voices from within Sudan. The director talks to ordinary Sudanese in outdoor tea shops, markets, refugee camps and living rooms about how deeply rooted prejudices could suddenly burst into a wild fire of ethnic violence."[42]

Director: Taghreed Elsanhouri *Distributor:* California Newsreel

Angola E A Nossa Terra (45 min.) [1988]

Abstract: "Angolan women are rarely heard describing the impact of South Africa's undeclared war against their country. This moving documentary, produced in conjunction with the Organization of Angolan Women (OMA), highlights the contribution women make to the reconstruction of a country

where war has consumed more than half the national budget and produced at least a million internal refugees."[43]
Director: Jenny Morgan *Distributor:* Women Make Movies

The Dream Becomes a Reality (48 min.) [1995]

Abstract: "Six young Eritrean women who participated in the 30-year military struggle for independence from Ethiopia are featured in this documentary.... The women speak about tragedies and accomplishments of the war, the gender egalitarianism among the liberation forces, and their current thoughts on the situation of women in postwar Eritrea."[44]
Director: Eva Beth Egensteiner *Distributor:* University of California Extension Center for Media

Flame (85 min.) [1996]

Abstract: "*Flame* is perhaps the most controversial film ever made in Africa—certainly the only one to be seized by the police during editing on the grounds it was subversive and pornographic.... [It] is the story of two close friends whose involvement in the liberation struggle leads to very different outcomes."[45]
Director: Ingrid Sinclair *Distributor:* California Newsreel

Going Home (31 min.) [1999]

Abstract: "Mohammed is 10 years old, but for most of 1997 he was forced to act as a young fighter with rebel forces in the forests of Sierra Leone. His duties included carrying heavy equipment, acting as a personal servant to other soldiers, and torturing and disciplining any of the other child soldiers who stepped out of line. Eventually he escaped to Guinea, where he is one of thousands lining up to register at the Gueckedou refugee camp. In 1997 Guinea was host to an estimated 430,000 refugees: 190,000 Sierra Leoneans, and 240,000 Liberians who had escaped the eight-year civil wars there. This film evaluates the success of the Guinean government and the UN High Commissioner for Refugees (UNHCR) in protecting the rights pledged this huge African refugee population under the OAU Convention."[46]
Director: Emily Marlow *Distributor:* Bullfrog Films

In the Wake of War (24 min.) [2004]

Abstract: "Philippe Mvuyekure has spent the last five years living in a refugee camp in Tanzania. Now, he's on his way home. He's among thousands of refugees convinced that the bitter, 10-year civil war that decimated his homeland of Burundi may be coming to an end. The civil war here between Hutu rebels and the Tutsi-dominated army uprooted over a million people and killed more than 300,000. But the benefits of a peace process are finally beginning to emerge. Using traditional mediation systems and peacemakers, Burundi is introducing innovative peace and reconciliation projects. The aim is to start a grass roots movement to bring a lasting peace to Burundi and its long-suffering citizens. This program examines the future for Burundi, for power sharing and for a rapprochement between warring factions."[47]

Director: James Heer *Distributor:* Bullfrog Films

Invisible Children (55 min.) [2006]

Abstract: "Can a story change the world? In the spring of 2003, three young Americans traveled to Africa in search of such a story. What they found was a tragedy that disgusted and inspired them. A story where children are the weapons, and children are the victims. The 'Invisible Children: rough cut' film exposes the effects of a 20 year-long war on the children of Northern Uganda."[48]

Directors: Jason Russell, Bobby Bailey, Laren Poole *Distributor:* Invisible Children

Liberia: A Fragile Peace (60 min.) [2006]

Abstract: "*Liberia: A Fragile Peace* is a perfect follow-up to *Liberia: An Uncivil War*, picking up the Liberian saga in October 2003, with the departure of the despotic Charles Taylor, the arrival of interim President Gyude Bryant and the deployment of a UN peacekeeping force. More than a historical record, however, this film is an ideal case study in how difficult it is to rebuild a society once it has lapsed into anarchy, a condition afflicting more and more nations around the world. The success or failure of the Liberian experience could have long-lasting impact on peacekeeping missions in the future."[49]

Director: Steven W. Ross *Distributor:* California Newsreel

Liberia: An Uncivil War (102 min.) [2005]

Abstract: "*Liberia: An Uncivil War* provides an in-depth case study of one of the many brutal civil wars which have sprung up like wild fires across Africa.

It is an exciting example of war-time journalism—white knuckles reporting with bullets ricocheting just feet from the camera placed in a historical context stretching back nearly two hundred years. Liberia can uniquely claim to be made in America and has always looked to the [United States] in its times of crisis. Reporter Jonathan Stack is besieged in the Liberian capital of Monrovia where President Charles Taylor says he will not leave until peacekeepers are in place. He is remarkably equable for a man who has just been indicted on 17 counts of crimes against humanity by the United Nations. James Barbazon is embedded with the LURD (Liberians United for Reconciliation and Democracy) who have pledged to pillage the country until President Taylor leaves. He introduces us to General Cobra, Col. Black Diamond and soldiers, slightly more than children, who eat their victims' hearts in the belief it will make them stronger. With the rebels at the bridges leading to Monrovia, the Nigerians are at last persuaded to send 750 peacekeepers and the UN follows soon with 14,000. But what remains in the viewers' mind is President Bush's empty promises of help during the darkest days of Liberia's civil war."[50]

Director: Jonathan Stack *Distributor:* California Newsreel

Mortu Nega (Those Whom Death Refused) (93 min.) [1997]

Abstract: "California Newsreel has released Flora Gomes' now classic, *Mortu Nega*, to commemorate three starkly dissimilar events. 1998 marked both the 25th anniversary of the independence of Guinea-Bissau and the assassination of its leader Amilcar Cabral but it was also the year that country virtually annihilated itself in a brutal civil war. Produced in 1988 near the midpoint of these dates, *Mortu Nega*, as its title implies, is a unique kind of elegy—not so much to the victims of the liberation struggle as to its survivors. . . . [It] is a bittersweet eulogy to those veterans who gave so much yet often benefited so little from the struggle. The film poses a question facing much of Africa at the start of the 21st century: with the goal of independence achieved, what can serve as an equally unifying and compelling vision around which to construct a new society? Or as Chris Marker observed in his 1980 documentary San Soleil, coincidentally contemplating the decay of Guinea-Bissau's revolution: 'What every revolutionary thinks the morning after victory: now the real problems begin.'"[51]

Director: Flora Gomes *Distributor:* California Newsreel

On the Frontlines: Child Soldiers in DRC (15 min.) [2004]

Abstract: This 15-minute "video was created by AJEDI-ka and WITNESS to advocate for the cessation of voluntary recruitment of child soldiers in

Eastern DRC. The region has been in active combat since 1996 with over 3.8 million people estimated to have died as a direct or indirect result of the war. The video features powerful footage, shot between 2003 and 2004, of the military training of children in several militia camps in South Kivu as well as compelling testimony from demobilized child soldiers recounting the horrifying memories of life as soldiers. More than ten militia groups operate in the region; every one of them has been reported to be using children as soldiers. The majority of these children are between the ages of 8 and 16 years old and [the children] include both girls and boys. It is estimated that children make up 60 percent of combatants in the region. Over 35 percent of these children are recruited voluntarily, led by a sense of patriotism or by ideas of prosperity. Parents and the community at large are often involved in this voluntary recruitment of children. ON THE FRONTLINES [was] screened throughout communities in Eastern DRC in January 2005 in an attempt to [stop] the voluntary recruitment of children from these communities."[52]

Director: AJEDI-ka *Distributor:* WITNESS

Operation Fine Girl (50 min.) [2001]

Abstract: Operation Fine Girl is "an intimate story about the tragic use of rape as a weapon of war told through the personal stories of three young girls who were abducted, taken to be 'rebel wives,' sex slaves, domestic servants and combatants held for many years against their will; and one boy abducted to be a child combatant."[53]

Director: Lilibet Foster *Distributor:* WITNESS

Women and War (53 min.) [2001]

Abstract: "Interwoven with footage from recent conflicts in the Middle East, Bosnia, northern Uganda, and South Africa, this program captures women's personal experiences of military violence, explains how they survived, and reflects on their growing resistance to war. The women's feelings of loss, uncertainty, and anguish are expressed through stories of cruelty, degradation, and psychological trauma, while their attempts to achieve reconciliation and rebuild shattered communities demonstrate their positive efforts to create a more peaceful future for everyone."[54]

Directors: Robyn Hofmeyr, Minky Schlesinger *Distributor:* Films for the Humanities and Sciences

Notes

1. E. Valentine Daniel, *Charred Lullabies: Chapters in an Anthropography of Violence* (Princeton, NJ: Princeton University Press, 1996), 4. See also Penelope Harvey and Peter Gow, eds., *Sex and Violence: Issues in Representation and Experience* (London: Routledge, 1994). For an excellent critique of the "pornography of violence," see Donald Donham, "Staring at Suffering: Violence as a Subject," in *States of Violence: Politics, Youth, and Memory in Contemporary Africa*, ed. Edna G. Bay and Donald L. Donham (Charlottesville: University of Virginia Press, 2006), 16–33.

2. Daniel, *Charred Lullabies*, 3. See also Michael Taussig, *Shamanism, Colonialism, and the Wild Man: A Study in Terror and Healing* (Chicago: University of Chicago Press, 1987).

3. Within this particular class, nine out of fifteen students were women of color. At least five publicly identified as lesbian or queer.

4. Feminist scholars resist military interventions for a number of different reasons. Many stem from the fact that women and girls experience war very differently than do men and boys. For one thing, as symbols of the nation, female bodies on both sides of the conflict often become the targets of assault. Others suggest that military interventions are damaging because they drain national coffers, thus resulting in reduced spending on important social and welfare initiatives. This may result in an increased labor burden for women if they are forced to compensate for services that the state fails to provide. Still other feminists cite larger, more global harms, such as environmental destruction or the rise of xenophobic, neoimperialist ideologies. A number of edited collections address these and other important critiques. See, for example, Lois Ann Lorentzen and Jennifer Turpin, eds., *The Women and War Reader* (New York: New York University Press, 1998); Marguerite R. Waller and Jennifer Rycenga, eds., *Frontline Feminisms: Women, War, and Resistance* (New York: Garland, 2000); Daniela Gioseffi, ed., *Women on War: An International Anthology of Writings from Antiquity to the Present* (New York: Feminist Press at CUNY, 2003); and Wenona Giles and Jennifer Hyndman, eds., *Sites of Violence: Gender and Conflict Zones* (Berkeley: University of California Press, 2004).

5. Much of Cynthia Enloe's work challenges the distinction between the "front lines" and the "home front." See, for example, Cynthia Enloe, *Does Khaki Become You? The Militarization of Women's Lives* (Boston: South End Press, 1983); and *Maneuvers: The International Politics of Militarizing Women's Lives* (Berkeley: University of California Press, 2000). See also Jacklyn Cock, "Keeping the Fires Burning: Militarization and the Politics of Gender in South Africa," *Review of African Political Economy* 45/46 (1989): 50–64.

6. For specific ideas on how to use these texts in the classroom, see Misty Bastian and Jane Parpart, *Great Ideas for Teaching about Africa* (Boulder, CO: Lynne Rienner, 1999).

7. For an excellent introduction to these types of issues, see Curtis Keim, *Mistaking Africa: Curiosities and Inventions of the American Mind* (Boulder, CO: Westview, 1999).

8. Sara Ruddick, for example, suggests that women are more peaceful than men because of their social or biological roles. See, for example, Sara Ruddick, "'Woman of Peace': A Feminist Construction," in Lorentzen and Turpin, *The Women and War Reader*, 213–26; and Sara Ruddick, *Maternal Thinking: Toward a Politics of Peace* (Boston: Beacon, 1989).

9. Cynthia Enloe describes this paradox in much of her work. See, for example, Enloe, *Does Khaki Become You?* and *Maneuvers*.

10. This is a good place to discuss the politics of naming. Ask students to think about the relationship between naming and identity formation. Who has the power to name a nation? Why did some countries change their names after independence while others did not?

11. Walter Rodney's classic text, *How Europe Underdeveloped Africa*, remains a useful reference for this discussion. See Walter Rodney, *How Europe Underdeveloped Africa* (Washington, DC: Howard University Press, 1972).

12. The African Studies Center at Michigan State University has excellent online resources for teaching about Africa. A map illustrating the placement of African railroads can be downloaded from the following website: http://exploringafrica.matrix.msu.edu/images/africarailroads.gif.

13. For women's experiences in the Zimbabwean liberation struggle, see Irene Staunton, *Mothers of the Revolution: The War Experiences of Thirty Zimbabwean Women* (Bloomington: Indiana University Press, 1990); Sita Ranchod-Nilsson, "'This, Too, Is a Way of Fighting': Rural Women's Participation in Zimbabwe's Liberation War," in *Women and Revolution in Africa, Asia, and the New World*, ed. Mary Ann Tétreault (Colombia: University of South Carolina Press, 1994), 62–88; Tanya Lyons, *Guns and Guerrilla Girls: Women in the Zimbabwean Liberation Struggle* (Trenton, NJ: Africa World Press, 2004); and W. O. Maloba, *African Women in Revolution* (Trenton, NJ: Africa World Press, 2007). The literature examining Eritrean women's participation is more limited. For a general overview of women's experiences, see Amrit Wilson, *The Challenge Road: Women and the Eritrean Revolution* (Trenton, NJ: Red Sea Press, 1991). For an analysis of women's postwar experiences, see Sondra Hale, "The Soldier and the State; Post-liberation Women: The Case of Eritrea," in Waller and Rycenga, *Frontline Feminisms: Women, War, and Resistance*, 349–70.

14. Tanya Lyons, "Guerrilla Girls and Women in the Zimbabwean National Liberation Struggle," in *Women in African Colonial Histories*, ed. Jean Allman, Susan Geiger, and Nakanyike Musisi (Bloomington: Indiana University Press, 2002), 305–26. For a more in-depth analysis of women's participation in Zimbabwe's liberation movement, see Lyons, *Guns and Guerrilla Girls*.

15. J. Nozipo Maraire, *Zenzele: A Letter for My Daughter* (New York: Dell, 1996).

16. *Flame*, DVD, directed by Ingrid Sinclair (San Francisco: California Newsreel, 1996). For a complete description of this and other recommended films, see appendix B.

17. Tanya Lyons offers a detailed explanation of the controversy in "The Forgotten Soldiers: Women in Zimbabwe's Liberation War," *Southern Africa Report* 12, no. 2 (1997): 12.

18. In 1952, a United Nations resolution joined Eritrea to Ethiopia in a federation. Although Eritrea initially retained some degree of independence, the emperor of Ethiopia, Haile Selassie, gradually usurped its autonomy. Military resistance to Ethiopia began in 1958 with the establishment of the clandestine Eritrean Liberation Movement. This was followed two years later by the founding of the Eritrean Liberation Front, and then in 1972, by the establishment of the Eritrean People's Liberation Front. After many years of struggle, Eritreans finally won their independence on April 27, 1993.

19. Amrit Wilson, *The Challenge Road*.

20. *The Dream Becomes a Reality*, DVD, directed by Eva Beth Egensteiner (Berkeley: University of California Extension Center for Media and Independent Learning, 1995).

21. Human Rights Watch, *The War within the War: Sexual Violence against Women and Girls in Eastern Congo* (New York: Human Rights Watch, 2002).

22. *Operation Fine Girl*, DVD, produced and directed by Lilibet Foster and Binta Mansaray (Brooklyn: Witness, 2001).

23. Audrey Macklin, "Like Oil and Water, with a Match: Militarized Commerce, Armed Conflict, and Human Security in Sudan," in Giles and Hyndman, *Sites of Violence: Gender and Conflict Zones*, 75–107.

24. *All about Darfur*, DVD, directed by Taghreed El Sanhouri (San Francisco: California Newsreel, 2005).

25. Human Rights Watch, *Seeking Protection: Addressing Sexual and Domestic Violence in Tanzania's Refugee Camps* (New York: Human Rights Watch, 2000).

26. The *UNHCR Handbook for the Protection of Women and Girls* (Geneva, Switzerland: Office of the United Nations High Commissioner for Refugees, 2008) outlines what practitioners need to do in the field to protect the rights and well-being of refugee women and girls. For information, see http://www.unhcr.org/protect/PROTECTION/47cfae612.html.

27. The United Nations passed Security Council Resolution 1325 in 2000. This resolution provides important protections for women in situations of armed conflict. For more information on this legislation, see http://www.peacewomen.org/un/sc/1325.html. Students should also become familiar with the Geneva Conventions, which outline the formal laws of war.

28. Alcinda Honwana, *Child Soldiers in Africa* (Philadelphia: University of Pennsylvania Press, 2006).

29. Some recent texts include chapters on girls' experiences of soldiering. See for example, Rachel Brett and Irma Specht, *Young Soldiers: Why They Choose to Fight* (Boulder, CO: Lynne Rienner, 2004); and Jimmie Briggs, *Innocents Lost: When Child Soldiers Go to War* (New York: Basic Books, 2005). Some texts include anecdotes involving girls in warfare but do not offer comprehensive gender analyses. See Charles London, *One Day the Soldiers Came: Voices of Children in War* (New York: Harper Perennial, 2007); and David Rosen, *Armies of the Young: Child Soldiers in War and Terrorism* (New Brunswick, NJ: Rutgers University Press, 2005).

30. P. W. Singer, *Children at War* (New York: Pantheon Books, 2005).

31. Ishmael Beah, *A Long Way Gone: Memoirs of a Boy Soldier* (New York: Farrar, Straus, and Giroux, 2007); Ahmadou Kourouma, *Allah Is Not Obliged* (New York: Anchor Books, 2006). China Keitetsi's *Child Soldier* is also quite good, and it captures the soldiering experiences of a young Ugandan girl. This book has not been published in the United States, though it is available for purchase through various Internet vendors. See China Keitetsi, *Child Soldier: Fighting for My Life* (Johannesburg: Jacana Media, 2005). *Girl Soldier*, by Faith J. H. McDonnell and Grace Akallo, explores similar issues but from an evangelical Christian perspective. See Faith J. H. McDonnell and Grace Akallo, *Girl Soldier: A Story of Hope for Northern Uganda's Children* (Grand Rapids, MI: Chosen Books, 2007).

32. *On the Frontlines: Child Soldiers in the DRC*, DVD, directed by Ajedi-Ka (Brooklyn, NY: Witness, 2004).

33. *Going Home*, DVD, directed by Emily Marlow and produced by Jenny Richards (Oley, PA: Bullfrog Films, 1999).

34. Els De Temmerman, *Aboke Girls: Children Abducted in Northern Uganda* (Kampala, Uganda: Fountain, 2001).

35. Human Rights Watch, *Stolen Children: Abduction and Recruitment in Northern Uganda* (New York: Human Rights Watch, 2003); Erin Patrick, "Surrounded: Women and Girls in Northern Uganda," Migration Policy Institute, Washington, DC, 2005, http://www.migrationinformation.org/Feature/display.cfm?id=310; and Women's Commission for Refugee Women and Children, *No Safe Place to Call Home: Child and Adolescent Night Commuters in Northern Uganda* (New York: Women's Commission for Refugee Women and Children, 2004). See http://www.migrationinformation.org/Feature/display.cfm?id=310.

36. *Invisible Children*, DVD, directed by Jason Russell, Bobby Bailey, and Laren Poole (Spring Valley, CA: Invisible Children, 2006).

37. African Women and Peace Support Group, *Liberian Women Peacemakers: Fighting for the Right to Be Seen, Heard and Counted* (Trenton, NJ: Africa World Press, 2004).

38. Elisabeth Rehn and Ellen Johnson Sirleaf, *Women, War and Peace: The Independent Experts' Assessment on the Impact of Armed Conflict on Women and Women's Role in Peace-Building* (New York: UNIFEM, 2002).

39. *Liberia: An Uncivil War*, DVD, produced and directed by Jonathan Stack (San Francisco: California Newsreel, 2005).

40. Enloe, *Maneuvers*.

41. Enloe, *Does Khaki Become You?*

42. For a complete description of this title, see http://www.newsreel.org/nav/title.asp?tc=CN0183.

43. For ordering information, see http://www.wmm.com/filmcatalog/pages/c48.shtml.

44. For additional information, see http://ucmedia.berkeley.edu/.

45. For a complete description of this title, see http://www.newsreel.org/nav/title.asp?tc=CN0034.

46. For ordering information, see http://www.bullfrogfilms.com/catalog/goh.html.

47. For ordering information, see http://www.bullfrogfilms.com/catalog/14in.html.

48. Excerpted from the DVD jacket. For ordering information, see http://www.invisiblechildren.com/movie.

49. For a complete description of this title, see http://www.newsreel.org/nav/title.asp?tc=CN0185.

50. For ordering information, see http://www.newsreel.org/nav/title.asp?tc=CN0176.

51. For a complete description of this title, see http://www.newsreel.org/nav/title.asp?tc=CN0061.

52. This film can be viewed online without charge at http://hub.witness.org/en/OnTheFrontlines.

53. See http://www.witness.org/index.php?Itemid=178&alert_id=20&option=com_rightsalert&task=view. For ordering information, see www.witness.org.

54. For ordering information, see http://ffh.films.com/id/4555/Women_and_War.htm.

5

Women and War

A Kenyan Experience

Pamela Wadende

Introduction

Kenya has suffered, and still suffers, violent conflicts of differing magnitudes: for example, the Mau Mau rebellion, resulting in Kenya's independence in 1963; cattle-raiding conflicts that frequently arise among neighboring communities; and the conflict that arose after the 2007 presidential election. Women played important roles in these conflicts, and it is important to record this fact as this chapter sets out to do. Andrea Cornwall, writing in 2005, notes that over the last thirty years an extensive literature has emerged on sub-Saharan African women.[1] However, "studies of African nationalist movements," according to Gloria Chuku, "seldom give evidence of any active participation by women. They tend to concentrate on the activities of men, while the roles played by women are, by and large, relegated to the background."[2] Robert Young reinforces the point Chuku makes, observing that

> just as colonial history is dominated by men, the generals, the admirals, the viceroys, the governors, the district officers and so forth, anti-colonial history of the liberation struggles is also dominated by the political theorists, communist activists, national party leaders, who were all largely (though by no means exclusively) male.[3]

However, Young then notes the "two landmark works [that] initiated the feminist response to the absence of women in colonial and anti-colonial histories," namely, Kumari Jayawardena's *Feminism and Nationalism in the Third World* (1986), and Kumkum Sangari and Sudesh Vaid's *Recasting Women: Essays in Colonial History* (1989).[4]

Waruhiu Itote's "*Mau Mau*" *General* is thus all the more remarkable, as he acknowledges the exemplary achievement of women fighters in the forest camps during the Mau Mau uprising. Writing in 1967, Waruhiu states: "Over and over again, during the Emergency, I noticed that a woman could keep a secret much better than a man; even under interrogation, relatively few[er] women than men would break down and reveal information."[5] Ngugi wa Thiong'o and Micere Mugo, in 1977, also acknowledge the achievement of women, in the play *The Trial of Dedan Kimathi*. They depict a woman character quite undaunted by the murderous white soldier she runs into on her way to supply the Mau Mau fighters with arms. She easily deceives him into not searching her entire basket.[6] When he pours out the contents of her basket and wishes to probe her parcel of concealed arms,

> The woman dramatically kneels on the ground, almost reaching out for his legs. He is shocked and again frightened by this unexpected move. He moves back a step, puts the bread down and points the gun at her. She talks all the time.[7] [stage directions]

The soldier does not know that what he puts down is not bread but arms for the Mau Mau fighters.

However, the concern here is not only with the role of women in Kenya's struggle for independence; instead, the chapter analyzes stories of selected Kenyan women to illustrate their experiences and roles in the context of the three conflicts mentioned above. By adopting a narratological approach, I place emphasis specifically on stories of individual women as told by those women—stories examined in the broader context of the conflicts. People are usually intimately involved in the society in which they live, and so they reflect the culture of that society through their stories.[8] (Auto)biography is one such form of story. The people relating their stories can then be said to be attaching meaning to their experiences. The places where they were raised and the ways in which they were raised, the paths they took, and the choices they made in life all come together to explain what they turned out to be.[9] The story, therefore, is at the center of narrative analysis, or narratology, and includes "personal narratives, family stories, suicide notes, graffiti, literary nonfiction, and life histories" as texts that "reveal cultural and social patterns through the lenses of individual experiences."[10]

Various examples of such stories are examined in this chapter. To take one example, *Mau Mau's Daughter* is the autobiography of Wambui Waiyaki Otieno. Otieno is one of the many women freedom fighters who took an active frontline role in Kenya's war of independence.[11] The story of her life lends itself to use here because it echoes the story of many Kenyan women at the time of the Mau Mau uprising.

A second example is the oral account provided to me by a Kenyan woman, Rose Kibet, on cattle conflicts.[12] Rose Kibet (a pseudonym) had been "stolen" as a child about fifty years ago, along with cattle during a raid on her home among the Luo in Western Kenya: members of the neighboring Kipsigis took her away to live with them. Cattle conflicts were in the past more of a traditional than a criminal activity, and warriors even obtained wives from among the women they captured along with the cattle.[13] This traditional practice has changed in that it has acquired a violent character, as indicated by the Tegla Loroupe Peace Foundation, active, for example, in Western Kenya,[14] and the Marsabit Women Advocacy and Development Organization of Northern Kenya (MWADO).[15]

A third set of examples draws on conversations and e-mail correspondence with other Kenyan women during January and February 2008 and mass media reports in order to address the disputed 2007 presidential election. This election conflict, intensely fought during January and February 2008, gave rise to the current grand coalition government, in a deal signed by the leaders of the warring parties in February 2008.[16] This chapter—as the following section explains—adopts a womanist rather than a feminist perspective to critique the social expectations for women in Kenya and to highlight both their traditional and their nontraditional roles in times of violent conflict.

Kenyan Women: A Womanist Perspective

In *Talking Back: Thinking Feminist, Thinking Black*, bell hooks criticizes the way women have traditionally been portrayed as "sex symbols" and men as those holding power.[17] In many societies, a woman's worth is calculated according to her association with the significant men in her life: her father, spouse, sibling, and even son. The woman tends to receive little recognition for her valuable role of mother in society. For hooks, this view undervalues women's status in society and her contributions to society, which has a negative effect on the growth and success of society as a whole.[18]

Despite the attitudes described above, however, raising children is a very important task, as it secures a society's future. Kenyan women, unsurprisingly, commonly spend more time with children than do men.[19] Nel Noddings describes "caring" as a moral and intellectual relation, a conscious and deliberate choice, and an important task in society, while she asserts that both men and women are capable of serving society in this way.[20] Caring for children in this sense requires a multiskilled approach, in which a mixture of gentleness, strength, intelligence, courage and other skills are found in the "carer."[21] Discussing and criticizing the societal expectation of the selfless woman who demands and receives little in life, bell hooks argues that total suppression of personal needs in order to serve others is unhealthy for both the individual woman and the people she serves.²² However, it is not necessarily unhealthy for a woman to suppress, from time to time, her needs in the interest of the greater good. The essence of successful motherhood and womanhood is giving and displaying both strength and modesty when they are appropriate—for the good of society. It is not uncommon to hear people affectionately refer to their mothers' ability to be strong enough to raise them but also humble enough to subordinate some of their ambitions for the sake of their family or society. The virtues of selflessness and charity are useful when society needs people such as foster parents for war orphans. Otieno, for example, talks of her decision to foster six children, adding them to her family when their mother and only surviving parent, Grace Wambui Arina, died in 1970.²³

Nevertheless, one has to agree with hooks that society should treat everyone fairly. It is important that women should be both appreciated for and identified with their traditional caring role, just as they should be for other roles in which they may excel but which are not directly related to care and motherhood. Being a "good" woman should not depend on a successful relationship with the men in a woman's life; it should depend on the woman herself and the way she relates to the world.²⁴ There are women who are successful in other roles but who do not have strong relationships with men. On the other hand, there are women who are successful in other roles and also live in relationships with men; and these women should not be judged only by the success of these relationships.

Alice Walker's womanism celebrates the way women negotiate the oppression in their world. Walker appreciates the strength of women and their ability to give of themselves by focusing this strength on the survival and "wholeness" of society.²⁵ As Marie Pauline Eboh formulates Walker's position.

> A womanist, Alice Walker would say, is in part a black feminist, a feminist of color committed to the survival and wholeness of an entire people, male and female, but who loves herself nevertheless. African womanism tends to marry African perturbation with the feminine problem.²⁶

Womanism, then, does not mean that women lose their femininity but rather that they exploit their potential in any arena in which they wish to involve themselves, with the aim of developing society as a whole, and that society gives them the credit they deserve. African womanists, then, have a double allegiance, to woman's emancipation and to African liberation.²⁷ This means that an African womanist "would rather identify more with the African man in the struggle for social and political freedom than with the middle class white feminist who ignores the fact that racism and capitalism are concomitants of sexism."²⁸

As Chikwenye Ogunyemi observes, African women have many issues to deal with at any one time. Ogunyemi says that, apart from her sexuality, the African woman needs to focus on her race, culture, the economy, and the politics in her country.[29] Thus, the African woman needs to develop an acute sense of priority so as to be able to survive, together with her society, in a difficult, oppressive environment. She has to have vast reserves of energy to negotiate successfully the issues that confront her, such as interethnic skirmishes, ethnic cleansing, religious fundamentalism, gerontocracy, and even "in-lawism."[30]

Kenyan women, in order to cope with the problems they have to deal with, usually form women's self-help groups called *chama* in Kiswahili, meaning "society" or "association." *Chama* are groups women form in different settings and contexts in Kenyan society, such as offices, churches, villages, and other living communities.[31] In these groups, women offer each other support of all kinds: for example, low-interest loans—useful for initiating income-generating activities; gifts of household goods—in most cases kitchenware; foodstuffs; and emotional support.[32] The *chama* constitute important support networks during times of conflict. Otieno talks of the women's group she belonged to and of the support its members gave her when her husband suddenly fell ill and died. They rallied around and helped her make the difficult transition into successful widowhood.[33]

The Mau Mau War of Independence

The Mau Mau war came about as a result of discontent that had simmered for many years before developing into an open confrontation with the colonial government, which led to a state of emergency being declared in 1952.[34] The war culminated in Kenya's independence in 1963. Both men and women actively participated in this conflict. During the Mau Mau war, many Kenyan women offered a strong backup service to the warriors. The women smuggled messages to and from groups of Mau Mau fighters;[35] supplied food to the fighters in the forest;[36] and enrolled people in the Mau Mau movement.[37] The women went as far as seducing colonial soldiers in order to steal their guns for the Mau Mau fighters.[38] These actions displayed their investment in and commitment to the war they were fighting. In using the common perception most men had of women—overvaluing their sexuality—against these same men, the women proved they were ready to do anything to free their country from the British colonial rulers.[39]

The women in this effort did not focus simply on their own immediate families but on the liberation of the whole country: they inextricably interwove their fate with that of the country. According to Otieno,

Scouting and gathering intelligence was not a simple task, and the war council knew that without scouts no war could be waged or won. As I mentioned before scouts had to be women for various reasons. Women normally look innocent and are able to change with every setting.... A spy had to go to an area that the fighters intended to attack and find out all the essential details. One would first have to make friends, find out the comings and goings thereabouts, and then assess the situation: Did the officers drink exceptionally heavily? Or were they fascinated by women?[40]

The story of Otieno putting her life in danger by confronting a brutish British district officer who had struck her mother further illustrates her selflessness, courage, and strength. Otieno had gone to the officer's superior to ask for his removal from their area.[41] This kind of reaction is a depiction of womanist traits in Otieno: she was not afraid to display her emotions and strength of character. She also recalls how she was arrested for her Mau Mau activities in 1960 and, together with her children, taken to detention in Lamu. During her detention, one of her children contracted malaria, and Otieno's confiners let her take the child to the local general hospital. She speaks of the kindness of a stranger, who met her on her way from hospital with her half-starved children:

Sheikh Ali gave my children money for food when they had starved for three days. This came about because one of the children had caught malaria and I was allowed to take her and the other two children to the general hospital.... Sheikh Ali was passing by and must have noticed the children were very hungry, for they were all lying on their helpless mother.[42]

Although the stranger's kindness was remarkable, Otieno herself was even more so: in spite of her extreme difficulties, she remained concerned for the well-being of her children. Ultimately, she had the strength to endure her traumatic experiences and remain active in Kenya's political scene after independence.[43]

Women could not easily be persuaded to relinquish their solidarity with the Mau Mau. Lisa Aubrey documents how the colonial government failed to destroy Mau Mau solidarity by using women's groups called Maendeleo ya Wanawake (MYWO), which loosely translated means "the development of women."[44] The colonial government attempted to use MYWO groups to work against the Mau Mau by giving these groups financial support and exempting some women from forced labor, with the aim of enticing them to reveal any Mau Mau secrets they had.[45] These efforts of the colonial government were largely unsuccessful. Many women were already personally involved in the Mau Mau resistance in various capacities; even the colonial government officers were aware of this.[46]

During the Mau Mau war, women took up some nontraditional roles, roles usually reserved for men. Women would at times combine their traditional roles with those of men and be quite successful, as the examples show. However, their more "traditional" roles remained just as important, as they continued to support one another in difficult circumstances. For example, when, in January 1961, Otieno and her three little children were released from political detention on the island of Lamu, she found that all her household goods had been stolen in her absence. She talks of a woman, a former neighbor, who gave her some money to help her solve her difficulties. She also recounts the welcome she received in the house of a former detainee, whose wife offered her a place to stay until she could reorganize her life. Otieno mentions many women who offered help when she needed it.[47]

Cattle-Rustling Conflicts

Particular ethnic communities in Kenya, bordering each other, would traditionally fight each other and seize each other's cattle. Examples of such neighbors are the Maasai and the Kikuyu of Central Kenya and the Luo and Kipsigis of Western Kenya.[48] With the cows thus acquired, men could pay bridewealth, perform traditional ceremonies in which cows formed an important part, increase their wealth, and provide food for their families.[49] Successful raiders received praise and respect. Revenge and counterrevenge raids occurred, going back and forth.[50] Wambui Otieno recounts the cattle-raiding adventures of one of her ancestors:

> Ole Kumale retained his Maasai name, settled down, and soon became friends with the young Kikuyu men of his age. However, he often visited his people in Maasailand. [But as] one of the many Kikuyu warriors, he would often raid Maasailand for cattle and women.[51]

Ironically, women were usually on the receiving end at such times, as young girls were equated with cattle and hence "raided" along with the livestock. Some of these girls became wives of the raiders.[52] Thus, the girls who had been "raided" made peace with their circumstances when they realized they had few if any means to rectify the situation. This provides evidence of a woman's emotional flexibility in daily negotiating the challenges in her life, which include racial, cultural, economic, and political considerations.[53]

Another example of cattle rustling together with the raiding of women comes from my conversation with Rose Kibet, an elderly woman who lives in Western Kenya's Rift Valley Province. In June 2007, she spoke of the raid about fifty years ago in which she was taken from her home in Nyanza

Province to Kericho in the Rift Valley Province, about two hundred kilometers away. As mentioned earlier, she became a wife of a member of the Kipsigis community living in the village she had been taken to. She describes her abduction:

> I cannot clearly recall what happened. I must have been three years old or so. The only thing I remember is waking up at night to a lot of noise. Men were shouting, and the women were screaming. I remember being grabbed by some man and being carried far away in the dark night. I cried until I was so tired I fell asleep. When I woke up I was in a strange place with people who did not speak my language. They were kind to me. I lived with an old woman who taught me their language and gave me a new name. As I grew up I would hear from people's talk that I was not from this community, but by then I was comfortable and never thought of going back to my home, which I could not remember.[54]

Rose's account illustrates her emotional flexibility and wisdom in opting for what worked best in her new situation. Mainstream feminism would have wished her to continually seek her freedom, but womanism would acknowledge the futility of such a move and rather encourage her to draw upon her reservoir of strength to make the most of her situation. Her options were limited, because she came from a community that rarely reaccepted any "once married" daughters. She made her peace with her captors for the sake of going on with her life and because they were "okay," as she says. Looking at Rose now, no one would imagine she was not born a member of the Kipsigis who live in Kericho. She is accepted and loved by her "relatives" just as if she were a blood relation. When she was in her teens, she was given the appropriate facial markings and had two lower teeth extracted, according to the rites families choose for their members.

However, in more recent times, cattle-rustling conflicts have become more violent and many people lose their lives in these frequent flare-ups.[55] Various women and women's groups have been formed to address this problem, which threatens to destroy Kenyan communities. In Marsabit, Northern Kenya, the Marsabit Women Advocacy and Development Organization (MWADO) works among the Gabbras, Rendille, Borana, and Burgi in order to avert conflict and promote peaceful coexistence. MWADO urges the women in the communities to refrain from encouraging the men to engage in cattle raiding and to withhold praise from successful raiders.[56] These women are focused on the security and well-being of the community as a whole.

Tegla Loroupe, an athlete who competes at national and international levels, has even formed a peace foundation focused on the issue. As Jeffrey Gettleman reported in the *New York Times* in 2006,

Her focus is bringing peace to her native area, an expanse in northwest Kenya that is hilly and dry, perfect for marathon training—and for rustling cattle. Each year, hundreds of people are killed there, as young men with long legs and automatic weapons steal one another's herds. Ms. Loroupe has lost friends, relatives and even her sister, in a way, to the neglect and turbulence of her homeland. . . . The battles rage on for days, shutting down schools, displacing families and keeping the area trapped in a development shadow, though Kenyan papers rarely deem the problems worthy of a headline.[57]

The Tegla Loroupe Peace Foundation, among many other activities, trains and develops athletes in exchange for their agreement to refrain from taking part in these deadly cattle raids.[58] When there are hostilities in the community, women who have to carry out domestic duties, such as fetching water, tending family kitchen gardens, and generally taking care of their families, are immediately exposed to danger.[59] They will mostly be unarmed and vulnerable at such times, as opposed to the men who will be armed and ready to confront the enemies. Tegla Loroupe, in starting her peace foundation, recognizes that when women and children are unable to go safely about their activities, society cannot develop. The cases of current cattle rustling described above clearly illustrate how important it is for members of society to focus on securing society as a whole by giving of themselves and their possessions.

The Conflict over the 2007 Presidential Elections

The trigger for the 2008 conflict situation was the alleged stealing of the presidential elections held at the end of December 2007. Members of the main opposition party, the Orange Democratic Movement (ODM), suspected fraud. There were major uprisings against the president's Kikuyu community. Members of the Kisii, perceived to be Kikuyu sympathizers, faced similar attacks from the opposition, but the Kikuyu fought back. Over a thousand people died and another estimated three hundred thousand were displaced by this conflict in which ordinary Kenyans—men and women—rose up against one another.[60] The media carried many pictures of women carrying all sorts of weapons in the streets along with their menfolk.[61]

Stephanie McCrummen noted in the *Washington Post's* Foreign Service section of January 2, 2008, that arsonists had burnt to death thirty-five people who had taken refuge in a church in the Western Kenyan town of Eldoret.[62] As usual, women made up the majority of victims, unable to escape their pursuers swiftly. They needed to secure the safety of their charges, children and elders, as well as to flee. Women also lost a great deal economically in this conflict when they were forced to flee from their homes: the crops they planted in their kitchen gardens; large tracts of family land that they farmed; and for some, even small businesses they ran to supplement their family's income.[63] On another level, these women suffered emotional losses as they had to part from their friends due to this "tribal-based" political conflict. Before the war broke out, Kenyans had mixed freely, and friendships transcended "tribal" barriers.

In a telephone conversation on January 25, 2008, my mother, who lives in Kenya, expressed her feelings about the conflict:

> We are terrified; it seems that this war has taken [on] a life of its own and it is like a bush fire during the dry season. The police are helpless, and they stand and watch as a house is burnt by protestors. We have decided that the best intervention measure is prayer and hope that our political leaders will come to their senses and ask their supporters to call off the fight. Parents should also ask their children to stop the destruction they are currently carrying out. Confronting these fighters with armed force will only make it worse.[64]

However, as of early May 2008, the process of resettling the people displaced by war had started, and the news media were full of pictures of families going back to their former homes in an effort to rebuild their lives.[65] Displaced women who were unable to return to their old homes were quickly invited to enter their new neighborhood's *chama*.[66]

A few women in the Kenyan diaspora expressed their sentiments about the violent flare-ups in the country. Paula Kipchumba, a Kenyan student in Texas, after getting news on January 4, 2008, that over thirty-five people had died in the church in Eldoret, said,

> You know, every time I read news from home I have this sinking feeling in the pit of my stomach. I do not know what to expect next because the relative peace that has prevailed in Kenya has never prepared me for this [the war]. I now know what people from wartorn countries daily undergo as they get news of the new and terrible atrocities that are taking place in their countries. I would listen to stories of war from my friends from countries at war and how they daily worried about the safety of their families back home and treat them just as such: stories. My country has been at war for only four days, yet I feel this helpless! It helps me a lot when I call and talk to my family. I find it therapeutic.[67]

Here Kipchumba expresses the shock that comes with the realization that peace is fragile. On January 20, 2008, she said,

> I have totally been caught off guard! In all this time I imagined war happened in other peoples' countries! I did not know that a seemingly cool country

could erupt into war in a space of two days. I spent sleepless nights worrying about my family back home, and at times I wish I could spend the whole day with them on the phone just to be reassured that they are all right. I have taken to praying every day for peace in my country so my family can be safe. I get strength from the act of talking to my family.[68]

In this conversation, Paula admitted seeking spiritual intervention over the fighting in Kenya. She also turned to offering and receiving emotional support through talking to family members, and she fell back on the coping mechanism favored by fellow women in Kenya, that is, seeking support from each other.

In an e-mail message of January 15, 2008, Jeanne (a pseudonym) asked her friends, myself included, to pray for the safety of her missing brother-in-law. Jeanne is a Kenyan woman living in Austin, Texas. Her brother-in-law, living in Kenya, had not contacted any family member since the conflict started and he had been where the fighting was most intense. Deeply spiritual, Jeanne realized that prayer was the best help she could ask for in such a situation.[69] The ability of the Kenyan woman to handle traumatic experiences and her reliance on the counseling of friends to help her get through difficult times is illustrated by Jeanne's message and request. As with the *chama*, reliance on others for emotional support works well in times of intense stress—women easily share their difficulties with others and readily accept help when others reach out to them.

The devastating effects of the 2007 Kenyan failed elections are illustrated by the conversations and message cited above. Reliance on the emotional support networks of friends and fellow women illustrates the wisdom of the Kenyan woman, born out of her need to survive in a male-dominated world. The women drew heavily on their upbringing to begin their recovery from the conflict.

Conclusion

This chapter discusses the role of Kenyan women in three conflict situations: the Mau Mau war of independence, cattle-rustling conflicts, and the conflict over the 2007 presidential elections. It presents Kenyan women as protagonists in war, exhibiting resilience, stoicism, strength of will, selflessness, comradeship, diligence, and determination. Many stories of Kenyan women at war remain undocumented, because the women's upbringing predisposes them to be modest about their achievements. More needs to be written about Kenyan women's contributions to the development of their country, especially now that there is a political climate favorable to the inclusion of more women in the country's leadership.

Muthoni Wanjira of Kenya has founded a project, the Literary Road to Empowerment, through which a group of African feminists, women scholars, and writers, revise oral literature narratives for use in Kenyan schools. In these revised stories, women are portrayed in a positive fashion.[70] Muthoni Wanjira began this project when she realized that the original stories represented as failures in society those women who were not submissive to the male figures in their lives. Such women characters were given bad endings, because of their refusal to submit to men. Wanjira says the group uses the revised stories, instead of the ones in which women are negatively portrayed, to instruct young people. The hope is that in a matter of ten years, society will have a crop of adults who are more sensitive to both the plight and the potential abilities of women and supportive of their development.[71] It is important that these changes of attitude be directed foremost to the youths, as they are the face of a country's future. Girls in Kenya also need to grow up knowing and appreciating their potential in society.

In similar vein, the Coalition on Violence against Women (COVAW), founded in 1995, notes that violence against women is the one major reason why women do not exploit their potential in nation-building activities.[72] Women who feel intimidated, or have been hurt, cannot fully engage in nation-building activities. If women are unable to participate fully in these activities, then Kenya Vision 2030 may not become a reality.[73] Kenya Vision 2030 is a plan for Kenya's journey to a more prosperous future by the encouragement of practices that foster peace among Kenya's citizens. Among the practices identified are the promotion of women's participation in economic, social, and political decision-making processes and the minimizing of retrogressive practices like female genital mutilation.[74] Such retrogressive practices minimize women in the eyes of society and by doing so diminish their nation-building potential.

At least, the current political climate has made it possible for qualified women to be appointed as heads of some of the country's powerful ministries, which less than ten years ago were the preserve of men. The Ministry of Public Health and Sanitation and the Ministry of Justice, National Cohesion and Constitutional Affairs are now headed by the Honorable Beth Mugo and Martha Karua, respectively.[75] However, if women are now able to fulfill such nontraditional roles, it is important to remember that their role as mothers and carers remains just as crucial as it has always been.

Notes

I would like to extend my gratitude to my academic supervisor, Dr. Clarena Larrotta of the College of Education at Texas State University–San Marcos, for her advice on matters of structure and style in this chapter. I particularly want to mention her patience during our meetings.

1. Andrea Cornwall, "Introduction: Perspectives on Gender in Africa," in *Readings in Gender in Africa*, ed. Andrea Cornwall (Bloomington: Indiana University Press, 2005), 1.

2. Gloria I. Chuku, "Women and Nationalist Movements," in Falola, *Africa*, vol. 4, *The End of Colonial Rule: Nationalism and Decolonization*, 109.

3. Robert J. C. Young, *Postcolonialism: An Historical Introduction* (Oxford: Blackwell, 2001), 360.

4. Ibid.

5. Waruhiu Itote, *"Mau Mau" General*, quoted in Marshall S. Clough, *Mau Mau Memoirs: History, Memory, and Politics* (Boulder, CO: Lynne Rienner, 1998), 142.

6. Ngugi wa Thiong'o and Micere Githae Mugo, *The Trial of Dedan Kimathi* (Oxford: Heinemann, 1977), 11.

7. Ibid.

8. Colette Daiute and Cynthia Lightfoot, eds., *Narrative Analysis: Studying the Development of Individuals in Society* (Thousand Oaks, CA: Sage, 2004), 39.

9. Ibid., 40.

10. Michael Quinn Patton, *Qualitative Research and Evaluation Methods*, 3rd ed. (Thousand Oaks, CA: Sage, 2002), 115.

11. Wambui Waiyaki Otieno, *Mau Mau's Daughter: A Life History*, with an introduction by Cora Ann Presley (Boulder, CO: Lynne Rienner, 1998).

12. Rose Kibet, conversations with the author, June 14 and 16, 2007 in Kipsiket market of Kericho, Kenya.

13. Otieno, *Mau Mau's Daughter*, 12.

14. Dennis Itumbi, "Kenyans Surrender Arms to Take Part in Race," *Africa News*, February 15, 2008, http//www.africanews.com. The Tegla Loroupe Peace Foundation "was formed to use the power of sport to bring peace to conflict-ridden areas of East Africa, to support children who are victims of conflict, and to enable economic development," http://www.tegla.org/TDec/Tegla_Loroupe_Peace_Foundation/Home.html.

15. Morten Bonde Pedersen, "Women Hold the Key to Peace," MS ActionAid (Denmark), November 22, 2007, http://www.ms.dk/sw87249.asp.

16. Njoroge Mwaura et al., "Kenya: Celebrating Power Deal," Kenya Television Network, February 28, 2008.

17. bell hooks, *Talking Back: Thinking Feminist, Thinking Black* (Boston: South End, 1989), 137–39.

18. Ibid., 60–61.

19. Lenah B. Ratemo, Alice Ondigi, and John Kebaso, "Is There Time for Family: Working Men in Nairobi-Kenya," February 12, 2007, www.womenofthemountains.org.

20. Nel Noddings, *Philosophy of Education*, 2nd ed. (Boulder, CO: Westview, 2007), 213–15.

21. Ibid., 224.

22. bell hooks, *Salvation: Black People and Love* (New York: HarperCollins, 2001), 34.

23. Otieno, *Mau Mau's Daughter*, 99.

24. Susan Arndt, "African Gender Trouble and African Womanism: An Interview with Chikwenye Ogunyemi and Wanjira Muthoni," *Signs: Journal of Women in Culture and Society* 25, no. 3 (2000): 713.

25. Alice Walker, *In Search of Our Mothers' Garden: Womanist Prose* (San Diego: Harcourt Brace Jovanovich, 1983).
26. Marie Pauline Eboh, "The Woman Question: African and Western Perspectives," in *African Philosophy: An Anthology*, ed. Emmanuel Chukwudi Eze (Oxford: Blackwell, 1997), 335.
27. Ibid.
28. Chioma Opara, quoted in Eboh, "The Woman Question," 335.
29. Arndt, "African Gender Trouble and African Womanism," 712.
30. Ibid.
31. Barbara Thomas-Slayter and Dianne Rocheleau, *Gender, Environment, and Development in Kenya: A Grassroots Perspective* (Boulder, CO: Lynne Rienner, 1995), 15–16.
32. Ibid., 14–15.
33. Otieno, *Mau Mau's Daughter*, 137–39.
34. Clough, *Mau Mau Memoirs*, 28–29.
35. Otieno, *Mau Mau's Daughter*, 42.
36. Ibid., 53.
37. Ibid., 37.
38. Ibid., 42.
39. Ibid., 43–46.
40. Ibid., 42.
41. Ibid., 36.
42. Ibid., 78.
43. Ibid., 211–23.
44. Lisa Aubrey, *The Politics of Development Cooperation: NGOs, Gender and Partnership in Kenya* (New York: Routledge, 1997), 45–46.
45. Ibid., 48.
46. Ibid.
47. Ibid., 89.
48. Otieno, *Mau Mau's Daughter*, 12.
49. Rose Kibet, conversations with the author, June 14 and 16, 2007.
50. Otieno, *Mau Mau's Daughter*, 14.
51. Ibid., 12.
52. Ibid.
53. Arndt, "African Gender Trouble and African Womanism."
54. Rose Kibet, conversations with the author, June 14 and 16, 2007.
55. Reuters, "65 Kenyans Killed in Cattle-rustling Violence," *New York Times*, July 14, 2005.
56. Pedersen, "Women Hold the Key to Peace."
57. Jeffrey Gettleman, "A Kenyan Runner Seeks Peace for Her Corner of the World," *New York Times*, November 18, 2006.
58. See Tegla Loroupe Peace Foundation. Also see Dennis Itumbi, "Kenyans Surrender Arms to Take Part in Race," *Africa News*, February 15, 2008, http//www.africanews.com.
59. Florida Karani, "The Situation and Roles of Women in Kenya: An Overview," *Journal of Negro Education* 56, no. 3 (1987): 422.

60. Muraya Kariuki, "Ranneberger Says U.S. to Assist Reconstruction," *Kenya Television Network*, March 2, 2008.

61. Ronald Rashid, "Kisumu Election Violence," Nation Television, December 29, 2007, http://www.ntv.co.ke.

62. Stephanie McCrummen, "Kenyans Killed Fleeing Violence: Dozens of Victims Trapped in Church That Mob Set Afire," *Washington Post*, Foreign Service Section, January 2, 2008.

63. Rashid, "Kisumu Election Violence," Nation Television, December 29, 2007, http://www.ntv.co.ke.

64. Author's mother, conversation with the author, January 25, 2008.

65. Harun Ochieng,' "Resettlement Operation for the Displaced Kenyans Starts," Nation Television, May 4, 2008, http://www.ntv.co.ke.

66. Ibid.

67. Coleen Kipchumba, conversation with the author, January 4, 2008.

68. Paula Anyango (pseudonym), conversation with the author, January 20, 2008.

69. Jeanne Kimaru (pseudonym), e-mail message to the author, January 15, 2008.

70. Arndt, "African Gender Trouble and African Womanism."

71. Ibid., 709–10.

72. Rosemary Mueni Mbaluka, *In Pursuit of Justice: A Research Report on Service Providers' Response to Cases of Violence against Women in Nairobi Province* (Nairobi: Coalition on Violence against Women, 2002), iv.

73. Ministry of State for Planning and National Development and Vision 2030, *Kenya Vision 2030* (Nairobi: National Economic and Social Council of Kenya, 2007), 11.

74. Ibid.

75. Njoroge Mwaura et al., "Swearing In of Kenyan Cabinet," Kenya Television Network, April 17, 2008, http://www.Africast.tv.

6

Mass Rape as a Weapon of War in the Eastern DRC

Jonathan Zilberg

> Rape is not an accident of war, or an incidental adjunct to armed conflict. Its widespread use in times of conflict reflects the unique terror it holds for women, the unique power it gives the rapist over his victim, and the unique contempt it displays for its victims.
>
> Amnesty International USA, 2005

Introduction

In 2007, the HBO documentary film produced and directed by Lisa Jackson, *The Greatest Silence: Rape in the Congo,* brought to American public attention, to a greater extent than ever before, the shocking nature of violence against women in the eastern Democratic Republic of Congo (DRC).[1] This chapter has the same objective as the film but with the Africanist academic community in mind, having been written specifically to document the emerging media coverage of and information on this continuing human rights crisis and to encourage active engagement within universities. It begins by outlining the efforts of governmental and nongovernmental organizations to bring the issue to public and academic attention and provides an overview of rape as a weapon of war in general and in the DRC in particular. Above all, it considers how expanding circles of concern are using the mass media, and increasingly new media forms as well, in an effort to encourage governments and the United Nations to control the violence against women in the DRC. The chapter then introduces some of the campaigns that are seeking to treat and prevent both nontraumatic (obstetric) and traumatic (rape-related) fistula, as well as the local and international efforts to protect and empower the victims through bolstering peace and security. After introducing the differences between obstetric and traumatic fistula, the chapter focuses on the symbolic violence and military/terrorist function of rape in a climate of complete impunity.[2] There is also a brief discussion of the limits of hope for any resolution of the conflict in the eastern DRC and thus of the plight of women and girls in these communities.[3] In addition, the chapter provides a brief overview of the broader history of the local and regional conflict, though this aspect of the crisis is largely relegated to references in the endnotes.[4] The conclusion recapitulates the efforts by Amnesty International, the United Nations, the U.S. government, and various local and international organizations to ameliorate this particularly extreme scenario of violence against women.[5]

The sheer scale of the problem and the horror it creates for the women trapped in the conflicts defies comprehension, not only among those formerly unaware of it but among doctors and judges dealing with the situation on the ground as well.[6] Moreover, since the publication of the Human Rights Watch report, *The War within the War: Sexual Violence against Women and Girls in Eastern Congo*—which provides one of the most detailed accounts of the scale of death and suffering, specifically on the perpetration of mass rape as a weapon of war—the situation has consistently continued to deteriorate.[7] This particular report, the numerous online reports and campaigns referred to in this chapter, and especially the United Nations resolutions and Senate and congressional meetings, attest to the ongoing urgent need to confront this grave humanitarian crisis. Indeed, the situation is so extreme that United Nations Resolution 1325 was passed in 2000, in order to enforce the Rome Statute of the International Criminal Court by making the use of rape as a weapon of war an international war crime. It was followed by United Nations Security Council Resolutions 1804 and 1820 in 2008, which have been no more effective than Resolution 1325.[8]

In terms of expanding circles of concern, there are a number of emerging interinstitutional initiatives, namely. the Congo Global Action Project, the ENOUGH and STAND campaigns, Friends of the Congo, the Harvard Humanitarian Initiative, and the HEAL Africa campaign. These and other humanitarian projects are framed here within the context of the emerging scholarship on the crisis in the eastern DRC as well as in relation to the all-important governmental and nongovernmental projects, particularly the efforts by the United Nations.[9] Though the crisis in Darfur has dominated the media reports on war in Africa since the Rwandan genocide, by late 2008, the DRC conflict was increasingly beginning to receive sustained media attention. In this larger context, in which many of the humanitarian campaigns are mobilizing support through e-blitzes on upcoming and past events, electronic petitions, and online social networks such as Facebook, there is significant potential synergy between all of them. Moreover, all of these campaigns and their media reach are progressively improving in the breadth and depth of their content and are slowly gaining traction in academic venues, having previously been obliged to rely largely on the celebrity and media nexus.[10]

Take, for instance, Friends of the Congo's recent screening in Washington, DC, of the film *The Anguish of War in the Congo*, on March 8, 2009, on the occasion of the International Women's Day Vigil. As with all the campaigns, the use of web pages is crucial. Friends of the Congo now has a weekly podcast on the latest situation in the Congo and recently managed the Break the Silence Speakers Tour, which ran from February through July 2009 and was an outgrowth of Congo Week 2008. This example of one evolving campaign highlights the fact that all of these campaigns are information-rich and have long- and short-term strategic goals. The communities formed by these campaigns can be imagined as an ever-expanding circle of concern, and together they arguably form an emerging global social justice movement focused on putting an end to rape as a weapon of war in the Congo.

This chapter is in essence an applied study of the role of the mass media, advocacy, and international relief as it concerns one aspect of one humanitarian crisis.[11] It illustrates how powerful the Internet has become as a tool for providing significant content, which allows the individual to monitor situations from afar, and it is specifically concerned with showing how the Internet has been used by advocacy groups and human rights organizations to transmit press reports and amplify media campaigns.[12] Written from the vantage point of a concerned African scholar working in Asia and Africa but not in the DRC itself, the chapter makes no claims to any firsthand knowledge of the situation. Originally written without access to any resources except those that had been posted on the Internet, it was subsequently significantly advanced by materials sent to me by individual scholars or individuals in the U.S. government, as well as by the continually emerging reports on the Internet through April 2009. Indeed, this is very much an engaged study of media and society, as I became aware of the issue of rape-related fistula in the DRC only through news of Eve Ensler's V-Day campaign, which popped up on my desktop's Yahoo web mail page in late 2006.

War and Rape in the DRC

Academic studies of the war in the DRC and the concomitant humanitarian problems are increasingly becoming available.[13] Such studies add critical and practical dimensions to the recent foundational studies and reports of the DRC conflict and the extremity of the violence and violation.[14] In addition, a great deal of material on the use of rape as a weapon of war in the DRC, mainly in the east, is to be found online in government documents and institutional and nongovernmental organization reports, which have provided the impetus to the necessarily more shallow and repetitive, if constantly updated, media coverage. For instance, Johann Hari's online article, "Congo's Tragedy: The War the World Forgot," in the *Independent* is a stark account, useful for those who may have little knowledge of the situation.[15] To provide another example, in all the documentary sources provided here, whether reports by campaigns or by organizations or observers relating victims' accounts in the media, no report stands out as a more shocking call to action than the online account given in "Rape as a Weapon of War in the Congo [Part 2: The Savagery]."[16]

More recently, Stephen Lewis, formerly the United Nation's envoy for AIDS in Africa, states that rape has become a "strategy of war."[17] Raping civilians is more effective than fighting, attracts less international attention than "piles of bodies do," and is considered by and large "not our problem" by the international community.[18] The 2002 Human Rights Watch report *The War within the War* presumably provided the impetus for the multifaceted efforts that followed.[19] However, as the ENOUGH campaign notes six years later, in 2008, "this spotlight has failed . . . to generate effective action; efforts to protect women and girls in the Congo are failing spectacularly."[20]

In the DRC, rape has become a calculated tactic so extreme in form and scale that it is hard for even seasoned relief workers to grasp—even given the 1994 Rwandan scenario, in which five hundred thousand women were reported to have been raped in the four months' genocide. As Chris McGreal reports, 75 percent of all the rape cases dealt with by Médecins Sans Frontières are in the DRC, and the situation in Darfur, as bad as it is, apparently does not compare.[21] One particularly visible foreign witness of this humanitarian disaster is Sarah Mosely, gender-based violence coordinator with the International Rescue Committee, based in Bukavu in eastern DRC. In an interview conducted with her in January 2008 available online, Mosely relates why rape is the most effective technique for punishing, intimidating, and thus controlling access to and support from local populations by militias and outlaws fighting against each other and the government.[22] Before we revisit Mosely's interview and comment upon its effects, it is important to put the media efforts toward advocacy and mobilization of resources into context with regard to academic, government, and institutional reports.

The emerging academic studies are obviously useful on a somewhat different level from the media reports. They introduce the level of complexity required to understand the nature of the conflict and attempts to ameliorate it and ultimately perhaps to strengthen government and civil society in order to control the rape epidemic. One critically relevant academic study is Lydiah Kemunto Bosire's online article, "The Limits and Possibilities of Transitional Justice," which aims to inform more effective policy and action.[23] Bosire's scholarship represents the cutting edge of emergent research in the field and is commendably focused on the practical challenges, explaining why sexual and gender-based violence remains inadequately addressed at the level of the International Criminal Court and the local civil and military courts. Bosire contributes in the legal, academic, and philosophical sphere just as Sarah Mosely contributes at a practical level in the DRC.

Regardless of the difficulties faced, or more correctly perhaps, precisely because of these limitations, injustices, and extremity of the cruelty involved, the central point of this chapter, which brings together disparate materials, is again simply to argue that greater concerted collective action through universities and professional societies would offer useful support to NGOs, governments, and the United Nations so as to provide more assistance for the victims. Of course, it goes without saying that without the establishment of the rule of law in the DRC through local political settlements, good governance, and economic development, the Hobbesian situation there is unlikely to change in the short to medium term, though, according to the most recent reports, the efforts in the legal sphere to end the climate of impunity are beginning to show results.[24] The painstaking academic work by political scientists and others, including Séverine Autesserre and Koen Vlassenroot, demonstrates how complex the situation is and why regional and international peace efforts have failed to bring peace and security to the eastern DRC.[25] This chapter focuses exclusively on the eastern DRC because this is the region where we see the most extreme use of rape as a weapon of war in the world today and the context in which it came to my attention. I leave it to other scholars who are specialists in the history and culture of the region to explain how and why this situation has come about.

Expanding Circles of Concern: The Media and the Campaign to End Fistula and Violence against Women

The material examined here has sometimes had a considerable impact on individuals, motivating them to become involved in the expanding and connecting circles of concern regarding sexual violence against women, particularly those working to end fistula. Take, for instance, the case of Megan G., who posted the following response on January 26, 2008, to the online article "Rape as a Weapon of War [Part 2: The Savagery]":

> This is unbelievable! I am only 15 and cannot even imagine how I would continue living if this happened to me. What can I do about this? I feel that it is my responsibility to do something and i [sic] need to do something about this but I also feel helpless because I dont [sic] know what I can do.[26]

The reply posted by Julie points Megan to the companion online article, "Rape as a Weapon of War in the Congo [Part 3: The Healing and What You

Can Do to Help]."²⁷ Julie also encourages Megan to watch the documentary *Lumo: One Woman's Struggle to Heal in a Country Beset by War*—the story of Lumo Sinai—directed by Bent-Jorgen Perlmutt and Nelson Walker III, produced by the Goma Film Project at the HEAL Africa Hospital, a project in which the women victims actively participated. Julie asks Megan to "tell people. Talk about these women. Blog about them."²⁸

Indeed, there is no shortage of projects and campaigns to join. Consider, for instance, in addition to the United Nations Population Fund's (UNFPA's) Campaign to End Fistula, the various governmental, international, and nongovernmental women's organizations referred to in the following pages. Moreover, some of the most vigorous efforts to combat fistula have come from individuals: concerned women and men in the West who have been impelled, often through the media, to become involved in the efforts to alleviate the suffering. For instance, in 2007, Natalie Imbruglia, supported by Joan Branson and Virgin Unite, the charitable arm of Virgin Atlantic, hosted a charity event in London to inaugurate the Natalie Imbruglia Campaign to End Fistula. It is important in following these celebrity campaigns to consider the order in which they emerged. As already mentioned, on V-Day in 2006, the issue of fistula was brought to the American public's attention through Eve Ensler, the well known author of *The Vagina Monologues*, and her City of Hope project in Bukavu.²⁹ In fact, however, coverage of the issue was not entirely new.

The problem of fistula in Africa had already been presented on the *Oprah Winfrey Show* on January 16, 2004, as recorded in the show's heartbreaking transcript. The tragic plight of the women victims had first been brought to the greater international public's attention the year earlier, in an equally compelling way, in a *New York Times* article, "Alone and Ashamed," by Nicholas Kristof.³⁰ Kristof's work, and that of Jeffrey Gettleman and others, provides a powerful example of the role of the media in educating the public about critical problems and the power of the media to generate, maintain, and expand circles of concern. The public sphere appears to be far in advance of the academy in awareness and engagement. Today, six years later, despite the media activism and even UN Security Council resolutions, the situation has become increasingly more extreme and the need for intervention arguably ever greater; yet belief in support for intervention, including prosecution, has become ever more contested, especially in Africa itself.

The examples of coverage of the medical condition and social consequences of fistula in the mass media noted above illustrate the vital role that such media events and articles have played in creating international awareness of the problems facing women in Africa. Yet, as the following account reveals, the incidence of rape and traumatic fistula resulting from rape has escalated sharply.

Obstetric and Traumatic Fistula: The Medical and Social Consequences of Poverty and Rape as a Weapon of War

Briefly put, aside from the long history of the use of rape and violence against women and children as a weapon of war, the definition of rape as a war crime and a crime against humanity came to international attention after the war in the former Yugoslavia in the 1990s. Rape was also used as a weapon of war in Liberia between 1989 and 1997—so extensively that it is now punishable by death.[31] Rape has become increasingly used as a strategic tactic for intimidating populations in Rwanda, Sudan, and Columbia in particular.[32] It has come to be systematically used by all parties in the DRC, that is, by the army and the police, by the opposition forces, by unaffiliated gangs known as Mai Mai, and increasingly by individuals.[33]

The situation has become so grave that on February 12, 2008, UNICEF appealed for $106 million for the DRC crisis. As Hilde Johnson, deputy executive director of UNICEF's United Nation's Children's Agency, reports, rape as a weapon of war has reached epidemic proportions in some African countries, having spread from armies to militias and now into the civilian population.[34] The UNICEF appeal was issued on the same day that the UN Security Council passed Resolution SC/9246, which is designed to enforce punitive measures against those committing acts of (sexual) violence against children in armed conflicts.[35] The appeal and the resolution followed significant political activity toward the end of 2007, when the governments of the DRC, Rwanda, the United States, and others agreed that it was imperative to resolve the conflict in the eastern DRC. It was crucial to bring the crisis under control before an even greater humanitarian crisis occurred, 5.4 million people having already died in the conflict by that time.[36]

Against the background of extreme violence against women, of war, and of poverty, it is necessary to provide a simple introduction to the medical condition of fistula and its treatment. Fistula is a significant problem in poor rural communities and traumatic fistula is one of the most immediate health problems in the DRC. According to the Johns Hopkins Bloomberg School of Public Health's Information Project report, "Obstetric Fistula: Ending the Silence, Easing the Suffering," fistula occurs when the connective tissue separating different parts of the body ruptures through tissue necrosis or physical trauma.[37] Nontraumatic fistulas result from complications during childbirth in which the fetus dies during a delayed delivery. These vesico-vaginal and recto-vaginal fistulas occur in a small percentage of problematic births in developing countries, mainly in rural areas that lack adequate health facilities to cope with a birth that would require a cesarian section. Because of the sustained pressure on the tissues of the upper cervix, which cuts off the blood supply during labor, and with further consequences caused by the unborn fetus, the tissues undergo necrosis. When these tissues slough off, a fistula may develop between the vagina and the urinary tract, or between the vagina and the rectum, resulting in an uncontrolled leakage of urine and feces. In the classic presentation of fistula, obstructed labor is the immediate primary cause, occurring in approximately 5 percent of pregnancies and accounting for 8 percent of maternal deaths—with 99 percent of the pregnancy-related deaths occurring in developing countries. The highest-risk group is composed of adolescent girls, particularly in Darfur, where girls are typically forced into marriage at a very young age. The same demographic is found in the case of sexual slavery among girls and women in the Ituri region, which was brought to the attention of the world through *National Geographic*'s special issue, *Africa: Whatever You Thought, Think Again*.[38]

In 2005, according to the Integrated Regional Information Network (IRIN) of the United Nations Office for the Coordination of Human Affairs (UNOCHA), the base count for obstetric fistula of all forms was estimated at two million cases worldwide with fifty thousand to a hundred thousand new cases being presented annually. Ethiopia and Sudan are the best-documented instances, as these countries have the longest history of hospitals providing treatment for the condition. The Fistula Foundation at the Hamlin Fistula Hospitals, specifically at the Addis Ababa Fistula Hospital, has been at the forefront of these efforts.[39] It was the *New York Times* article "Alone and Ashamed," mentioned earlier, that first brought attention to this issue in the American press and inspired the making of the documentary *A Walk to Beautiful*.[40] Tragically, as the documentary, Kristof, and many others have recorded, the social consequences of fistula are as devastating as the physical consequences.

Typically, the victims are shunned, divorced, and ultimately ostracized by their communities, and several case studies have documented the fall into extreme poverty that occurs when husbands divorce their wives. For instance, in Jos, Nigeria, it was found that 71 percent of women with fistula were divorced. In India and Pakistan, the figure ranges from 70 to 90 percent, and in Addis Ababa one in five such women resort to begging to survive.[41] The plight of such African women has been recorded by the Women's Dignity Project through *Faces of Dignity: Seven Stories of Girls and Women with Fistula*.[42] In many (post)conflict situations, these women and their children can only survive by earning a living through "survival sex," becoming known as the "One-Dollar UN Girls."[43]

Traumatic fistulas, on the other hand, present far more complex challenges than the comparatively simple surgical challenge of repairing normal recto-genital, poverty-based fistulas. Traumatic fistulas result from the violent sexual abuse of women, ranging from octogenarians to girls and to infants only months old, by multiple men, often followed by radical genital and vaginal mutilation involving knives and guns and other sharp objects.[44] The author of "Rape as a Weapon of War in the Congo [Part 2: The Savagery]" writes as follows:

It is difficult to write this section because what I am about to describe is nearly unimaginable. But it is true and it is happening. Not to one woman. Not to ten, or one hundred, or one thousand. Not to ten thousand. It's happening to *hundreds of thousands* of women throughout the DRC. It is happening right now, this second, as you read this. Women, children, babies. Raped, tortured, mutilated. Many times in front of their families. Many times for days on end. They are gang raped. They are raped with objects. Sticks. Rocks. Bayonets. Guns. They are raped with the sheer intent to destroy—body and soul. Women have had firearms discharged into their vaginas, blowing out their female anatomy, yet surviving. Girls under the age of three, women over eighty.[45]

The author goes on to quote Christine Schuler [Deschryver], a Congolese human rights activist, who records that

the last baby who was raped, it was in April. She was ten months old, so a very small baby. She was raped. The same gang raped the mother during two weeks. Then they came to Bukavu into my office. I wanted to bring the baby to the hospital, but she was so injured she died in my arms.[46]

Other reports, available on the Internet, written by witnesses or aid workers visiting hospitals in the eastern DRC confirm these accounts. It is also vital to emphasize, according to Judithe Registre of Women for Women, that

when a woman is raped, it's not just her that's raped. It's the entire community that's destroyed. . . . When they take a woman to rape her, they'll line up the family, they'll line up other members of the communities to actually witness that. . . . They make them watch. And so, what that means for that particular woman when it's all over, is that total shame, personally, to have been witnessed by so many people as she's being violated.[47]

Moreover, as many reports document through survivors' accounts, the perpetrators commonly attempt to force people to rape their own family members, and being largely unsuccessful in doing so, conclude by killing them. We will never know how many tens of thousands of women and children, and even men and boys, have been killed after being raped and tortured, nor what forms of extreme violence have been employed and how many pregnant women were disemboweled during gang rapes for additional effect—not that the exact numbers should matter.[48] In fact, the few shocking statistics on the incidence of rape in various provinces provided in the next section of this chapter "almost certainly represent only a tiny proportion of the total."[49] In addition, a large number of the female victims who survive, and whose cases are reported because they are brought to hospital, are not only pregnant but will have contracted HIV and other sexually transmitted diseases, adding yet more long-term consequences in addition to the women being ostracized by their families and communities.[50]

In bringing attention to the ongoing work to assist such victims, the following interview with Sarah Mosely on DRC International Relief Committee projects is especially significant. As she relates, the IRC project in the DRC is attempting to help the victims to "recover some sense of normality and some sense of hope and healing, physically and emotionally, so they can ideally move forward with their lives."[51] Mosely adds that there is an intergenerational issue here as well: "We do see victims as young as 2, 3 and 12 at times who have been sexually assaulted. . . . you have quite a longstanding history now and two or three generations of women who have really suffered in the form of sexual violence on quite a large scale."[52]

Mosely also makes the point that there is a deeply destructive psychological and social process at work, affecting the male psyche and society at large:

> I think it really does affect men especially because they are in this culture specifically seen as protectors and more often than not they are not able to protect their families. . . . So there's a lot of guilt and sense of culpability on the part of fathers and spouses that's not really spoken or dealt with which then again probably heightens the rejection factor. I think the rejection factor we're seeing by spouses rejecting their wives probably stems from an element of guilt that they're not able to deal with and it's easier out of sight out of mind than to work through the issues of "demasculinization" which is the term that gets thrown around.[53]

On CBS's *60 Minutes* program, "War against Women," aired on January 11, 2008, Dr. Mukwege, director of Panzi Hospital, said:

> I used to think that when men fled they were irresponsible, but now I understand things differently. . . . They haven't fled because their wives have been raped, but because they feel they've been raped. They have been traumatized . . . humiliated . . . because they weren't able to do anything to protect their wives and children.[54]

Mosely reflects on the larger social and psychological consequences of rape as a weapon of war:

> one thing that has become quite clear is that ALL the armed groups are doing it [including the national army—FARDC] and they do it to terrorize communities. It's often done in conjunction with looting and often in front of family members and communities in a public manner and that's not really related to desire, that's related to power and humiliation and shame. When families see

their own women and children raped that destroys communities. It's opening up wounds that are very hard to heal.[55]

Significantly, she adds that many of the perpetrators are adolescents, who, as child soldiers, have grown up in environments of extreme violence, hardship, and insecurity. While this is not an attempt to rationalize their actions, it introduces the long-term challenge for the future: how to rehabilitate boys and men who for years have acted with total impunity outside the conventions of basic social norms, whether or not they were initially coerced (as their testimonies all too often reveal).[56]

Symbolic Violence

Rape serves an antisocial psycho-pathological purpose and is used as an instrument of terrorism.[57] Claudia Card's article, "Rape as a Weapon of War," lays bare the foundational logical and psychological anatomy of rape in war:

> The ubiquitous threat of rape in war, like that of civilian rape, is a form of terrorism. The aim in war, however, may not be service (the aim generally served by civilian rape) but expulsion or dispersion.... There are often two targets, sacrificial victims and others to whom their sacrifice is used to send a message. Martial rape domesticates not only the women survivors who were its immediate victims but also the men socially connected to them, and men who were socially connected to those who did not survive.[58]

Aside from the highly questionable use of the word "domesticates," Card's discussion contributes to an understanding of the effects of the tactic beyond the violation of the individual:

> If there is one set of fundamental functions of rape, civilian or martial, it is to display, communicate, and produce or maintain dominance, which is both enjoyed for its own sake and used for such ulterior ends as exploitation, expulsion, dispersion, murder. Acts of forcible rape, like other instances of torture, communicate dominance.... Rape is a cross-cultural language of male domination (that is, domination by males; it can also be domination of males). This is its symbolic social meaning.[59]

While the truth of these observations on the symbolic power of rape to intimidate defenseless civilian populations is only too obvious, the following passage from the same article goes further, exploring the social motivations for rape in war with particular insight and relevance:

> Martial rape aims to splinter families and alliances and to bind not women to men but warrior rapists to one another. The activity of martial rape, often relatively public, can serve as a bonding agent among perpetrators and at the same time work in a variety of ways to alienate family members, friends, and former neighbors from each other, as in cases where the perpetrators had been friends or neighbors of those they later raped.[60]

In addition, Yakin Ertürk records that "The extreme sexual violence used during the armed conflicts in DRC has eroded all notions of humanity, unleashing the exercise of brutal fantasies on women's bodies simply because it was possible to do so."[61]

In concluding this section, we must turn to an International Alert report, *Women's Bodies as a Battleground*, written by Omanyondo Ohambe, Bahananga Muhigwa, and Wa Mamba. The report provides an extraordinary analysis of the motivations for rape, its use, and its effects as well as an analysis of its incidence and the affiliations of the perpetrators. The report shows that rape is being used to settle scores and to gain and neutralize power through ritual and magic. It considers the local history of rape and rebellion, and shows how rape is also being used as an act of economic violence, as a reward for bravery in battle, for the humiliation of enemies, and for purposes of genocide.[62]

This report is particularly valuable because of the insights it offers on better ways of dealing with the problem. For instance, we learn that, contrary to general impressions demonizing the Mai Mai militias, these militias have ritual restrictions on contact with women. This has led local communities to support them; it is "false Mai Mai" militias who are using rape as a terror tactic. Moreover, elderly women are guardians of the *dawa* and *mangona* protective war magic, administering it to the fighters, which explains in some instances why elderly women are raped and murdered in particularly appalling ways.[63] The value of social science in increasing our understanding of the context and nature of the violence is striking.

Impunity

Sexual violence as a weapon of war used against women and children has spiraled out of control. In six months in 2004, between May and October, there were 12,000 reported cases of rape alone in eastern DRC.[64] In one province, South Kivu, in 2005, the United Nations estimated that 45,000 women had been raped in that year.[65] By late 2007, an estimated 16,000 rape victims had been treated, and at Panzi Hospital in Bukavu, ten victims a day were being hospitalized.[66] As an ENOUGH report emphasizes, in the absence of authority, both militias and the general population are able to act with impunity, which is not just a problem for remote rural areas but a problem for large cities as well. For instance, 3,500 rape victims were treated in hospitals in Goma alone between January and September 2006. Moreover, in parts of North Kivu, civilian rapes are threatening to eclipse those committed by the militias and the army, and these reported figures constitute some indeterminable, but in all likelihood small, percentage of the real incidence of rape.[67]

This dire and escalating crisis has led to such a state of concern at the United Nations among those member states committed to protecting and assisting women in such circumstances that on February 12, 2008, Radhika Coomaraswamy, the UN secretary-general's special representative for children and armed conflict was compelled to deliver a special address to the UN Security Council. She argued that it is imperative for punitive measures, "concrete and targeted," to be taken against violators so as to transform the current "climate of impunity" in which these crimes are committed.[68] She noted that

> in the Great Lakes region, particularly in the Democratic Republic of Congo and Burundi, we have received information that there are appalling levels of sexual and gender-based violence. Impunity for these acts is widespread. It is imperative that perpetrators of acts of rape and other sexual violence which leave a long-term, devastating impact on the victims are prosecuted in accordance with the gravity of such crimes. Like the recruitment and use of children, sexual violence is always deliberate, targeted and a direct consequence of criminal intent. We cannot tolerate such action in any context but when it involves children, it is especially abhorrent.[69]

Furthermore, as Amanda Beltz concludes, while rape is currently prosecuted because it is used as an instrument of genocide—a view that most Congolese victims in the eastern DRC would share, as they consider rape to be part of a deliberate process of extermination—it needs to be criminalized as a war crime in and of itself.[70] As part of a larger international effort toward the eventual local enforcement of justice, the DRC United Nations mission announced on February 8, 2008, that the first military justice officials were being trained in sex crime investigation and that the military would attempt to lead the way in reducing sexual violence.[71]

In assessing official statements, particularly the DRC government's 2006 commitment to prosecuting sexual violence as a "new form of criminality," the critical response must be that the continuing reality of impunity on the ground consistently outpaces and makes a mockery of such addresses and attempts. As the March 2008 ENOUGH report emphasizes,

> Even though adjustments have been made to the Congolese penal code to help deal with the epidemic of sexual violence, the foremost problem in Congo is

a culture of impunity because of the lack of a strong Congolese state. For the women and young girls who have had the courage to publicly identify their rapists, prosecutions are slow to non-existent. . . . Even worse, because there is no witness protections program in Congo, many perpetrators are able to find and terrorize their accusers again. There are numerous accounts of victims being re-raped in revenge.[72]

Anneke van Woudenberg, a senior researcher at Human Rights Watch, declares in the same report: "In Congo, if someone starts an armed group or kills people, they have a better chance of becoming a senior minister or a general than being put behind bars."[73]

Despite the ceasefire of January 2008, and UN Resolution 1325, the use of rape as a weapon of war has continued to escalate in an environment of virtually complete impunity where there is effectively no rule of law—either local or international. Furthermore, despite the Rome Statute, which provided the International Criminal Court with jurisdiction over rape as a war crime, and despite the ongoing symbolic trials of three key warlords at The Hague, the problem of rape in the eastern DRC continues and can be expected to do so for many years to come.[74] Bosire concludes that, at best, limited "attenuated justice" can be achieved.[75] For practical and political reasons, truth and reconciliation commissions are in effect being used as alternatives to legal mechanisms for justice.

Marion Pratt, Leah Werchick, and colleagues note that "oversimplified initiatives encouraging 'global forgiveness' for war-related and other violence are at best not realistic and at worst mock the suffering experienced by individuals and communities through the country."[76] Keeping in mind this reality, the future would appear to be one of intensifying impunity and injustice. Accordingly, considering the sheer magnitude of the expanding incidence of rape in this only nominally centralized state with a culture of impunity and a severely limited and easily compromised justice system in which the largely ineffective army and police forces (integrated with former militia members) are prone to committing rampant human rights abuses, the best case scenarios for the DRC are not encouraging.[77]

Efforts to Assist

Although the brute fact of the matter is that impunity will by and large continue, at least the UNFPA and other organizations have responded as best they can to this crisis and have put small-scale programs in place to address the medical needs of the victims.[78] In addition, programs are in place to support these women and attempt to reintegrate them into society. Lewis Wall writes that medical services need to consider the "whole person" when dealing with the "obstructed labor injury complex."[79] However, such treatment, never mind prevention, is exceedingly difficult in an environment in which the prospects for peace and security are tenuous at best, and in which hospital admissions, at those few hospitals that exist, exceed these hospitals' capacity for longer-term postoperative care. Nevertheless, though the scale and nature of the problem is daunting if not unmanageable, these relief efforts are proving effective to some degree.

In some cases, women victims have become leading spokespersons for victims' rights and for the need to bring more and more attention to this humanitarian crisis; and they are creating and managing programs and social networks for supporting survivors. Significantly, a key aim of efforts at the United Nations and on the political agenda of aid programs is to attempt to incorporate women into the political process, peace initiatives, reform, and governance, however unlikely and limited the prospects of this in the DRC. In an effort toward the fostering of such developments—and specifically toward international assistance and intervention to protect women—on April 1, 2008, the Congo Global Action group visited Capitol Hill in an attempt to bring pressure on the U.S. House of Representatives to take more proactive measures against the uncontrolled use of rape as a weapon of war in the DRC. Workshops held on March 30 and 31 in preparation for this visit were conducted at the U.S. Holocaust Memorial Museum and focused on gender-based violence, children as victims of war; economic realities, national resource exploitation and conflict, the postconflict stabilization of the nation, governance concerns, and effective advocacy.

These efforts can be seen as part of a growing social movement, in which more and more concerned individuals are being drawn into the orbit of expanding humanitarian organizations and coalitions attempting to address the conflict and the consequences for women. In very large part, this is a consequence of media attention and the power of the Internet.[80] There one finds exceedingly useful firsthand accounts and accounts of the work of humanitarian relief organizations and individuals such as Sarah Mosely's. Mosely's knowledge is directed, as discussed earlier in this chapter, toward very specific and active agendas in a deeply disturbing professional context. The first response to the women victims is to provide medical help. Further explaining the focus of the IRC program, Mosely comments upon the essential social component in humanitarian projects mandated to heal the victims of rape. The program focuses on the psychosocial and specifically on social reintegration. Counselors work with individual women and girls, and with groups—this latter is also designed to promote socialization with women who have endured the same experience. These two methods turn out to be very effective, especially as they encourage the women to set up their own support systems and enable them to generate their own income.[81]

The challenge is gargantuan and, as events in North Kivu continue to show, increasingly difficult. Toward meeting this challenge, studies of trauma and recovery, military intervention, peacekeeping, gender training, security construction and transition, and women waging peace are essential for assisting victims of this war and ultimately perhaps, resolving this conflicts.[82]

What Hope for the Eastern DRC?

Given the extent of the violence and the fact that its recent roots lie in large part in the Rwandan genocide, these gender-based crimes may come to be seen as among the most spectacular examples of violence and inhumanity in the twentieth and twenty-first centuries. However, inhumanity aside, what is perhaps unique here is that the case of the Congo provides us with an opportunity to compare the contemporary, postcolonial events with a similar moment in the history of colonialism. Just as the extraordinary excesses of King Leopold's cruel extractive rule stimulated people of conscience almost a century ago to join the Congo Reform Association to document, protest, and end the crimes against humanity of the time, so we find today a new global movement emerging, in response to similar suffering, to achieve the same ends. The goal of the former was to bring the gravity of the situation to international attention with the specific aim of doing something about it, that is, to achieve justice, to ameliorate the suffering of the victims, and to transform society for the better. In this sense, we see history repeating itself.

Adam Hochschild concludes in *King Leopold's Ghost* that the earlier movement's long-term contribution was that "it kept alive a tradition, a way of seeing the world, a human capacity for outrage at pain inflicted on another human being, no matter whether that pain is inflicted on someone of another color, in another country, at another end of the earth."[83] The relevant questions are whether a movement of equivalent force might emerge to revitalize this tradition in the same, but now postcolonial, nation, and whether peace and the rule of law can be established in the DRC. The fact that women survivors move forward with hope is a testimony to the resilience of the human spirit, especially considering the appalling fact that they will in many instances be raped again, and that if they have the extraordinary bravery to testify, they may even have their lips cut off—the ultimate message.[84]

The time depth and scale of the violence in the DRC make it very difficult to be hopeful. For the problem of rape—since it has become endemic and the incidence of noncombat rape in places exceeds the incidence of combat rape, notably in urban environments—the worst-case long-term scenario is very grave indeed. For instance, Fatima Kayingeli of the women's collective in Kamanyola, where the conflict has been largely resolved, notes that the culture of war has become part of normal life,

Boys who were teenagers before the war and are young adults now grew up seeing people not punished for rape. . . . So they go and get a girl and rape her and know they won't be punished. It's not just men in uniform anymore. It's civilians too.[85]

In postconflict situations, these men and boys, who have in remarkable cases even been assisted by women, will continue to entrench their positions in the emerging power structure, whether in the national army, the police, or the UNHCR, or at local levels from cities down to village households. What is now a rape epidemic will simply become a brutal fact of life for the foreseeable future. As a consequence, the realistic scenario for the eastern DRC is sustained conflict with periodic eruptions of significant violence and the persistent use of rape as a means to terror and domination.

Perhaps then, considering the vast difference between current U.S. supported democratization projects and the role of foreign "assistance" in the Mobutu era during the Cold War, it is fitting to revisit Karl Meyer's *The Dust of Empire*, in which he quotes John F. Kennedy's speech at the University of Washington on November 16, 1961. Kennedy concluded: "In short, we must face problems which do not lend themselves to easy or quick or permanent solutions. And we must face the fact that . . . we cannot right every wrong or reverse every adversity."[86] Today, in a period in which the wisdom of foreign engagements is increasingly becoming the subject of critical debate, there is a tendency simply to accept the situation in places such as the DRC. This is because the problem is seen as insurmountable, as there is insufficient local and international will, and because a great many states see crimes such as rape in war as internal matters, outside the jurisdiction of international conventions.[87]

Conclusion

While the systematic use of rape as a weapon of war first became an international issue during the Bosnian conflict and subsequently led to legal resolutions at the United Nations and developments in international law,[88] in the case of the eastern DRC it is occurring on a wholly new scale and with a degree of brutality that defies comprehension. In an effort toward understanding this situation, the Raise Hope for Congo campaign on October 21, 2008, posted an Internet document titled "Ten Reasons Why Eastern Congo Is the Most Dangerous Place on Earth for Women."[89] In brief, the reasons given in this document are as follows: "predatory security forces," "lawless militias," "culture of impunity," "resource curse," "poverty," "collapsed health care system," "internal displacement," "a failing education system," "gender inequality and cultural barriers," and "inaction."[90] Not surprisingly, petitions are circulating, such as the Talk Future Petition's "Global Call for Action: Demand End to War Rapes in Goma," and there are increasing calls to boycott electronic firms using "blood minerals."[91]

UN resolutions and laws are proving wholly ineffective as deterrents, particularly due to political deals declaring universal amnesty except for leaders such as General Nkunda and others currently on trial at the International Criminal Court. At the same time, the continuing rape crisis is driving the circles of concern that are attempting to assist victims and advocate for conflict resolution in the DRC to expand and intensify their work. For instance, the ENOUGH project's *Past Due: Remove the FDLR from Eastern Congo* has urged political advocacy and encouraged individuals to contact their senators and notify them that they support the Conflict Coltan and Cassiterite Act of 2008, which requests greater accountability and transparency in U.S. importation of potential conflict minerals from the DRC that profit the FDLR.[92] In addition, the ENOUGH campaign requests that U.S. citizens press their representatives to condemn the use of rape as a weapon of war by the FDLR and other groups by cosponsoring House Resolution 1227, Condemning Sexual Violence in the DRC. This all-important resolution has three key goals. The first is to motivate the U.S. secretary of state to appoint a special envoy to the DRC so as to increase assistance to the victims. The second is to pressure the government of the DRC to end the use of sexual violence by holding all armed groups accountable. The third is to call for the "full implementation" of United Nations Security Council Resolution 1325, which stipulates the protection of women and girls and their rights.[93]

More recently, HEAL Africa added yet another urgent call for the protection of women in North Kivu in a situation that had been steadily worsening since August 2008.[94] It advocated for the prevention of war rape and the protection of the victims through increasing the scale and power of the MONUC forces and their mandate.[95] Responding to a large demonstration in early November 2008 in Goma against the ever-increasing prevalence of war rape, the call for action emphasized that "*We have heard their voices and we stand in active solidarity with them, demanding world leaders, and all belligerents in the DRC conflict act immediately to stop the violence, including rapes in Congo*" (italics in the original). The statement called for six specific and immediate courses of action: (1) the implementation of UN Security Council Resolution 1820 on women, peace and security, that is, the "immediate and complete cessation by all parties to armed conflict of all acts of sexual violence against civilians" and affirming that "rape and other forms of sexual violence can constitute war crimes, crimes against humanity or a constitutive act with respect to genocide"; (2) the use of MONUC to prevent war rape in North Kivu and in particular the gang rapes by the Congolese army taking place in Goma; (3) the deployment of more MONUC soldiers to protect civilians attempting to return to their homes; (4) the application of pressure on representatives of the United Nations and the United States, specifically in the U.S. State Department African Affairs section, to develop a mandate with the authority and resources needed for brokering a durable peace initiative; (5) the creation of a MONUC sexual violence rapid response unit and (6) an increase in the delivery of food aid to North Kivu through the World Food Program. In addition, the statement called for support of local initiatives in both North and South Kivu, including the creation of a local emergency plan; an NGO network with mobile medical teams; IDP relief teams trained to prevent rape and enabled to provide postrape counseling, medical referral, and support services.[96] Predictably, after each highly unpredictable shift in the fortunes of various parties in the conflict, and despite the presence of MONUC in Goma and its expansion after the near-fall of Goma, the rape epidemic has continued to escalate.

In closing, it is necessary to highlight the problems facing the United Nations, the DRC, and the U.S. government, as well as the various humanitarian efforts to end the conflict and in particular the rape of women in war. All the efforts so far have in large part failed, due to a culture of absolute impunity in which the military, the warlords, and the militias profit from violence and uncertainty, not from peace and security.[97] The ultimate purpose of this article, however, is to stimulate any form of advocacy, practical engagement, or financial contribution—no matter how minor, no matter how apparently futile.

Notes

I appreciate the opportunity to present and advance this essay as a visiting research fellow at the National Museum of African Art at the Smithsonian Institution, Washington, DC. In particular, I thank Nicolas Cook, Séverine Autesserre, Jonathan Benthall, Adam Hochschild, and Denise Roth.

I dedicate this chapter to the memory of Nicole Dial, who worked in Indonesia before moving to Afghanistan to work with former child soldiers. In Afghanistan, she paid the ultimate price for her belief in the importance of human rights and development work.

1. Lisa F. Jackson, prod. and dir., *The Greatest Silence: Rape in the Congo* (New York: Jackson Films, 2007), http://www.thegreatestsilence.org/. For Lisa Jackson's testimony to the United States Senate Hearing on Rape as a Weapon of War, see http://tobefree.wordpress.com/2008/04/11/rape-in-the-congo-the-gruesome-picture/. Also see Institute for War and Peace Reporting (IWPR), *Special Report: Sexual Violence in the Democratic Republic of Congo*, ed. Caroline Tosh and Yigal Chazan (The Hague: Institute for War and Peace Reporting, 2008), http://www.iwpr.net/pdf/IWPR_NL_DRC_special_102008.pdf. See also CongoWarResource, at http://www.congowarresource.org, which "provides the tool needed to cast light on a very dark subject."

2. For the need for a functioning justice system in order to prevent future impunity for rape in Liberia, see Amnesty International, *Liberia: No Impunity for Rape: A Crime against Humanity and a War Crime* (London: Amnesty International, 2004), http://www.amnesty.org/en/region/liberia.

3. For examples, a decade apart, of media coverage of the intractability of the conflict, see Charles Krause, "Conflict in Congo," *Online NewsHour*, PBS, October 22, 1998, http://www.pbs.org/newshour/bb/africa/july-dec98/congo_10-22.html; and, more recently, Katy Glassborow and Peter Eichstaedt, "Paralysis over Deepening Goma Crisis," *Africa Report* 192, Institute for War and Peace Reporting (IWPR), November 2008, http://www.ipr.net/?=acr&s=f&o=347730&apc_state=henh. For important studies of the larger conflict, see Thomas Turner, *The Congo Wars: Conflict, Myth and Reality* (London: Zed Books, 2007); Human Rights Watch/Africa, Human Rights Watch Women's Rights Project, Fédération Internationale des Ligues des Droits de l'Homme, *Shattered Lives: Sexual Violence during the Rwandan Genocide and Its Aftermath* (New York: Human Rights Watch, 1996).

4. For in-depth analysis of the crisis, see Fabrice Weissman, ed., *In the Shadow of "Just Wars": Violence, Politics and Humanitarian Action* (Ithaca, NY: Cornell University Press, 2004); John Tatulli, "Resolving Africa's Longest Civil War: Updates on the Case concerning Armed Activities in the DRC," *New York Law School Journal of Human Rights* 9, no. 3 (2003): 903–12; Marie Claire Omanyondo Ohambe, Jean Berckmans Bahananga Muhigwa, and Barnabé Mulyumba Wa Mamba, *Women's Bodies as a Battleground: Sexual Violence against Women and Girls during the War in the Democratic Republic of Congo, South Kivu (1996–2003)*, ed. Martine René Calloy, Ndeye Sow, and Catherine Hall (Paris: International Alert, 2005). For the problem of internal displacement, see Norwegian Refugee Council, *Profile of Internal Displacement: Democratic Republic of the Congo* (Geneva: Norwegian Refugee Council/Global IDP Project, 2001), http://www.nrc.no/?aid=9167171; Mike P. Anastario, "An Analysis of Violence, Victimization and Women's Mental and Reproductive Health in Two Internally Displaced Populations" (PhD diss., Boston College, 2007); and Internal Displacement Monitoring Center (IDMC), *Focus on North Kivu Province: IDPs on the Move Face Grave Human Rights Violations.* IDMC Report, November 21, 2008, http://www.internaldisplacement.org/idmc/website/countries.nsf/(httpCountries)/554559DA500C858802570A7004A96C7?OpenDocument&count=1000.

5. Amnesty International, *It's in Our Hands: Stop Violence against Women* (London: Amnesty International, 2004), http://www.amnesty.org/en/library/asset/ACT77/001/2004/en/dom-ACT770012004en.pdf; Yakin Ertürk, *Promotion and Protection of All Human Rights, Civil, Political, Economic, Social and Cultural, Including the Right to Development. Report of the Special Rapporteur on Violence against Women, Its Causes and Consequences* (New York: United Nations General Assembly, 2008); United States Department of State, *Country Reports on Human Rights Practices 2006* (Washington, DC: Bureau of Democracy, Human Rights, and Labor, 2007), http://www.state.gov/g/drl/rls/hrrpt/2006/; USAID/OTI, *Democratic Republic of Congo Field Report*, Field Report no. 19 (Washington, DC: USAID, 2003), http://www.usaid.gov/our_work/cross-cutting_programs/transition_initiatives/country/congo/rpt1103.html.

6. Integrated Regional Information Network (IRIN), "Our Bodies—Their Battle Ground: Gender-based Violence in Conflict Zones," United Nations Office for the Coordination of Humanitarian Affairs (UNOCHA), September 2004, http://www.irinnews.org/

InDepthMain.aspx?InDepthID=20&ReportID=62817. Also see Jeanne Ward, *If Not Now, When? Addressing Gender-based Violence in Refugee, Internally Displaced, and Post-conflict Settings: A Global Overview*, The Reproductive Health for Refugees Consortium, 2002, http://www.womenscommission.org/pdf/ifnotnow.pdf.

7. Human Rights Watch, *The War within the War: Sexual Violence against Women and Girls in Eastern Congo* (New York: Human Rights Watch, 2002), http:www.hrw.org/reports/2002/drc/Congo0602.pdf. For more recent reports, see Jeffrey Gettleman, "Rape Victims' Words Help Jolt Congo into Change," *New York Times*, October 17, 2008; and Bob Herbert, "The Invisible War," *New York Times*, February 21, 2009. In the latter, Herbert wrote: "Despite the presence in the region of the largest UN peacekeeping mission in the world, no one has been able to stop the systematic rape of the Congolese women," http://www.nytimes.com/2009/02/21/opinion/21herbert.html?_r=2.

8. Physicians for Human Rights, U.S. Senate Committee on the Judiciary, Human Rights and the Law Subcommittee, *Rape as a Weapon of War: Accountability for Sexual Violence in Conflict*. United States Senate Hearing on Rape in the DRC, Washington, DC, April 2008. For the resolution itself, see http://www.peacewomen.org/un/sc/1325.html. For the testimony, see http://physiciansforhumanrights.org/library/documents/testimony/rape-as-a-weapon-of-war.pdf. Also see Feminist Majority Foundation, "Senate Committee Hearing on Rape as a Weapon of War," *Feminist Daily News Wire*, April 3, 2008, http://feminist.org/news/newsbyte/uswirestory.asp?id=10919; Aningina Tshefu Bibiane and the PeaceWomen Project, "Women Advocating for Resolution 1325 in the Democratic Republic of Congo." *Project for the 1325 Peace Women E-News*, no. 10, 4 October 2002, http://www.peacewomen.org/1325inaction/Africa/DRC13251ist.html; NGO Working Group on Women Peace and Security, *Resolution 1325: Two Years On*, October 31, 2002, http:www.peacewomen.org/un/ngo/ngopub/NGOWGTwoYearsOn.pdf.

9. John Prendergast and Colin Thomas-Jensen, *Averting the Nightmare Scenario in Eastern Congo*, ENOUGH Strategy Paper 7, September, 2007, http://www.enoughproject.org/publications/averting-nightmare-scenario-eastern-congo; Congo Global Action, http://www.congoglobalaction.org/. For information on the Harvard Humanitarian Initiative's collaboration with Dr. Dennis Mukwege, chief surgeon and director of Panzi Hospital in Bukavu, see http://www.hsph.harvard.edu/news/press-releases/2007-releases/press10112007.html. For the Panzi Hospital's official website, see http://www.panzihospitalbukavu.org/. For the attack on the hospital and the City of Hope and continuing difficulties and media attention, see Katherine Goetze, "No Sign of End to Epidemic," in Institute for War and Peace Reporting, *Special Report: Sexual Violence*, 4–5. Other initiatives besides those mentioned in the above reports include programs run by the Women to Women International Congo Program, the International Rescue Committee Aid in Congo, and the Stephen Lewis Foundation. Also see the combined V-Day, Stop Rape Now, and UNICEF campaign, Stop Raping Our Greatest Resource: Power to Women and Girls of Democratic Republic of Congo, http://www.stoprapeindrc.org/.

10. As regards emerging academic activism, see, for instance, Samuel Martínez, "Making Violence Visible: An Activist Anthropological Approach to Women's Rights Investigation," in *Engaging Contradictions: Theory, Politics, and Methods of Activist Scholarship*, ed. Charles R. Hale (Berkeley, CA: University of California Press, 2008),

183–212; and "Symposium on Women in Conflict Zones," University of California, Los Angeles, Burkle Center for International Relations and Department of Women's Studies, April 10, 2009, http://www.international.ucla.edu/burkle/calendar/showevent.asp?eventid=7318.

11. For an important recent article on international relief and the media, see Jeremy Benthall, "The Disaster—Media—Relief Nexus," *Anthropology Today* 24 (2008): 4–5.

12. For a particularly useful study of networks and international advocacy work, see Margaret E. Keck and Kathryn Sikkink, *Activists beyond Borders: Advocacy Networks in International Politics* (Ithaca, NY: Cornell University Press, 1998).

13. Séverine Autesserre, "Local Violence, National Peace? Post-war 'Settlement' in the Eastern DR Congo," *African Studies Review* 49, no. 3 (2006): 1–29; Amanda Beltz, "Prosecuting Rape in International Criminal Tribunals: The Need to Balance Victim's Rights with the Due Process Rights of the Accused," *St. John's Journal of Legal Commentary* 23, no. 1 (2008): 167–209.

14. Héritiers de la Justice, *Congo, terre d'impunité et d'arbitraire* (Bukavu, DRC: Héritiers de la Justice, 2003); International Crisis Group, *The Kivus: The Forgotten Crucible of the Congo Conflict*, ICG Africa Report 56, 2003, http://www.crisisgroup.org/home/index.cfm?id=1630&1 =1; International Crisis Group; *Congo Crisis: Military Intervention in Ituri*, ICG Africa Report 64, 2003, http://www.crisisgroup.org/home/index.cfm?1 =1&id=1626; Koen Vlassenroot,"Violence et constitution des milices dans l'Est du Congo: Le cas des Mayi Mayi," in *L'Afrique des Grands Lacs, Annuaire 1999–2000*, ed. Stefaan Marysse and Filip Reyntjens (Paris: L'Harmattan, 2003), 115–52; Koen Vlassenroot and Timothy Raeymaekers, *Conflict and Social Transformation in Eastern DR Congo* (Ghent, Belgium: Academia Press Scientific Publishers, 2004); Nancy Farwell, "War Rape: New Conceptualizations and Responses," *Affilia* 9, no. 4 (2004): 389–403; Meredeth Turshen, "The Political Economy of Rape: An Analysis of Systematic Rape and Sexual Abuse of Women during Armed Conflict in Africa," in Moser and Clark, *Victims, Perpetrators, or Actors?* 55–68.

15. Johann Hari, "Congo's Tragedy: The War the World Forgot," *Independent*, May 5, 2006, http://www.independent.co.uk/news/world/africa/congos-tragedy-the-war-the-world-forgot-476929.

16. Julie Ann Marra, "Rape as a Weapon of War in the Congo [Part 2: The Savagery]," http://blackbirdwhistlingwordpress.com/2007/12/07/rape-as-a-weapon-of-war-in-the-congo-part-2-the-savagery/. Also see Jeffrey Gettleman, "Rape Epidemic Raises Trauma of Congo War," *New York Times*, October 7, 2007, http://www.nytimes.com/2007/10/07/world/africa/07congo.html; Nicholas Kristof, "The Weapon of Rape," *New York Times*, June 15, 2008, http://www.nytimes.com/2008/06/15/opinion/15kristof.html; Eoin Young, "MONUC Calls on Armed Groups in Eastern DRC to End the Suffering of the Kivu Peoples," July 23, 2008, July 23, 2008, http://allafrica.com/stories/200807231102.html; Stephen Leahy, "Congo-Kinshasa: Activists Slam World's 'Grotesque Indifference,'" Inter Press Service News Agency, December 3, 2008, http://allafrica.com/stories/200812030892.html.

17. Kristof, "The Weapon of Rape."

18. Ibid. The DRC is a "State Party" to the Rome Statute of the International Criminal Tribunal (Beltz, "Prosecuting Rape," 208). For criminal prosecution of rape as a war crime at the International Criminal Court (ICC), see William A. Scha-

bas, *An Introduction to the International Criminal Court*, 2nd ed. (Cambridge: Cambridge University Press, 2005). For a discussion of attitudes toward the plight of rape victims, including the view that the violation is normal, see Marion Pratt and Leah Werchick et. al., *Sexual Terrorism: Rape as a Weapon of War in Eastern Democratic Republic of Congo: An Assessment of Programmatic Responses to Sexual Violence in North Kivu, South Kivu, Maniema and Orientale Provinces, January 9–16, 2004* (Washington, DC: USAID/DCHA, 2004), 13. For the gender-based violence in Africa and Asia, see Integrated Regional Information Network (IRIN), *Our Bodies—Their Battle Ground.*

19. Human Rights Watch, *The War within the War.*

20. Rebecca Feeley and Colin Thomas-Jensen, *Getting Serious about Ending Conflict and Sexual Violence in Congo*, ENOUGH Strategy Paper 15, March 2008, http://www.enoughproject.org/publications/getting-serious-about-ending-conflict-and-sexual-violence-congo.

21. Chris McGreal, "Hundreds of Thousands of Women Raped for Being on the Wrong Side," *Guardian* (London), November 12, 2007. In the case of Liberia, rape was so widely used as a weapon of war between 1989 and 1997 that legislation was enacted making the crime punishable by death.

22. Jeb Sharp, "Interview with Sarah Mosely of the International Rescue Committee," January 9, 2008, http://www.theworld.org/?q=node/15207.

23. Lydiah Kemunto Bosire, "The Limits and Possibilities of Transitional Justice," *Pambazuka News*, July 14, 2008, http://pambazuka.org/en/category/comment/49421. *Pambazuka News* is a weekly forum for social justice in Africa published online by FAHAMU. AWID, the Association of Women's Rights in Development, is another vital source of information. See, for instance, Kathambi Kinoti, "What Are the Challenges in Using Transitional Justice Structures to Address Sexual Violence in Situations of Conflict?" AWID, July 25, 2008, http://www.awid.org/eng/Issues-and-Analysis/Library/Transitional-Justice-and-Rape-in-Conflict.

24. Peter Eichstaedt, "Militias Seen as Main Perpetrators," in Institute for War and Peace Reporting, *Special Report: Sexual Violence*, 6–7.

25. See, for instance, Séverine Autesserre, "DR Congo: Explaining Peace Building Failures: A Study of the Eastern DR Congo, 2003–2006," *Review of African Political Economy* 34, no. 113 (2007): 423–42; Autesserre, "Local Violence, National Peace?"; and Vlassenroot, "Violence et constitution des milices dans l'Est du Congo"; Vlassenroot and Raeymaekers, *Conflict and Social Transformation in Eastern DR Congo*. Also see Herbert Weiss, *War and Peace in the Democratic Republic of the Congo* (Uppsala, Sweden: Nordiska Afrikainstitutet, 2000).

26. Marra, "Rape as a Weapon of War [Part 2: The Savagery]."

27. Ibid. See also Julie Ann Marra, "Rape as a Weapon of War in the Congo [Part 3: The Healing and What You Can Do to Help]," http://blackbirdwhistling.wordpress.com/2007/12/13/rape-as-a-weapon-of-war-in-the-congo-part-3-the-healing-what-you-can-do-to-help/.

28. Marra, "Rape as a Weapon of War [Part 2: The Savagery]."

29. See V-Day website, www.vday.org/contents/vday/vcampaigns/amea/congo. Also see Centre d'Espoir pour Filles et Femmes (CEFF-ONG), http://www.centrefillefemme.org.tripod.com.

30. Nicholas Kristof, "Alone and Ashamed," *New York Times*, May 16, 2003, http://query.nytimes.com/gst/fullpage.html?res=9C06E4D7163EF935A25756C0A9659C8B63.

31. See Lois Ann Lorentzen and Jennifer Turpin, eds, *The Women and War Reader* (New York: New York University Press, 1998); Michael L. Pen and Rahel Nardos, *Overcoming Violence against Women and Girls: An International Campaign to Eradicate a Worldwide Problem* (Lanham, MD: Rowman & Littlefield, 2003); Patricia Rozée, "Forbidden or Forgiven? Rape in Cross-Cultural Perspective," *Psychology of Women Quarterly* 17 (1993): 499–514; Shana Swiss, "Rape as a Crime of War: A Medical Perspective," *Journal of the American Medical Association* 270, no. 5 (2001): 612–15). For a discussion of the 1949 Geneva Convention with regard to protecting women and children during war, see Omanyondo Ohambe, Bahananga Muhigwa, and Wa Mamba, *Women's Bodies as a Battleground*.

32. For cases relating to Rwanda, see Donatella Lorch, "Wave of Rape Adds New Horror to Rwanda's Trail of Brutality," *New York Times*, May 15, 1995. For Bosnia, see Christine Chinkin, "Rape and Sexual Abuse of Women in International Law," *European Journal of International Law*, 5 (1994): 326–41; Lene Hansen, "Gender, Nation and Rape: Bosnia and the Construction of Security," *International Feminist Journal of Politics* 3, no. 1 (2001): 55–75; and Alexandra Stiglmayer, "The Rapes in Bosnia-Herzegovina," in *Mass Rape: The War against Women in Bosnia-Herzegovina*, ed. Alexandra Stiglmayer, trans. Marion Faber (Lincoln: University of Nebraska Press, 1993). For the use of rape as a political weapon in Zimbabwe, see Jane Parpart, "Masculinities, Race and Violence in the Making of Zimbabwe," in *Manning the Nation: Father Figures in Zimbabwean Literature and Society*, ed. Kizito Muchemwa and Robert Muponde (Harare, Zimbabwe: Weaver, 2004), 102–14. For Rwanda, see Ann Nkirote Kubai, "Living in the Shadow of Genocide: Women and HIV/AIDS in Rwanda," in *Women, Religion and HIV/AIDS in Africa: Responding to Ethical and Theological Challenges*, ed. T. M. Hinga, A. N. Kubai, P. Mwaura, and H. Ayanga (Pietermaritzburg, South Africa: Cluster Publications, 2008), 51–74. On the work of Amnesty International and Médecins Sans Frontières, see Laura Smith-Spark, "How Did Rape Become a Weapon of War?" *BBC News*, December 8, 2004, http://www.news.bbc.co.uk/1/hi/in_depth/40788677.stm.

33. Médecins Sans Frontières, *Ituri: "Civilians Still the First Victims." Permanence of Sexual Violence and Impact of Military Operations* (Geneva: Médecins Sans Frontières, 2007). For useful background articles on relevant aspects of the security situation in the DRC, see MONUC (Mission de l'Organisation des Nations Unies en République Démocratique du Congo), "First Assessment of the Armed Groups Operating in DR. Congo," April 5, 2002, http://www.reliefweb.int/rw/rwb.nsf/AllDocsByUNID/ae88f282e0390a95c1256b98004585f6. See also Eugène Bakama Bope, "Comment: North Kivu's Fragile Peace," *Africa Report* 154, Institute for War and Peace Reporting (IWPR), February 4, 2008, http:www.iwpr.net/?p=acr&o=342445&apc_state=henh; Lisa Clifford, "Ituri's Fragile Peace," *Africa Report* 194, Institute for War and Peace Reporting (IWPR), December 3, 2008, http://www.iwpr.net/?p=acr&o=342445&apc_state=henh; and Daniel Ngeno, "Africa: Making Sense of the DRC," *All Africa* (2007), http://www.allafrica.com/stories/200711020337.html. For a brief clarification of the term Mai-Mai, or Mayi-Mayi, see http://en.wikipedia.org/wiki/Mai-Mai; and for a more accurate and detailed understanding of the difference between "true" and "false" Mai Mai," see Omanyondo Ohambe, Bahananga Muhigwa, and Wa Mamba, *Women's Bodies as a Battleground*; and Vlassenroot, "Violence et constitution des milices dans l'Est du Congo."

34. Reuters, "Rape 'Epidemic' in African Conflict Zones," February 12, 2008, http://www.africa.reuters.com/top/news/usnBAN324178.html.

35. UN Security Council SC/9246, *Press Release* (New York: United Nations Department of Public Information, February 12, 2008), http://www.un.org/News/Press/docs/2008/sc9246.doc.html.

36. Richard J. Brennan, Michael Despines, and Leslie F. Roberts, "Mortality Surveys in the Democratic Republic of Congo: Humanitarian Impact and Lessons Learned," *Humanitarian Exchange Magazine* 35 (2006), http://www.odihpn.org/report.asp?id=2838. For mortality figures for the early colonial period and the statistics and details of the scale of death for the Belgian colonial period (upwards of ten million people are said to have died), are still a Belgian state secret. See Adam Hochschild, *King Leopold's Ghost: A Story of Greed, Terror, and Heroism in Colonial Africa* (New York: Houghton Mifflin, 1999), 297; Jules Marchal, *L'Etat libre du Congo: Paradis perdu; L'Histoire du Congo 1876–1900*, vols. 1 and 2 (Borgloon, Belgium: Editions Paula Bellings, 1996); and Jules Marchal, *E. D. Morel contre Léopold II: L'histoire du Congo 1900–1910*, vols. 1 and 2 (Paris: L'Harmattan, 1996).

37. Johns Hopkins Bloomberg School of Public Health, "Obstetric Fistula: Ending the Silence, Easing the Suffering." *Info Reports* 2, 2004, http://info.k4health.org/inforeports/fistula/index.shtml.

38. Paul Salopek, "Who Rules the Forest?" *National Geographic: Special Africa Issue; Africa: Whatever You Thought, Think Again*, September 2005, 74–93.

39. See the Fistula Foundation, http://www.fistulafoundation.org/.

40. *A Walk to Beautiful*, DVD, prod. Steven Engel, dir. Mary Olive Smith (New York: Engel Entertainment, 2007), http://www.walktobeautiful.com/.

41. Johns Hopkins Bloomberg School of Public Health, "Obstetric Fistula: Ending the Silence, Easing the Sufffering."

42. Women's Dignity Project, *Faces of Dignity: Seven Stories of Girls and Women with Fistula*, stories compiled, written, and edited by Kristina Graff and Maggie Bangser (Dar es Salaam, Tanzania: Women's Dignity Project, 2003), http://www.womensdignity.org/Face_of_Dignity.pdf.

43. Emily Wax, "Congo's Desperate 'One-Dollar UN Girls': Shunned Teens, Many Raped by Militiamen, Sell Sex to Peacekeepers," *Washington Post Foreign Service*, March 21, 2005, http://www.washingtonpost.com/ac2/wp-dyn/A52333-2005Mar20?language=printer.

44. ACQUIRE Project, *Traumatic Gynecologic Fistula: A Consequence of Sexual Violence in Conflict Settings* (New York: ACQUIRE Project/Engender Health, 2005), www.acquireproject.org/fileadmin/user_upload/ACQUIRE/Publications/TF_.

45. Marra, "Rape as a Weapon of War [Part 2: The Savagery]."

46. Quoted in ibid.

47. CBS News, "War against Women: The Use of Rape as a Weapon in Congo's Civil War," *60 Minutes*, January 11, 2008, updated August 14, 2008, http://www.cbsnews.com/stories/2008/01/11/60minutes/main3701249_page3.shtml.

48. See Goetze, "No Sign of End to Epidemic."

49. Yakin Ertürk, *Promotion and Protection of All Human Rights*; Médecins Sans Frontières, *Ituri. "Civilians Still the First Victims."* According to this report, 1.8 percent to 4 percent of recorded victims in Ituri between 2003 and 2007 were boys and men. The

percentage of child victims is on the increase and children are increasingly being raped by civilians.

50. Cecile Pouilly, "Can Congo Turn the Page?" *Refugees* 145, no. 1 (2007): 14.
51. Sharp, "Interview with Sarah Mosely."
52. Ibid.
53. Ibid.
54. CBS News, "War against Women."
55. Sharp, "Interview with Sara Mosely."
56. Human Rights Watch, *Reluctant Recruits: Children and Adults Forcibly Recruited for Military Service in North Kivu*" (New York: Human Rights Watch, 2001/2005), http://www.hrw.org/reports/2001/drc3/. Also see Projet Enfants Soldiers, http://www.ajedika.org/index.html.
57. On rape as an act of symbolic violence, see Susan Brownmiller, *Against Our Will: Men, Women, and Rape* (New York: Simon and Schuster, 1975); Susan Griffin, *Rape: The Power of Consciousness* (New York: Harper & Row, 1979). Also see Bülent Diken and Carsten Bagge Laustsen, "Becoming Abject: Rape as a Weapon of War," *Body and Society* 11, no. 1 (2005): 111–28.
58. Claudia Card, "Rape as a Weapon of War," *Hypatia* 11 (1996): 518.
59. Ibid.
60. Ibid.
61. Statement by Yakin Ertürk at the SIDA Conference on Gender Based Violence, September 12, 2008, Stockholm.
62. Omanyondo Ohambe, Bahananga Muhigwa, and Wa Mamba, *Women's Bodies as a Battleground*.
63. Ibid., 51.
64. Pouilly, "Can Congo Turn the Page?" 5. For recent political developments and the use of rape as a weapon of war by the FDLR, see James Karuhanga, "Congo-Kinshasa: North Kivu Governor Accuses FDLR of Using Rape to Destroy Families," *New Times* (Kigali, Uganda), December 9, 2008, http://allafrica.com/stories/200812090300.html. FDLR is the acronym for Forces Démocratiques de Libération du Rwanda.
65. Hari, "Congo's Tragedy: The War the World Forgot."
66. Integrated Regional Information Network (IRIN), "Congo-Kinshasa: Campaign against Sexual Violence in South Kivu," United Nations Office for the Coordination of Humanitarian Affairs (UNOCHA), November 29, 2007, http://www.irinnews.org/report.aspx?ReportID=75580.
67. Feeley and Thomas-Jensen, *Getting Serious about Ending Conflict and Sexual Violence in Congo*. For a record of reported individual acts of human rights violations, see United States Department of State, *Country Reports on Human Rights Practices 2006*. For a description of the contributing background practices in nonconflict settings in the DRC, see Integrated Regional Information Network (IRIN), "Congo-Kinshasa: Sexual Abuse of Minors Doubles in Kasai Occidental Town," December 5, 2008, http://www.irinnews.org/Report.aspx?ReportId=81836.
68. Radhika Coomaraswamy, "Statement in the Security Council on the Occasion of the Open Debate on Children and Armed Conflict," February 12, 2008, http://www.un.org/children/conflict/english/12-feb-2008-open-debate-security-council.html.

69. Ibid.
70. Beltz, "Prosecuting Rape in International Criminal Tribunals."
71. See William Elachi Alwiga, "Congo-Kinshasa: Military Justice Officials Trained in Sex Crime Investigation," February 8, 2008, http://www.monuc.org/News.aspx?newsID=16653.
72. Feeley and Thomas-Jensen, *Getting Serious about Ending Conflict and Sexual Violence in Congo*.
73. Ibid. Technically, sentences for sexual violence range from six months to twenty years in prison. In instances where the victim dies, a life sentence is technically mandatory.
74. See NGO Working Group on Women Peace and Security, *Resolution 1325: Two Years On*.
75. Bosire, "The Limits and Possibilities of Transitional Justice."
76. Pratt and Werchick, *Sexual Terrorism*, 19.
77. See Human Rights Watch, *Renewed Crisis in North Kivu* (New York: Human Rights Watch, October 2007), http://hrw.org/reports/2007/drc/007/; and International Crisis Group, *Congo: Bringing Peace to North Kivu*, ICG Africa Report 133, 2007, http://www.crisisgroup.org/home/index.cfm?id=5134.
78. For United Nations Population Fund (UNFPA) programs, see http://www.unfpa.org. The NGO Working Group on Women, Peace and Security is composed of the following organizations: The Hague Appeal for Peace (HAP); the Women's International League for Peace and Freedom (WILPF); the International Women's Tribune Centre (IWTC); the Women's Caucus for Gender Justice on the International Criminal Court (WCGJ); the Women's Commission for Refugee Women and Children (WCRWC); and International Alert (IA).
79. Johns Hopkins Bloomberg School of Public Health, "Obstetric Fistula: Ending the Silence, Easing the Suffering."
80. See Feeley and Thomas-Jensen, *Getting Serious about Ending Conflict and Sexual Violence in Congo*. Also see Rebecca Feeley and Colin Thomas-Jensen, *Past Due: Remove the FDLR from Eastern Congo*, ENOUGH Strategy Paper 22, June 3, 2008, http://www.enoughproject.org/publications/past-due-remove-fdlr-eastern-congo.
81. Sharp, "Interview with Sarah Mosely."
82. On trauma and war, see Judith L. Herman, *Trauma and Recovery* (New York: Basic Books, 1992); on military intervention, see International Crisis Group, *Congo Crisis: Military Intervention in Ituri*; on peacekeeping gender training, see Nadine Puechguirbal, "Gender Training for Peacekeepers: Lessons from the DRC," *International Peacekeeping* 10, no. 4 (2003): 113–28; and on women waging peace, see Swanee Hunt and Cristina Posa, "Women Waging Peace," *Foreign Policy* 124 (2001): 38–47.
83. Hochschild, *King Leopold's Ghost*, 395.
84. Pratt and Werchick, *Sexual Terrorism*, 18.
85. Quoted in ibid.
86. Quoted in Karl Meyer, *The Dust of Empire: The Race for Mastery in the Asian Heartland* (New York: PublicAffairs/A Century Foundation Book, 2003/2004), 214.
87. Cato Institute, "Can We Export Democracy?" *Cato Policy Report* 30, no. 1 (2008): 11–13, http://www.cato.org/pubs/policy_report/v30n1/cpr30n1.pdf.

88. Doris Buss, "Prosecuting Mass Rape: Prosecutor v. Dragoljub Kunarac, Radomir Kovac and Zoran Vukovic," *Feminist Legal Studies* 10, no. 1 (2002): 91–99.

89. Raise Hope for Congo (ENOUGH campaign), "New! Ten Reasons Why Eastern Congo Is the Most Dangerous Place on Earth for Women," October 21, 2009, http://www.raisehopeforcongo.org/tenreasons.

90. Ibid.

91. Heal Africa, "Global Call for Action: Demand End to War-rapes in Goma DRC," October 30, 2008, healafrica.org/cms/files/media/Goma%20Global%20Action%20Petition.doc.

92. On the FDLR, see Feeley and Thomas-Jensen, *Past Due: Remove the FDLR from Eastern Congo.*

93. Cory Smith, "Bring Peace to Eastern Congo. End Violence against Women and Girls," ENOUGH NEWS, July 11, 2008, http://www.enoughproject.org/news/bring-peace-eastern-congo-faith-action.

94. Heal Africa, "Global Call for Action: Demand End to War-rapes in Goma DRC."

95. MONUC is the acronym for Mission de l'Organisation des Nations Unies en République démocratique du Congo (United Nations Organization Mission in the Democratic Republic of the Congo). Set up on November 30, 1999, its mission and projects are provided online at http://monuc.unmissions.org/.

96. Heal Africa, "Global Call for Action: Demand End to War-rapes in Goma DRC."

97. Autesserre, "Explaining Peace Building Failures: A Study of the Eastern DR Congo, 2003–2006."

7

Mozambique

The Gendered Impact of Warfare

Zermarie Deacon

Introduction

Men's and women's relative social positions, as well as their differential access to rights and resources, have important implications for their experiences during and after war.[1] However, there is still a tendency to overlook women's experiences of warfare in favor of a male-centered paradigm that governs responses to survivors of armed conflict.[2] Because of the assumption that women's experiences mirror the experiences and needs of men, gendered postwar recovery processes often do not receive sufficient attention. In fact, prior to about the 1990s, Western social scientists and practitioners not only failed to fully consider women's experiences of trauma, but they also ignored the experiences and needs of non-Western communities impacted by armed conflict.[3] As a result, programming aimed at African war survivors often does not sufficiently consider factors that support women's postwar recovery. In order to address this gap in social science and practice, I carried out a qualitative investigation of factors that have facilitated Mozambican women's recovery from the impact of warfare. In-depth, semi-structured interviews were conducted with forty-seven women who had lived through the recent war.

In recent wars, as many as 90 percent of all casualties have been civilians, the majority of whom are estimated to have been women and children.[4] However, civilian women who survive wars also endure significant aftereffects. These women's war experiences result from their differential gender roles and related needs, but women are also often deliberate targets of violence.[5] For example, women who perform gender-specific tasks, such as fetching water and firewood or working in agricultural fields, may be particularly vulnerable to land mines or attack by enemy combatants. In addition, as a result of their responsibility for children and elderly family members, women may not be as mobile as men and may not be able to flee violence as readily, rendering them more susceptible to harm.[6] Finally, during wartime, women may be targets for sexual violence for a variety of reasons, ranging from the offering of their bodies as rewards to soldiers to the use of sexual violence as a deliberate attack on the integrity and identity of an opposing side.[7]

However, in spite of the nature of their wartime experiences, women's needs often go unmet, because their devalued social status provides them with access to fewer resources than men. It is also because service providers often overlook women's specific biological needs, related to pregnancy, childbirth, lactation, and so forth.[8] Women's gender roles, their gender-specific experiences, and their unique biological needs interact with the resources available to them within their environments.[9] Thus it is essential that the postwar context within which women reside be one in which they receive support for their recovery from the gendered results of armed conflict. As Stephen Lubkemann suggests, warfare alters both the physical and the social landscapes of a community in a profoundly gendered manner.[10] Therefore, it is necessary to understand how individuals and communities reconstruct their lives in the wake of warfare with particular attention to factors that support women's recovery.

The War in Mozambique

The war in Mozambique, fought between the Frente de Libertação de Moçambique (FRELIMO) government and the externally supported Resistência Nacional Moçcambicana (RENAMO), lasted from 1976 to 1992. Until it gained independence in 1980, Rhodesia provided support for RENAMO; at this point, South Africa took over Rhodesia's role. The South African government aimed to deliberately destabilize the FRELIMO government in an attempt to end its support of the African National Congress (ANC). As a result, the war was especially brutal, and civilians, women in particular, were routinely targeted by RENAMO.[11] Apart from the destruction of infrastructure and the terrorization of civilians, women were routinely raped and kidnapped in order to perform domestic as well as sexual labor for RENAMO troops.[12] However, at the time of my investigation, thirteen years had passed since the end of the war, providing women with an opportunity to reflect on the period of postwar reconstruction. This allowed not only for an examination of the consequences of the war for women, but also for an investigation of the ways in which they have sought to recover from these consequences.

For women, the consequences of the war were multiple in character and resulted both from their individual experiences and from the sociocultural meaning attached to these experiences by their larger communities.[13] Various authors, including Victor Igreja and colleagues, Carolyn Nordstrom, Tina Sideris, and Meredeth Turshen, have documented the ways in which the war impacted civilian women.[14] During the period immediately following the war, survivors were found to be suffering psychological, physical, and sociocultural symptoms of trauma, such as intrusive thoughts, nightmares, poor appetite, somatic complaints, and general feelings of malaise and depression described as an injury to the spirit.[15] In addition, several authors have noted that some women who had been raped, particularly those who became pregnant by enemy soldiers and who were living in patrilineal communities in the south of Mozambique, were ostracized by their families and rejected by their husbands.[16]

Women sought to recover from the war within a context where civilians have had inadequate, if any, access to physical and mental health resources. The situation was exacerbated by postwar economic reforms forced by the structural adjustment policies (SAPs) imposed upon Mozambique as it made its transition to a capitalist economy.[17] These reforms led to reduced government spending on social provisions and health care, which further limited women's postwar access to formal health resources, economic support services, education, and supportive services such as childcare.[18]

The immediate postwar context in Mozambique was thus largely unsupportive of women's recovery from the impacts of warfare. Therefore, in order to reconstruct their lives, Mozambican women have had to rely largely on indigenous support structures available to them within their communities, such as familial support and traditional and religious healers, as well as services provided by nongovernmental organizations (NGOs). For example, as Edward Green and Alcinda Honwana, as well as Victor Igreja, point out, some communities have attempted through the use of traditional healers to overcome the long-term impact of the war and to provide ways for victimized women to be reintegrated into their larger communities.[19] An improved understanding of these indigenous factors that have contributed to women's postwar recovery may lay the foundation for improved service provisions aimed at these, as well as other, women residing in nations recovering from war.

Methods

In 2005, I conducted in-depth, semistructured interviews with forty-seven women living in the rural areas of Nampula Province in northern Mozambique, in order to elucidate factors that supported these women's recovery from the war. These women came from six farmers' associations in Meconta District, which were located within a fifteen-kilometer range, and they shared some services, such as health care posts and agricultural extension services. All of the participants had direct experience of armed conflict and ranged in age from twenty-five to sixty-one years, with an average age of forty years. Forty-five of the women were married at the time of their interview, and two had been widowed in the years following the war. Finally, all the participants were subsistence farmers, selling some of their produce in exchange for cash. Discussions with local NGO staff members revealed that families living within the Meconta District survived on an average of one U.S. dollar a day.

I told women within each targeted farmers' association about the study and invited them to participate in an interview, provided they were aged twenty-five or over, were able to recall their wartime experiences, and had lived in their community during and since the war. All the women who volunteered to participate were interviewed once in a private location at the site of the farmers' associations in the area where they lived (for example, in the community meeting hall). The investigator conducted all interviews in Portuguese with the assistance of a Macua translator. As discussions with Mozambican NGO staff revealed that the communities would be particularly wary of outsiders and would most likely be unwilling to be interviewed in the presence of unfamiliar translators, local women, fluent in both Portuguese and Macua, were recruited for this purpose.

The interviews lasted for approximately an hour, during which the participants answered questions about their experiences both during and after the war. The women were asked whether or not they considered themselves to have recovered from the war and whether or not they considered themselves to have attained well-being in its wake. Additional questions centered upon factors that either facilitated or inhibited their postwar recovery. Finally, the women were asked to define what it meant for them to be well following the war. The findings revealed the ways in which these women, with the help of their families and communities, sought to recover from the long-term impact of armed conflict.

Factors That Facilitated Women's Recovery from Warfare

The women who participated in this investigation all had some direct experience of warfare, ranging from having their belongings taken and homes destroyed to having been kidnapped by soldiers. Women were reluctant to identify the affiliation of the combatants who attacked them (likely from fear of retaliation), but at least one participant spoke about being attacked by RENAMO troops, while another indicated that both sides, that is, RENAMO and FRELIMO, were responsible for attacks. Participants additionally identified a number of results of the war, including the loss of resources necessary for survival, for example, their homes, crops, and livestock; physical injuries;

lingering psychological effects, such as thoughts about the war; and social consequences, such as the breakdown of respectful relationships among individuals, which has led to increased crime and generalized violence. However, the findings indicate that, in spite of all this, women considered themselves to have recovered from the war.

Factors at all levels of the socioecological system supported women's postwar recovery. These ranged from the individual to the macro level. First, individual women expressed a significant determination to recover from the war as well as a willingness to do what was necessary to put their lives back together. Women worked both individually and collectively to overcome the immediate economic devastation wrought by the war. As one participant noted, "Women formed organizations for women.... They were together with other women, they worked together in a group."[20] It was this determination to persevere in the face of significant adversity that laid the foundation for their recovery. They not only believed that it was possible for them to recover but also believed that they were able to do so by drawing upon their personal and collective strength. In this way, Mozambican women are similar to war survivors worldwide who strive to restore their health and well-being in the wake of warfare.[21]

The microlevel support that women received from their families was also crucial to their physical and psychological recovery. Both during and after the war, family members assisted one another in small ways, by sharing food and clothing when necessary. This was particularly important when kidnapped women returned:

> When those who were kidnapped returned home, they [the family members] took some food and gave it to them.... They came back from there and had nothing.... Their family gave them what they purchased.[22]

Furthermore, this support allowed women to mitigate some of the economic and nutritional health results of the war. Given that women were also largely responsible for caring for their families' nutritional and other needs, this support alleviated some of the pressure upon them. In other cases, family members arranged for their wives and daughters to receive treatment for the physical and psychological consequences of their wartime experiences. Women and girls were either taken to medical facilities, where they were available, or were treated by *curandeiros* (traditional healers) in order to find relief from the social and psychological consequences of war.

It is particularly notable that family members accepted back—regardless of what had been done to them—those women and girls who had been kidnapped and provided them with whatever support was available. Given that the majority of kidnap victims were women who may have been raped, this assistance was significant, as it provided them with a supportive context within which to recover. When asked if families were sometimes unwilling to accept back these women, as was the case in some other areas, one participant said, "It was not the same here like there; when these people came back, they were received by their families."[23] This assertion was supported by several women among the interviewees who had been kidnapped and had subsequently returned to and remained within their communities. It may be that the matrilineal kinship structure of the Macua communities, as opposed to the patrilineal kinship structures of the communities in which the majority of other investigations have been conducted, had implications for the ways in which women's experiences of sexual assualt were perceived. This is, therefore, a finding that requires additional future investigation.

Communities additionally found multiple ways to support the survivors of wartime violence. For example, in some cases, community members allowed women returning from their kidnap ordeal to maintain secrecy regarding their experiences. In this way, even though community members knew what had happened to these women, they provided them with a method for disassociating themselves from these experiences. Thus, both these women and their communities were spared some of the social consequences of these experiences, for example, the stigma associated with rape. One participant described her feelings toward returned kidnap victims as follows: "I am not going to go after those who entered into the bush so that they don't have to speak about the taboos that occurred there in the bush."

Notably, no participant in this investigation reported having been raped or having become pregnant as a result of rape. It is likely that fear of stigma prevented women from admitting to having been raped. In addition, it is possible that women who were raped or became pregnant by enemy combatants did not volunteer to participate in the investigation for fear of having to discuss this potentially stigmatizing experience. Therefore, the postwar experiences of women who were raped may have been obscured.

As discussed earlier in this chapter, another source of postwar support available to women was their access to *curandeiros,* or traditional healers. These healers play an important role in Mozambican society and are often the only source of health care available to residents of rural communities.[24] *Curandeiros* treat individuals for both physical and spiritual ailments, and they may be sought out if a mainstream medical cure is unavailable. *Curandeiros* frequently treated women who had suffered wartime violence and, apart from treating their physical ailments, performed rituals meant to cleanse them of their negative experiences in an attempt to break the link between the experience of violence and their current and future lives. This treatment thus provided women with a culturally appropriate manner through which to reintegrate into their communities. One participant described her feelings after receiving treatment from a *curandeiro*, referring to her freedom from the consequences of her kidnapping: "After being treated by that doctor [*curandeiro*], I was free." This availability of culturally appropriate resources and indigenous interpretations of distress and well-being was particularly important to the postwar recovery process for both individual women and their larger communities. These resources allowed women to participate in the social structures of their communities without suffering stigma as a result of any violence they may have suffered or even participated in.

In later years, as postwar development proceeded, the participants in this investigation also gained access to various resources that contributed to their empowerment and their related capacity to pursue their own versions of what it meant to be well after the war. These resources included access to farmers' associations; to programs provided by nongovernmental organizations, for example, women's savings groups; and to government-funded adult education programs. These new resources complemented the familial and community resources available to women and facilitated their capacity to achieve life goals and to mitigate the immediate economic consequences of the war.

Participants in general identified the opportunity to obtain an education—a resource that has become available to them in recent years—as a facilitating factor in their postwar recovery. This allowed them to strive for larger life goals that had previously been closed to them. The participants also indicated that schooling could potentially facilitate their ability to earn an income and to assist their families in better meeting their needs. Educational opportunities thus contributed to women's postwar recovery and their related attainment of well-being. Other postwar changes have also allowed women to access rights and resources they did not have before. For instance, multiple laws have been implemented in order to ensure gender equality with regard to access to employment, schooling, and so forth, which has resulted in an improvement in women's social status, thus contributing to their postwar recovery.

The participants were aware of the rights they had now acquired and were able to take advantage of some of the resulting new opportunities. One participant provided the following description of some of the changes in the social system that she has observed since the war:

> Because of democracy we are recovering, and men are feeling this difference. They are discovering that they cannot treat their wives badly. We also cannot treat our husbands badly; we are equal.[25]

She then goes on to say that "We have human rights." The participants also discussed women's greater access to education: "We women were not able to go to school, but now we are already going to school." Finally, one participant discussed some of the improvements that she has noticed as a result of the changes to the social system, including women's increased access to political power:

> Today women are studying and have jobs, yes, because back then women didn't work, only the men worked, but today women work as well, like men; if someone says "that woman over there, she is a [government] minister," she really is a minister, while before it wasn't like that.[26]

As a result of their greater access to these multiple resources, participants felt that they were able to live their daily lives as they saw fit, and, moreover, that they were able to work toward a better future. As one participant observed,

> We are recovering, now, today, we are moving forward, we really are moving forward; women are already studying, because before the war, and during the war, it was before we moved forward, but today women are studying and are going to work.[27]

It should be noted that while it is possible that participants' discussions of their postwar recovery process were skewed by the circumstances of their interviews—they were being interviewed by an outsider who was of a different race, nationality, and language group and in the presence of a member of their community—there was no evidence to suggest that women had not recovered from the war. However, it is certainly the case that, as a result of the war, the buffers that protect women and their communities from economic hardship are not well developed. For example, at the time of the investigation, members of the targeted communities were experiencing a food shortage. Delayed annual rainfalls coupled with a short rainy season the year before the interviews had eroded families' food stores, and many people were facing significant hunger. While the rains did eventually arrive, the problems highlighted the narrow margins upon which women residing in rural Mozambique subsist. Additionally, although significant strides have been made toward the improvement of women's status—and the participants clearly identified major, positive changes in their postwar social and political status—Mozambican women still do not have equal and complete access to all the rights and resources that are available to men. Disparities between rural and urban areas still deeply affect women and girls, and legal equality does not guarantee their equality within the home. Thus, while women did recover from the war, they are still feeling its effects, and more needs to be done to facilitate women's attainment of postwar well-being.

Conclusion: Implications for Policy and Practice

The findings from this investigation provide a framework for understanding women's postwar recovery: the particular significance of these findings lies in the synthesis of factors affecting women's attainment of postwar recovery at all levels of the social system. This allows for the development of a comprehensive understanding of women's postwar recovery and facilitates the development of maximally effective programming aimed at women in developing nations recovering from warfare. Thus, various implications for policy and practice emerged from this investigation.

First, it is important to listen to the women themselves and to design postwar interventions that take into consideration their own interpretations of their experiences. For example, the interpretations of trauma and recovery provided by participants in this investigation were different from those of women in Western communities. It would therefore be inappropriate to design services aimed at Mozambicans without taking this into account. As noted by Honwana, as well as Igreja, Kleijn, and Richters, Mozambican communities actively worked toward recovering from the impact of the war.[28] It would be important to support this recovery process in an appropriate manner rather than hindering it through the application of potentially inappropriate measures, for example, relying upon counseling methods that require individuals to discuss their experiences in situations where silence is culturally more appropriate.

Second, it is important to support the reintegration into their communities of women who have experienced war-related trauma. These women often derive significant psychosocial benefits from such acceptance. One of the ways this can be done is by working within communities in order to strengthen preexisting support structures such as those involving traditional healers and families that assist women and their communities to make sense of and recover from their wartime experiences. Such interventions should be designed to address gaps in the capacity of these structures to support women's postwar recovery. This allows for interventions that draw upon indigenous interpretations of women's wartime experiences, while it does not impose Western interpretations of trauma and healing upon recipients. Postwar interventions should, therefore, be developed in conjunction with the targeted communities in order to ensure that the interventions are maximally appropriate. Accordingly, it would be useful to consult members of targeted communities regarding the most appropriate manner in which to respond to war survivors. Community members may also identify those areas in which they require the most assistance in their support of survivors.

Third, it is essential for postwar interventions to focus upon strengthening women's access to economic resources, for example, assisting women to regain access to agricultural land and related resources such as tools and seeds, or assisting them to develop skills that facilitate their employment. This not only allows women to recover from the significant economic effects of war, but also helps to provide a buffer against future economic setbacks. Moreover, if women are continuously preoccupied with their own and their families' survival needs, they are not able to pursue activities that may further improve their postwar well-being (such as attending school). Supporting women's postwar economic recovery thus has long-term implications for their continued well-being.

Finally, interventions that capitalize on postwar changes in social systems, for example, postwar social changes that give women increased rights and access to resources, can support women's increased empowerment after war. Given that various authors, including Lillian Comas-Diaz, M. Brinton Lykes, and Renato Alarcón, and also Pilar Hernández, consider the empowerment of those victimized by war to be essential to the postwar recovery process and the prevention of future warfare, such postwar development is almost essential.[29]

The findings from this investigation additionally emphasize that social policy should not only focus on women's individual needs after war but should also consider the influence of the larger social system on their recovery. Such policies should take into account the fact that women's war experiences are often the result of their relative lack of (gendered) social power.[30] Therefore, it is important to support women's postwar access to rights and resources that improve their capacity for empowerment. Policies should focus on improving women's access to economic resources, educational resources, and human rights. Such policies would also support the implementation of the interventions discussed above, allowing for the development of supportive contexts within which women can recover from war.

In conclusion, while it is possible to encourage women's recovery from armed conflict, it is necessary to do so in a manner that acknowledges their experiences as profoundly gendered and different from those of men. Through the provision of appropriate postwar services and the implementation of gender-sensitive policies, it is possible to facilitate women's recovery from the gendered impacts of warfare.

Notes

The findings in this chapter have previously been reported in Zermarie Deacon and Cris Sullivan, "An Ecological Examination of Rural Mozambican Women's Attainment of Postwar Wellbeing," *Journal of Community Psychology* 38, no. 1 (2010): 115–30, http://dx.doi.org/10.1002/jcop.20355. The author also acknowledges all previous indebtedness as well as the contributions of her coresearcher.

1. Cynthia Cockburn, "The Gendered Dynamics of Armed Conflict and Political Violence," in Moser and Clark, *Victims, Perpetrators or Actors?* 14; Caroline Moser, "The

Gendered Continuum of Violence and Conflict: An Operational Framework," in Moser and Clark, *Victims, Perpetrators or Actors?* 44.

2. Tina Sideris, "War, Gender and Culture: Mozambican Women Refugees," *Social Science and Medicine* 56, no. 4 (2003): 713–24.

3. Edna B. Foa, Terence Martin Keane, and Matthew J. Friedman, eds., *Effective Treatments for PTSD: Practice Guidelines from the International Society for Traumatic Stress Studies* (London: Guilford Press, 2000), 53; Bessel A. van der Kolk, Lars Weisaeth, and Onno van der Hart, "History of Trauma in Psychiatry," in *Traumatic Stress: The Effects of Overwhelming Experience on Mind, Body, and Society*, ed. Bessel A. van der Kolk, Alexander C. McFarlane, and Lars Weisaeth (New York: Guilford Press, 1996), 59; Lisa Cosgrove and Maureen C. McHugh, "Speaking for Ourselves: Feminist Methods and Community Psychology," *American Journal of Community Psychology* 28, no. 6 (2000): 815–38.

4. Susan McKay, "The Effects of Armed Conflict on Girls and Women," *Peace and Conflict: Journal of Peace Psychology* 4, no. 4 (1998): 381–92; Margo Okazawa-Rey, "Warring on Women: Understanding Complex Inequalities of Gender, Race, Class, and Nation," *Affilia* 17, no. 3 (2002): 371–83.

5. Cockburn, "The Gendered Dynamics of Armed Conflict," 21; Libby T. Arcel, "Deliberate Sexual Torture of Women in War: The Case of Bosnia-Herzegovina," in *International Handbook of Human Response to Trauma*, ed. Arieh Y. Shalev, Rachel Yehuda, and Alexander C. McFarlane (New York: Kluwer, 2000), 185.

6. Cockburn, "The Gendered Dynamics of Armed Conflict," 23.

7. Ibid., 29; Arcel, "Deliberate Sexual Torture of Women in War," 189; McKay, "The Effects of Armed Conflict on Girls and Women," 383; Meredeth Turshen, "The Political Economy of Violence against Women during Armed Conflict in Uganda," *Social Research* 67, no. 3 (2000): 803–24; Moser, "The Gendered Continuum of Violence and Conflict," 49.

8. Elizabeth Colson, "Gendering Those Uprooted by 'Development,'" in Indra, *Engendering Forced Migration*, 35; Indra, "Not a 'Room of One's Own': Engendering Forced Migration Knowledge and Practice," in Indra, *Engendering Forced Migration*, 19; Moser, "The Gendered Continuum of Violence and Conflict," 38.

9. Hasida Ben-Zur and Moshe Zeidner, "Gender Differences in Coping Reactions under Community Crisis and Daily Routine Conditions," *Personality and Individual Differences* 20, no. 3 (1996): 331–40; Sideris, "War, Gender and Culture," 719.

10. Stephen C. Lubkemann, *Culture in Chaos: An Anthropology of the Social Condition in War* (Chicago: University of Chicago Press, 2008), 25.

11. Alcinda A. de Abreu, "Mozambican Women Experiencing Violence," in *What Women Do in Wartime: Gender and Conflict in Africa*, ed. Meredeth Turhsen and Clotilde Twagiramariya (New York: Zed Books, 1998), 87; Meredeth Turshen, "The Political Economy of Rape: An Analysis of Systematic Rape and Sexual Abuse of Women during Armed Conflict in Africa," in Moser and Clark, *Victims, Perpetrators or Actors?* 58.

12. Victor Igreja, "'Why Are There So Many Drums Playing until Dawn?' Exploring the Role of Gamba Spirits and Healers in the Post-war Recovery Period in Gorgongosa, Central Mozambique," *Transcultural Psychiatry* 40, no. 4 (2003): 460–87; Lina Magaia, *Dumba Nengue: Run for Your Life; Peasant Tales of Tragedy in Mozambique* (London: Karnak House, 1989), 8; Turshen, "The Political Economy of Rape," 60.

13. Sideris, "War, Gender and Culture," 721.

14. Igreja, "Why Are There So Many Drums Playing until Dawn?" 480; Victor Igreja, Bas Schreuder, and Wim Kleijn, "The Cultural Dimension of War Traumas in Central Mozambique: The Case of Gorongosa," *The International Forum for Psychiatry* (2004), http://www.priory.com/psych/traumacult.htm; Victor Igreja, Wim Kleijn, and Annemiek Richters, "When the War Was Over, Little Changed: Women's Post-traumatic Suffering after the War in Mozambique," *Journal of Nervous and Mental Disease* 194, no. 7 (2006): 502–9; Carolyn Nordstrom, *A Different Kind of War Story* (Philadelphia: University of Pennsylvania Press, 1997), 79; Sideris, "War, Gender and Culture," 722; Turshen, "The Political Economy of Rape," 58.

15. Igreja, Schreuder, and Kleijn, "The Cultural Dimension of War Traumas"; Nordstrom, *A Different Kind of War Story*, 90; Sideris, "War, Gender and Culture," 719.

16. Igreja, "Why Are There So Many Drums Playing until Dawn?" 475; Turshen, "The Political Economy of Rape," 64.

17. Judith Marshall, "Structural Adjustment and Social Policy in Mozambique," *Review of African Political Economy* 17, no. 47 (1990): 28–43.

18. Ibid., 35; Kathleen E. Sheldon, *Pounders of Grain: A History of Women, Work, and Politics in Mozambique* (Portsmouth, NH: Heinemann, 2002), 99.

19. Edward C. Green and Alcinda Honwana, "Indigenous Healing of War-affected Children in Africa," *Africa Policy E-Journal* 10 (1999), http://www.africaaction.org/docs99/vio19907.htm; Igreja, "Why Are There So Many Drums Playing until Dawn'" 477.

20. Participant interview, 2005. Subsequent participants' responses are all from January–March 2005.

21. Murray Last, "Healing the Social Wounds of War," *Medicine, Conflict and Survival* 16, no. 4 (2000): 370–82; Carolyn Nordstrom, "(Gendered) War," *Studies in Conflict and Terrorism* 28, no. 5 (2005): 399–411.

22. See also Zermarie Deacon and Cris Sullivan, "An Ecological Examination of Rural Mozambican Women's Attainment of Postwar Wellbeing," *Journal of Community Psychology* 38, no. 1 (2010), 115–30, http://dx.doi.org/10.1002/jcop.20355, 123.

23. Ibid.

24. Igreja, Schreuder, and Kleijn, "The Cultural Dimension of War Traumas."

25. See also Deacon and Sullivan, "An Ecological Examination of Rural Mozambican Women's Attainment of Postwar Wellbeing," 124.

26. Ibid., 125.

27. Ibid., 125.

28. Alcinda Honwana, "Sealing the Past, Facing the Future: Trauma Healing in Mozambique," *Accord* 3 (1998), 77; Igreja, Kleijn, and Richters, "When the War Was Over, Little Changed," 507.

29. Lillian Comas-Diaz, M. Brinton Lykes, and Renato D. Alarcón, "Ethnic Conflict and the Psychology of Liberation in Guatemala, Peru, and Puerto Rico: International Perspectives," *American Psychologist* 53, no 7 (1998): 778–92; Pilar Hernández, "Trauma in War and Political Persecution: Expanding the Concept," *American Journal of Orthopsychiatry* 72, no. 1 (2002): 16–25.

30. Elizabeth Colson, "Gendering Those Uprooted by 'Development,'" 25; Indra, "Not a 'Room of One's Own,'" 17; Moser, "The Gendered Continuum of Violence and Conflict," 39.

Part Three

Narrative Strategies and Visions of Peace

8

Acting as Heroic

Creativity and Political Violence in Tuareg Theater in Northern Mali

Susan Rasmussen

Introduction

In Tuareg communities of northern Mali, actors call themselves, and many others call them, *ibaraden*. This plural term (sing. *abarad*) in the Ifoghas dialect of their language, Tamajaq, denotes approximately "courageous (brave) people" or "notables." Why is this so? What are the nuanced and multiple meanings of this term, often translated as "brave" by French-speaking Tuareg? How are these meanings historically, socially, and culturally constructed?

The present chapter explores these questions in the urban performance context of Kidal, in the Adragh-n-Ifoghas Mountains of northern Mali, the primary setting of my 2006 project on theatrical performance, modernity, and memory. The theoretical perspective and methodology are interdisciplinary: the disciplines involved include anthropology, history, and aesthetics/performance. This chapter also addresses the broader issue of how performers cope, through their creativity, with recurring political violence and oppression in alternating periods of armed conflict and peace mediations, and how their performances express the cultural consequences of war. The chapter includes an analysis of these performers and their performance poetics (aesthetics as lived, practiced experience) and their politics (power) but also of their creativity in resistance to oppression—in terms of how they convey retrospective historical memory and contemporary social commentary on the causes and effects of political violence, and how these experiences shape their aesthetics.[1]

The Tuareg data also suggest that these contemporary local performances are in some respects, as Stoller terms Songhai possession rituals, a "sensory arena of countermemory" in their dramatic and satirical conveying of past and current events, and of fears over future socioeconomic and political experiences.[2] Courage in the face of fear is central here: in efforts to reclassify and distinguish friend from foe, to reestablish boundaries that have become blurred in the sporadic resurgence of the Tuareg armed rebellions and among the new, "lost" youthful generation returning from flight and exile as refugees.[3]

This essay draws from approaches to theater in Africa as crisis management.[4] Yet theater in Africa, as elsewhere, is also an art form, albeit historically situated in broader power systems.[5] This analysis is intended to contribute to anthropological theories of performance, memory, and narrative.[6] More broadly, the performances studied here contest, but also reproduce, cultural ideologies of power—for example, long-standing and changing distinctions in social relationships and emerging nation-state and global hierarchies. I argue that the sketches/plays narrate, but also critique, nationhood. That is to say, the actors, the plays, attitudes to them, and commentaries about them represent narratives of nationhood but also encode resistance to the state and other bureaucracies.

There is no precise correspondence between these Euro-American categories and the Tuareg plays popularly called "sketches" in Kidal; nor is there a clear-cut division, traditionally, between local actors and other verbal art specialists. The dividing line between actors and other oral historians is not rigid in the telling of mythico-histories, though only the *ibaraden* actors perform these origin tales in the form of scripted plays and more modern scripted sketches involving edutainment. Yet recently in the urban and bureaucratic setting, an increasingly "marked" status of the *ibaraden* actors has developed. In other words, in the Tuareg acting case, some Euro-American aesthetic concepts, genre categories, and performance styles are being imposed upon local aesthetics.

Ibaraden perform oral histories, legends, and tales, sometimes in scripted form, and nowadays they also perform scripted theatrical plays called by the French term *des sketches*. The last-mentioned types of performances, although not entirely new, are considered by many local residents to be more "modern" than other types. Often, though not always, these plays are organized by urban health, education, and media bureaucracies. In northern Mali among the Ifoghas (a major Tuareg descent group and political confederation, which includes many of the people of Kidal, within the larger regional Kel Adagh confederation), these plays or sketches emerged from older local oral poetry and folk tales—themselves still enduring and vital. All these performances have historically occurred during stressful periods in and around the Sahara: flight from droughts and invasions, life in exile, the repatriation and sedentization of nomads, unemployment, and sporadic armed conflicts with French colonial states and later postcolonial nation-states. Most recently, such periods have included the Tuareg separatist rebellions, the first in 1990–96, and now the current resurgence of rebellion, from around 2007, against the central governments of Mali and Niger.

In many Tuareg communities, there are rich traditions of verbal art, with diverse specialists. Yet only those specialists in theatrical plays are called *ibaraden*, or "brave or courageous notables." Among some Tuareg groups, griots and smith/artisans also perform oral art, but these specialists are neither known by the term *ibaraden* nor given the same status or prestige as the actors.

I show how the *ibaraden* actors, with regard to aesthetics (poetics and creativity in spirit) and to politics (power and oppression in the reality surrounding their art), attempt to provide voices of dignity and resistance in difficult times. They are often, though not always, successful in achieving these goals. In some respects, I argue, their performances become therapeutic; in other respects, they are appropriated by the central state and NGO agencies.

Historical and Ethnographic Background

Most Tuareg, sometimes called Kel Tamajaq after their language in the Berber group of Afro-Asiatic languages, reside in Mali, Niger, Algeria, Libya, and Burkina Faso, and they are seminomadic. Many combine herding livestock with oasis gardening, work as artisans, labor migration, and caravan and other itinerant trading. These occupations no longer correspond to inherited social statuses in the old stratified system: aristocratic *illallen* or *imajeghen;* tributary *imghad;* artisans called *inaden;* and (formerly) client and servile persons of various degrees of servitude, called *iklan, ighawalen,* and Bella in Mali and Buzu in Niger.[7] Although the older client-patron system has broken down, particularly in the towns, some client-patron roles and relationships persist in modified form in the countryside.[8] Aristocratic descent groups or clans, who together comprise several large regional confederations, remain prestigious, but many are now impoverished as a result of droughts and aid policies detrimental to nomadic interests.[9]

Tuareg and other Berber groups in North Africa converted to Islam between the eighth and eleventh centuries CE.[10] To varying degrees, pre-Islamic local cultural and ritual influences persist: in matrilineal ancestor-founder mythico-histories; in spirit possession and non-Qur'anic healing; and in legal institutions, as in the interweaving of local matrilineal and Qur'anic, Arabic, and nation-state patrilineal inheritance laws. Most Tuareg women enjoy high social status, independent property ownership, and free mobility. Most are not secluded or veiled (rather, it is men who wear the face-veil/turban), may visit male nonkin, may travel, and may initiate divorce.

There is relatively free social interaction between the sexes: a great deal of cultural emphasis is placed upon courtship, witty conversation, poetry, and musical performances by both women and men, as well as on festivals and mixed-sex gatherings.[11]

French colonial policies in French West Africa, which included the present-day nations of Niger and Mali, tended to favor the sedentarized farming peoples predominant in these countries' southern regions, including the Hausa, Songhai, and Bambara. These policies marginalized many Tuareg, who were predominant in the northern regions, which the French neglected until the discovery of uranium deposits in northern Niger, beginning around February 2007.[12] The historical marginalization of many Tuareg and the horrific massacres of them by some national militia members have resulted in the recent armed rebellions against the central governments of Niger and Mali. The roots of these conflicts were primarily regional and economic. The rebel leaders' goals have been cultural autonomy, equal economic opportunities, equal political representation, and the integration of the predominantly Tuareg northerners into the national armies, the civil service, and universities.[13]

Most Tuareg who reside in and around the town of Kidal in northern Mali belong to the Ifoghas confederation, within the larger regional Kel Adagh confederation, headed by the traditional *amenukal* with modified powers, one of whose sons is mayor of this town. Several descent groups and factions arrived in the Adragh-n-Ifoghas, including the Kidal area, from different regions, such as Gao and Menaka.[14] As of 2007, the population of Kidal was about twenty thousand, though this fluctuates markedly. Many inhabitants attempt to remain nomadic, even in this urban setting, by spending part of the year (the rainy season) out in rural pastures and camps with their herds. Others depart periodically for labor migration and itinerant trade. Many sporadically flee, not by choice but to save themselves and their families from the intermittent outbreaks of armed violence between the Malian national army and the Tuareg rebels.

Besides seminomadism, occupations include small-scale commerce (in markets and small boutiques); overland trading with other Saharan towns; Islamic scholarship; artisanry; and governmental, civil service, and military work. Many new NGO and other aid projects, as well as the plots of some plays, implicitly encourage sedentarizing nomads, or at least keeping track of them, but the nomads prefer their freedom in traditional stockbreeding and caravan and other itinerant trading, and they resent surveillance or limitations on their mobility in towns or rural areas and across national borders.

Many adults complain that youths (that is, adolescents) fall prey too easily to the rebels because youths today "do not have enough work, and want too much money," but adults also acknowledge the difficulty of living off dwindling herds and of increasing monetization. One goal of theatrical productions now, in the words of adult coordinators at a local youth center, is to "keep youths busy . . . otherwise they make trouble." Adolescents belong to an age-cohort popularly known as *ichumaren* (a Tamajaq term some persons explain as deriving from *chemmer*, to resist, and others explain as deriving from the French term *chomeur*, "unemployed person"). They comprise one of several generations since the 1970s who have felt displaced from traditional occupations and alienated from some of the values of their parents and elders. Many have dropped out of school and have traveled and spent periods away from Tuareg society in labor migration and political exile. This age-cohort has a distinctive style of dress, music, and lifestyle, different from those of its parents and elders. NGOs, aid agencies, schools, and clinics encourage many of these youths to form theatrical ensembles and join job-training programs. However, these modern acting ensembles are not entirely new; they have a long-standing precedent in, but also differ from, the older Tamajaq verbal art performance traditions.

Kidal is diverse, but its most prominent cultural and artistic symbols and musical events, as well as its major ceremonial traditional political offices, are dominated by the aristocratic Ifoghas Tuareg and their Tamajaq language. Yet these Ifoghas Tuareg cultural and political forces have historically been in conflict with and currently compete with other forces, including state and regional governmental authorities (namely, the prefecture and the prefect or governor), Kunta Arabs from the north (with whom Tuareg groups have alternately fought, intermarried, and studied the Qur'an), and other ethnic groups from the south, such as Bambara and Songhai, who, with Mauritanians and North African Arabs, are active in markets, boutiques, and other places of commerce.

Many of the southerners (Bambara, Songhai) are active in military occupations at the Malian army base in Kidal—this is a source of ongoing tension with Tamajaq-speakers and some others. Recent arrivals from other African countries have opened shops catering to the army base. Others from outside Mali descend from Senegalese *tirailleurs*, who came with the French colonial military forces. Even at Radio Tisdas, its importance as a Tuareg cultural center notwithstanding, the staff is made up predominantly of Bella Tuareg (former slaves, the first in the region to be educated, at a time when aristocratic Tuareg resisted schools), although they speak Tamajaq and self-identify as Tuareg.

Yet identities and allegiances are complex. The lines of division are not strictly ethnic: some Tuareg have been integrated into the army, from which they intermittently defect and to which they return, and not all Tuareg support the rebellion. Not all dissident movements in the Sahara are ethnically Tuareg, and armed conflicts there are not exclusively between Tuareg and central state armies. Other dissidents, exiles, and refugees traverse this vast desert corridor, fleeing distant conflicts. The widely used phrase "the Second Tuareg Rebellion" tends to imply a rigid binary opposition between the Tuareg and central governments. Although Tamajaq-speakers indeed hold grievances with regard to some policies (they are impatient, for example, with progress toward keeping the promises made in the peace accords that ended the First Tuareg Rebellion), some issues crosscut ethnicities. Regional disparities in development stemming from colonial policies are the source of many grievances.

Thus, the atmosphere in Kidal is pluralistic, but also tense, due to historical conflicts and the political violence caused by successive raids and invasions. One older actor explained why the name Kidal derives from a Tamajaq term, *egdela*, from the verb meaning to refuse or resist. He likened Kidal to a well-secured house or camp. "This," he explained, "refers to the local refusal to be dominated. Kidal is on a hill [gesturing] over there, that was fought over." He and others traced the word "Ifoghas" to a Tamajaq term meaning to be strong. Historically, Tuareg descent groups fought over the hill and water source in the area before Kidal became a town. Later, in 1963, just after Mali's 1962 independence from France, Tuareg armed rebellion broke out; this preceded the two more recent and larger-scale rebellions, the first lasting from 1990 to 1996, and the second seen in the current resurgence of fighting, especially in Niger.

The causes of the 1963 conflict in Kidal included tensions over drought food aid distribution, taxes, massacres, genocide, and other atrocities committed by some government militia commanders in that region. Modibo Keita, at the time the first president of newly independent Mali, around 1960 or 1961 chose a commander for the Kidal region who massacred many Tuareg; he forced them to dig a pit, and then shot them and buried them in it. He forced Tuareg adolescent girls to sing in the Bambara, Bobo, and Songhai languages, and forbade them to sing in Tamajaq. This commander was finally brought to justice by Moussa Traore and sent to a notorious prison (now closed) at the Taoudeine salt mines.

Today, most local residents yearn for peace and welcome the integration of Tuareg into national institutions such as universities, the civil service, and the army. However, a few army recruits, dissatisfied with the government's progress on policies promised in the peace accords of the mid-1990s, stockpiled weapons and defected. They conducted sporadic attacks, thus far on primarily military rather than civilian targets. Rebel leaders have demanded a paved road, a second hospital, better supplies, and more access to communications, and have criticized the Malian army for "foot-dragging" in withdrawing bases from northern areas. The Kidal local authority is encouraging people who have fled to return to the town, assuring them that it is secure. Officials attempt to draw people into town by organizing festivals and performances at the town's stadium and through youth centers and the radio.

The *ibaraden* actors in Tamajaq theater, in contrast to West African griots or oral historians, do not constitute a hereditary, endogamous occupational group or social stratum based strictly upon descent, although the specialty tends to predominate in certain families and clans. Actors also have other occupations, such as herding and migratory labor, and many are often dispersed outside Kidal. Yet Kidal is also a magnet and center for vibrant trading, art, and media. Organized religious and secular festivals are frequent during peaceful times. There are cell phones, televisions, radios, and a new Internet center.

What is striking about Kidal and relevant to its urban theater is its strong artistic heritage (its many prominent singers, poets, and theatrical specialists, as well as silversmiths and leatherworkers), on the one hand, and its highly militarized ambience and history of violence, on the other. In the early twentieth century, Kidal was a headquarters of the French colonial militia and there was a prison there, nearly as infamous as the one at the Taoudeine salt mines. Recently, Kidal and Gao have been visited by U.S. Pan-Sahel Initiative forces, organized by the Bush administration upon African government leaders' requests for aid to fight bandits and "terrorists."[15] Some national leaders obtain U.S. aid by defining all Tuareg fighters as "terrorists," though they have, as yet, no documented connection to terrorist organizations. This trend is worrisome, for it alienates many local residents who are already exhausted from successive waves of violence.

Given these tensions, many actors in their creativity face a choice between shunning political themes altogether (in fear of reprisals) or "setting the record straight" through critique and countermemory—a rigid binary that becomes more nuanced in practice, as shown in the following sections.

Actors, Acting, Performances, and Verbal Art in Tuareg Society

What Is a Sketch, and Who Are "the Courageous Ones?"

Actors' plays/sketches are usually informally organized, on an ad hoc basis, by individuals, families, schools, hospitals, and the radio. Some ensembles record their sketches and the radio broadcasts them. Plays and sketches may be either humorous or serious. The themes include labor migration to Libya, which youths believe will be rewarding, but they are disappointed because Khadaffi has used them to fight his wars or employers have cheated them and refused to pay them. One sketch, for example, is about a family's sacrifice of its camel and all its goats for its son who has fallen ill in Libya. The message is that it is not as healthy there as in Kidal. Other plots/themes concern poverty and orphaned children.

Ahoulou (pseudonym), an actor/composer/poet and founder of a popular ensemble lamented to me that "People tend to stereotype northern Malians as bandits, though most are not. We are not like the Mafia!" This sentiment—widely held, but not always so explicitly stated—motivated Ahoulou and his ensemble to perform some sketches/plays for me. Ahoulou explained that he writes his plays in Tifinagh, the Tamajaq script. He sometimes composes and performs plays independently, and sometimes specifically for agencies and festivals. He is about twenty-six years old, and his parents were also actors. When young, he saw his parents' sketches, became interested, and began converting poems into plays. Ahoulou described a sketch as "a file or a paper, like a message to transmit. A good play is clear. In the beginning, there can be some metaphor or allusion [*tangalt*], but at the end, there should be clarity [*tedit*]."

After converting a poem into a play with monologue or dialogue, Ahoulou gathers his friends together to act in a sketch. The actors in his ensemble discuss the sketch, but he directs, using his ideas. Some of his works are very personal. At the beginning of one monologue, a man is alone in the desert; his friends have abandoned him. Ahoulou laments here, "It is like a drought. Tuareg are all dispersed. We need to return to the Sahara and be together." He has composed other plays, however, for less personal and more "official" bureaucratic purposes. For example, one sketch, called "Girls' Education," promoted nomads' support of girls' schooling and was performed at the end of the schools' vacation. Another, entitled "The False Marabout," critiques charlatans who make false diagnoses of illnesses for financial gain. "Go to the Hospital!" exhorts sick persons to seek biomedical care, which is feared by some rural Tuareg. A play called "Merchants on Caravan" portrays the problem of betrayal on business trips and in caravans to Algeria.

There are between thirty and forty actors in and near Kidal. Traditionally, they perform upon a personal request for a specific occasion, such as a name day or wedding. Families organize many performances. Nowadays, some more "modern" innovations (locally defined as "different from the past" or "new" plays/sketches) have emerged from neighborhood organizing for educational purposes by Radio Tisdas, by schools, clinics, hospitals, and youth centers. In addition, actors now often don facial makeup and costumes.

Local terms abound for theatrical and other verbal art performance specialties, though these are traditionally very fluid, flexible, and overlapping. Comedians, *kel isatsagh*, those who joke or make people laugh, are sometimes also *ibaraden*, but not all *ibaraden* are also *kel isatsagh*. *Iswat* in the Ifoghas dialect denotes an evening festival. One term for artistry is *le théâtre*, a French loan term. Many contemporary plays have a goal described in Tamajaq as *asemeter* (in French, *la sensibilisation*), meaning consciousness raising in English. *Awahetajet* denotes a role, a character in a play. *Kel Isuha* denotes an artist, and *suha* denotes songs. *Isatsa* denotes laughter; *Kel Isatsagh* refers to comedians. *Agna* denotes art and tradition. *Tanfust*, plural *tinfusen*, denotes tale(s). *Tisiway* refers to poems. *Tanzort* denotes a riddle. *Tenzoghen*, plural, refers to traditional plays/sketches, also, broadly speaking, traditional tales, legends, or epics. *Tisiwey* refers to a modern scripted sketch, and also a poem.

Traditional epics are often performed as plays by acting ensembles such as Imesli-n-Tenere (Voices of the Desert) and Togeghamanes or the Visionaries (Those Who See Far), and these are performed in the countryside, as well as in the town. Others, *tisiwey*, are performed with the goal of consciousness raising; Bourgault terms this "edutainment,"[16] by ensembles such as Tilwat Jeunesse, the youth branch of an ensemble called Tilwat, or Joy, and a youth center–based group, Temekrist. Many ensembles, even today, flexibly alternate sketches with music and song. When I expressed an interest in local theatre, or *isatsa*, I had to specify performances including words, plots, and dialogue (*majaret*), otherwise many local residents tended to assume that I meant musical performances. This is very telling, for it implies that most Tuareg still consider performance to be primarily musical.

The ensemble called Tilwat, or Joy, grew out of competitions between neighborhood teams of artists. Its president is a renowned woman poet, singer, playwright/composer, and actor whom I shall call Tekres (pseudonym). There were, as of 2007, about fifteen men and women members of Tilwat and about eight youths in Tilwat Jeunesse. Tekres considers herself first as an artist or *kel isuha*. She says she is primarily a singer, and Tilwat was originally mostly musical, but the ensemble now also performs a mixture of singing and sketches with dialogue.

Tekres, both a widow and a divorcée, born around 1949, of *tamghit* (masc. *amghit*) or tributary social background, came from a small clan called Tarat Mellet. She married several times and had eight children. Originally from Agelhok, she came to Kidal as a young girl. Her parents were not performers. Tekres insisted that "anyone can be a *kel setsegh*, anyone who is witty and jokes." The acting of *ibaraden* combines these skills, as was explained to me during interviews and conversations. Tekres founded Tilwat when she saw neighborhood associations forming performing ensembles. At first, as noted, Tilwat mostly performed traditional songs, but more recently, since around 2000, they have agreed to requests from the youth center, Radio Tisdas, and the hospital for more contemporary performances, called *manifestations*, to raise consciousness about current issues, such as health and education. Tilwat Jeunesse is composed mostly of Tekres's children and their friends, who perform plays composed by Tekres. Tilwat has also performed in Belgium. There, before international audiences, Tilwat emphasized traditional Tuareg music and song, rather than plays/sketches.

According to Tekres, "a sketch involves consciousness raising and chatting. Their purpose is to relate the experience of youth [*tichumera*]." To Tekres, an *abarad* is "a brave or courageous person who seeks [that is, searches for some goal; seeks to do something]; actors do that. There are many actors: Kel Essuk marabouts; Ifoghas nobles; and the tributary social stratum, all include some actors among them. Their motivation is to relate their experience, since they have lived in very difficult times." Tekres described her criteria for a good sketch/play as follows:

> People must receive a serious message. Older persons usually give me ideas, and others complete them. Since my childhood, I have sung. I learned plays/sketches as I listened to others. I began [my career] by singing nomads' songs. There are numerous changes in dialogue: older traditions include themes based on, and left to us by, our ancestors: namely, poems and tales. [These often tell, for example, of ancient battles, of the origin of nearby Essuk-Tademeket and its rock art, and they also discuss morality, such as the need to beware of, but also forgive, thieves.] Modern ones are based on actual current events. Taboo subjects are love and sex, since marabouts disapprove of their open discussion. The role of Kel Isuha in society is to give pleasure and earn a livelihood, and to provide an education on serious matters, for artists must bring something to society, also.

Actors traditionally performed sketches in neighborhood spaces and inside household compounds. Modern plays are performed at the stadium and in youth centers, and broadcast on the radio. Scripts are written in advance in Tifinagh, the Tamajaq script, though they may change if the composer finds in discussion during rehearsals that others in his or her ensemble have good ideas.

During a Tilwat Jeunesse rehearsal I observed, Tekres dictated the script (called *tisiwey*, which is also the Tamajaq term for poetry) orally to the actors and singers. The actors in the ensemble learned their lines orally by rote memory. They sat in a circle on the floor inside Tekres's house and rehearsed informally. Tekres sometimes interjected comments and prompted them. They did not rehearse with costumes or props.

Over time, I learned more about Tekres's life and art, and the ways in which they were connected. Tekres has won prizes and recognition for the advocacy role she played during youth festivals, and she has often been honored for her contributions to youth programs. Tekres expressed much concern about, and had been involved in many efforts to assist, abandoned or lost children. Perhaps this is why she often plays cards with her sons and their friends, to keep them busy and at home until they return to school or find jobs, and she has informally adopted the son of a sister who resides in Mecca, Saudi Arabia. Tekres is also active in an association in Kidal promoting searches for lost children.

Tekres related to me how she went to Brussels, Belgium, in 2002 for the International Voices of Women Festival, held at the Grande Place to support women in countries involved in wars and other upheavals, and in which children have gone missing:

> A car took us from the Charles de Gaulle airport in Paris to Brussels. There were international songs, foods, and music at the Brussels festival. [But] this was also a sad occasion. Many women wore on their bodices photos of disappeared and/or missing children, [still not knowing] whether they were alive. Some children have been abandoned, others kidnapped into slavery. This also happened here in Mali during the May 2006 attack, when many families fled from Kidal and lost children. We have found some and arrested those who took advantage of children.

As we became more closely acquainted with each other, Tekres related to me events from her youth. "I spent my childhood in the countryside. My parents, like many Tuareg in the past, opposed secular schools," she explained one day as we listened to a Radio Tisdas play encouraging girls' education, "Tuareg tend to mistrust girls' education, from fear of censuses, taxes, destruction of their culture, and in the case of girls, sexual harassment by some teachers." Tekres offered particularly rich insights into the connections between gender, youth, age, power, and creativity in performance. She and other women tend to play more subdued acting roles in the modern sketches; indeed, most women prefer to perform solo in songs and poems. This is due to the fact that sketches/plays involve more bodily motions such as gestures (*sikbar*), which are shameful for women of aristocratic and tributary origins, who, in contrast to smiths and former slaves, emphasize the cultural value of reserve in public. Performance per se, however, is not a problem for women, only gestures and body motions. I noticed that the women who did perform in plays often participated in the dialogues but usually remained seated much of the time.

Thus, male actors tend to outnumber female actors in the modern urban sketches, but this is for reasons related to female reserve and social prestige, not because women are secluded, veiled, or restricted. There are, however, also political reasons for this gender difference: that is, many women feel ambivalent about male attempts to control performances by women. For example, at Radio Tisdas a staff member wanted only rural girls to act in sketches there because he preferred what he defined as a "more traditional" appearance: indigo clothing, for example, rather than urban dress.

Much more traumatic are some of Tekres's memories, from her adolescence, of performances that resulted from coercion by the former Kidal military commander, a Bobo. This commander, in the early 1960s, rounded up Tekres and other Tuareg girls in the countryside, brought them to Kidal at gunpoint, and ordered Tekres and the other girls to sing songs in Bambara, Bobo, and Songhai. Therefore, some performances were associated with oppression and fear in some actors' memories, in Tekres's case specifically associated with early abuse of youths by outsider army members. This undoubtedly shaped her art, the plots of her plays, and her social advocacy for uprooted children.

Acting in Relation to Other Verbal Art in Tuareg Society

Actors and acting among the Tuareg cannot be understood in isolation from the more general verbal art performance heritage. Traditionally, the verbal (oral and written) performance arts are not separate from life, and the various genres of verbal art performance, while given different names in Tamajaq, were often not entirely separate from each other, but rather blurred and overlapping. Women and men of diverse social origins compose and perform poetry and songs, and relate tales and legends, though different musical genres and instruments were associated with different social strata in the past.[17] Skills in poetry, song, and informal witty conversation and jokes, as well as more embodied performance aspects such as gestures or mime, have always been highly admired routes to respect, regardless of social origin.

Aesthetic performance categories are highly elaborated, yet flexible and fluid. Any translations of these categories are only approximate, however, for they are not precisely equivalent to categories and distinctions in Western theater or in the French and English languages. "People of the Word" is a general phrase designating all those who are clever and witty: in the Air dialect, it is rendered as Kel Awal; in the Ifoghas dialect, Kel Tisiwey. Within this category are included the Kel Setsegh comedians, the Kel Isuha singers/artists, and the *ibaraden* actors and poets. Smiths and griots are distinguished from Kel Tisiwey. Actors and nonactors alike explained to me that "*ibaraden* denotes *les braves* in French." Actors call themselves *ibaraden*, and others also overwhelmingly use this term for them. The *ibaraden* are named after ancient knights/warriors who traditionally protected nobles by raiding and trading for them. The only exception to the general agreement I encountered came, significantly, from a playwright and journalist of Bella (former servile) background, who reacted sarcastically to the label, and was scornful of its allusions to past social categories. For him, rather than evoking heroism, the term *abarad* (the singular form) evoked past slavery. However, all other performers and audiences with whom I spoke about this matter used the term as evoking heroism.

Abarad is indeed metaphorically apt. As simultaneously metonymy and synecdoche, this designation attaches dignity—an all-important Tuareg aristocratic cultural value—to all contemporary actors' art. An intellectual and poet who worked for an aid organization in Kidal felt that "there is no exact translation of 'actor' in Tamajaq, since [the new urban] sketches are not traditional." This man defined an *abarad* as "a warrior, an old knight or *chevalier*, a man esteemed by women and courageous." *Tabaradt*, the feminine form, originally meant a woman who conformed to the rules of conduct, for example, being hospitable, defending her own rights, and defending those of others. The term for dignity, *imouhar* or *imoujagh*, in many Tamajaq dialects is etymologically related to the term for the aristocracy. Other terms for members of the aristocracy, such as *illilen*, have reference to a free (rather than enslaved), proud, dignified, and reserved person. Hence the close relationship between acting, dignity, and pride in local traditions—despite the varied social backgrounds of actors—which centers upon selective reminiscences of historical relationships among Tuareg and between Tuareg and others. The intellectual and poet referred to above distinguished between ensembles that perform music and songs in contrast to those that perform modern theater, but I found that these genres often overlap. Some musical ensembles have added sketches to their repertoire and now also act, including Tekres's Tilwat.

It is instructive here to examine the finer analytical distinctions among the diverse Tamajaq verbal art performers. Kel Sikbar make gestures only during individual storytelling. Some plays/sketches are collective versions of storytelling, for as noted, they grew out of, or developed from, traditional storytelling by individual raconteurs, with gestures. There is some overlap between them. Ibaraden, Kel Isuha, and Kel Setsegh roles may therefore overlap in one performer, but each specialty also involves distinct skills. The same person can be two, or all three at once; others specialize in only one skill. Actors come from diverse social origins, though in and around Kidal there are many *imghad* (of tributary background) and some youths from *maraboutique* clans (though not older practicing Islamic scholars) in them, perhaps reflecting on one level these groups' numerical prevalence and social prominence in the Adragh-n-Ifoghas region in general, as both these groups served aristocrats in the precolonial system. "People who make one laugh," or Kel Seghser, belong to a very flexible and fluid category. They may be performing comedians, or simply very witty persons who make others laugh during informal conversation, as was illustrated when a tailor joked that some embroidery designs on a woman's robe resembled cow's urine when I enquired about the symbolism of the design.

Isatsa is a broad category, approximating to the English term "theater," though *isatsa*, too, does not correspond exactly to our own categories, except in the modern play/sketches organized by NGOs and aid and government agencies. Indeed, until recently, most Tuareg were more interested in music, song, and poetry performances.

The Wider Dynamics: Aesthetics, Sociopolitical Concerns, and "Culture Wars"

The Poetics and Politics of Acting

In some respects, the aesthetic style of most Tuareg plays in the town of Kidal continues to reflect long-standing, continuing cultural emphasis upon oral and verbal skill. At the beginning of each play, actors always greet each other, though not the audience, in Tamajaq. In most plays costumes are used, but no masks or stilts, except in a few new edutainment plays influenced by outside European and Malian organizers. Such edutainment plays include, for example, those performed by Temekrist at the local youth center and the AIDS prevention plays performed by an itinerant national ensemble, Caravan without Borders, on visits to Kidal several times a year. The use of masks, stilts, and marionette puppets by Caravan without Borders receives mixed responses. These props are somewhat controversial. Many youths adore them, but some older and religious Tuareg disdain them as "not true Tuareg performance [techniques]." Some even stoned the actors during one performance. In this performance context, therefore, actors were viewed as not local heroes protecting local culture and art, but rather as invaders to be resisted by the audience.

The usual emphasis in Tuareg plays is upon verbal wit, plot complexity, and gestures—especially in the plays/sketches performed by Voices of the Desert and Travelers of the Desert, which are recognized by many as more "traditional" than others. There is always much conversation: predominantly this takes the form of dialogues, but there are also some monologues, which grew out of the older poetry and epic recitation traditions of specialists generally called "people of words," "people of gestures," and comics. There are also some action-oriented sketches. For example, one plot depicted a swordfight in a battle over a well. Another portrayed a tragic death from thirst in the desert. Other plays use both verbal and action-oriented techniques to warn youths against going to Libya, joining armed rebels, and other actions viewed as dangerous. This merging of aesthetics with sociopolitical concerns pervades many performances.

Although concepts of verbal art performance and its many genres in Kidal remain very fluid, spontaneous, and overlapping, as in long-standing cultural practice, the traditional genres, styles, and actors' roles are becoming more sharply delineated and compartmentalized. Following a play performance portraying the history of Esuk-Tedemeket, I spoke to the oldest son of Tekres, who acted in an ensemble called Sons of Azawagh, who sadly commented on what he viewed as unwelcome changes in Tuareg performance tradition over the past few years:

Acting in the more "modern" sketches began with schoolchildren at twelve years, called Young Pioneers, or scouts associated with the national youth organization and at youth centers. They had three camps, schools, where one performed sketches and other activities. Also, there were competitions between schools; these were frequent, [but] now they are rare because there is now a lack of recruitment. . . . Youths now require money. There is no more discipline between teachers and students. There are several causes of this. Because of the rebellion, youths have a different mentality now, lack of motivation except money. Before, sketches were obligatory; they were required by elders and teachers. Youths interpret democracy as implying a lack of discipline. The importance of the actor is to make a presentation, to show oneself to spectators, to bring harmony among people. Of all arts, theater brings the most love and ties of unity.

Since the Tuareg rebellion, there are fewer plays, except at festivals. Yet there is now a real need for theater on the part of youths; it is therapeutic. But recently, performances have declined because of the social breakdown in relationships between generations and diminished authority of elders and teachers.

Additional changes include those in performer-audience relationships. Significantly, when I interviewed a group of Tuareg women refugees from rural Niger who had fled Niger's recent locust invasion, drought, and war and were now residing in Kidal, these rural women expressed a preference for actors who were "nice," and who were their relatives. By contrast, Tuareg women, who had resided in Kidal longer and followed a more sedentarized and urban lifestyle, without hesitation named their favorite actors according to their criteria of skill: conveying important messages, performing interesting plays, being courageous, and defending the town. They did not always know a particular actor personally, and he/she was almost never a relative. According to another actor in Sons of Azawagh, "the traditional relationship between actor and audience was personal. Also, traditional theater was expressive of our Tuareg history and culture. Whereas now, modern theater is more didactic, and has the goal of education. The modern actor/spectator relationship is less personal."

The reason why actors take the name *abarad*, even in modern sketches, many local residents and performers explained, is that earlier heroes inspire actors in the sketches. Most traditional sketches (that is, those based upon earlier stories) are several centuries old, and tell legends of war. There are several types of sketches now, with diverse plots and themes. One actor explained that "before, one followed the footsteps of the ancients. Now, we are trying to make themes more relevant." The writer can be original but is often inspired by old stories.

In and around Kidal, actors tend to predominate in certain families and clans, among the *imghad* tributaries of the Ifoghas and in the Kel Essuk *maraboutique* clan, though not exclusively. Some actors indicated that "predominantly tributaries were *ibaraden* at first, although today these specialists come from diverse social backgrounds." Actors are also described as "notables" who perform sketches intended to influence people, to change their ideas, and give them moral insights. Kel Essuk marabouts are traditionally mediators and peacemakers and bring people together: that is the meaning of the term Kel Essuk, or "people of the market." Many contemporary actors come from *maraboutique* clans because they customarily give advice, but marabouts' sketches usually shun politics, except for younger actors among the marabout groups. Marabouts can also make people laugh, in order to illustrate good versus evil. A few sketches resemble morality plays or sermons in the mosque, with themes based on old religious legends. In one such play, a victim of a theft knows who the thief is, but continues to do kind things for him, knowing that only God punishes thieves. In another morality-type play, a marabout settles a conflict between two men over a well. So the plays do not always center on warriors or heroic deeds, though many people trace most plays to the inspiration of courageous warriors and heroic accounts.

Art, Resistance, and Accommodation

Sketches and actors often become arenas for discourse on conflicts, resistance, and accommodations between different social forces: women and men, rural and urban, youths and elders, nomadism and sedentarism—not always polarized binaries or diametrically opposed categories, yet nonetheless salient distinctions in much local thought. The free social interaction between women and men in Tuareg society and nomadic women's, as well as men's, property ownership have been threatened recently by the loss of livestock herds, an important source of wealth and independence, and also endangered by encroaching national and urban forces bringing violence to the region. This was shown in Tekres's traumatic childhood experience. However, responses to these traumas vary in their effects.

According to an actor in Travelers of the Desert, "[our] actors' role is to warn and protect our culture and to advise people." Yet this actor's example of a modern theme—which he called "revolution" (also the title of that play)—revealed ambivalent attitudes toward women. This play, performed inside a family compound, was about a young girl from the countryside who went into town and succumbed to its temptations in terms of commodities and a devious suitor/shopkeeper who tried to take her away from her rural fiancé. Accordingly women's independence, previously as respected property-owners within the safe confines of rural and nomadic society, was now represented as threatened and also threatening in the urban setting. Despite the prevalent respect for women and the high social status of most of them, there are hints here of transformations in property relations that cast women more as jural minors or wards of men, assumed as "going wild" and becoming irresponsible unless supervised by male kin.

Yet, paradoxically, there is also more critical and antiauthority use of gendered themes in resistance to outside forces of violence. Oppressors and dangers are often evaded through a transgender theme or cross-dressing—both within the plots of sketches and outside them, in everyday life. The transgender theme is greatly appreciated, inside and outside the performance context, and it is often deployed to resist powerful others or elude potential harm (violence or loss of dignity). Some male actors, for example, cross-dress and play female characters in plays, although as noted, female actors appear in some plays as well. In the play entitled "The False Marabout," for example, performed by Voices of the Desert, the character of a woman client seeking Qur'anic amulets was played by a male actor, Bidi (pseudonym). Bidi frequently cross-dressed and played female characters in his ensemble's plays, because the female actors who belong to this group are often outside the town herding in pastures.

Cross-dressing occasionally occurs in everyday life as well, as a joke or for purposes of cleverness, hiding, and resistance. It can be extended beyond the theater, in effect, as a performative act of resistance. The actor whom I call Bidi related to me how he once knew a military commander who wanted women; Bidi dressed as a woman and flirted with him:

> I pretended to be available. I waited for him inside his room. I asked for 10,000 CFA [about $20] each evening, and some more for removing each item of clothing. I gave him little excuses, so as not to have sex, for example, I said I had my "period" [some Tuareg believe that during her period, a woman "loses her essence" and should not engage in sexual relations]. Finally, a month went by, and I said I was still "menstruating." Eventually, that military man found out my ruse, but he was not angry because people do this sort of thing as a joke all the time.

Thus, resistance to the military regime here took a form of a very elaborate comic performance, and fortunately it was received as such by the commander.

There are additional foci of resistance in these unstaged, transgendered performances in everyday life, these "tactics," to use Michel de Certeau's term, used in contexts outside the sketches/plays.[18] Men sometimes disguise themselves as women to get a man to treat them to a guitar concert or play performance, so they can enter free of charge. Women also sometimes wear the men's face-veil in order to be able to return from an evening festival or performance and not be accosted. On all these occasions, cross-dressers change not only their appearance but also their voice and way of talking. Life and art are intertwined here in performative resistance.

In one play, I saw greater empathy for preserving women's independence, in its theme of marriage and girls' education. During one of my visits, Tekres spontaneously composed and orally dictated a sketch to a youth who is president of (Youth) Development. However, the script was flexible: the two also debated particular points and Tekres accepted and incorporated many of the youth's suggestions. Her play's theme and title was "Early Marriage and Schooling," and it was to be performed during National Children's Week in order to raise consciousness/awareness about children who are not in school; then at the Women's and Children's House by members of the regional Children's Parliament (each region in Mali has such a parliament); and again by students during Youth Week in Bamako. Each region, or *cercle*, was represented in a contest there. Tilwat also performed this sketch as part of a festival. The plot of the sketch is as follows: the father of a girl wants her to marry a certain man, Ahmed. The girl is upset because she prefers to remain in school. Her mother goes to the local PTA and asks its chief for assistance. Eventually, the latter convinces the girl's father to cancel the marriage arrangements and allow his daughter to remain in school.

Sketches/plays therefore serve as a forum for reflection and discussion of such processes and the issues they raise. The issue is how effective these actors' messages are in social life. Although there is still some resistance to sending girls to school, attitudes are changing, particularly in the towns. Many women's associations also promote girls' education and provide job-training programs. The age of marriage, on the other hand, appears in some cases to remain low; many poorer families, and in particular, those of aristocratic background who have lost many herds, are marrying off their daughters early, preferably to economically better-off men, in order to collect bridewealth and alleviate their poverty.

Actors often emphasize their roles as critical social commentators. A female actor in Travelers of the Desert remarked that "*ibaraden* are champions. The role of the actor, since he[/she] is brave, is to defend and protect people." Indeed, some actors are warriors; they have been literally and recently involved in armed conflict; they are not simply warriors metaphorically speaking, or in terms of inspiration from the remote precolonial past. The father of an actor in the Travelers of the Desert ensemble, who was himself also an actor, participated in battles during the 1990s Tuareg rebellion at Toxamen (in the Tukseme region, about 160 kilometers from Kidal, near Taghaghaghagh). To this actor, "an *abarad* is someone who frightens, has strength or force. Why do actors take that name? In order to imitate their ancestors." Another actor explained that "[We] actors seek to be like the brave ones of the past, in spirit, in battles in the past."

As a result, memory does not operate here solely as an ethereal ideal or nostalgic yearning; inspiration from the past may involve active practice.

Narratives of nationhood can produce very real effects, and narrators can alternately resist and accommodate. The connections among heroism, acting, performing in plays, and performing beyond plays in the wider society include, but also transcend, metaphor, recalling some of James Fernandez's observations about the active and performative, rather than merely referential or descriptive, mission of tropes.[19] Yet in contrast to Fernandez, I argue, here the "figurative/literal" divide, although fluid, remains salient when historicized. One actor related to me that he learned folktales first, and then he started acting in sketches:

> Before, traditional acting related stories of the past, acts of nobles and fathers. Modern acting begins with current events, for example, economic problems. A good actor must have peace inside and be rested, to defend. He/she cannot be upset, and so forth. The problem now is fear and tension in the political atmosphere; also, people have less time for the old warrior traditions, and also, money is less good for our traditions.

A female musician and actor in the Tilwat ensemble lamented:

> There are problems now; people are not in the mood for theater. But agencies [here] are trying to organize people for plays. Actors used to be males, who recounted heroic exploits and gave gifts to women. They did not traditionally act for money. Now, since the education efforts from NGOs and state agencies, there are also women actors in modern sketches and ensembles. People here are forgetting, or are too troubled and/or busy for conversation and other social relaxation, for example, tea drinking.

She explained that

> an *abarad* is like Rambo, like a warrior. In the past, actors were mounted knights for nobles. At first, actors represented warriors, knights in traditional sketches. At first, these were the same people, who acted out heroic epics and deeds. In sketches now, many actors are descendants of *imghad chevaliers* [tributary knights] who accompanied nobles to war. . . . The first actors were all men. But actors respected women; they were not in principle, at least, supposed to be their lovers; rather, they gave gifts to aristocratic women for God.

This role recalls that of the troubadours in medieval Europe. Women became actors later, with the consciousness-raising programs of state and NGO agencies. While griots play for money, traditionally, actors do homage "for the sake of God and nobles." Some themes are now provided by agencies but written up by local composers, for example, themes about topics such as well digging.

A female actor in an ensemble whose plays were often broadcast on the radio explained that she has temporarily stopped acting because she is married and has too much work as a housewife. When I became more closely acquainted with her, however, she hinted at additional reasons for her hesitation to act: "The May attacks [referring to fighting between dissidents and the army] have spoiled everything. There is no peace." Another actor in the same ensemble commented that "acting is good for the heart and soul, but now, it [creativity] is difficult because there is a no liberty."

A young actor in Sons of Azawagh elaborated on these ideas: "When one acts, one must not wound or do harm." One must be gallant, only protect. He discussed changes: traditional sketches and actors attempt to use humor to make a connection between actor and spectator; the traditional actor's role is to express culture and its traditions. By contrast, the contemporary actor in modern sketches expresses the actor's individual personality and often educates. There is a less personal relationship with the audience.

A popular comedian and musician described an actor's role "as seeking a solution to problems. In the past, he was a warrior; now, he is someone who follows his spirit or mind, reflects well before doing something. There are many kinds of *ibaraden*." He continued: "Now, modern plays mix past with present." As an example of a current theme, he related an antidrug joke with the moral that drugs blur thought. He lamented that "many Tuareg youths now do drugs or smoke cigarettes from foreign influences during travel; they think it [smoking] is modern. In the past, over ten years ago, elders would strike youths if they smoked, but not now; their authority has been breaking down since the early 1990s."

Nonactors who attend Tuareg theater as members of the audience, or listen to plays broadcast on the radio, also discussed continuity, change, conflict, and challenges in actors' roles. One woman felt that the role of the actor is to resolve problems in life: for example, "if there is a battle, they can do a sketch encouraging peace." Another woman wanted to see more sketches with advice, ideas from the brave ones. A male tailor identified the actor's role as "to combat bad things, such as corruption and illnesses, to correct problems. An actor teaches people, is a notable in the memory or spirit [*tayte*] of people, does good works, is admired, and so has influence." Others said, "Actors bring things out into the open." Actors defend and protect relatives and parents, make people aware, and instruct. One nonactor commented: "There are few traditional *ibaraden* now, because before, in the past, they told of war; now, people do not like that topic because they want peace." Another sadly surmised that "actor's roles with our current problems are difficult; they must give happiness, but this is difficult because of the [military] occupation here."

Conclusion

The acting tradition in Kidal emerges as a refashioned medley of traditions: its roots are in the old chivalrous, gallant, troubadourlike tradition of precolonial Tuareg warriors and their courtship of women. This tradition may have been reemphasized due to the influence of French and other European NGO youth agencies who underwrite modern sketches, but its local Tuareg historical and cultural salience also remains. Hence, the intercultural translation of performance tropes is not altogether dissonant, despite the domination of some alien ideologies. Acting remains associated with protection, warning, and gallantry, but in state- and NGO-orchestrated edutainment plays, this status may become blurred for the audience as well as the actors. What many local residents call "modern plays" are organized in part to redefine and redirect actors' older, classic roles within the same genre or style, but often to foster different goals. The new agenda is double-edged: liberating, but also risky.

Warriors and actors alike should protect those in distress; for example, aristocratic women in the past. They now warn against social ills, although some audiences regard some novelties—such as AIDS edutainment and calls to educate girls—as instead introducing potential dangers or social ills. A recurrent theme throughout acting is protecting people from harm and danger, and raising awareness or consciousness. This is why contemporary actors call themselves *ibaraden*, or brave people, after the old warriors of the past. The question arising here is, given the difficulties faced and the widely acknowledged challenges to actors' roles, to what extent and in what ways are actors effective in these roles today? What is the efficacy of their art?

Kidal officialdom (that is, the mayor's office and the prefecture) is trying to dissuade youths from various actions, from joining the rebellion or going to Libya to overspending or disobeying parents and elders. Thus, we see emerging and intensifying rural/urban cleavages here: a growing gap between the town bourgeoisie with its multiethnic and technological bases of influence and the rural nomadic herders. Yet these divisions are not static or clear-cut. A rural, nomadic actor in two ensembles, Voices of the Desert and Travelers of the Desert, also participated in a national Malian theater festival in Ségou in 2004. The sketch performed at that festival had the theme of arms smuggling. In its plot, a chief's son smuggles arms, a woman becomes romantically involved with him, and finds out about the smuggling; and the authorities are able to stop him.

As has been shown, various modern concerns are revealed in the themes of sketches: labor migration; democracy; health; and educating children and girls. How far do these performances challenge, and how far do they reproduce, cultural ideologies of power—for example, long-standing and changing distinctions in social relationships and emerging nation-state and global hierarchies? To what ends are actors' powerful and respected roles being directed, and by whom? Do we see empowerment or appropriation of their performance values? The data suggest that many transformations in acting and plays, acts of resistance notwithstanding, are impacted by the increasing bureaucratization and militarization of the state, and other powerful official institutions impinging upon the more sedentarized Tuareg communities. The emergent category of the "modern" sketch/play represents, to a large degree, an attempt at a crystallized or "freeze-frame" genre, developed into a spectacle from the more fluid long-standing traditions of Tamajaq verbal art performance. However, this attempt from the top down is not always successful. On one level, the actors, the plays, and the attitudes and commentaries expressed by and about them represent narratives of nationhood, but, on another, they encode resistance to the state and other bureaucracies.

Each performance act is informed by a sense of the past that derives its meaning from the present. This is the realm of what Victor Turner called "social dramas"—the infusion of present experience and action with the resurrection of key events from the past.[20] Whether as invocations of long-forgotten cosmologies, or as ritual, dance, and bodily gesture, social and artistic performances may reassure actors and audiences of their dynamic past, however redefined it may become in new, more powerful agendas. That past is not merely reproduced but is selectively remembered and forgotten. There may be circumstances under which specificity is dangerous, ambiguity a virtue.[21] All narratives are selective, and forgetting can also be an active strategy. Cultural performances are occasions on which, as a culture or society, we reflect upon and define ourselves, dramatize our collective myths and histories, present ourselves with alternatives, and eventually change in some ways while remaining the same in others; such performances range from rituals to plays and films to sports events. The Tuareg actors' art explores sometimes conflicting, contradictory, and threatened understandings of cultural identity.

To Don Handelman, modern spectacles are public masks of the bureaucratic ethos. Bureaucracy is a paradigmatic form of organization in the modern state: no state can exist without it, and its logic affects even the logics of oppositional discourses, if only by inversion or distortion.[22] I respect the local conceptual frameworks or endogenous theories of the actors under study, but like Handelman, I am also interested in the role of overarching and hegemonic logics in relating agency (whether of individuals or of groups) to powerful agendas of regimentation, and in the role of "displays of order" as a way of avoiding the ritual/spectacle dichotomy. In the Tuareg acting case, some Western, Euro-American aesthetic concepts, genre definitions, and acting performance categories are becoming imposed upon local

Acting as Heroic 177

aesthetic genres in bureaucratic processes. These displays both reflect and shape social transformations. Yet "courageous notables" critique and assert alternative identities and "scripts" in their creativity.

Notes

1. Michael Herzfeld, *The Poetics of Manhood: Contest and Identity in a Cretan Mountain Village* (Princeton, NJ: Princeton University Press, 1985); Michel Foucault, *Discipline and Punish* (New York: Vintage, 1979); Michel de Certeau, *The Practice of Everyday Life*, trans. Steven Rendall (Berkeley: University of California Press, 1988); James C. Scott, *Domination and the Arts of Resistance: Hidden Transcripts* (New Haven, CT: Yale University Press, 1990).

2. Paul Stoller, *Sensuous Scholarship* (Philadelphia: University of Pennsylvania Press, 1997), 63.

3. Hélène Claudot-Hawad and Hawad, eds., *Touaregs: Voix solitaires sous l'horizon confisqué* (Paris: Ethnies, Documents 20–21, 1996); Hélène Claudot-Hawad, *Voyager d'un point de vue nomade* (Paris: IREMAM, Editions Paris-Méditerranée, 2002); Susan Rasmussen, "Between Several Worlds: Images of Youth and Age in Tuareg Popular Performances," *Anthropological Quarterly* 73 (2000): 133–44.

4. Catherine M. Cole, *Ghana's Concert Party Theatre* (Bloomington: Indiana University Press, 2001); Louise M. Bourgault, *Playing for Life: Performance in Africa in the Age of AIDS* (Durham, NC: Carolina Academic Press, 2003).

5. Mary Jo Arnoldi, *Playing with Time: Art and Performance in Central Mali* (Washington, DC: Smithsonian Institution Press, 1995); Karen Barber, "Popular Arts in Africa," *African Studies Review* 30 (1987): 1–78; Margaret Thompson Drewal, "The State of Research on Performance in Africa," *African Studies Review* 34 (1991): 1–64; Daniel B. Reed, *Dan Ge Performance: Masks and Music in Contemporary Côte d'Ivoire* (Bloomington: Indiana University Press, 2007).

6. Don Handelman, *Models and Mirrors: Towards an Anthropology of Public Events* (Oxford: Berghahn Books, 1998); John J. MacAloon, *This Great Symbol: Pierre de Coubertin and the Origins of the Modern Olympics Games* (Chicago: University of Chicago Press, 1981); John J. MacAloon, ed., *Rite, Drama, Festival, Spectacle: Rehearsals toward a Theory of Cultural Performance* (Philadelphia: Institute for the Study of Human Issues, 1984); Richard Schechner, *Between Theater and Anthropology* (Philadelphia: University of Pennsylvania Press, 1985); Richard Schechner and Willa Appel, eds., *By Means of Performance: Intercultural Studies of Theatre and Ritual* (Cambridge: Cambridge University Press, 1990); Victor Turner, *Dramas, Fields, and Metaphors: Symbolic Action in Human Society*, Symbol, Myth, and Ritual Series (Ithaca, NY: Cornell University Press, 1974.

7. The Tuareg, like neighboring groups, practiced slavery until approximately the mid-twentieth century, until independence from France in 1962. Servile persons were found in varying degrees of bondage and tended to be absorbed into Tuareg society as fictive kin over several generations. Today, their status varies considerably. Some, sent to schools shunned by nobles as a threat to local cultural autonomy, have jobs in the new urban infrastructure; others continue to do menial work, albeit for

pay, for their former owners in the countryside. The aristocrats or "noble" strata before colonialism monopolized the caravan trade, most large livestock, and weapons and jewelry, and they held military dominance over peoples of tributary and other degrees of "client" status; tributaries raided and traded for nobles; artisans/smiths manufactured jewelry, weapons, and tools and in some regions, performed praise-songs, and acted as ritual specialists and ambassadors for their aristocratic patron families; Islamic scholars or "marabouts" interpreted the Qur'an. The two last-mentioned social categories continue some of their traditional work, with modifications, though many aspects of the older client-patron relationships have broken down. See Edmond Bernus, *Touaregs nigériens: Unité culturelle et diversité régionale d'un peuple pasteur* (Paris: Editions de l'ORSTOM, 1981); Ida Nicolaisen and Johannes Nicolaisen, *The Pastoral Tuareg: Ecology, Culture and Society* (Copenhagen: Rhodos, 1997).

8. Nicolaisen and Nicolaisen, *The Pastoral Tuareg*; Susan Rasmussen, *Healing in Community: Medicine, Contested Terrains, and Cultural Encounters among the Tuareg* (Westport, CT: Bergin & Garvey, 2001); Susan Rasmussen, *Those Who Touch: Tuareg Medicine Women in Anthropological Perspective* (DeKalb: Northern Illinois University Press, 2006).

9. Pierre Boilley, *Les Touaregs Kel Adagh; Dépendances et révoltes: Du Soudan français au Mali contemporain* (Paris: Khartala, 1999); Jeremy Keenan, *Tuareg: People of Ahaggar* (London: Allen Lane, 1976); Hélène Claudot-Hawad, *Touaregs: Portrait en fragments* (Aix-en-Provence, France: Edisud, 1993); Nicolaisen and Nicolaisen, *The Pastoral Tuareg*.

10. Most Tuareg groups have matrilineal origin mythico-histories emphasizing female founder/ ancestresses/culture heroes, whose symbolism extends into healing, rituals, cosmology/philosophy, and some informal property endowments. These mythico-histories, however, compete with "official" Qur'anic-derived mythico-histories, rituals, and legal systems, as well as with nation-state laws that tend to favor patriliny. Most groups today have bilateral inheritance, descent, and succession systems. Susan Rasmussen, *Spirit Possession and Personhood among the Kel Ewey Tuareg* (Cambridge: Cambridge University Press, 1995); Rasmussen, *Healing in Community*; Rasmussen, *Those Who Touch*.

11. François Borel, "Rythmes de passage chez les Touaregs de l'Azawagh," *Cahiers de musiques traditionnelles* 2 (1989): 28–38; Dominique Casajus, *Gens de parole: Langage, poésie et politique en pays touareg* (Paris: Editions La Découverte, 2000); Marceau Gast, "Relations amoureuses chez les Kel Ahaggar," in *Amour, phantasmes et sociétés en Afrique du Nord et au Sahara*, ed. Tassadit Yacine, 151–73 (Paris: L'Harmattan-Awal, 1993); Kristyne Loughran and Thomas Seligman, eds., *Art of Being Tuareg: Sahara Nomads in a Modern World* (Los Angeles and Stanford. CA: Fowler Museum and Cantor Arts Center, 2006); Susan Rasmussen, *The Poetics and Politics of Tuareg Aging: Life Course and Personal Destiny in Niger* (DeKalb: Northern Illinois University Press, 1997); Rasmussen, "Between Several Worlds"; Susan Rasmussen, "Gendered Discourses and Mediated Modernities: Urban and Rural Performances of Tuareg Smith Women," *Journal of Anthropological Research* 59, no. 4 (2003): 487–509.

12. The most recent outbreak of Tuareg armed nationalist/separatist rebellion, beginning around February 2007, has been particularly intense in northern Niger, where there are tensions over the allocation of contracts, resources, and lands in the wake of the central government's granting of uranium mining contracts to transnational companies.

13. Mano Dayak, *Touareg, la tragédie* (Paris: Editions J. C. Lattès, 1992); Samuel Decalo, *Historical Dictionary of Niger* (London: Scarecrow, 1989).

14. Akly Ag Wacawalen, "Contribution à l'histoire des Kel Tamacheq de la conquête arabe à la veille des indépendances. Le cas des Kel Tamacheq de l'Adrar des Iforas" (PhD diss., Ecole Normale Supérieure de Bamako, Mali; section Histoire et Géographie), 1988.

15. Jeremy Keenan, verbal communication, African Studies Association meeting, 2008.

16. Bourgault, *Playing for Life*.

17. Caroline Card, "Music and Social Identity in Tuareg Society" (PhD diss., Indiana University, 1978); Borel, "Rythmes de passage."

18. de Certeau, *The Practice of Everyday Life*.

19. James W. Fernandez, *Persuasions and Performances: The Play of Tropes in Culture* (Bloomington: Indiana University Press, 1986).

20. Turner, *Dramas, Fields, and Metaphors*.

21. Michael Herzfeld, *Anthropology: Theoretical Practice in Culture and Society* (Malden, MA: Blackwell and UNESCO, 2001).

22. Handelman, *Models and Mirrors*.

9

Representations of War and Peace in Selected Works of Ben Okri

Kayode Omoniyi Ogunfolabi

Introduction

Ben Okri's works are often seen as quintessentially postcolonial or postmodern texts, but such terms may be said to "aspire to name the ocean."[1] The aim of this chapter is not to demonstrate whether Okri's works are postcolonial or postmodern; rather, the focus will be on one of the short stories, "Laughter beneath the Bridge," and the novella *Astonishing the Gods*, with particular emphasis on the importance of language and naming in both texts and of (in)visibility in the novella. It is pertinent to recognize Robert Fraser's exploration of the intersection of naming, language, and violence in Okri's writings. Once people possessed

> the tool of language . . . "they no longer understood one another. They broke into tribes. They had wars all of the time. And they moved away from the great garden that was their home." . . . Language is the harbinger of violence. Most damaging is naming—the kind of language that takes aim and declares "I name this. This is mine."[2]

Okri's focus on the divisive effects of language in "Laughter beneath the Bridge" is in the context of the Nigerian civil war, when people are required to identify themselves through their language in order to determine whether they belong to the "enemy tribe." Language, therefore, is linked to a person's ethnic identity. When ethnicity is a marker of difference that is used against the person concerned, it is obvious that difference is not a cause for celebration, as it is in so many postmodern discourses.[3] On the contrary, Okri's short story reveals the far-reaching consequences when ethnic identity is used against people in times of war and conflict.

Since the publication of Ben Okri's first collection of short stories, *Incidents at the Shrine* (1986), it has been evident that war and conflict have become major subjects in his writings.[4] Although the only archetypal war story in this collection is "Laughter beneath the Bridge," the second collection, *Stars of the New Curfew* (1988), features three stories of war and conflict, namely "In the Shadow of War," "Worlds that Flourish," and "Stars of the New Curfew."[5] The novel *Dangerous Love* (1996) reconstitutes the Nigerian civil war through the memories of some of the major characters, who experience its traumatic effects.[6] Because of the general violence of war and its aftereffects, Okri's writings project a grim and at times pessimistic perspective. However, it is his novella *Astonishing the Gods* (1995) that mediates this gloomy representation by destabilizing the notion of ethnic labeling and naming.[7] Despite the fact that *Astonishing the Gods* is not a war narrative as such, the theme of naming nevertheless continues and by implication that of ethnic labeling.[8] However, the narrative creates the possibility of imagining peace by transcending the limitations that naming and ethnic labeling impose on people—in *Astonishing the Gods*, ethnicity does not play a role at all.

This chapter critiques Okri's view of language and ethnicity, and Fraser's analysis of Okri's works as they emphasize the role of language as "the harbinger of violence." While Fraser's emphasis is on the limitations of language in general, which are overcome in *Astonishing the Gods*, this chapter will take the argument further. A brief discussion of the Nigerian civil war is followed by an overview of some of the literary works with the war as their subject. The next section examines "Laughter beneath the Bridge" in relation to the grim role that ethnic affiliation comes to play in wartime. The analysis of *Astonishing the Gods* represents Okri's vision of peace from a utopian perspective. Then the chapter examines the role of (ethnic) identity and how it functions with particular reference to Africa in order to propose an alternative solution that, rather than getting rid of ethnicity altogether, recognizes not only its reality but its possibilities as well.

The Nigerian Civil War: Historical and Literary Background

It is undeniably true that ethnic rivalry was a major factor in the Nigerian civil war (1967–70), in which the 1945 Richards Constitution played an important role as "the regions created in the northern, eastern and western parts of the country coincided largely with the three major ethnic nationalities that dominated the Nigerian political scene."[9] Although the Richards Constitution in later years seemed to Nigerians "to have been a policy of divide and rule, many nationalists supported various forms of federalism at the time."[10] Moreover, Northerners regarded it as an essential provision, "if they were not to be perpetually dominated by the educated men of the south,"[11] but the three regions were competing "among themselves for offices, and dominant positions in the government, civil service," and so forth.[12] According to Udida Undiyaundeye, the crisis of ethnic chauvinism deepened when the military took over the government on January 15, 1966. He observes that the North became suspicious of the aim of the coup leaders when the pattern of casualties emerged: only one casualty from the East, a few from the West and Midwest, and many from the North.[13] More important were the promotions after the coup, which, Undiyaundeye argues, "only reinforced Northern fears of Igbo domination of the country as the Igbo were eighteen out of the twenty-one Officers promoted."[14] To worsen the problem, the officer who had emerged as the head of state, General Aguiyi Ironsi, "promulgated Decree no. 34 abolishing the regions on May 24, 1966."[15] The North interpreted Ironsi's decree that aimed at unifying the country by abolishing regionalism as "a confirmation of an Igbo agenda to dominate the North";[16] it should not be surprising then that Igbo officers were massacred in the countercoup of July 29, 1966 and Igbo people were massacred in the infamous pogrom of September 1966.[17] The then military governor of the Eastern Region, Colonel Chukwuemeka Odumegwu Ojukwu, "had appealed to the Igbo who had fled to the East in May to go back only to be killed in greater numbers."[18] Judging from this brief discussion of the origins of the Nigerian civil war, it is clear that ethnic chauvinism played a major role in the crisis.

However, regional or ethnic divisions cannot provide the only explanation for the civil war, precisely because there were other immediate political factors that led to the crisis. For example, while accepting the abovementioned antecedents of the Biafra conflict, Eghosa E. Osaghae and Ebere Onwudiwe contend that "it was the proclamation of independence of the Eastern Region of Nigeria, christened the 'Independent Republic of Biafra,' by the military Governor of the region, Col. Emeka Odumegwu Ojukwu on 30 May 1967 that proved to be the final trigger for the war."[19] To Osaghae and Onwudiwe, the federal government's determination to keep the country whole superseded any other reason for the war. They argue that

> although Biafra had a just cause and enjoyed tremendous support all over the world, in view of the widely publicised pogrom against Easterners in the North and West, the regime of hatred and hostility against the Igbo, and the alleged persecution of Igbo Christians by Hausa/Fulani Muslims overlords, the option of preserving the state at all costs carried the day.[20]

In *The Nigerian Civil War: A Study in Class Conflict*, Ikenna Nzimiro suggests that one must "treat the Civil War of Nigeria as one of the world upheavals which should be seen in the context of the class structure of Nigeria which is part of the world capitalist social order."[21] Nzimiro contends that in order to discover the historical character of the war it must be studied in the context of world revolutions.[22] Taking into account the government's determination to safeguard the unity of the Nigerian state, the intraethnic violence,[23] and the global significance of the conflicts, no single perspective can fully explain the circumstances that led to the crisis. However, in Okri's "Laughter beneath the Bridge" ethnicity does play an important role.

The Nigerian civil war has resulted in a significant corpus of literary works. Obi Nwakanma begins his review of *Half of a Yellow Sun* by recounting how in 2000 he had submitted for publication a story set at the end of the Nigerian civil war.[24] The story was rejected with a note: "thanks very much; your story is beautiful and touching, but I'm afraid the subject of the Nigerian civil war has been exhausted."[25] And then, in 2006, Chimamanda Ngozi Adichie published—to great acclaim—*Half of a Yellow Sun* to join the growing corpus of war literature,[26] which included Elechi Amadi's *Sunset in Biafra* (1973), Flora Nwapa's *Never Again* (1975), Cyprian Ekwensi's *Survive the Peace* (1976), Chukwuemeka Ike's *Sunset at Dawn* (1976), Buchi Emecheta's, *Destination Biafra* (1982), Ken Saro-Wiwa's *Sozaboy* (1985), and Festus Iyayi's *Heroes* (1986).[27]

"Laughter beneath the Bridge"

In "Laughter beneath the Bridge," the narrator recounts his experience of the civil war when he was a ten-year old boy, somewhat surprisingly remembering it as a beautiful time.[28] His mother rescues him from his abandoned boarding school but is unable to take his friends with her. While waiting for his mother to arrive, the narrator is continuously thinking—reflecting his emerging sexuality—about his friend Monica, who is still in his hometown. Along the way to their town, there are a hundred checkpoints.[29] At one of them, the soldiers search and question them for a long time.[30] The soldiers ask his mother

> where she came from in the country.... They shouted to mother to recite the paternoster in the language of the place she claimed to come from.... Then mother recited the paternoster fluently in father's language. She was of the rebel tribe but father had long ago forced her to master his language.[31]

Whereas Fraser surmises that the father's language is Urhobo and that of the mother Igbo, the text at this point does not name or specify the "rebel tribe," or the language of the narrator's parents, which makes the scene representative of civil war situations in general.[32] The moment the boy's mother realizes that the interpreter does not know very well the language he is supposed to verify, she vents her anger and ridicules the whole process by abusing the soldiers' mothers and fathers.[33]

When the narrator is asked to recite the Hail Mary, he tells the soldier that he cannot speak "our language that well."[34] His mother urges him to speak the language of his father, but the narrator is unable to remember a word.[35] He bursts out laughing when the interrogator says that he cannot be his mother's son if he is unable to speak her language.[36] The narrator, however, is overcome by fear when he is dragged into the forest, and he shouts the oldest word he knows. His mother screams, "The boy has spoken, he has just said he wants to shit."[37] The soldiers think this extremely funny and let him go, while mother and son wait "for the others to prove they were not of the enemy."[38] The mother chastises her son, explaining, "They shoot people who can't speak their language."[39]

Although mother and son survive this particular checkpoint, at which the soldiers require them to make known their ethnic identity through language, it is clear that other people are not so fortunate. It is for this reason that the soldiers' checkpoints assume such catastrophic dimensions. The narrator says as the lorry continues its journey, "We . . . saw numerous corpses along the road."[40] Then there is the rape of a woman whom the narrator describes simply as being light-complexioned.[41] As the interrogation intensifies, so does the violence of the sexual assault. The brutality of the act becomes evident when the boy declares that "The soldier in the bush had finished wrecking his manhood"[42] and "the woman on the ground began to wail tonelessly."[43] Then the lorry leaves without her.[44] Therefore, although the story is set outside of battlefields, the tragic effects are evident in the number of deaths, the general violence, and the rape.

When mother and son finally arrive in their hometown, the narrator asks his mother where Monica is. She tells him that people of the town have chased Monica's family from their house and that they are now in the forests and that Monica's brother has been killed.[45] The narrator finds Monica; together with two other children, they go out in spite of the curfew that is in force, and they find there is a roadblock just on the other side of a bridge.[46] Monica insists on going past the roadblock. One of the soldiers tells Monica to come closer and asks, "You be Yamarin?"[47] The term "Yamarin" is crucial here because it reveals the existence of ethnic animosity in Nigeria. Generally, it is a derogatory expression used to refer to or to denigrate the Igbo people. Although the term originally applied to the Igbo people of Biafra, it is not uncommon for some people from the North and West of Nigeria to use the term to describe not only the Igbos but also minorities in the eastern part of Nigeria and the southwestern and southern parts of Biafra such as the Urhobos, Itsekiris, Ijaws, Kalabaris, Ikwerres, and Ogonis. The entire Eastern Region is often homogenized as being Igbo. Therefore, when the soldier poses the question it is the narrator who replies, "haltingly, in our language," that they are from the town[48] and the soldiers let them go. However, when Monica participates in an Egungun masquerade, one of the soldiers tears off the mask and slaps her face: "'Speak your language!' he screamed, as she urinated down her thighs and shivered in her own puddle. Then she jabbered. In her language."[49] Monica thus proves she belongs to the "enemy tribe" and is subsequently dragged off to the jeep by the soldiers. The narrator never sees Monica again.[50]

Astonishing the Gods

If language is all-important for the main protagonist and the other characters in "Laughter beneath the Bridge," in *Astonishing the Gods* this is no longer the case. The novella is Okri's bold step to reinvent a world, albeit a fictional one,[51] in which war and carnage disappear and peace and harmony become the norm. While "Laughter beneath the Bridge" is narrated in a realist mode, *Astonishing the Gods* is a utopian narrative, although not in a conventional sense, as it "transcends the static felicity of the classical utopia."[52] Ralph Pordzik contends that

> Okri... conceives of the novel as a kind of "testing-ground" for various approaches to utopianism in fiction as they have been developed in Western literary history... subverting the notion of one single and uniform concept of utopia.[53]

Such an experimental move on the part of Okri is not unjustified in a world "where totalitarian rule—effectuated in the name of justice, unity and equality—has been established at the expense of democracy and individual freedom."[54] Indeed, self-realization is central to the narrative.

Astonishing the Gods is a novella that may be seen as Okri's attempt to dismantle ethnic totalizations not only in relation to Nigeria but in relation to the African continent as a whole: "They built a new world of beauty and wisdom and protection and joy to compensate for their five hundred years of suffering and oblivion beneath the ocean."[55] The concern is with "an imaginative space for the unremembered people" of Africa.[56] The novella tells the story of an unnamed protagonist who leaves his country in search of visibility, because he discovers in books that he and his people have been banished from historical time and space; that is to say, they do not exist.[57] The protagonist associates history with visibility—a clear reference to the invisibility of African peoples in (Western) history and historiography, an observation that justifies his "quest for the secret of visibility."[58] The protagonist travels through time and space, from ignorance toward the moment of self-realization.

On the protagonist's arrival at the island of the Invisibles,[59] the guide explains to him, "On this island of ours learning what you know is something you have to do every day, and every moment" and goes further to develop a critique of amnesia by alleging that "In the places where I have been, forgetting is what you do every day."[60] Arthur, the major character in the short story, "Stars of the New Curfew," confirms his people's tendency to forget when he says, "human beings are notorious for having such a short memory."[61] In *Astonishing the Gods,* the guide explains, "Too much forgetting led to our great suffering. We always have to relearn here," a statement that serves as a constant reminder of the implacably cruel world of *Incidents at the Shrine* and *Stars of the New Curfew,* which is mediated in *Astonishing the Gods.*[62] In other words, the novella challenges the reader's attitudes toward wars and conflicts; if there is no conscious awareness of the brutality of wars, their harsh consequences will forever be perpetuated.

The protagonist's desire for visibility and his quest for knowledge are reinforced when he expresses the desire to understand things by their name. The protagonist asks, "Where is this place?" and his guide replies, "It doesn't have a name. We don't believe in names. Names have a way of making things disappear." When the protagonist indicates he does not understand what is being said, the response is, "When you name something it loses its existence to you. Things die a little when we name them."[63]

At this point, the reader may well begin to wonder how the protagonist communicates with the invisible guide, being aware that the language with which they communicate will not have a name. It is a language that the protagonist is unable to decode in its written form: it is a language that is no longer spoken.[64] The protagonist realizes that "all along he had assumed a similarity of language, when in fact he had been communicating with his guide beyond words."[65] At one point, the protagonist tries to read the words he sees on a scroll[66] but is unable to do so. He becomes aware that if he cannot read the words, he will not be able to enter the city.[67] He is unable to master his incomprehension and unable to think, and it is as if he is dissolving, until the more he trembles, the clearer the words become. Somewhat paradoxically and enigmatically, he is even becoming the words.[68] This experience could refer to the guide's remark that the first law of the city is that what somebody thinks becomes real,[69] which Pordzik views as "highlighting the fictional status of the world he inhabits."[70] The guide's remark appears to indicate that human beings think in words. The protagonist finally reads the indecipherable signs.[71] When he asks a dwarflike figure who he is and where he comes from, the reply is that his name, like all names, is unimportant.[72]

Astonishing the Gods vigorously challenges the reader's attitudes to naming, which have become a matter of routine.[73] That is, people's attitudes to naming have become so perfunctory that the protagonist has to go through a rite of passage in order to destroy the habit of naming,[74] presumably because names are incapable of adequately representing human beings, or objects and ideas.[75] Applying this view to ethnicity, Okri's idea appears to be that, because of their inadequacy, ethnic distinctions—as a corollary of naming—tend to introduce more violence, as already seen in "Laughter beneath the Bridge." The experience of the protagonist in *Astonishing the Gods* suggests on the one hand that emphasizing difference leads to pain and grief as in war and, on the other, that renouncing the preoccupation with naming signifies the acquisition of peace. As the novella shows, the less visible the protagonist becomes, the more peaceful he becomes. Without breaking the habit of naming, he is trapped in the cycle of "violence, corruption, and war in post- and neocolonial African societies."[76]

The significance of the protagonist's education on the normativizing discourse of naming lies in the connection that *Astonishing the Gods* establishes between the protagonist's desire to name in order to know and the moment when he learns the value of namelessness and invisibility. However, before the protagonist becomes completely invisible himself, the dwarflike figure tries to induce him to leave the island of the Invisibles, explaining that it is a rigorous land, where everyone lives without illusion. It is boring to live always in perfection,[77] while visibility amounts to living with one's life, one's mortality.[78] He advises the protagonist to leave, because if he stays on the island too long, he will end up "crying out for places where you can participate in some useful struggle and where there are a thousand useful and beautiful illusions."[79] The protagonist decides to stay and is once more led into temptation, this time by a beautiful woman who wants him to accept her love. He does not give in, and because he rejects her love, she curses him: because he refuses to love an illusion, he will have to love without illusion.[80]

According to Fraser, the protagonist initially communicates with the islanders "beyond words" because of their distrust of language and the detrimental effects of name calling.[81] While going through the process of purification, the protagonist finds himself among "the earliest heroes of the Invisibles."[82] He notes that there are no hierarchies, that all persons are equal participants and creators, and that the lack of distinction between people means that "men fed children while women constructed temples."[83] During the purification ceremony, the protagonist is unable to understand what is being said, but then the words begin to change the hall in which the ceremony is being held,[84] and the words are even changing the universe around him.[85] Here the words appear to take on a performative aspect and lose their inadequacy to represent—presumably because of their purity, coming as they are from his pure heart, and because they are now representing what is real and not mere illusion.[86] These changes appear to reflect the protagonist's universe, which is, therefore, a highly subjective one.[87]

Having gained a new consciousness and as he successfully goes through the "rite of passage," the protagonist finally becomes one of the Invisibles himself, this being a higher invisibility than the one he started off with. This is the invisibility of the blessed.[88] Before he attains this blessed invisibility, he has to answer three questions correctly, the first relating to the purpose of invisibility, the second to the dream of the invisibles, and the third to the mystery of the bridge. The purpose of invisibility is perfection; the dream of the invisibles concerns the creation of "the first universal civilization of justice and love"; and the mystery of the bridge concerns creativity and grace.[89] Interestingly, there is here an appeal to the universal in spite of the emphasis on the subjective. Not only are the limitations that language imposes made to disappear, but the introduction of invisibility means that visual distinctions, that is, distinctions discernible to the eye, are erased as well.

Ethnicity Revisited

Robert Fraser remarks how in *Infinite Riches* (1998) the nation of which Madame Koto dreams is not unlike Nigeria, whose citizens "were too many, too different, too contradictory; the nation was composed not of one people but of several mapped and bound in one artificial entity by Empire builders."[90] The nation is divided; there are too many different "tribes," that is, too many different ethnicities. Indeed, ethnicity in Africa tends to be seen as a problem,[91] but it is useful to remind ourselves that everyone has ethnicity.[92] Patrick Chabal and Jean-Pascal Daloz argue that ethnicity "is not an essentialist attribute of the African, but more simply one of several components of identity."[93] Amartya Sen notes in his discussion of identity that in everyday life

> we see ourselves as members of a variety of groups. . . . A person's citizenship, residence, geographic origin, gender, class, politics, profession, employment, food habits, sport interests, taste in music, social commitments, etc., make us members of a variety of groups. . . . None [of these collectivities] can be taken to be the person's only identity or singular membership category.[94]

However, it is also the case that

> within-group solidarity can help to feed between-group discord. We may suddenly be informed that we are not just Rwandans but specifically Hutus. . . . A Hutu laborer from Kigali may be . . . incited to kill Tutsis, and yet he is not only a Hutu, but also a Kigalian, a Rwandian, an African, a laborer, and a human being.[95]

Sen, therefore, sees identity as "a source of richness and warmth as well as of violence and terror, and it would make little sense to treat identity as a general evil."[96] We might add that it would not make much sense either to treat ethnicity as a general evil. It is necessary to distinguish the concept of ethnicity from its political instrumentalization;[97] that is to say, historically and conceptually, ethnicity may have been misinterpreted.[98] *Infinite Riches* mentions "the artificial entity" created by the empire builders, and the ethnic map of Africa was indeed formalized by the colonial state.[99]

Belonging to one particular ethnic group may lead to disastrous consequences, as "Laughter beneath the Bridge" and Fraser's analysis demonstrate: "The sentries want to know where [the protagonist's friend Monica] is from so that they can *label her ethnic group*. Their probing takes the form of *linguistic interrogation:* "Speak your language!" [emphases added]."[100] During the interrogation, as discussed earlier, a woman is being raped because she belongs to the enemy tribe, and if the protagonist's mother is unable to speak the required language, the same may happen to her. It is more than likely that the narrator's friend Monica is raped before she is killed; as Fraser points out, "we, who have witnessed the fate of the woman in the bush, do not need to be told what her fate might be."[101] It is because of her ethnicity that the mother is unable to take the other boys with her, because it poses too great a risk—to them, as she does indeed originate from the enemy's geographical area. She expresses her anxiety clearly when she tells her son and his friends, "I'm not a wicked person to leave behind children who are stranded . . . but how will I rest in my grave if the soldiers we meet hold them, because of me?"[102] Apart from ethnicity, class plays a role too, as suggested by the soldier's remark to the narrator: "All you children of rich men. You think because you go to school you can behave anyhow you want?"[103] Nevertheless, in "Laughter beneath the Bridge," it is ethnicity that becomes all-important, and for the women gender as well, if they happen to belong to the enemy's ethnic group.

In *Astonishing the Gods*, ethnicity and linguistics no longer play a role, and therefore, they no longer have the disastrous effect they have in "Laughter beneath the Bridge." Okri's works, then, denounce the existence of tribes, or, put differently, the classification of people according to ethnicity. Rather than emphasizing one particular aspect of someone's identity, we should realize that

> the force of a bellicose identity can be challenged by the power of *competing* identities. These can . . . include the broad commonality of our shared humanity but also many other identities that everyone simultaneously has. This . . . can restrain the exploitation of a specifically aggressive use of one particular categorization.[104]

Astonishing the Gods is indicative of "our shared humanity" and becomes a strategy for getting rid of all the differences that result in racial, ethnic, and gender oppression and in wars and violent conflicts.

However, another solution is possible as well, as Chabal and Daloz point out in *Africa Works*. They note, as does Sen, that ethnicity is "one of several components of identity."[105] Following John Lonsdale, Chabal and Daloz ask the question "whether ethnicity could be or become the foundation myth" in Africa[106] and find that the clear implications of Lonsdale's argument are as follows: "it is political tribalism that suppresses the politically constructive role moral ethnicity could play in African politics."[107] Ethnicity would then be "central to the development of more accountable politics,"[108] and in this way it becomes a legitimate instrument rather than overt political tribalism. Thus, a number of questions arise: "Can a workable notion of national identity . . . encompass a diversity of ethnic affiliations? Can there be ethnically based governmental institutions which function efficiently and for the common weal?"[109] In other words, "is an ethnic federal state viable?"[110] According to Chabal and Daloz, both Lonsdale and Mwayila Tshiyembe argue that "ethnicity is creatively compatible with present African modernity."[111] To Tshiyembe this means there should be space for a political framework that is based in this multiethnic reality,[112] in order to devise a political structure that is, as summarized by Chabal and Daloz, "both legitimate in the eyes of the population and accountable in its operation."[113] However, at this stage it is impossible to say whether such a structure would be viable or not.[114]

Conclusion

Language plays an important role in the texts examined in this chapter: speaking a particular language can have disastrous consequences, as in "Laughter beneath the Bridge." However, as the case of the narrator's mother demonstrates, speaking a particular language is not necessarily proof of one's ethnic origin. Language becomes the harbinger of violence and has the capacity to destroy. The theme of name calling continues in *Astonishing the Gods,* and here the words themselves become reality and the universe itself appears to be nothing but a discursive formation, having overcome the limitations of language. The individual creates his or her own world, and individuals' worlds will not be identical with each other. In other words, there is a recognition of difference, a recognition that becomes a radical imperative—"a call for the empowerment of differences."[115] *Astonishing the Gods,* then, may be said to be a postmodern narrative in that it creates a universe that is highly subjective; on the other hand, it also appeals to the universal, which evokes connotations of Enlightenment thinking. Although the novella eliminates all the distinctions that lead to strife and wars and although its vision for peace does possess a certain appeal, in the real world of wars and all forms of oppression, it is necessary to seek concrete solutions.

It is not the different languages themselves that lead to wars and conflicts; nor do ethnicities in themselves create conflicts. In the discussion of ethnicity in Africa, it is always necessary to make conceptual and historical distinctions.

It is when ethnicity is singled out as determining someone's identity that problems arise. It should be remembered that other aspects of people's identities play a role in conflicts as well, as "Laughter beneath the Bridge" demonstrates in relation to gender and class; that is to say, ethnicity is not always "the only significant aspect of African identity."[116] However, ethnicity in Africa too often becomes an instrument in political power struggles. To end this state of affairs, the solution proffered by Lonsdale and Tshiyembe appears to be attractive: rather than seeing ethnicity in Africa as an eternal problem, it may be put to use to create nation-states that are accountable and acceptable to their peoples. Such a solution takes into account the multiethnic reality of Africa and moves, by doing so, "beyond words." The reason why *Astonishing the Gods* turns out to be so thought provoking is probably precisely the fact that it is a fictional narrative, divorced from reality as it is.

Notes

1. Robert Fraser, *Ben Okri: Towards the Invisible City* (London: Northcote House, 2002), 10. The author of the present chapter would like to thank Hetty ter Haar for her assistance in expanding the scope of the chapter.
2. Fraser, *Ben Okri*, 3, 4.
3. Iain Hamilton Grant, "Postmodernism and Politics," in *The Routledge Companion to Postmodernism*, 2nd ed., ed. Stuart Sim (London, Routledge, 2005), 25.
4. Ben Okri, *Incidents at the Shrine* (London: Vintage, 1993; originally published 1986).
5. Ben Okri, *Stars of the New Curfew* (London: Vintage, 1999; originally published 1988).
6. Ben Okri, *Dangerous Love* (London: Phoenix, 1996). For a useful discussion of the novel, see Andrew Armstrong, "Speaking through the Wound: Irruption and Memory in the Writing of Ben Okri and Festus Iyayi," *Journal of African Cultural Studies* 13, no. 2 (2000): 173–83.
7. Ben Okri, *Astonishing the Gods* (London: Phoenix, 1995).
8. See Fraser, *Ben Okri*, on naming/labeling.
9. Udida A Undiyaundeye, "Issues and Causes of the Nigerian Civil War," in *The Nigerian Civil War Forty Years After: What Lessons?* ed. Armstrong Matiu Adejo (Makurdi, Nigeria: Aboki, 2008), 3.
10. Elizabeth Isichei, *A History of Nigeria* (New York: Longman, 1984), 407.
11. Ibid.
12. Undiyaundeye, "Issues and Causes of the Nigerian Civil War," 8.
13. Ibid.
14. Ibid.
15. Ibid., 10.
16. Ibid.
17. Ibid., 14.
18. Ibid.

19. Eghosa E. Osaghae and Ebere Onwudiwe, "General Introduction: The Relevance of the Nigerian Civil War," in *The Nigerian Civil War and Its Aftermath*, ed. Eghosa E. Osaghae, Ebere Onwudiwe, and Rotimi T Suberu (Ibadan, Nigeria: John Archers, 2002), 3.

20. Ibid., 3.

21. Ikenna Nzimiro, *The Nigerian Civil War: A Study in Class Conflict* (Enugu, Nigeria: Frontline, 1982), 13.

22. Ibid.

23. See Nabo B. Graham-Douglas, *Ojukwu's Rebellion and World Opinion* (London: Galitzine, Chant, Russell, and Partners, 1968), 1–2. Graham-Douglas stresses the atrocities committed by Biafrans against minority groups within Biafra.

24. Obi Nwakanma, review of *Half of a Yellow Sun*, by Chimamanda Ngozi Adichie, *Vanguard* (Lagos, Nigeria), April 15, 2007.

25. Ibid.

26. Ibid.

27. See also "The Story behind the Book," at Chimamanda Ngozi Adichie's website http://www.halfofayellowsun.com/content.php?page=further_reading&n=5&f=2, which provides a useful bibliography.

28. Okri, "Laughter beneath the Bridge," in *Incidents at the Shrine*, 3.

29. Ibid., 5.

30. Ibid., 6.

31. Ibid., 7.

32. Fraser, *Ben Okri*, 50.

33. Okri, "Laughter beneath the Bridge," 7.

34. Ibid.

35. Ibid., 8.

36. Ibid.

37. Ibid.

38. Ibid.

39. Ibid., 9.

40. Ibid., 5.

41. Ibid., 7.

42. Ibid.

43. Ibid., 8.

44. Ibid., 9.

45. Ibid., 11.

46. Ibid. 15.

47. Ibid., 16.

48. Ibid.

49. Ibid. 21.

50. Ibid., 22.

51. Ralph Pordzik, "An African Utopographer: Ben Okri's *Astonishing the Gods* and the Quest for Postcolonial Utopia," *ZZA: A Quarterly of Language, Literature and Culture* 48, no. 1 (2000): 44–56.

52. Ibid., 51.

53. Ibid., 47.

54. Ibid.

55. Okri, *Astonishing the Gods*, 27.
56. Pordzik, "An African Utopographer," 48.
57. Okri, *Astonishing the Gods*, 3.
58. Ibid., 4.
59. The protagonist is visible; what he seeks is a different kind of visibility, a historical one. To his astonishment, the inhabitants of the island are invisible. It is a kind of invisibility (he later discovers) that is far superior to the visibility he originally seeks.
60. Okri, *Astonishing the Gods*, 17.
61. Ben Okri, "Stars of the New Curfew," in *Stars of the New Curfew*, 86.
62. Okri, *Astonishing the Gods*, 17.
63. Ibid., 6.
64. Ibid., 35.
65. Ibid., 35–36.
66. Ibid., 60.
67. Ibid., 61.
68. Ibid., 62.
69. Ibid., 46.
70. Pordzik, "An African Utopographer," 51.
71. Okri, *Astonishing the Gods*, 71.
72. Ibid., 102.
73. See also Fraser, *Ben Okri*.
74. Pordzik, "An African Utopographer," 49.
75. See also Fraser, *Ben Okri*, 92.
76. Pordzik, "An African Utopographer," 47.
77. Okri, *Astonishing the Gods*, 107.
78. Ibid., 107.
79. Ibid., 108.
80. Ibid., 121.
81. Fraser, *Ben Okri*, 91.
82. Okri, *Astonishing the Gods*, 130.
83. Ibid., 131.
84. Ibid., 137.
85. Ibid., 141.
86. Ibid., 157.
87. See Pordzik. "An African Utopographer," 49.
88. Okri, *Astonishing the Gods*, 154, 159.
89. Ibid., 155.
90. From Ben Okri, *Infinite Riches* (London: Phoenix, 1998), quoted in Fraser, *Ben Okri*, 4.
91. Patrick Chabal and Jean-Pascal Daloz, *Africa Works: Disorder as Political Instrument* (Oxford: James Currey, 1999), 56.
92. Ibid.
93. Ibid., 58.
94. Amartya Sen, *Identity and Violence: The Illusion of Destiny* (New York: Norton, 2006), 4–5.
95. Ibid., 2, 4.

96. Ibid., 4.
97. Chabal and Daloz, *Africa Works*, 56.
98. Ibid., 57.
99. Ibid.
100. Fraser, *Ben Okri*, 7–8.
101. Ibid., 51.
102. Okri, "Laughter beneath the Bridge," 3.
103. Ibid., 6.
104. Sen, *Identity and Violence*, 2.
105. Chabal and Daloz, *Africa Works*, 58.
106. See ibid., 60, note 8, for Lonsdale's two chapters (11 and 12) on the Kikuyu in B. Berman and J. Lonsdale, *Unhappy Valley: Conflict in Kenya and Africa*, book 2 (London, James Currey, 1992); and Lonsdale, "Ethnicité morale et tribalisme politique," *Politique Africaine* 61 (March 1996): 98–115.
107. Ibid., 59–60.
108. Ibid., 60.
109. Ibid., 61.
110. Ibid.
111. Ibid., 62.
112. Ibid.
113. See ibid., 61, note 10, for Mwayila Tshiyembe, "La science politique africaniste et le statut théorique de l'Etat africain: Un bilan negative," *Politique Africaine* 71 (October 1998): 109–32.
114. Ibid.
115. David Simpson, *Romanticism, Nationalism, and the Revolt against Theory* (Chicago: University of Chicago Press, 1993).
116. Chabal and Daloz, *Africa Works*, 58.

10

Visions of War, Testaments of Peace

The "Burden" of Sierra Leone

Cheryl Sterling

> Take up the White Man's burden
> Send forth the best ye breed—
> Go bind your sons to exile
> To serve your captives' need;
> To wait in heavy harness,
> On fluttered folk and wild—
> Your new-caught, sullen peoples,
> half devil and half child.
>
> Rudyard Kipling, "The White Man's Burden" (1899)

Introduction

Kipling's poem "The White Man's Burden" is the ultimate aesthetic signifier of the role of white colonialists around the world, but even more significantly, it carries within it a greater burden, one shouldered by the subjugated, the object of its derisive lens, who must forever live in the shadow of their assumed inferiority.[1] The poem lives beyond the colonial era, for its implications—the nobility of white Westerners, their transcendent humanism manifested in their ever-present willingness to give to those unfortunate "sullen" peoples—encapsulate a Western vision of the world that still defines, categorizes, codifies, and judges everything that darker peoples do, from defecation to spiritual elevation. When we examine the present-day aesthetic signifiers and depictions of the real, of the realities of the darker "other" as still perpetuated by the center "white," we are left with variegated concepts of the white man's burden. When we specifically move toward a cinematic lens, the visual field recodes, reifies, and makes even more obvious the need for the white man's rationality, stability, strength, intelligence, and dignity in the face of the ruthlessness, violence, chaos, irrationality, ignorance, and ineptitude of the darker being.

This chapter examines both visual and textual depictions of the Sierra Leone war and its aftermath. The analysis focuses on three vectors: the films *Blood Diamond* and *Ezra*, the text *A Long Way Gone* by Ishmael Beah, and the e-book *Don't Let Me Die* by Adisa Andwele (ÁJA). My intention in this chapter is to provide a critique of the paternalistic, problematic vision of Africa inherited through the discourse of the white man's burden, reflected in the film *Blood Diamond*, by debunking its representational myths about the continent or, as they are described by Achille Mbembe, its "imaginary significations."[2] The critique thus hinges on comparing and contrasting differing versions of the representation of the Sierra Leonean civil war and its aftermath as seen in the film *Ezra*, the memoir *A Long Way Gone*, and the e-book *Don't Let Me Die*. Crucial to the overall analysis is establishing an aetiological relationship between populist fiction and the construction of Africa in the midst of turmoil. The chapter will therefore highlight the perspectivism of human rights narratives and the ways in which the social location of the speaker, writer, and filmmaker determines the material-rhetorical context into which these depictions are projected.

Achille Mbembe suggests that the imaginary significations of Africa are both an imbrication of Western invention of self and its "apologetic concerns and exclusionary and brutal practices towards others."[3] Representations of African conflicts generate a discourse of self-deception or perversion as it is rarely about Africa but rather about the subjectivity and subconscious of the Western interpellator. Such myth making spawns the dialectic that entraps the African subject in a constant counterhegemonic stance, rather than as an agentative subject constructing one's own discourse and lived worldview. I contend that *Blood Diamond*, as it uses the lived reality of the Sierra Leone civil war, still encodes and endorses the mythic constructs of the "darker" Africa. When *Blood Diamond* is questioned in relation to an independent film like *Ezra*, which features the life of its eponymous child soldier, and contrasted to the autobiography of Ishmael Beah, who is also a former child soldier, its anti-African narrative is made obvious, as these two other stories from African perspectives broaden the analysis and enlarge our understanding of conflicts such as the Sierra Leone civil war as more than grotesque perversions of power that are irrationally self-destructive and without causation. Further, when *Blood Diamond* is contrasted to the human rights agenda of the e-book, *Don't Let Me Die*, its sensationalism belies its reformatory intent. The highlighting of an alternative construct of a human rights narrative in *Don't Let Me Die* makes apparent how the sensationalism of a film like *Blood Diamond* belies its reformatory intent.

When we examine the ways in which Hollywood and its pundits fetishize Africa and African conflicts, we are subjected to another form of what I consider ethnographic spectacle. Hollywood films become cinematic trauma, as they are built on the foundation of empire building, the causative narrative of the civilizing mission. They presuppose and reaffirm an understanding of the African world as a world in chaos, a world in perpetual need that only Western intervention can save. They are crafted to appeal to a sense of philanthropy, a desire to give humanitarian aid that can only come from a privileged center that sees its own culture, its own economic order, and its own political vector as a standard of well-being that must be exported around the world. How can we forget, in *Hotel Rwanda* (2004), the character of Colonel Oliver, the head of the United Nations troops, played by Nick Nolte, who ostensibly protects the hotel from the marauding Hutus? It may be facetious to point this out at this date, but in Rwanda at that time, the UN troops were long gone, and the protection provided to the hotel was given by a general in the Rwandan military and his troops, who were in fact Hutu.[4]

At a panel on Hollywood's representations of Africa at the 2007 African Studies Association conference, Maryellen Higgins spoke on the ways in which Hollywood perpetuates "the ethos of Empire." She gave a five-fold explication of how this rhetoric is cinematically reproduced that bears revisiting here:

1. white protagonists . . . mediate the narrative point of view, while African perspectives and African actors, even in films that are specifically concerned with African suffering, are marginalized;
2. exposition about Africa and Africans . . . relies primarily on the authority of white protagonists, who lecture other naïve characters about Africans;
3. European or American power . . . is used to rescue good Africans from evil ones;
4. Africa [is] the site of horror, an Inferno, hell, or heart of darkness, à la Conrad; and
5. infantilized African leaders, . . . [positing] "the political immaturity of colonized or formerly colonized peoples."[5]

Blood Diamond gives us all these tropes of empire building. If we examine the trajectory of this type of narrative, we can return to one of the first of these narratives, *Robinson Crusoe*, which introduced what becomes a "positional superiority," as it is termed by Edward Said, through a master/slave dialectic between whites and the darker others.[6] On his deserted island, Crusoe makes himself lord and master, and when a darker being finally appears, Crusoe thinks, "now is my time to get me a servant."[7] We can just imagine the character of Danny Archer, played by Leonardo DiCaprio, when he learns that Solomon Vandy (Djimon Hounsou) has that rare large, pink diamond in his possession, thinking, "I'm going to make this man my servant and he will make me rich." In fact, the actual words of the Archer character, as he attests to the horror that is Africa, are "This diamond is my ticket out of this God-forsaken continent."

The intention of any film, we may presuppose, is to manipulate the subjective identification of the audience. Hence, it is important to establish the tone of *Blood Diamond* through its stance as human rights advocacy and its underpinning narrative of testimony, which attempts to engage with the representations of the experiences of the oppressed. Like many human rights narratives in the West, it establishes a problematic pattern of having the privileged speak *for* rather than *with* the oppressed. Privilege is situated as an authenticating presence and underscores the alienation of the subject of trauma, who remains without voice. Foregrounding its political agenda, the film begins with flashing epigraphs:

> Sierra Leone 1999.
> Civil war rages for control of the diamond fields.
> Thousands have died and millions have become refugees.
> None of whom has ever seen a diamond.[8]

It ends with "Sierra Leone is at Peace. There are still two hundred thousand child soldiers in Africa."

Like *Blood Diamond, Ezra* is a human rights narrative, but it is researched, written, and directed by an African filmmaker, Newton Aduaka from Nigeria. Aduaka's imperative is more subtly choreographed through the aesthetic style he employs. In some ways, he undermines the human rights narrative as seen in the extremely fine print at the film's end; it is only with difficulty that it can be read, but the message it contains stands in direct contrast to the narrative of *Blood Diamond:*

> By the year 2000, it was reported that an
> Estimated 300,000 children were serving as soldiers
> In armed conflicts in more than thirty countries
> Around the world, and that nearly 120,000 of these
> Were engaged in various conflicts
> On the African continent
> The arms continue to pour in, the Blood Diamond,
> Oil and other natural resources continue to be shipped out.
> Children continue to fight and a future generation
> Continue to be laid to waste.[9]

Delimiting the issue of child soldiers as an African problem, *Blood Diamond* bolsters the image of a continent warring on itself; whereas *Ezra* enlarges the narrative to include all the nations facing the same horror. Aduaka creates a fictional conflict zone and never explicitly ties the story line to Sierra Leone. By implication, Africa for him simply becomes one of the contested terrains that exemplify the global trauma of war and its impact on children.

Manthia Diawara terms the works of black filmmakers as new forms of cultural authority, participating in alternate subjectivities that allow us to consider them as rewriting their own narratives.[10] Ella Shohat and Robert Stam also speak of the role of Third World filmmakers as reclaiming or remapping colonial fictions, or proposing "truths" and "narratives" from a cultural wellspring from which they generate powerful interruptions of what they call the "flawed mimesis of Hollywood films."[11] *Blood Diamond* and *Ezra* are emblematic of the divide between Hollywood and African films and the clash of the reals/reels, a clash of authenticating narratives propelled by differentiated voices in the global divide. The materiality and consumerism of the Hollywood-scape undoubtedly influence the types of films produced and the tropes used, and if *Blood Diamond* could be typed as a simple adventure film or action drama, its sensationalism would be less contentious. However, its aim of generating a human rights critique makes its visuality infinitely problematic, as not only does it code Africa, but it becomes AFRICA for its viewers.

The Colonial Narrative: *Blood Diamond*

The opening sequences of *Blood Diamond* flash between an attack on a village in Sierra Leone by the Revolutionary United Front (RUF)[12] and speakers at the G8 Conference in Antwerp, Belgium. Evoking the infamous Berlin Conference of 1884–85, black faces are conspicuously absent from the room. Yet the shifting dynamics of global power relations are depicted, as two Asians are allowed to sit at the table. The meeting immediately acquires an element of righteousness as the U.S. ambassador, played by Stephen Collins,[13] proclaims in a stentorian tone:

> Throughout the history of Africa, whenever a substance of value is found, the locals die in great numbers and in misery. Now this was true of ivory, rubber, and oil and it's now true of diamonds. According to a report by Global Witness, these stones are being used to purchase arms and finance civil war. *We must act to prohibit the direct or indirect import of all rough diamonds from conflict zones.*

The scene flashes between the conference room, emblematic of the apparent logic and rationality of the West, and the desecration and death of a village attacked by rebel soldiers, underscoring African irrationality and the "inferno" of life on the continent.

The following sequences, as they switch between the conference and scenes of Sierra Leoneans forced to mine the diamonds, reinforce Collins's speech. The commander of the rebel unit, tellingly dubbed Captain Poison (played by David Harewood), becomes the archetypical representative of the maniacal local leadership, ironically shouting at the enslaved workers: "The Freetown government and their white masters have left their land to feed their greed. The RUF has freed you, no more slave and master here." The raging presence of the captain belies the revolutionary context of his words, just as the actual brutality of RUF actions erased their egalitarian aims and Marxist ideals, as he continues with his proclamation: "RUF is fighting for the people. RUF is fighting for Sierra Leone."[14] What could have been a trenchant indictment of neocolonial Africa is erased by the captain's subsequent actions, as he spies a miner pocketing a diamond and shoots him casually in the head. The miner, supposedly, is one of the people the RUF is fighting for.

According to Shohat and Stam, "cinema is consumed in *communitas*, spectatorship can take on a national or imperial thrust."[15] Wendy Hesford questions to what extent observing the suffering of others positions viewers as "tourists amid their landscapes of anguish."[16] In this film, which combines narrative and spectacle, the human rights objective seemingly allows viewers to become voyeurs. The scene, as it flits between the halls of European officialdom and examples of African brutality, points to the limits of empathetic identification, for it does not foreground the trauma suffered by the victims of war. It is not a bearing of witness to atrocious acts, but a witnessing, a spectacle even, that only confirms the audience's conditioning that Africa is a horrific place, where human life is devalued, and that African peoples are by their nature savage or are victims of savagery and we must help them to become better people, develop stabilized governments, and introduce rational forms of discourse that bypass the obscene cruelty.

What is less noticeable to the audience is that Captain Poison, before he begins his diatribe, is looking at a *Hooters Magazine*. In what becomes an amusing aside, Commander Zero gives Archer the diamonds, asking him to bring back a satellite television so that he can view *Baywatch*. What is not commented on is the fact that Africa is not a separate universe or simply the "hell" of the Western imaginary, but a participatory member of the global community, and that its inhabitants too desire the material conditions that Westerners take for granted. Imbedded instead in the narrative is the way the desire for materiality engenders and reinforces corrupted practices; only secondarily, through the story of Solomon, do we begin to comprehend the exploitative nature of the global market in relation to the wealth the continent provides.

Foreshadowing this story line, in the conference chambers, we are briefly introduced to members of Van de Kaap, a thinly veiled reference to the

De Beers Corporation, which controls 70 percent of the diamond trade in Africa. Their calm, smiling faces are juxtaposed against the brutality of the RUF captain in such a way as to presage the culpability of the capitalist agenda and the hypocrisy of those who benefit from exploiting Africa's resources.

Yet those in the domains of power are never allowed to appear irrational or illogical, for they give their commands from pristine, ordered spaces; they never truly encounter the "other"; nor do they actually dirty their hands in effecting their orders. Greed, then, becomes rational; it is a naturalized process that allows for the exacting of human suffering without contact with humanity. Manichean dichotomies are reinforced as the white/black, good/evil, self/other separation remains unchallenged in this ode to capital gain. Characters like Danny Archer, however, elide these boundaries and nullify the binaries, for his role demands a repositioning of the trope of darkness. Archer exhibits and inhabits a measure of immorality and heartlessness that allows him to be the exploiter/explorer, the man of action, who can and will do whatever nefarious deeds those in the halls of power demand. Simultaneously, Archer is both hero and antihero, for he dares to go, if you will forgive the quip, "where no white man has gone before," but his actions retell the same story of the *conquistadors*, the conquerors in search of wealth, who exploit and kill anyone who impedes their progress.

Not only are we contending with the tropes of empire building in this film, through the character of Danny Archer, but we are revisiting the topos of the foreign legionnaire, or as John Eisele suggests, the "realist-colonialist type."[17] It must be acknowledged that the legionnaire figure is a stock character in orientalist films, but when we extend the metaphor to the normative gaze that the West casts over Africa, it becomes a trope with which to understand the ways in which the West assumes a right to control, to determine Africa's destiny. In the filmic narrative, the legionnaire figure undergoes predictable behavioral and attitudinal shifts that underscore his role as survivor and savior. Eisele considers these shifts to be transgression, separation, abduction, reduction, induction, seduction, redemption, revelation, reaffirmation, and mutilation.[18] Before we examine the legionnaire model, we must also underscore what Stuart Hall refers to as an inferential racism, "Those apparently naturalized representations of events and situations . . . which have racist premises and propositions inscribed in them as a set of unquestioned assumptions."[19] The assumption is that a film about an African conflict cannot have an African character as its leading man.

Danny Archer is a self-identified white Rhodesian, a mercenary, arms dealer, diamond trader, and general exploiter of conflicts in Africa. His introduction takes on heroic signification as he arrives in a small white plane and is immediately subjected to a clash of masculinities with one of the subcommanders, whose alias, Rambo, dually encodes individual hyperbolism tied to the globalized and mediatized model of the ideal warrior. In the memoir *A*

Long Way Gone, Ishmael tells of the popularity of the Rambo films during his days as a soldier, adding that "we all wanted to be like Rambo; we couldn't wait to implement his techniques."[20] When confronted with a Rambo impersonator, Archer quickly shows that he is not the easily terrorized white man in Africa. He, after all, is the model of the conqueror, and he walks away from the macho posturing even after Captain Rambo pulls out a gun. He meets with Commander Zero, another tropic figure, who adds humor to a jarring situation, as he is a little runt, who appears too harmless to command any respect, let alone lead a battalion of crazed "freedom fighters." These parodies of power stand in sharp contrast to Archer's courage, as he reifies what constitutes manliness in his ability to overcome the darker others just through his force of personality.

Archer's quintessential manliness manifests itself in his autonomous actions and independence. His aloneness is fostered through his exilic existence, for his original transgression and separation are found in his departure from Rhodesia. He is forced to go to South Africa, because, as he says, the "munts overran us." "Munts," I was told by Tim Stapleton, at the 2008 University of Texas at Austin Africa conference on "Wars and Conflicts in Africa," is a derogatory term for blacks used by white Rhodesians. It is derived from the Bantu word *muntu,* signifying "human being." The distanciation in meaning does indeed make one reconsider Derridean deconstruction and the manner in which binary pairs are significations of each other, for surely "munt" signifies "nigger," and "muntu" signifies "person"; hence the imbrication of the two occurs only through a racist's lens.

Following Eisele's model, the abduction and reduction phase of Archer's personal journey are referenced in his abduction by his own boss, Colonel Coetzee (played by Arnold Vosloo), after he loses a cache of diamonds when he is arrested for smuggling. This kidnapping scene, too, becomes an affirmation of the logic, order, and progress of white rationality as we are taken to Cape Town and Coetzee's farm. An enormous white villa is situated in this panoramic scene, surrounded by manicured lawns, flowing down to a vinery where Coetzee confronts Archer. This idyllic existence is juxtaposed against flashes of Freetown, where everything is ragged and broken down, where the streets are crowded and filthy—a site fitting for the ensuing chaotic attacks. Yet a decentering of power does take place, as Coetzee tells Archer that the Sierra Leone government has asked for the help of his mercenaries. Archer points to the irony of the situation, as it is Coetzee who sells arms to the RUF in exchange for diamonds and, when the situation escalates, comes to the rescue of the government. In the process, Coetzee receives dual compensation. In this situation, however, the compensation is even more profitable, as Coetzee gains mining concessions in return for his military intervention. This is a moment of mimesis in the film, paralleling the real-life operations of the mercenary group Executive Outcomes in Sierra Leone.

Executive Outcomes (EO) was a partly British-based company, staffed by veterans of the South African Defence Force who fought in Mozambique and Angola.[21] The group launched an airborne campaign and later a ground campaign to protect Freetown and take control of the mining area. While Ndumbe and Gershoni give credit to EO for reducing the warfare,[22] Richards argues that EO's success was in controlling government decision making through its propagation of military intelligence. When it finally launched ground attacks against RUF bases in 1995, he states, its aim was to psychologically disrupt the rebels and as a result it left a scattered force that, when it regrouped, committed the most atrocious acts of the war.[23] While *Ezra* too points to manipulation from outside, as the supplier of the drugs to the rebels also provides the government troops with arms, it does not engage with such details of the struggle. Its perspective from the point of view of child soldiers lends itself to this overarching framework, for even if they realize that they are pawns in a complicated game of external and internal manipulation, the children will not know who exactly the global players are.[24]

The process of induction into the conflict begins for Archer when Freetown is attacked by the RUF. As Archer conveniently rescues Solomon during the attack, Solomon becomes a child that must be led and saved. This scene serves as an extreme contrast to the Solomon we meet at the beginning of the film, who bravely runs into a RUF attack to save his family, rather than hiding in the bush like the other villagers. The privileged position of whiteness is affirmed when Archer tells Solomon, "I know people. White people. Without me, you're just another black man in Africa." The visual impact of their escape encourages the audience in its affirmation of the heroic Archer. His skill and calm when dodging rapid gunfire, explosions, and careening wreckage, is juxtaposed against the masses of Sierra Leoneans running in fear through the streets, dying pell mell in the midst of flying debris. We are indeed assured that Solomon is in capable and experienced hands.

Metonymically, the music in the background encodes the devastation inflicted by the RUF. Shohat and Stam point out that music is crucial to spectatorial identification:

> Lubricating the spectatorial psyche and oiling the wheels of narrative continuity, music "conducts" our emotional responses, regulates our sympathies, extracts our tears, excites our glands, relaxes our pulses, and triggers our fears, in conjunction with the image and the service of the larger purposes of the film.[25]

In narratives of empire building, the drum sounding across the colonially dominated landscape signifies uprising; its mimicking of the rhythm of the human heartbeat, and its intensity felt through the increasing decibels, allows for its perception as ominous and threatening. It causes white women to shudder in fear, and white men to run for their guns. In *Blood Diamond,* rap music replaces the drum rhythm. Whenever the RUF appears, hip-hop is played: not just any type of hip-hop but gangsta' rap. Aligning rap with violence, the filmmakers play on spectatorial identification and misidentification.

Gangsta' rap in the public imagination is a celebration of all antisocial behaviors, outright violence, and denigrating misogyny, and, while it contains all these elements, it is also the wordsong of the U.S. ghettos that tells of the alienation of young black and Latino youths from mainstream culture, political access, and economic options. When exported, it stresses what is now considered a politically incorrect stereotype, but not a false premise that links blackness and brutality. Rap is used in one of the first scenes as the RUF attack on Solomon's village, evoking the circling savage motif; the RUF fighters indeed circle the village in their Land Rovers with guns drawn, killing the villagers at random. The music briefly stops, only to begin again when they start to chop off the hands of their captives.

Reprising the now infamous siege of Freetown—called, by the rebels, "Operation No Living Thing"[26]—with the victory of the RUF in the city, the night scene shifts to silhouettes of dancing black bodies, much like scenes in the popular advert for the I-Pod Nano pasted on billboards and elsewhere. As mere outlines against a backdrop of devastation, these dancing bodies lose all aspects of three-dimensionality and humanity; they stir the imagination of the savage "other" bent on reckless abandonment. It is only through Ishmael Beah's narrative that we are given the nuances of the siege as a combined effort by the Armed Forces Revolutionary Council (AFRC) and the RUF. While Ishmael witnesses the fact that "the entire nation crumbled into lawlessness,"[27] the Hollywood version of the narrative reinforces a level of sensationalism, as it reinterprets this crucial moment in the Sierra Leonean civil war as black bodies dancing to rap, while drinking, shooting, and torturing at random. This is not to deny the brutality that the AFRC/RUF perpetrated, but the provocative nature of the representations ultimately reduces the actual victimization that took place, in which people were randomly and deliberately killed, starved to death, and faced constant torture while the rebel forces were in control.

Rap music is also recoded in the narrative structure of *Ezra* and *A Long Way Gone.* In *Ezra,* rap and reggae are used to underscore the humanity of the child soldiers and their everydayness in the midst of trauma. In contrast to both films, in *A Long Way Gone* rap music becomes an essential tool for the survival of Ishmael and his friends. Made homeless by the war, they wander around the country looking for a safe space, but as a band of young men, they represent to the people they encounter the feared child soldiers, the machines of war that kill without inhibition. As they change from being just boys to being predatory brutes, it is only when they perform a rap song that they are seen differently. This unique verbal virtuosity, combined with obvious skills in speaking English, then marks them as "safe" and recodes them as simply children in need of help.

Archer's seduction into the cause begins when he meets the journalist Maddie Bower (Jennifer Connelly). Through his attempts to use her, we see the unfolding of his story. Their scenes together become a confessional narrative that begins to expunge Archer's internal darkness. In the same way, Maddie's representation also exposes the limits of the ethos of empire, for she embodies the role of the female colonizer, the one who is more compassionate to the natives but who still ultimately wields power over them. Abena Busia and Ania Loomba point to the confluence of sexual and racial tension in the role of the female colonizer. For Busia, white female power is limited, because the female too is the object of male desire,[28] and Loomba suggests an (in)voluntary naturalized subordination as she takes on the characterizations (the simultaneous pity and loathing of the "other" evident in the white man's burden) of white patriarchal institutions.[29] Stephanie Athey and Daniel Alarcón bring together these two disparate stances as they argue in a reading of *Oroonoko* that white women complicate the oppression/resistance dyad yet do not fundamentally change the male-contra-male antagonism in colonial discourse.[30]

Although cast in the role of the female sympathetic to Africans and Africa's problems, it must be noted that Maddie does not shift the essential agonistic positioning of Archer and Solomon. All the same, her positional superiority to Solomon is evident in her role as a foreign journalist and, as such, she becomes a representative of whiteness as the authenticator of and "expert" on black suffering. She has the ability to transcend borders, helping Solomon to locate his family in Guinea. Yet she remains unscathed and unviolated after multiple RUF attacks, because her role as "reporter" guarantees her access to safe transport away from danger. Her cynicism and her knowledge of her own power are betrayed, however, when Archer asks for her help and she responds, "The whole country is at war. Why should I help just one person?" She immediately recants, adding, "I can't believe I just said that," but her agreement comes at a price, which is Archer's story. Even though this war is taking place in Sierra Leone, and Solomon is its direct victim—his village was destroyed, his family was scattered, and he was enslaved by the RUF—it is Archer's story that matters, for Solomon is indeed only another black man in Sierra Leone, while Archer gives access to the domains of power.

Thus, it is only through Archer that Solomon's story becomes relevant. Maddie as the writer and human rights worker can now put a white face in the midst of all the black faces, allowing Western readers to see themselves imbricated in this story of a land so far away from them. It fosters the identification desired in a film such as this. Yet it is not empathy with the victims of trauma but empathy with the heroes who save the victims from themselves. Whites can reinforce their mythic presence as the bringers of civilization. This is the insidiousness of the global reach of white privilege, for whites are endowed with the power to transform the dynamics of this national struggle, and they can still absolve themselves of any blame in its causation.

At the end of the film, we briefly glimpse Maddie's article in Solomon's hands, as he stares woefully at a prominent picture of Archer. Since the essential conflict revolves around Archer and Solomon, when Archer dies, Maddie's relevance to the storyline is significantly reduced, for she no longer speaks. Instead, we see her trailing Solomon, taking pictures of his encounters with a Van de Kaap representative. We see a quick vignette in which Solomon is called to testify in South Africa. Yet even though she is silenced in the film, Maddie still has more voice than Solomon, for she is now the expert. Shohat and Stam point out that stereotypes are based on assumptions of superiority/inferiority; hence, "whites are the objective ones, the experts, the uncontroversial ones, those who cause no problems, those who judge, those 'at home' in the world, whose prerogative it is to create laws in the face of alien disorder."[31] Still, the unvoiced Maddie is not the same as the silenced darker woman; she is the documenter, the white witness that the Western world needs to validate the "authenticity" of Solomon's tale of horror. Her power has such sacred authority that she dares to speak to and even take pictures of the Kamajoh, the traditional warriors who are said to have mystical power, when even Solomon looks down at their feet.

Maddie's role as the compassionate female stands as a direct foil to the role of Archer, as she tells him "maybe I just give a damn" about the turmoil all around her. Maddie and Archer's moments of togetherness both reveal his "heart of darkness" and begin his catharsis. Yet this is only the beginning, for in a scene whose tropic significance inverts the savage "other" dichotomy, Archer threatens to kill Solomon. Hiding in the bushes from an oncoming truck filled with soldiers, Solomon shouts out "Dia!" in the hope of finding his son, only to have the soldiers chase and attempt to kill him and his companions. Camouflaging them with bushes and thus ensuring their escape, Archer shows why he is the hero of the film. When Solomon wakes up, he finds Archer in the background with a bloody knife, skinning something; in this tense moment, the audience can only speculate whether it is an animal or a human being. The ensuing dialogue reveals the depths of brutishness and brutality in the life of a mercenary. Solomon is left without doubt that to Archer he is just like the animal Archer has just skinned, for Archer tells him, "You risk my life like that again, and I will peel your face back off your head." He moves the bloody knife closer to Solomon and adds, "You understand," for emphasis. Flinging the dead baboon at Solomon, he orders him, "Make us a fire." For Archer, Solomon's servitude is complete.

A period of redemption and revelation is triggered by a clash with Solomon, when they near the village that holds the diamond and Solomon's child, Dia. This scene becomes an archetypical clash of masculinities, as Archer tries to exert his control over Solomon. Thus far, Archer has been the leader. The irony cannot be overstated: Archer has been the one to lead Solomon through his own country, even though Archer does not know the geographical terrain. He finally encounters resistance when he attempts to stop Solomon from entering the village. Solomon counters, not as the Hegelian slave[32] that Archer fabricates in his imaginary, but as an agent within this journey, by shouting, "You're not the master!" Archer responds, "That is exactly what I am and you'd better remember it, kaffir!" Archer can only win the ensuing physical struggle when he pulls a gun. But he loses, for he learns that it is just folly to kill a man whose only motivation is love for his family. This confrontation changes the dynamics between the two, and in moments of revelation, they are able to share their story.

The limited nature of Archer's life allows the growing empathy of the audience and the validity of his redemption. His humanization substantiates the belief that the Western subject is innately compassionate and giving. It is through Solomon that we see the reaffirmation of the Western narrative, in Solomon's denunciation of Africa. Solomon confesses to Archer, "I understand why people want our diamonds, yes. But how can my own people do this to each other? I know good people that say that there is something wrong with us, inside our black skin, that we were better off when the white man ruled. But my son is good." In this one statement, Solomon affirms the power of empire building as an antidote to the inferiority of the empire's subjects. Pathologizing blackness and normalizing whiteness are key factors in the tropes of empire and, seemingly unwittingly, Solomon endorses the dichotomies inherited from Enlightenment discourse, such as reason versus emotion; mind versus body; culture versus nature; objectivity versus subjectivity, that privilege whiteness and disdain blackness.[33] Such relational superiority is reinforced even when Solomon uncovers the site of the diamond: no element of ownership of the gem on his part is ever recognized. His knowledge and agency are never acknowledged; conveniently he becomes "the digger."

Yet, Solomon is neither the Buck, nor the Coon, nor the Tom stereotype.[34] He is rather ennobled, and he claims and retains his humanity as seen in the profound love he demonstrates for his child. Recast as the noble savage, his complexity as a speaking being, his capacity to challenge oppression, and his psychological opacity are never the subject of the filmic gaze. We only catch glimpses of his multidimensionality when he resists the attempts to make him a subject of empire. He maintains his dignity and displays sarcasm in response to Archer's greed and corruption that demonstrates his autonomy. It is also obvious that Solomon is using Archer, because of the access the latter provides to information, to transport, to his family, that Solomon does not have as yet another internal refugee. Solomon follows because Archer is leading him where he wants to go—to his son. In the end, their shared journey and story allow them to bond and see their mutual humanity, but before Archer's metamorphosis, to Solomon he is just another person who is "crazy for our diamonds."

Archer undergoes a fatal mutilation as he is wounded during the final escape scene, leading to one of the two endings of the film. The first, the emotional ending of the film on the mountaintop where Archer dies, signals the ending of the *communitas* shared by the audience, as the protagonist has achieved redemption by giving his life for a black man and his child. The second is the actual ending, in which Solomon is called to testify in Kimberley, South Africa, before the G8 tribunal.[35] He is called to witness. The story ends as it begins, with Steven Collins's voice proclaiming that "The Third World is not a world apart and the witness you will hear today speaks on its behalf. Let us hear the voice of that world. Let us learn from that voice, and let us ignore it no more." Significantly, the film ends, yet Solomon never speaks. Maryellen Higgins points to the reductionism of having one man speak for the entire Third World, and this point must be taken into consideration, but when even that voice is silenced, the audience must question the relation of power to discursive authority.[36] As Gayatri Spivak notes, the subaltern does not speak,[37] and a narrative such as this one that purports to speak for the oppressed must interpellate and decenter the discursive authority of the writers, speakers, and filmmakers who claim such authority, but my argument here is that it does not.

The Testimonial Narrative: *Ezra* and *A Long Way Gone*

While Solomon is not allowed to speak, Ezra does. As he stands in the midst of the Truth and Reconciliation Commission, he reveals to the judges:

> We were fighting for our freedom. If killing in a war is a crime, then you have to charge every soldier in the war. War is a crime, yes, but I did not start it. . . . Our government was corrupt. Lack of education was their way to control power. . . . Your country talk about democracy but you support corrupt government, like my own. Why? Because you want our diamonds. Ask anyone in this room have you ever seen real diamond before. No!

Here, *Ezra* inverts the Eurocentric focalization of the Hollywood narrative by giving pathos and multidimensionality to the child soldier. It is a stance that critiques the neocolonial order, for it discerns that in spaces like Sierra Leone, people are manipulated by insiders/outsiders to commit atrocious acts. This does not negate their culpability, but it provokes a clamant quality, demanding recognition of child soldiers as thinking, feeling, albeit manipulated, human beings. *Ezra*, like *A Long Way Gone* and *Don't Let Me Die*, belongs to the genre of testimony. Straddling both sides of the divide in a civil war, *Ezra* gives a fictional account of the life of a rebel inductee, and Beah's memoir tells of his life as a child soldier inducted by governmental forces. Analogically, in *Don't Let Me Die*, ÁJA inhabits the roles of author and activist simultaneously, and, as this poetic account is also a photo montage, it allows him to craft an unabashedly emotional evocation of the effects of warfare. Testimonial literature is usually written in the first person and aims to bring to the forefront the silenced, subaltern voices. Its success is tied to the generation of an "ethical sense of obligation in the reader" based on an empathetic response that triggers social consciousness.[38] It is a self-representational discourse by those deemed as the "other," allowing them to be subjects rather than objects of someone else's gaze. Inherently, it promotes acts of redefinition and reaffirmation of the redeeming aspects of political activism. Crafted as "truth," its thematic must by its nature subsume its aesthetic considerations to bolster its counterhegemonic positioning.

Newton Aduaka succeeds in recreating a testimonial in filmic form, borrowing from the cyclic, often shadowy, domain of memory to craft the story. Transfiguring the Western linear narrative, Aduaka uses flashback sequences to create an aesthetic circularity that mirrors the erratic nature of free-flowing thought. In a film based on Ezra's recollections, Ezra's interiority is the focus of the narrative as the story weaves back and forth through time and space. As the story is told before the Truth and Reconciliation Commission (TRC), we are called to witness the processes of indoctrination, fellowship, terror, and brutality that define the life of a child soldier. The film forces a comparison with the way in which *Blood Diamond* treats the issue of child soldiering, given that the focus of *Blood Diamond* never wavers too far from the character of Archer, as if to emphasize the "incidentalness" of Africans to the storyline. What makes Aduaka and, as will be discussed, Beah more successful in their approaches is the fact that they allow African perspectives to come to the forefront through more nuanced considerations of the motivations, actions, and daily struggles of the child soldier as a victim of war.

The issue of child soldiers has become one of the most complex human rights issues. Recent studies attempt to give it coherence and understandability, but the horror of it all is not lessened, even when filtered through academic jargon. Although her case studies are of Mozambique and Angola, Alcinda Honwana gives a compelling overview of the rise of the phenomenon in Africa. Linking the growing proliferation of child soldiers to the spiraling crises of the postcolonial state—its internal economic collapse, mounting external debt, and growing health crises—allows these nations to commodify child labor, she argues, which, in turn, prevents an organic, orderly progress from childhood to adulthood. Coupled with growing ethnic tensions, a state's inability to protect its citizens and the massive migrations to cities to look for nonexistent employment generate a pool of disaffected and displaced youths who are co-opted into various conflicts.[39] Missing, though, in the analysis is the neocolonial component, which sets forth the role of the global economic forces that feed off Africa's resources.

Specifically focusing on Sierra Leone, Paul Richards documents the earliest phases of the civil war and characterizes the tactics used to induct children as tactics of "sodality versus sodality."[40] Indoctrination is equated to initiation in a secret society and, thus, each side had its initiates, who were coerced and psychologically manipulated to such an extent that they fully identified with the causative narrative and goals of their indoctrinators. They even came to believe that victory for their particular side was the only way to end the war. Richards's explanation of why governmental forces began using child soldiers is even more disquieting, as the reasoning behind the use of child soldiers rationalized the killing of children by children. Adult soldiers, Richards explains, found it psychologically difficult to kill children, even though they were enemy combatants. Apparently, the children's inexperience in warfare and lack of understanding of its fundamental rules compounded adult soldiers' inability to consider them as enemies.[41] We can only speculate that a war between children may have been viewed as more winnable but definitively psychologically less devastating to the soldiers. When the government embarked on the policy of using child soldiers, however, it could not have known that the war would continue for years to come and create a generation of incredibly damaged youths.

Understanding how children are made into agents of warfare is essential to any human rights initiative on their behalf. William Murphy's analysis of induction rituals provides a framework through which to exercise such interpretative agency. Warfare, we know, typically breaks down the family unit, and Murphy suggests that kinship bonds are reconfigured for the child through the processes of indoctrination. What is forged instead is a system of patronage and clientelism between the adult commanders and the children to replace the familial bond. Brutality, benevolence, and reciprocity characterize these patron-client relationships and, as rituals of power, they become infinitely more complex.[42] In validation of Murphy's constructs, the induction rituals are seen to be remarkably similar in all three narratives, as they revolve around the profound psychological reconditioning of the children.

In *Ezra*, after the children are abducted, fear is immediately instilled in them as a boy is shot because he cries too much. Once they arrive at the rebel camp, as symbolized by passing through a threshold containing the proverbial sign of danger, a skull and crossbones, they begin their training. The mise-en-scène extends an understanding of the patrimonialism fostered in the relationships between the children and the adult soldiers, for the commander becomes simultaneously teacher, father, protector of the children, and, as in any deviant relationship, their abuser. The scene begins with the children standing in formation, wearing identical army uniforms. The commander hovers above them and commences the process of indoctrination. The call to action becomes a Machiavellian tour de force as he blatantly manipulates them in his quest for power: "Soldiers, you are going to fight a battle, so you must get ready and willing to die." An antiphonal sequence follows each line and the children respond as a chorus, "Get ready and willing to die." The commander's masterstroke is in his revelation of the reason for the war: "From now on, you are walking corpses.... What are we fighting for? Justice, Justice. There is no justice in this country. The people are suffering. I am ready to change the system. Our success is guaranteed but only through the barrel of a gun." The commander raises the gun in the air and the children repeat "The barrel of a gun." The argument is simple enough for a child to understand: evil is outside and we must fight it.

The popular interpretation of the preference for child soldiers, Honwana suggests, is that children are better at soldiering because they are more susceptible to ideological conditioning:

> They are easier to manipulate and control; they are readily programmed to feel little fear in combat or revulsion at atrocious acts; and they can simply be made to think of war and only war. Their abductors and commanders believe that children possess excessive energy so that, once trained, they carry out brutal attacks with greater enthusiasm than adults.[43]

Scenes such as the one described above are obviously geared toward manipulation. The deceptively simple repetition of the call and response sequence becomes a deliberate form of brainwashing that allows both the words and the intensity of their delivery to reverberate and become embedded in the psyche of the children. The commander is both nemesis and hero as he asserts the ideals of the revolution in this inculcation process: "Our ideology for this country is simple. We must bring our country to greatness. Free education. Free health. Electricity. Running water for everyone.... You are now children of the revolution!" Murphy likens the patrons' comportment to a metaphorical conflation of nationalism and patriarchy and, as the commander creates an alternate society and an alternate mode of belonging for the children, he validates this tropic significance:

> Forget about everything you learned till now. Forget it all. History, religion. Forget it. Forget home. Forget your family. They no longer exist. This is your home! And the brotherhood is your family. From today you are born again as new children of this nation. And you will fight and die for her.

A paradox of identification and separation is recoded in this antiphonal ritual as the children mimetically repeat: "Fight and die for her."[44] Indoctrinated into what Murphy terms the "revolutionary model" of clientelism,[45] children such as these become the agents of a socially active discourse and efficient little killing machines. Fanon speaks of violence as a cathartic act in the revolutionary struggle, but he could not have envisioned a struggle in which children are the perpetrators of that violence.[46] As politicized insurgents, they now act in response to the corruption of the state and its failed infrastructure. Warfare becomes revolution, they believe, and they justify their actions as righting the wrongs of failed governmental policy and practice—just as we see with Ezra.[47]

In *Blood Diamond*, while the induction scene is just as forceful, what is crucially missing is the ideological content of the commander's speech. Captain Poison reprises his maniacal behavior as he tells the children:

> Your parents are weak. They are farmers. They're the fishermen. They do nothing but suck the blood from this country. But you are the heroes who will save this nation. You're not children anymore You're MEN! . . . No one has ever given you respect. But with this in your hand [he holds up an AK 47] they fear you! If you don't get the respect you deserve, you will take it by shedding their blood. . . . Repeat after me. Shed their blood!

The children then repeat, "Shed their blood," again and again. To complete the initiation process, Dia is encouraged to kill his first victim. Blindfolded, he is urged to shoot. Evocatively, within the story line, the commander in this scene is the commander who enslaves Solomon and swears to get the diamond. He is a foil to Archer; while Archer is on the road to redemption, he, as Archer's darker doppelganger, can only become more brutish and sadistic. Yet, again, this model of indoctrination is rendered by Murphy as the "coerced youth" model, in which the children are passive victims of the insurgency movements, brutally forced into military service.[48]

In contrast, in *A Long Way Gone*, Ishmael may belong to the model of the "delinquent youth," children drawn into the struggle at times for economic or social gain, but also because of social alienation and dispossession.[49] We see how Ishmael is irrevocably changed because of the loss of his family, the loss of his home, and the constant danger to which he and his friends are subjected. Ishmael and his friends are made into internal refugees due to successive rebel attacks and, as they run away, they find limited spaces of refuge because, as a band of boys, they too are suspected of being rebels. Further traumatizing their already traumatized psyches, those who are kind to them during this forced dispersal are killed and, just before Ishmael is reunited with his family members, they too are killed in a fire during a rebel attack. The village that becomes their safe haven, the only home they have known since their original displacement by the war, comes under attack and, for Ishmael, his anger at his victimization is transformed into a desire for revenge.

The boys' instinctive predisposition to hate the rebels is reinforced by the lieutenant-in-charge as he inducts them into the war. He reinforces in their already fragile psyches the idea that the rebels "have lost everything that makes them human. They do not deserve to live. That is why we must kill every single one of them. Think of it as destroying a great evil. It is the highest service you can perform for your country. . . . We must kill them all. We must make sure they never walk this earth again."[50] Before going into battle, Ishmael psychologically replays the lieutenant's urgings to "*visualize the enemy, the rebels who killed your parents, your family, and those who are responsible for everything that has happened to you.*"[51] Giving concretion to the ordeals suffered and an explicit face to the enemy, ideological brainwashing is transformed into a systematic introduction to violence as a way of life.

A highly relevant but recondite issue is the responsibility that these children have for their actions. According to Honwana, child soldiers exercise tactical agency, rather than strategic agency.[52] Strategic agency implies some modicum of power and comprehension of the political, economic, or ideological consequences of actions. Tactical agency is the agency of contingency. It is the agency of the weak, who take advantage of any given opportunity to manifest aspects of their humanity that have to remain hidden to ensure survival.[53] Ezra's and Ishmael's stories become narratives of tactical agency. In fleeting moments of connectedness, the protagonists allow themselves to speak of a halcyon past, with home and family; they enjoy being alive; they listen to music, dance, and animate themselves in unexpected ways.

The marriage of Ezra (Mamodou Turay Kamara) and Miriam (Mamusu Kallon) evokes the seeming impossibility of love and its ability to grow and survive in the midst of the most horrific conditions.[54] As the children share their lives, these times of unguarded communication are their only moments of joy, because their reality is one of collective suffering due to hunger, drugs, and violent reprisals from the commander. When Miriam becomes pregnant, it causes universal celebration, and the scene dissolves into a big party. *Ezra*'s revisionist perspective when compared to *Blood Diamond* is evident even in the music played. Instead of moving against a background of raucous gangsta' rap, the children are all "skankin" to reggae music. Yet, as the battalion embarks on a raid to avenge the death of Ezra's family,[55] the incongruence between the lyrics and the action can only be an ideological commentary imbedded by the filmmaker in response to the violence of the children's lives. Fully armed, they leave the camp in step with the lyrics by Nasio Fontaine, from his CD *Living in the Positive*. The lyrics tell the listener to live positively, with untroubled hearts, wiping away tears and fears, because love will conquer evil.[56]

For Ezra and his compatriots, reggae remains a source of psychological escape in the midst of the daily trauma. To Beah, however, reggae becomes an aesthetic and affective signifier of his narrative of redemption. Memorizing the lyrics of Bob Marley's *Exodus*, Beah discusses them and Rastafarian philosophy with his counselors and, as his reticence lessens, he forges what becomes a cathartic relationship with his nurse, Esther. It allows him to trust again and to bond with his uncle and his family; for a time, he finds moments of relative peace—until the infamous siege of Freetown. The siege precipitates his departure from the country, for he knows that if he does not escape, he will be drawn back into the warfare.

Tactical agency also co-opts will and volition, states Honwana; such velleities are seen in the child soldiers' unwavering obedience to the commands that are given and to the commander in the misguided desire to gain his favor.[57] Through the horrific deeds they commit, both Ezra and Beah demonstrate their devotion to their commanders. As a result, Ezra is tormented by this past, and he cannot admit to his most atrocious act, that of killing his own parents. Fundamentally, he does not know the truth of his actions, for he led the attack on his village in a drug-induced haze and, from the action sequences, we as the viewers do not know the truth either. This section of the tale evolves from the recollections of Ezra's sister, Onitcha (played by Mariame N'Diaye), who sees Ezra bombarding the house of their parents, but Ezra is not prepared to accept what he has done. In fact, Beah attests, cocaine, "brown brown" (a mixture of cocaine and gunpowder), and amphetamines were commonly taken by the children to fortify them when they were commanded to do the unthinkable. In between the drugtaking and the killings, they watch *Rambo* movies.[58]

Central to Ishmael's interior dialogue is his quest for the approval of the commander, who becomes for Ishmael both a father and teacher. It is one of his proudest moments when the lieutenant dubs him "Green Snake," because of his ability to hide and kill the enemy.[59] Ishmael feels the most profound betrayal when the commander allows him to be taken to the capital to be rehabilitated. Ishmael appears to be a boy who enjoys the adulation that comes with his skills as a warrior. In one scene, he graphically describes slitting a man's throat in a competition to establish which of them was the quickest and most efficient killer:

> I grabbed the man's head and slit his throat in one fluid motion. His Adam's apple made way for the sharp knife, and I turned the bayonet on its zigzag edge as I brought it out. His eyes rolled up and they looked me straight in the eye before they suddenly stopped in a frightful glance, as if caught by surprise. The prisoner leaned his weight on me as he gave out his last breath. I dropped him on the ground and wiped my bayonet on him. I reported to the corporal, who was holding a timer. The bodies of the other prisoners fought in the arms

of the other boys, and some continued to shake on the ground for a while. I was proclaimed the winner, and Kanei came second. The boys and other soldiers who were the audience clapped as if I had just fulfilled one of life's greatest achievements. I was given the rank of junior lieutenant and Kanei was given junior sergeant. We celebrated the day's achievement with more drugs and more war movies.[60]

Such shocking scenes impel the narrative of testimony to the point of a "crisis of witnessing" and to the point at which it is impossible to generate empathy between the witness and the audience.[61] Kimberly Nance speaks of the processes that limit empathetic engagement in human rights narratives. Surprisingly, it is principally the reader who subverts the narrative, by skipping pages in the text that are too intense, or by closing the book before finishing it.[62] Generating her own oppositional dynamic to resist the call to social action, the reader may, unthinkingly or otherwise, undermine the intent of the testimony, so that it remains only a textual construct rather than a lived engagement.

Through his actions, Beah affirms the trope of child soldiers as mindless monsters that commit perverse, abnormal, and deviant acts. He may in fact lose audience identification, since it is now difficult to perceive him as a passive victim of circumstances. This point in the narrative does, however, generate a polemic that must be spoken about when dealing with memoir and acts of remembrance: that is, how faithful is such a narrative of trauma to the actual events? Can it be believed? How far is Beah's tale constructed, in the effort to emphasize his personal suffering to fill his own pockets? It is commonly known that the validity of events in the story has been challenged; consequently, should we read this text as fiction?[63] For the purposes of this essay it may be more useful, however, to question Beah's role in reifying constructs of the "darker" Africa.

Just as Beah offers a compelling affirmation of the "dark continent," he presents an equally undeniable distanciation from this trope in his description of the rehabilitation process. In the rehabilitation camps, at first, the youths reorganize and reconfigure themselves into the particular factions in which they fought; thus perpetuating the violence. In whatever form, whether or not personally directed, they are consistently mollified by the staff and constantly told, "None of what happened to you was your fault." Such blamelessness establishes their positions as victims. This is an important reformulation of their roles in Sierra Leonean society, for during the early part of the war they were shunned and condemned. This vital change of policy and behavior allows the community to embrace these children and to reinforce the value they have for the community, and it tells of a society seeking its way out of its tumult.[64]

Significantly, Ishmael's relationships with Esther and his uncle prefigure the possibility of redemption and a return to a normalcy that previously existed only in his imagination. In comparison, even before the convening of a TRC in *Ezra*, the elder of the village, Ezekial, links the acts of confession and redemption. He tells Ezra's sister Onitcha that Ezra's "parents' spirit will not rest until he admits what he has done and begs forgiveness. This is a serious matter, *serious* matter. He must beg forgiveness. Atone. Make a sacrifice." This elder harkens back to a time in which the cultural values of the society made sense to the people. This is not an atavistic reminder of a dead past, for imbedded in the TRC discourse is the desire for healing, reconciliation, and recovery of basic human dignity.

The setting up of a TRC always involves ambivalence, because the justice that many victims long for is retributive, while, at best, the TRC process offers mediation and a forum in which to share one's story.[65] For someone like Ezra, who cannot remember all the atrocities he committed because of the complex combination of drugs, trauma, and denial, the TRC is even less effective. Thus, he cannot expunge his guilt as the process demands, and he confesses to the court that "I cannot say what you want me to say. I don't remember. I don't remember. I don't remember." In the effort to eradicate an internalized psychical barrier that limits memory, the aim of such confessionals is for the participants to retell their personal narratives of trauma. Yet these confessionals often evoke a self-censorship that is endemic to any ritual of testimony, and thus limit the personal transformation produced in cathartic exegesis. Ishmael, however, is able to take the confessional narrative to its ultimate point in his autobiography, and his story becomes documentary evidence during the United Nations First International Children's Parliament in 1994. Unfortunately, but not surprisingly, even with testimonials by children, the war in Sierra Leone continued for several more years.[66]

In Sierra Leone, the TRC operated under the principle of transitional justice, to "establish a historical record of past abuses, prevent future abuses through legal and institutional reform, provide remedies to victims, and punish perpetrators."[67] Mbembe presents a noteworthy critique of the neoliberal agenda in relation to Africa that is particularly relevant to the TRC: "The current fads for 'civil society,' 'conflict resolution,' and alleged 'transitions to democracy,'" he states, are "primarily concerned, not with comprehending the political in Africa or with producing knowledge in general, but with social engineering."[68] Hence, to a critic like Mbembe, the TRC's role is not one of catharsis or the personal healing of victims and perpetrators, but is instead predicated on fulfilling imposed models of accountability, geared to preventing further abuses. In its operation in Sierra Leone, the TRC established two sections: a commission that collected personal records and a special court that placed on trial only those who had committed the worst atrocities.[69] This is not to deny the TRC's expurgatory function, for it did indeed allow many of the victims and victimizers to tell their stories and ask for forgiveness.

Films such as *Ezra* give pathos to these institutional apparatuses, and Aduaka forgoes mimesis to generate a fictive recreation of the effects of the TRC process. In the case of Sierra Leone, the commission that wrote its charter unequivocally agreed that children under eighteen would not publicly testify.[70] Aduaka's exposition of the TRC allows us to explore its inherent contradictions: if the narrative of healing is predicated on confession and forgiveness, how does one forgive atrocities that are so recent, we must wonder? Moreover, how does one heal when the wounds and the scars are still so visible? In *Ezra*'s last words, we see that fatal conundrum:

> I don't remember what happened in my village on the 6th of January 1999. The psychiatrist says it was the mixture of drugs and trauma. She says it is called amnesia. My memory blanked out for my protection. Maybe it is better that way. I killed people. Plenty of people. Other people's parents, brothers, sister, and wife. May the spirit of everyone that died in this war forgive me.

The movement from amnesia to anamnesis involves a deliberate psychical excavation and atonement. It signifies the utterance of what Toni Morrison calls "unspeakable things, unspoken,"[71] and connecting to the lived world in a way that the visuality and narrative cannot.

ÁJA and *Don't Let Me Die*

It is in the work of ÁJA that we see the effects of the human rights narrative, its triggering of spectatorial identification, and its resultant political activism.[72] *Don't Let Me Die* is unapologetically crafted to appeal to a universal sense of humanism. This is not the humanism of the Enlightenment, which recognized only a limited few in its concepts of humanity and equality,[73] but a transcendental humanism that projects beyond concepts of race, class, gender, and ethnicity to create a utopic Ur-world in which beings are seen as part of the divine. Thus, ÁJA begins his narrative with the word-thought "inspiration," seeing the creation of this e-book as the result of a divine calling:

> The inspiration informed me that I must write an anthology about war, poverty and HIV-AIDS and that it must be published with photographs to compliment [*sic*] the written word. The latter would involve me experiencing abject poverty and suffering of war firsthand in order to take the photographs.[74]

As a result, this photographic essay/choreopoem also becomes a witnessing. It too becomes a testimonial, not just to the effects of warfare but to the agency of the human rights activist who engages in social restructuring. It belongs to a form of rhetorical witnessing that Hesford characterizes as that of "the viewer/listener who witnesses/hears the testimony of another."[75] As a witness, ÁJA becomes irrevocably changed by his spectatorship, and his personal commitment to humanitarianism extends globally, structured by his faith as a Rastafarian and his calling as an artist. Whether consciously or not, ÁJA's narrative intersects with the thrust of empire building, for it assumes, as Mbembe suggests, that the "*idea of a common human nature, a humanity shared with others,* long posed, and still poses, a problem in Western consciousness."[76] ÁJA's call for a "higher existence that humans have to reach in order to subordinate religion, heritage, culture, and national and racial philosophies and perspectives to the oneness of life" is predicated on the absence of such a higher existence, and his narrative attempts to narrow the gap between "other" and "self."[77]

ÁJA blends his poetic narrative with a series of photographs taken from countries all over the world.[78] Sierra Leone is given the primary focus, to chronicle the effects of war and poverty on children. Among the first visuals is one of children in the slum of Kroobay, just outside Freetown, standing in a long gutter flowing with water that is filled with detritus. A subsequent photograph reveals the other end of the gutter with its contents flowing into a stream in which a mother is bathing her child. In the overall context of the work, the poems and visuals form an apposite, integral whole, even though they are constructed separately. Its duality conveys ÁJA's distress, astonishment, and dismay in a way that a singular narrative could not. In the poem attached to the photographs of the gutter, "Nutten Can Prepare Yuh Fuh This," the repetitiveness of the choral chant intensifies ÁJA's emotions to emphasize his horror at the conditions under which human beings live:

> nutten can prepare yuh fuh this
> nutten can prepare yuh fuh this
> nutten can prepare yuh fuh
> de instinctive intense reaction.
> nutten can prepare yuh fuh
> when all yuh senses explode.
> nutten can prepare yuh fuh this
> nutten can prepare yuh fuh
> de level of anger and anguish
> trust muh
> nutten, uh mean nutten
> can prepare you fuh this.[79]

ÁJA begins his narrative with an imperative: he has to experience poverty firsthand in order to continue his activism. Testimony by its very nature causes discomfort, and his reaction is beyond visual voyeurism. As the observer and the chronicler, his shock, perturbation, and disgust are communicated through the poem in such a way that they cannot be communicated by the images alone. His words unfurl with such anguish that the repetition of the phrase "nutten can prepare yuh fuh this" reverberates and replays the initial shock. Attempting to nullify any immunity to the visuality of horror, the verse generates pathos, a profound empathy, to push the boundaries of spectatorial identification, to create an emotional engagement that shifts human rights discourse from something outside oneself to the level of one's personal transformation.

It is through this poetry that ÁJA addresses such issues as child soldiers, girls as victims of war, and the lives of amputees. The visuals without the poetry are open to interpretation, but ÁJA uses them to direct the viewer's gaze; thus, the image of a child outlined in a doorway holding a toy is likened to that of a child soldier.[80] The poem titled "Victim of Heritage" combines with the image to provide a profound commentary on children trapped by violence:

> a quick glimpse of me
> may reveal an innocent child,
> but if you look long enough,
> you may eventually see
> a victim of my heritage
> that will blow you up tomorrow
> for my flag
> and the policies of my president.[81]

The poem speaks to the essential conundrum when facing these children, as they are victims of war who are only children, but they are also deadly killing machines that, as witnessed through Beah's confession, can seemingly operate without any conscience. The juxtaposition of ÁJA's poetry and images, as Hesford suggests, "allows the viewers to consider the relationship between testimony and visual evidence, and the distance between what one sees and what one hears or reads."[82]

Any distanciation between image and narrative collapses, however, when ÁJA tackles the issue of child prostitution. The images appear quite innocent as they are simply those of young girls on the streets, but when combined with the following poem, entitled "Legacy of Poverty," the visuality is recoded as the narrative becomes the image:

> sometimes I wonder
> if they see me as a child
> but then again their only aim
> is to have a good time
> at first it hurt
> for my little body

couldn't handle their explosive bursts
but now I have learnt
there is no more blood and pain
they disappeared with my innocent frame
which now shows the passion for the game.[83]

Instantaneously, a vision of innocence is replaced by imagined representations of grotesqueness and perversion. To say the poem evokes the horrifying nature of rape and sexual abuse is reductive; rather, it repositions the narrative as the image. Such a narrative reverses and reinscribes the image by reflecting the thoughts and reactions of the viewer back to him- or herself. It becomes a self-reflexive moment predicated on a surreal imaginary construct, for it is impossible to see the young girls in the frame. What replaces the image is an interior construct of their distorted, broken bodies, writhing in pain. Hence, the image becomes the representation of the viewer's ability to become more than a spectator. Appreciably, it is the most compromising position of all, because it requires the viewer to take on the subject position as either the perpetuator or the victim of this violence. It shifts subjectivity into the photographic frame and demands a response. This is the brilliance of ÁJA's text, because it allows the spectatorial identification of film and the evocation of written narrative to combine in the subjectivity of the reader/viewer.

"Images are ideological," suggests Lola Young: "no image is neutral or innocent of the past whether or not that past is acknowledged."[84] ÁJA's work as testimony allows the past to live in the present, and the present to question itself as the unfolding point leading to the future. A poem such as "Poor People Dead," taken together with the image of an old man sitting in front of a shack as he is fed by a young girl, ultimately encapsulates ÁJA's reformatory political agenda and human rights initiative:

an' yuh tell muh
that de worl' progress
yuh tell muh to look ahead
but all i see is dread
all i see
poor people dead
poor people dead
all i see
poor people dead.[85]

The commentary on the image tells us that the young girl is the granddaughter of the old man and, when we examine the image closely, it becomes obvious that he is an amputee. In that moment, all that we know of the Sierra Leonean civil war comes back into focus. The commentary may as well read that the past has not passed, as generations are living with their victimization. The poem thus unfolds into a critique of the discrepancy between the wealthy nations and the poor, U.S. foreign policy, and its effects in the world market. The images of this man and child are then interpolated into the drama of world domination, to be seen as the direct recipients of nothing good from the West. Part of the goal of human rights narratives is to reposition the subjects of trauma to propel action in regard to rebuilding societies, generating agendas for restitution and justice, and advancing human rights causes globally. ÁJA's axiological vantage point removes the separation of these conflicts into the self/other dichotomy. Collectively, ÁJA's work demands from the spectator a natural entanglement in the issues at stake, and it demands an understanding that acts of terror, acts of horror, are not outside the self but are universal human actions and that, by extension, the desire for recuperation, transformation, and justice is also universal and human.

Conclusion

The roles the cinematic and photographic lens plays in the construction of difference are profound and go back to their use as ethnographic tools to document "others" all over the world. When the visuality privileges Western culture and values, it often casts a derogatory gaze. The camera, as an extension of the imperial eye, becomes an instrument of power and control over the representations of the "other," and that control is only wrested back when those subjugated by the derisive lens create their own visuals and their own discourses. A film such as *Blood Diamond* seizes the right to define and speak for the "other." Based on its human rights thrust, it naturalizes whiteness as both interrogator and champion of human rights causes around the world. Even with its critique of the global power structure, it still affirms white male superiority and authority, and it consolidates power outside the realm of the black subject that it so blatantly misrepresents. Western discourse thus becomes tautological, trapped in its own binary impulses that disallow any shading, self-referentiality, or agency to the subjugated of empire.

The narratives of *Ezra*, *A Long Way Gone*, and *Don't Let Me Die* serve as empirical contrasts. They reverse what has often been an anthropological gaze by representing different versions of the "real." These narratives focus on the struggle for legitimacy and power, and they deconstruct discourses of power as complex workings of internal forces and international actors. Taken together, these works succeed in questioning the constructs of subjugation, and they examine the ways in which domination is created and validated. By focusing on the construction of terror as the limits of humanity, they consider a relational humanism, generated in regard to the human family and in relation to transcendence and divinity. ÁJA states that "war is the manifestation of conflicts within the minds of men and it is there where the battle against war has to be fought and won."[86] Confronting the effects of war through these narratives ultimately demands that we face ourselves and our responses, whether they generate concrete action or more passivity, not just in reaction to the texts or the images but in reaction to the realness of the world.

Notes

1. Rudyard Kipling, "The White Man's Burden: The United States and the Philippine Islands," originally published in *McClure's Magazine* 12 (1899); see http://209.85.229.132/search?q=cache:Z1mIdizQTIQJ:en.wikisource.org/wiki/The_White_Man%27s_Burden+the+white+man%27s+burden,+in+public+domain&cd=3&hl=en&ct=clnk.

2. Achille Mbembe, *On the Postcolony* (Berkeley: University of California Press, 2001), 2.

3. Ibid., 2.

4. Paul Rusesabagina has become a controversial figure, having been accused by Tutsi activists of being a Hutu supporter. Tutsi activists have charged that he uses the monies he has gained to support Hutu causes, and that he negates the genocide by referring to it as a tribal conflict. It has also been stated that during the period of the genocide, he extorted money from the Tutsis he saved in exchange for protecting them. See http://www.friendsofrwanda.com/rwanda/articles/Hotel%20Rwanda%20ohero%20CNN.pdf; http://www.commondreams.org/archive/2007/12/09/5719; and http://www.petitionspot.com/petitions/rwandangenocide.

5. Maryellen Higgins, "Human Rights in Hollywood's Africa: *Blood Diamond* and *The Last King of Scotland*" (paper presented at the annual African Studies Association Annual Meeting, New York, October 18–21, 2007), 2. In the last part of the quotation, Higgins cites Ella Shohat and Robert Stam, *Unthinking Eurocentrism: Multiculturalism and the Media* (New York: Routledge, 1994), 140. I must also give credit to Higgins for inspiring the formulation of this chapter.

6. Edward Said, *Orientalism: Western Conceptions of the Orient* (New York: Penguin Books, 1991; originally published 1978), 7.

7. Daniel Defoe, *Robinson Crusoe* (New York: Penguin Books, 2003; originally published 1719), 160.

8. *Blood Diamond*, DVD, directed by Edward Zwick (Burbank, CA: Warner Home Video, 2007). All subsequent quotations are taken from this DVD.

9. *Ezra*, DVD, directed by Newton Aduaka (San Francisco: California Newsreel, 2007).

10. Manthia Diawara, *African Cinema: Politics and Culture* (Bloomington: Indiana University Press, 1992).

11. Shohat and Stam, *Unthinking Eurocentrism*, 201–2.

12. The RUF was formed as early as the 1980s in response to the All Peoples Congress and the regimes of Siaka Stevens (1968–85) and his successor Joseph Momoh

(1985–91). Fighters were trained in Libya along with Liberian forces that included Charles Taylor. They first gained battle experience in the Liberian conflict, beginning in 1989, before launching their push for territorial control in Sierra Leone. See Paul Richards, "War as Smoke and Mirrors: Sierra Leone 1991–2, 1994–5, 1995–6," *Anthropological Quarterly* 78, no. 2 (2005): 377–402; J. Anyu Ndumbe, "Diamonds, Ethnicity, and Power: The Case of Sierra Leone," *Mediterranean Quarterly* 12, no. 4 (2001): 90–105; Yekutiel Gershoni, "War without End and an End to a War: The Prolonged Wars in Liberia and Sierra Leone," *African Studies Review* 40, no. 3 (1997): 55–76, for more in-depth analysis of the earliest phases of the civil war.

13. Collins undoubtedly has resonance in the American psyche as a humanitarian, due to his most recent role in the television miniseries, *7th Heaven*, in which he played a clergyman, do-gooder, and family man.

14. Foday Sankoh and his rebels first advocated a quasi Marxist/Pan-Africanist revolutionary model that pushed for democracy as a source of "equal opportunity and access to power to create wealth through free trade, commerce, agriculture, industry, science and technology," as quoted in Elizabeth M Evenson, "Truth and Justice in Sierra Leone: Coordination between Commission and Court," *Columbia Law Review* 104, no. 3 (2004): 734. It is universally agreed that Sankoh was influenced by the Pan-Africanist, anti-West sentiments of Muammar Qaddafi, who saw himself as the inheritor of Nkrumah, and by the megalomania of Charles Taylor in his bid for control of Liberia. The RUF initially garnered support among those disaffected due to governmental policy, who saw within the movement a chance to redress the unbalanced exploitation of the country's resources. Yet this was not done in the subsequent history of the movement, as it quickly dissolved into a war of greed over the control of diamond mining areas and into the use of the civilian population to service the RUF's needs: see Richards, "War as Smoke and Mirrors"; and Gershoni, "War without End and an End to a War."

15. Shohat and Stam, *Unthinking Eurocentrism*, 104.

16. Wendy S. Hesford, "Documenting Violations: Rhetorical Witnessing and the Spectacle of Distant Suffering," *Biography* 27, no. 1 (2004): 108.

17. John C. Eisele, "The Wild East: Deconstructing the Language of Genre in the Hollywood Eastern," *Cinema Journal* 41, no. 4 (2002): 70.

18. Ibid., 73–77.

19. Stuart Hall, "The Whites of Their Eyes: Racist Ideologies and the Media," in *Silver Linings: Some Strategies for the Eighties*," ed. Georges Bridges and Rosalind Brundt (London: Lawrence & Wishart, 1981), 40.

20. Ishmael Beah, *A Long Way Gone: Memoirs of a Boy Soldier* (New York: Farrar, Straus and Giroux, 2007), 121.

21. Richards, "War as Smoke and Mirrors," 394.

22. Ndumbe, "Diamonds, Ethnicity, and Power," 99–105; Gershoni, "War without End and an End to a War," 55–76.

23. Richards, "War as Smoke and Mirrors.," 394–97.

24. The RUF was aided by nationals from Liberia, Burkina Faso, The Gambia, Guinea, Belgium, Israel, Kenya, the Netherlands, Russia, South Africa, Tajikistan, Ukraine, and the United States. See Ndumbe, "Diamonds, Ethnicity, and Power," 99–100.

25. Shohat and Stam, *Unthinking Eurocentrism*, 209.

26. Evenson, "Truth and Justice in Sierra Leone," 736.

27. Beah, *A Long Way Gone*, 203.

28. Abena Busia, "Silencing Sycorax: On African Colonial Discourse and the Unvoiced Female," *Cultural Critique* 14 (1989–90): 89.

29. Ania Loomba, "Seizing the Book," in Ania Loomba, *Gender, Race, Renaissance Drama* (New York: Manchester University Press, 1989), 156–58.

30. Stephanie Athey and Daniel Cooper Alarcón, "Oroonoko's Gendered Economies of Honor/Horror: Reframing Colonial Discourse Studies in the Americas," *American Literature* 65, no. 3 (1993): 421–22.

31. Shohat and Stam, *Unthinking Eurocentrism*, 200.

32. The Hegelian master/slave dialectic is predicated on a mythic construct in which two self-consciousnesses meet. In a fatal duel, one (the master) achieves victory over the other (the slave), as the other voluntarily sublates himself because of his fear of death. The slave longs for recognition by the master and the master cannot exist without the recognition of the slave. See *Hegel's Phenomenology of Spirit: Selections*, trans. Howard P. Kainz (University Park: Pennsylvania State University Press, 1994).

33. See Lola Young, who examines how these binaries function in the imagining and visual representation of the black subject. Lola Young, *Fear of the Dark: "Race," Gender and Sexuality in the Cinema* (New York: Routledge, 1996), 43. See also David Hume, *Essays, Moral, Political, and Literary*, ed. Eugene F. Miller. Library of Economics and Liberty, 1987, http://www.econlib.org/library/LFBooks/Hume/hmMPL21.html), originally published 1741; and Immanuel Kant, *Observations on the Feeling of the Beautiful and Sublime*, trans. John T. Goldthwait (Berkeley: University of California Press, 1960; originally published 1764), for examples of the way in which racist concepts were naturalized in Enlightenment discourse.

34. Donald Bogle explores the ways in which these stereotypes were simultaneously employed in Hollywood films and subverted by the actors who played them. Donald Bogle, *Toms, Coons, Mulattoes, Mammies, and Bucks: An Interpretive History of Blacks in American Films* (New York: Continuum, 1995).

35. The principles agreed to in the May 2000 Kimberley conference include the following: (1) the importance of establishing a global certification process for diamonds; (2) the need for a formal code of conduct to govern the practices of the industry, producing states, and marketing centers; (3) the creation of an independent monitoring agency to supervise the implementation of the certification scheme and the code of conduct; and (4) the establishment of a working group to make recommendations on specific mechanisms for implementing these agreements. A certification of origin specifying where a diamond was last exported from was later added to the resolutions, as well as a ban by G8 members on the importation of diamonds from conflict zones. See Ndumbe, "Diamonds, Ethnicity, and Power," 102.

36. Higgins, "Human Rights in Hollywood's Africa," 5.

37. Gayatri Spivak, "Can the Subaltern Speak? In *Colonial Discourse and Post-Colonial Theory: A Reader*, ed. Patrick Williams and Laura Chrisman (New York: Columbia University Press, 1994), 66–111.

38. Arturo Arias, "Conjunctions, Disjunctions: Similar Goals, Contradictory Strategies," *Modern Fiction Studies* 46, no. 4 (2000): 1018.

39. Alcinda Honwana, *Child Soldiers in Africa* (Philadelphia: University of Pennsylvania Press. 2006), 46.

40. Further, Richards speaks of the ways in which the first inductees into the RUF were viewed as "witch children," initiated as if into the secret Poro society. Families disowned them, and they were routinely killed by government troops at the instigation of the locals because they were seen as irrevocably damaged and, as a result, would continue to behave like enemies and spies in their home territories. See Richards, "War as Smoke and Mirrors," 385–88.

41. Richards, "War as Smoke and Mirrors," 385–86.

42. William P. Murphy, "Military Patrimonialism and Child Soldier Clientism in the Liberian and Sierra Leonean Civil War," *African Studies Review* 46, no. 2 (2003): 61–65.

43. Honwana, *Child Soldiers in Africa*, 44.

44. In my conversation with Newton Aduaka, he stated that he was given the text by former soldiers inducted into the RUF, and that it is an almost verbatim representation of the indoctrination process (African Literature Association Conference, April 26, 2008).

45. Murphy, "Military Patrimonialism," 64.

46. See Frantz Fanon, *The Wretched of the Earth*, trans. Constance Farrington (New York: Grove, 1991).

47. Murphy, "Military Patrimonialism," 64.

48. Ibid.

49. Ibid.

50. Beah, *A Long Way Gone*, 108.

51. Ibid., 112.

52. Honwana, *Child Soldiers in Africa*, 70–71.

53. Ibid., 70–73.

54. Although Aduaka never explicitly names Sierra Leone and Liberia in the film, it is obvious that they are his points of inspiration. Even the induction of the children points to these countries, as Ezra and his friends were kidnapped, but Miriam joins the struggle as the daughter of a revolutionary journalist from a neighboring country.

55. It must be noted that, at this stage, Ezra believes that the enemy faction attacked his village.

56. The verse is influenced by the Biblical passage John 14:2–3: "Do not let your hearts be troubled. Trust in God; trust also in me. In my Father's house are many rooms; if it were not so I would have told you. I am going there to prepare a place for you. And if I go and prepare a place for you, I will come back and take you to be with me that you also may be where I am." See Nasio Fontaine, *Living in the Positive*, Sanctuary/RAS compact disc B0002XMF12.

57. Honwana, *Child Soldiers in Africa*, 71–72.

58. Beah, *A Long Way Gone*, 121–22.

59. Ibid., 144.

60. Ibid., 125.

61. Hesford, "Documenting Violations," 107.

62. Kimberly Nance, "Disarming Testimony: Speakers' Resistance to Readers' Defenses in Latin American *Testimonio*," *Biography* 24, no. 3 (2001): 572.

63. The controversy is well documented on the Internet. I found the following article quite illuminating with regard to problems with the text: Clarence Roy-Macaulay, "Ex-boy Soldier Back in Sierra Leone," *Seattle Times*, May 21, 2008, http://seattletimes.nwsource.com/html/entertainment/2004429288_apsierraleonebeah.html.

64. This must be contrasted with Richards's article, which tells how these children were deliberately exterminated as they were seen as threats to the society: see Richards, "War as Smoke and Mirrors." In the aftermath of the war, Sierra Leoneans adopted war orphans, which contrasts sharply with the reaction of nationals from other countries facing the same issue. See Richard Wilson, "Children and War in Sierra Leone: A West African Diary," *Anthropology* 17, no. 5 (2001): 20–22.

65. Evenson, examines the policies set by various truth commissions. Evenson, "Truth and Justice in Sierra Leone," 730–67.

66. See Gershoni, who analyzes the way in which the wars in Sierra Leone and Liberia were prolonged due to the unwillingness of the United States to intervene in these domestic theaters; the inability of the UN and OAU to deploy effective peacekeeping strategies; the failure of ECOWAS to broker a lasting accord with Charles Taylor; and the corruption of ECOMOG forces, whose acronym came to stand for "Every Commodity or Movable Object Gone." Gershoni, "War without End and an End to a War."

67. The Lomé Peace Accord of 1999 also established a TRC, with the mandate "to address impunity, break the cycle of violence, provide a forum for both the victims and perpetrators of human rights violations to tell their story, [and] get a clear picture of the past in order to facilitate genuine healing and reconciliation." See Evenson, "Truth and Justice in Sierra Leone," 737.

68. Mbembe, *On the Postcolony*, 7.

69. Evenson, "Truth and Justice in Sierra Leone," 741.

70. Wilson was one of the international members who drafted the TRC process. He writes about the universal consensus in regard to the role of children. Of primary consideration was guarding the confidentiality of the children and lessening the sensationalism surrounding their roles in the war. Hence, it was agreed that private statements instead of public confessions were to be taken. If the children did not testify, they were allowed to draw, or to give dramatic enactments of their roles in the war. No attempt was to be made to get them to ask for forgiveness or to be publicly shamed. See Wilson, "Children and War in Sierra Leone," 22.

71. Toni Morrison, "Unspeakable Things Unspoken: The Afro-American Presence in American Literature," in *Within the Circle: An Anthology of African American Literary Criticism from the Harlem Renaissance to the Present*, ed. Angelyn Mitchell (Durham, NC: Duke University Press, 1994), 368–98.

72. ÁJA is a dub poet and social activist from Barbados, who has become a United Nations Development Program (UNDP) spokesman for peace. His work stands as testament to the issues facing Sierra Leone as it rebuilds and grows.

73. See primary sources, such as David Hume, *Essays, Moral, Political, and Literary*; Kant, *Observations on the Feeling of the Beautiful and Sublime*; Thomas Jefferson, *Notes on the State of Virginia* (Chapel Hill: University of North Carolina Press, 1995); and Georg Wilhelm Friedrich Hegel, *The Philosophy of History*, trans. J. Sibree (New York: Dover, 1956). Each of these authors questions the mental capacities of African peoples; Jefferson states categorically that blacks are mentally inferior to whites. Secondary sources include Robert J. C. Young *Colonial Desire: Hybridity in Theory, Culture and Race* (New York: Routledge, 1996), who examines how Enlightenment theories on race affected colonial discourse; and Louis Sala-Molinas, *Dark Side of the Light: Slavery and the French Enlightenment*, trans. John Conteh-Morgan (Minneapolis: University of

Minnesota Press, 2006), who examines the paradoxes in Enlightenment discourse with regard to transatlantic slavery.

74. Adisa Andwele, *Don't Let Me Die* (St. Philip and St. Michael, Barbados: ÁJA Productions and Acute Vision, 2005), 6.

75. Hesford, "Documenting Violations," 106.

76. Mbembe, *On the Postcolony*, 2.

77. Andwele, *Don't Let Me Die*, 12.

78. ÁJA traveled to Jamaica, Haiti, Sierra Leone, South Africa, and Palestine. He explained that he appealed to Virgin Airlines to help him in his journey. Therefore, his destinations were predetermined by the countries they serviced.

79. Andwele, "Nutten Can Prepare Yuh Fuh This," in *Don't Let Me Die*, 50. It must be noted that this poem was written in response to a picture taken in Haiti, depicting food vendors surrounded by a mountain of garbage. "Victim of Heritage," 22; "Legacy of Poverty," 32; "Nutten Can Prepare Yuh Fuh This," 50; and "Poor People Dead," 68 are reprinted from *Don't Let Me Die* (St. Philip and St. Michael, Barbados: ÁJA Productions and Acute Vision, 2005), with the permission of the author and publisher, Adisa Andwele (ÁJA).

80. During ÁJA's presentation of the material on April 4, 2008, he told his audience that when he came upon this child, he did not know that he was carrying only a toy gun, and he expressed his surprise and relief that it was not real. The image is from South Africa.

81. Andwele, "Victim of Heritage," in *Don't Let Me Die*, 22.

82. Hesford, "Documenting Violations," 117.

83. Andwele, "Legacy of Poverty," in *Don't Let Me Die*, 32.

84. Young, *Fear of the Dark*, 53.

85. Andwele, "Poor People Dead," in *Don't Let Me Die*, 68.

86. Andwele, *Don't Let Me Die*, 13.

Part Four

The Duty to Remember

11

(Re)Writing the Massacre of Thiaroye

Sabrina Parent

Introduction

Over the past sixty years, West African writers have continuously examined the massacre of Thiaroye, a violent reprisal inflicted by the French army on its African soldiers.[1] While the French cultural discourse remains silent on the event, the meaning of Thiaroye continues to be explored by West African artists. Generally speaking, the present chapter is concerned with the multiple literary (re)writings of a historical event. More specifically, it argues that the various interpretations of Thiaroye are not univocal and that they depend on each author's critical intentions and sociopolitical agenda. In order to provide support for this argument, the content and the form of various works are closely analyzed and related to their historical contexts of production.

At dawn on December 1, 1944, the French army opened fire on West African *tirailleurs* repatriated in the Thiaroye camp on the outskirts of Dakar. Although figures may vary from source to source, sociology professor Armelle Mabon speaks of twenty-four infantrymen killed, eleven dead as a result of their injuries, thirty-five wounded, and forty-five imprisoned mutineers.[2] Naked force was the only response provided by France to the soldiers' legitimate demands for pay. For the most part, the contingent of 1,280 men stationed in Thiaroye, according to historian Myron Echenberg, consisted of "ex-prisoners of war . . . held in German camps from the collapse of France in June 1940, until the Liberation in the summer and fall of 1944."[3]

As a sign of gratitude for their participation in the conflict, de Gaulle discharged soldiers of African origins before the war ended.[4] Demobilized and sent to transit camps first in France and then in Senegal,[5] the infantrymen logically expected to receive the same treatment as their French comrades, that is, the payment of back pay, war allowances, and demobilization bonuses by the French authorities. In France, under various pretexts, their complaints had been dismissed. French journalist Yves Bénot adds that "They were promised that everything would be done in Senegal. Yet, there, nothing was being done either."[6] In Thiaroye, they just received an order to go back to their remote African villages. As a result, the infantrymen protested, demonstrated, and "went as far as to capture General Dagnan [the Commanding General of Dakar and the region] and hold him prisoner for a few hours,"[7] until Dagnan promised they would receive the monetary compensation that was due to them.

Despite the legitimacy of the African soldiers' claims, the French colonial authorities ignored them from the outset, on the grounds that these claims came from soldiers who, according to an officer in charge, "by arrogance, vanity or jealousy [dared to demand] a status identical to the French."[8] Obviously, the French military authorities were not ready to cope with the demands for *égalité* coming from colonial subjects, even though these same subjects had defended French territory and fought, along with French soldiers, against the Nazis and their racist ideology. In fact, the French seem to have feared a more global "black uprising" and wanted to make Thiaroye "an object lesson."[9] The deployment of armed violence against soldiers who were deprived of weapons tends to confirm that Thiaroye was meant, as Bénot suggests, to be an example of "preventive repression."[10]

To my knowledge, the massacre of Thiaroye has not been, totally or even in part, the subject of any French artistic representations, as if this event has completely disappeared from France's collective memory. Although some French historians and journalists have mentioned and analyzed Thiaroye as an episode that reveals the darkest side of French colonial history, French cultural discourse remains silent on this particular event.

However, over the past sixty years, West African artists have continuously provided representations of the massacre: the Senegalese poet-president Léopold Sédar Senghor wrote a poem, "Tyaroye,"[11] in 1944, a few days after the events took place; the Guinean artist Fodeba Keita wrote and staged a narrative poem, "Aube africaine,"[12] in 1957; the Senegalese writer Boubacar Boris Diop published a play, *Thiaroye terre rouge*, in 1981;[13] an author of Malian origins, Doumbi-Fakoly, published a novel, *Morts pour la France*;[14] in 1987, Senegalese filmmakers Sembene Ousmane and Thierno Faty Sow directed a film, *Camp de Thiaroye*, in 1987;[15] a French director of Algerian origin, Rachid Bouchareb, created a short animated movie, *L'Ami y'a bon*, in 2004;[16] and the Senegalese author Cheikh Faty Faye published a play, *Aube de sang*, in 2005.[17] A first look at the list indicates that the works were produced before the independence of Senegal in 1960 (Senghor and Keita), twenty to twenty-five years after independence (Diop, Doumbi-Fakoly, and Sembene Ousmane), or quite recently, in the so-called new era of globalization (Bouchareb and Faye).

In this chapter, three of these works are closely examined, each of them belonging to a different historical moment: Senghor's poem, "Tyaroye"; Diop's play, *Thiaroye terre rouge;* and Faye's play, *Aube de sang*. The main relevant stylistic, textual, and rhetorical strategies utilized in the works will be discussed, in order to assess how each author represents the past event according to his contemporary context of production.

Senghor's Thiaroye: The Myth of Resistance and the Prototype of Sacrifice

"Tyaroye"[18] belongs to Senghor's collection of poems, *Hosties noires*. Written between 1936 and 1945, the collection was only published in 1948. It is a transitional book in the sense that its period of composition corresponds in Senghor's life to his passage from an intellectual awareness embodied in the concept of Négritude—a celebration of "blackness" that he developed along with Aimé Césaire and Léon-Gontran Damas in the 1930s[19]—to more pragmatic and concrete ways of *acting* in the world. Senghor began his political career in 1945 when he and Lamine Guèye were elected as deputies to the French constituent assembly. During all these years, Senghor did not dream of an independent Senegal but envisioned "a French Union based on equality and free consent."[20] He hoped that France would be willing to grant full citizenship to the overseas populations of its empire on the basis that they had actively participated in the war effort.

The collection *Hosties noires* is oriented toward a French audience, whom Senghor wanted to convince of the worthiness of his political ideas. This required a delicate touch in 1948 in the aftermath of the Liberation, when the prevailing, even exclusive, discourse was one that promoted the Resistance network. The historian Marc Michel[21] argues that Senghor, in a very subtle way, set up the *tirailleurs sénégalais* who participated in World War II as figures belonging to the Resistance movement in order to insert them into the collective memory of the French people. Michel also notes that one of the means used by Senghor to achieve his goal was to resort to the theme of sacrifice, as confirmed by the title of the collection, which can be translated as "Black Hosts." The English translation of the title, by Melville Dixon, literally translates the French *Hosties noires*, both versions referring to the consecrated communion wafer. This symbolizes Christ's body and represents the life he sacrificed for humanity. In the same way, the *tirailleurs sénégalais* are (black) sacrifices for France.

Considering the overall tone of *Hosties noires*, the poem "Tyaroye" may at first sound out of tune, since it is devoted to soldiers who, from a French perspective, were not heroes at all, but mutineers, rebels against French authority. However, Senghor succeeds in transforming the rebellious infantrymen of Thiaroye into the heroes of a just cause by choosing poetry as his vessel, in order to evoke, rather than describe, the events that took place.

According to Marc Dominicy, a cognitive linguist, the evocation of a prototype, as opposed to the episodic representation created by detailed descriptions and narratives, prevails in poetry, because of parallelisms and repetitions found at different levels of the language code (phonemes, syllables, syntax, semantics, and so forth). These parallelisms prevent readers from constructing a detailed picture of what happened, conveying instead a prototypical image that is stored in the long-term memory.[22] In Senghor's poem, repetitions of words ("prisoners," repeated twice in line 1 of the English translation; "blood," repeated three times in line 10; "our," repeated three times in lines 21–22)[23] and syntactical structures ("is it true," repeated three times in the first stanza; "you have not died in vain" and "you are the witnesses of," each repeated twice in the last stanza)[24] are examples, among others,[25] of parallelisms. These favor, according to Dominicy's theory, the construction of a prototypical representation of the event. This process goes along with another strategy, that of blurring the circumstances of the massacre.

Except for the place and date, Senghor mentions no other relevant details in the poem. For a broad French audience not already familiar with what happened, it is impossible to grasp, from the poem only, that Thiaroye is synonymous with rebellion. That essential aspect is kept silent. Instead, the poet emphasizes in the first stanza what makes Thiaroye an unfair reprisal or, better said, an unjust event. If France is in effect blamed, the reasons for this remain vague and are not developed into specific details: "is it true / That France is no longer France?" (lines 1–2).[26] Moreover, the use and repetition of the question mode tends to attenuate the strength of the accusation while accentuating the poet's disbelief and dismay.

These textual (generic) and stylistic strategies transform the *tirailleurs* of Thiaroye into victims and Thiaroye itself into the prototype of a sacrifice. The structure of the poem itself reflects the process that leads to complete purification. The first stanza, by the repetition of the question mark and the same syntactical phrase ("is it true"),[27] displays incredulity and a total lack of rational comprehension of what happened. The second stanza depicts the emotional ("anguish," line 12)[28] and even corporeal ("sweat," line 12)[29] impact of the events on the poet, whereas in the last stanza a reinterpretation of what happened is taking place, which reinserts the atrocity into a more adequate system of beliefs: "No, you have not died in vain. / . . . / You are the witnesses of the new world to come" (lines 23 and 25).[30] In Senghor's vision of the world, Thiaroye is interpreted as a step toward the purification of the "white race" in the hope of creating a new civilization in which the criterion of humaneness would supersede the notion of race. Thiaroye is explained as necessary for the coming of the famous *civilisation de l'universel*, or the dream of a society based on fraternal relationships between Western and African peoples, that would eventually overcome any bias about each other and take the best from what each has to offer to the other.

Diop's *Thiaroye*: A Reflection on Rebellion and Treason

Twenty years after the independence of Senegal, the play by Diop, more noticeably than the poem by Senghor, denounces the French colonizer. The play focuses on aspects of the story that Senghor did not develop: an *uprising* that was savagely *suppressed* by the French military. Unlike Senghor, Diop clearly presents the injustice and the barbarism of the authorities and does so by presenting to the audience two points of view concerning the events: the French point of view and the African.

On the French side, the prevailing representation is a pitiful one of colonizers who, without exception, are cruel, immoral, and perverted. The characters are stereotypes of racist individuals who have a strong sense of hierarchy regarding races and civilizations. On the African side, the idea arises that a just and fair armed struggle is a relevant concept, mainly because dialogue with colonizers is impossible and doomed to fail, given the fact that the French do not keep their promises and that they have lost their sense of honor.

The play may initially appear to be adopting a Manichean perspective: the Colonizer on the evil side and the Colonized on the good side. Two elements qualify this judgment and transform the apparent Manicheism into a textual strategy that consists of inviting the audience to challenge preconceived opinions and to consider the complexity and the paradoxes of the (neo)colonial situation. The first element concerns the depiction of Africans.

The play stresses the fact, for instance, that colonization was not disadvantageous to all strata of African society, but rather had the effect of reinforcing structures based on social inequalities existing in traditional communities well before colonization. The play also suggests that the failure of the uprising was due to a betrayal from the African side. The figure of the traitor is actually embodied in different characters, all of them African. If the play clearly denounces the French and the desire for gain that led them to immoral behavior, *Thiaroye terre rouge* is also an African autocritique in which the author, without necessarily providing answers, raises the painful issue of Africans' own involvement in the misery of (neo)colonialism. In order to do this, Diop uses yet another device, delegating authorship of the play to a fictional character.

The play was actually published in the same volume as a novel by Diop, *Le Temps de Tamango*. As the scholar Fredric Michelman argues, this is no coincidence.[31] Michelman notes that in the fictional world of the novel, the play was written between 1960 and 1970 by N'Dongo, a character who, besides being a chemist and writer, is an opponent of the regime that follows the independence of an unidentified African country. Michelman also points out that N'Dongo's *nom de guerre* is Tamango, a name he has chosen in remembrance of a character in the eponymous short story by the nineteenth-century French writer Prosper Mérimée. Tamango is famous for being a cruel slave trader who eventually becomes a slave himself:

> Tamango led a successful slave revolt at sea, but having killed the entire European crew, he realized that neither he nor his fellow rebels knew how to control the vessel or where to go with it. Sole survivor of the inevitable disaster that followed . . . he was rescued and brought to Jamaica where . . . he died . . . probably as the result of health problems created by heavy drinking.[32]

Michelman therefore suggests that choosing Tamango as his *nom de guerre* means for N'Dongo questioning not only his own legitimacy as a revolutionary but also, and more fundamentally, questioning the validity of revolution itself, considering the outcome of Tamango's revolt. Consequently, the play by N'Dongo/Diop conveys another tone: less Manichean than it may appear to be at first sight, it also sounds more dubious, not only about the achievements of the *tirailleurs*, however righteous their battle, but also about the achievements of African independence.

Faye's Thiaroye: Understanding the Perpetrator's Psyche

Published in 2005, Faye's play is the most recent representation of Thiaroye analyzed in this chapter. The event at Thiaroye is described by one of the characters, Le Mossi, in terms of the "logic" of repression.[33] While Thiaroye may be an example of the violent suppression of mutinies, it is more particularly an emblematic example demonstrating the logic of the colonial system. In the foreword to the play, the author states that Thiaroye is "one of the many humiliations done to Africa by colonization."[34] Faye blames the historical machinery (of "colonization") instead of particular nations, as he does not refer to any specific countries. He therefore insists on abstract historical forces shaping the destiny of particular continents or countries, and on dividing the world's population between the Colonized on the one hand and the Colonizer on the other—both of these, in a way, "victims" of their times. The binary opposition, Colonizer/Colonized, however, is deconstructed in two different ways. First, the binary pair is challenged to the extent that it appears not as absolute but as anchored in historical circumstances that can transform the Colonizer of yesterday into the Colonized of today. Second, the dichotomy is deconstructed in a further way because the author is convinced, as we shall see, that men can learn something from history and its hazardous forces, and build a new type of society.

Like Diop, Faye presents the viewpoints of both the African soldiers and the French authorities, and shows how these two forces oppose each other, to the point where a violent response from the stronger becomes inevitable. Yet the play goes beyond the simple representation of the two sides, since the *tirailleurs* go so far as to be concerned with the "white" psyche and wish to grasp the motives behind the whites' behavior. Via a device that resembles a maieutic dialogue—a dialogue from which the truth eventually emerges— the soldiers finally point to the logic of colonial thinking: that the colonizers need to maintain an indisputable position of power.[35] If they fail to do so, and the colonized see their failure, the colonizers' solution to the problem, to restore their initial authority, will most likely be to get rid of the embarrassing witnesses. Because the soldiers of Thiaroye had witnessed France's defeat in 1940, and because in Thiaroye they were objecting to the "double standard that France applies to her soldiers,"[36] it became necessary to silence them.

Underscoring the French authorities' position does not indicate a desire to condemn the French people. It must rather be understood in the context of forgiveness and true cooperation between peoples, which is an issue Faye feels very strongly about. Faye's play belongs to a specific interpretative stage. Sixty years after Thiaroye, and forty-five years after independence and supposedly the end of colonization, the event at Thiaroye can be approached with less passion and more serenity by a writer coming from a region of the world that had formerly been colonized. The play is, indeed, less a play "against," like B. B. Diop's, in which the African characters display legitimate anger, than it is a play "for," in which the African characters believe that "history teaches us that those who oppress always end up losing,"[37] and that the Africans are able to overcome their rage to the benefit of a greater understanding between peoples. On the cover of his published play, Faye, who is also a history professor, states that "By duty of memory, we owe it to our peoples to provide responses to these powerful questions [on colonization] in order to build between peoples solid relationships of cooperation."[38] In his reference to "peoples" and "relationships of cooperation," Faye certainly includes the French people. His play is therefore meant to overcome the injuries of the past by allowing Thiaroye to become a historical moment, able to teach us a lesson about blatant injustice and magnanimous forgiveness.

Conclusion

Belonging to the past, the massacre of Thiaroye remains in the field of Senegalese literature an event open to interpretation. In fact, it is a "site of memory"[39] for Africans, an event that writers revisit and engage with from the perspective and vantage point of their own historical situation. Because Léopold Sédar Senghor, when he wrote his poem, envisioned that Senegal would be part of the French Union under French authority, his text aims to include the event in the discourse of the French Resistance. The play by Boubacar Boris Diop, *Thiaroye terre rouge*, was published a year after Senghor resigned from his position as president of Senegal in 1980. Diop's play, by examining the reasons why the rebellion of Thiaroye was a failure, is meant to reflect on the responsibility of Africans themselves in the construction of neocolonial ties. In Cheikh Faty Faye's play, Thiaroye is the means to reconsider and revaluate the colonialists' past mistakes and motivations in order for Africans to forgive them and move forward.

The fact that the interpretation of what happened in Thiaroye remains not only open but alive (considering the continuous production of cultural works over the past sixty years) proves that, for the Senegalese population, Thiaroye was a traumatic event. It is an event that points to the atrocities committed by the colonizers as much as to the ambiguities experienced by the *tirailleurs*, the "Empire's black watchdogs"[40] who eventually rebelled against the empire in Thiaroye.

Notes

1. This chapter is based on various chapters of my PhD dissertation: Sabrina Parent, "West African Representations of World War II: (Re)Writing the Massacre of Thiaroye," University of Texas at Austin, 2008. I would like to thank Dina Sherzer, Chay Baker, and Hetty ter Haar, coeditor of this volume, for their insightful comments, which helped me improve these pages.

2. Armelle Mabon, "La tragédie de Thiaroye, symbole du déni d'égalité," *Hommes et migrations* 1235 (2002): 90.

3. Myron J. Echenberg, "Tragedy at Thiaroye: The Senegalese Soldiers' Uprising of 1944," in *African Labor History*, ed. Peter C. W. Gutkind, Robin Cohen, and Jean Copans (Beverly Hills, CA: Sage, 1978), 109.

4. The discharge is, however, given another interpretation by French historian Bernard Mouralis, who suggests that "this 'whitening' of the Free French Forces troops responded to a twofold concern: to give back to the metropolis the role that should always have been its own [in the Liberation of the French territory] and to integrate into the regular forces the Resistance, which the provisional government wanted to control as rapidly as possible" (ce 'blanchissement' des troupes des Forces Françaises Libres répondait au double souci de redonner à la métropole le rôle qui aurait toujours dû être le sien et d'intégrer dans les forces régulières les maquis que le Gouvernement provisoire souhaitait contrôler le plus rapidement possible). Bernard Mouralis, *République et colonies. Entre mémoire et histoire: la République française et l'Afrique* (Paris: Présence africaine, 1999), 226. All translations from French to English are mine, unless otherwise noted.

5. They reached Senegal on November 21, 1944.
6. Yves Bénot, *Massacres coloniaux 1944–1950: La IVe République et la mise au pas des colonies françaises* (Paris: La Découverte, 1994), 77.
7. Echenberg, "Tragedy at Thiaroye," 116.
8. In the original French, "par orgueil, vanité ou jalousie ... un statut identique à celui des Français": these were the words of a French officer reporting on the massacre, quoted in Charles Onana, *La France et ses tirailleurs: Enquête sur les combattants de la République 1939–2003* (Paris: Duboiris, 2003), 130.
9. Janet G. Vaillant, *Black, French, and African: A Life of Léopold Sédar Senghor* (Cambridge, MA: Harvard University Press, 1990), 173.
10. In the original French, "répression préventive": see Bénot, *Massacres coloniaux*, 77.
11. Léopold Sédar Senghor, *Hosties noires* (Paris: Seuil, 1948), 77–78.
12. Keita Fodeba, *Réveil* 351 (1949): 3.
13. Boubacar Boris Diop, *Le temps de Tamango*, followed by *Thiaroye terre rouge* (Paris: L'Harmattan, 1981).
14. Doumbi-Fakoly, *Morts pour la France* (Paris: Karthala, 1983).
15. Ousmane Sembene and Thierno Faty Sow, writers and directors, *Camp de Thiaroye*, perf. Ibrahim Sane, Sigiri Bakara, Hamed Camara, Ismaila Cisse, and Ababacar Sy (Enaproc and Société nouvelle de promotion cinématographique, 1987).
16. Rachid Bouchareb, writer and director, *L'Ami y'a bon* (The Colonial Friend), prod. Jean Brénat (Tessalit Production, 2004).
http://www.tadrart.com/tessalit/lamiyabon/home.html (accessed October 5, 2008).
17. Cheikh Faty Faye, *Aube de sang* (Paris: L'Harmattan, 2005).
18. My analysis is based on a translated version of the poem in English: in Léopold Sédar Senghor, *The Collected Poetry: Léopold Sédar Senghor*, trans. Melvin Dixon (Charlottesville: University Press of Virginia, 1991), 354.
19. Mongo Beti, *Dictionnaire de la négritude* (Paris: L'Harmattan, 1989).
20. Vaillant, *Black, French, and African*, 206.
21. Marc Michel, "*Hosties noires* entre mémoire et reconnaissance," in *Léopold Sédar Senghor: Africanité–universalité*, ed. Jacques Girault and Bernard Lecherbonnier (Paris: L'Harmattan, 2002), 110.
22. Marc Dominicy, "Prolégomènes à une théorie générale de l'évocation," in *Sémantique textuelle et évocation*, ed. M. Vanhelleputte (Leuven, Belgium: Peeters, 1990), 9–37.
23. In the original French version, "prisonniers," repeated twice in line 1; "sang," repeated three times in line 12; "notre," repeated twice in line 23.
24. The phrase "est-ce (donc) vrai," repeated three times in the first stanza; "vous n'êtes pas morts gratuits" and "vous êtes les témoins," each repeated twice in the last stanza.
25. I have chosen repetitions that can be seen both in the English translation and in the original French version. Repetitions of phonemes would obviously have depended on the language that was used.
26. In the original French, "est-ce donc vrai que la France n'est plus la France?" (line 2).
27. In French, "est-ce (donc) vrai."

28. In French "angoisse" (line 14).

29. In French, "sueur" (line 14).

30. "Non, vous n'êtes pas morts gratuits. / . . . / Vous êtes les témoins parturitaires du monde nouveau / qui sera demain" (lines 25 and 27–28).

31. Fredric Michelman, "From Tamango to Thiaroye: The Revolution Back on Course?" *Research in African Literatures* 21 (1990): 59–65.

32. Ibid., 62–63.

33. The word "logique" is used in Faye, *Aube de sang*, 80.

34. In the original French, "une des humiliations faites à l'Afrique par la colonisation." Ibid.

35. "All colonization has one absolute necessity: that of maintaining the colonized in the condition of inferior human being in all matters relative to the colonizer, always strong. Thus, the defeat of May–June 1940 is a scathing disclaimer to French colonial claims. Accordingly, we infantrymen on the front lines of fire, and therefore eyewitnesses to the defeat, we appear as a bad conscience to the colonial truth. So within the colonizers' logical framework, we have to disappear." (Toute colonisation a une nécessité absolue: celle de maintenir le colonisé dans la condition d'homme inférieur à tout égard par rapport au colonisateur toujours fort. Aussi, la défaite de mai–juin 1940 est-elle un cinglant démenti aux affirmations coloniales françaises. En conséquence, nous les tirailleurs aux premières lignes du feu, donc témoins oculaires de la défaite, apparaissons comme mauvaise conscience pour la vérité coloniale. C'est donc dans le cadre logique de ces données qui sont les leurs qu'il faut que nous disparaissions.) Faye, *Aube de sang*, 79–80.

36. "S'agirait-il d'une politique de deux poids deux mesures que la France applique à l'égard de ses soldats?" Faye, *Aube de sang*, 29.

37. "L'histoire nous enseigne que ceux qui oppriment finissent toujours par perdre." Faye, *Aube de sang*, 83.

38. "Par devoir de mémoire, nous devons à nos peuples d'apporter des réponses à ces interrogations fortes pour mieux asseoir, entre les peuples, des relations solides de coopération." Faye, *Aube de sang*.

39. This notion, "lieu de mémoire," is borrowed from Pierre Nora, ed., *Les lieux de mémoire* (Paris: Gallimard, 1997), 23–43.

40. This expression is the literal translation of the French "les dogues noirs de l'Empire." It is extracted from the poem "Prayer for Peace" (Prière de paix). See Senghor, *The Collected Poetry of Léopold Sédar Senghor*, 72; and Senghor, in *Hosties noires*, 84.

12

In Search of Lost Kabyles in Mehdi Lallaoui's *La colline aux oliviers*

Aména Moïnfar

> Ce sont des âmes d'ancêtres qui nous occupent, substituant leur drame éternisé à notre juvénile attente, à notre patience d'orphelins ligotés à leur ombre de plus en plus pâle, cette ombre impossible à boire ou à déraciner.
>
> [We are busy with our forefathers' souls, subjecting their ongoing ordeal to our youthful expectations, our impatience that of orphans who are bound to these fading ancestral shadows, shadows you can neither drink nor uproot.]
>
> Kateb Yacine, Nedjma (1956).

Introduction: Forefathers' Souls

The first pages of Mehdi Lallaoui's *Kabyles du Pacifique,* on the subject of the deported Algerian Kabyles punished by the French for their uprising in 1871, incorporate this chapter's epigraph—a quotation from the famous twentieth-century Kabyle poet Kateb Yacine.[1] According to Patricia M. E. Lorcin, "The Berbers of Algeria comprise the Chaouia of the Aurès mountains in southeastern Algeria, the Kabyles (the largest group) of what is now known as Kabylia, the Mozabites of the Mzab in the northern Saharan region and the Tuareg of the central Sahara."[2] Lorcin adds that "Individual exceptions apart, all but the Mozabites are, like the Arabs, Sunni Muslims of the Maleki rite. They are distinguished from the Arabs by their culture and language, of which there are several dialects, but there are none the less Arabic-speaking Berbers and Berber areas, among the Chaouia for example, where Arabic culture has been absorbed into their own."[3] Kateb Yacine fought all his life for Algeria's diversity and, in particular, for the right of Kabyles to have their language recognized as one of the national languages.[4]

It is significant that Mehdi Lallaoui, a writer born and raised in France but nevertheless considered in France as "second generation of Algerian descent," pays tribute to Yacine by quoting from the latter's masterpiece, *Nedjma*.[5] Lallaoui thus acknowledges the place of the poet in his own intellectual journey to research, share, and publish the Kabyle experience within and outside Kabylia itself. The "forefathers' souls" contributed to shaping the destiny of many victims of and actors behind colonialism, and they occupy a crucial space in Lallaoui's works.[6] As with so many other contemporary writers belonging to a dual cultural heritage, Lallaoui's birth as a writer corresponded with and, one could even argue, was triggered by particular socioeconomic factors connected to colonialism.

This chapter will examine the way in which Lallaoui's second novel, *La colline aux oliviers* (The Olive Grove), revisits the concept of collective memory in relation to one of too many episodes of confrontation between France and Algeria.[7] The idea of collective memory in Lallaoui transcends geographical borders and is resurrected beyond these borders by the descendants of this collective memory. I will explain why it is that Lallaoui occupies a distinctive place in what is called Beur literature, that is, literature produced by French writers of North African descent. In the same vein as Richard Derderian's "Algeria as a *lieu de mémoire*: Ethnic Minority Memory and National Identity in Contemporary France,"[8] my analysis of the novel will also use Pierre Nora's concepts of *lieux de mémoire* (realms of memory) and how they engage in the *devoir de mémoire* (the duty to remember).[9] Before moving to the main argument of Lallaoui's innovative novel, I will first summarize the way in which the 1980s contributed to the presence of writers such as Lallaoui.

Indeed, the 1980s opened a decade of political and racial turmoil in France. First of all, the 1980 presidential election saw the socialist candidate François Mitterrand putting a momentary end to the conservative and mostly Gaullist power that had prevailed on the French political scene ever since the birth of the Fifth Republic in 1958.[10] Second, a new political party, le Front National, and its controversial leader, Jean-Marie Le Pen, came onto the political scene, shamelessly voicing racist comments that resonated with, and within, a particular sector of the French population.[11] The Front National's slogans resurrected the most abject colonial discourses on immigrants in general and on North Africans in particular. According to the French historian of immigration Gérard Noiriel, the appearance of the Front National gave birth to the third crisis of French xenophobia. In *Le creuset français,* Noiriel identifies the first two crises as corresponding respectively to the Dreyfus Affair in the 1890s, and the fascist discourse in the 1930s that led to the Vichy Regime.[12] Noiriel shows that these first two crises had appalling consequences: abject anti-Semitism, xenophobia, and homophobia that led to the deportation of Jews, homosexuals, Africans, and Roma people living in France.[13]

The third wave of xenophobia found fertile soil in the middle of the period of catastrophic unemployment that hit France after the 1973 oil crisis. Foreigners and North African immigrants in particular were blamed for taking away French citizens' jobs. The Front National brought these once off-the-record discourses into the national and public arena. Sadly, this xenophobic party not only found an audience but also found supporters for its limited and limiting doctrine on the French economic crisis.[14] Discourses against North Africans and foreigners in general had always been present in France. There was nothing new there. However, I would like to show that, if in the past the North African community had silenced itself or had been silenced into not protesting against racist discourse and practices, this time the children (born or raised in France) of this community could not and would not be silenced.[15]

In fact, during the 1980s a new wave of French literature erupted on the French literary scene. These writers were French citizens born or raised in France but were Muslims of North African origin, most of them of Algerian descent.[16] In *Voices from the North African Immigrant Community in France,* Alec G. Hargreaves explains that these writers were the children of Algerian, Moroccan, and Tunisian immigrants who had come to France to take jobs that French citizens did not want to do anymore. Their fathers had worked in mines, factories, and in subways, but

> until the 1950s, very few immigrant workers brought their wives and children with them from North Africa. When the Algerian war of independence broke out in 1954, there were only 6,000 families of Algerian origin in France.... A wave of Algerian families settled in France during the war of independence, carrying the total from 6,000 at its inception to 30,000 when the conflict ended in 1962.[17]

This influx of people remained invisible to the citizens of the French Republic. The vast majority of these families could afford only to live on the outskirts, in the *banlieues,* of major French cities.[18] Shantytowns (*bidonvilles*) and, later on, horrific subsidized public housing estates[19] for low-income families constituted the places to which the French Republic relegated these particular workers and their families.[20] Mothers and fathers from this community were for the most part illiterate and unaware of their legal rights. The French-Algerian war (1954–62) accentuated discrimination and resentment, and this increased especially after Algeria's independence in 1962. If the parents lacked the tools necessary to claim and affirm their presence on French soil through literature, their children turned to cultural media such as literature, music, especially rap, and urban art, such as graffiti and street theater.[21]

However, before this new literature, known as "Beur literature," emerged, a Francophone Algerian literature already existed.[22] Kateb Yacine's *Nedjma* is acknowledged as the first Francophone Algerian literary masterpiece, and Yacine is proclaimed as the first "serious" Francophone Algerian writer. In 1962, Assia Djebar published *Les enfants du nouveau monde* (Children of the New World).[23] Nevertheless, as Hargreaves demonstrates, it became quickly apparent that

> unlike the older generation of North African writers ... the Beurs have undergone their formative experiences as part of an ethnic minority within France, where they have shared through the family home in both the material disadvantages and the cultural traditions associated with first-generation immigrants. Beur authors have in this sense been the first to write from within the immigrant community itself.[24]

Writing in French from a localized Algerian standpoint is radically different from writing in French and coming from an ostracized community in France. The Beurs are French but unlike other children of immigrants, they experienced the same forms of racial, social, and judicial discrimination as their parents.[25]

In the passage quoted above, Hargreaves points out that the sense of self of these "second-generation" writers was molded within the "immigrant community itself," since French social practices put them into ethnic ghettos. Moreover, the French authorities deliberately emphasized the origins of these children in order to deny them their right to Frenchness. However, as Hargreaves underlines in *Multi-ethnic France*, their North African heritage was also "widely portrayed as a serious threat to French national identity and social cohesion."[26] Therefore,

> the central notion in political discourse about those minorities was the need for "integration." To the extent that "integration" was not proceeding at the desired speed, this was commonly blamed on the alleged inability or unwillingness of Muslims to adjust to the cultural norms dominant in France.[27]

On the one hand, as Hargreaves shows, what was seen by the French as the slowness of Muslims to integrate was seen by the Muslim community itself as prejudice from the French. On the other hand, Hargreaves is rightly critical of the fact that socioeconomic factors and discrimination were not taken into account in assessing the potential for the integration of the members of the second generation.

One could ask a simple rhetorical question: how is one to be integrated when one is born, raised, and educated in France itself? "Failure of integration" was an almost ontological view of the children of this community, whereas the true causes of the failure were mainly ignored, since in the 1980s France had been to a large extent a nation in denial, with many refusing to believe that immigrant minorities originating in former colonies in Africa and elsewhere could be incorporated into French society. Symptomatic of this conceptual blockage was the refusal to use terms which might appear to give recognition or legitimacy to immigrant minorities as structural parts of French society.[28]

What Hargreaves refers to as "the refusal to use terms" to reflect the reality, that these children were French citizens, gave birth to a linguistic phenomenon I will refer to as *citizenship euphemisms*. Terms such as "integrated" and "second generation" are applied only to these children of North Africans, and not, for instance, to the children of other immigrants. Noiriel emphasizes this unevenness by arguing that

in France, the expression "second generation" has only been widely used for the past ten years [since 1979]; it is applied essentially to the children of North African immigrants. . . . In fact, the expression "second generation" came from outside the realm of scholarship and has yet to receive a specific definition, which for some is reason enough to disqualify the concept.[29]

The term "second generation" carries an ambiguous and somewhat insulting connotation in French popular discourse, since it is *only* applied to one specific category in France's immigrant population. Conscious of this, Noiriel offers a more positive definition of "second generation," that it "designates individuals who have been exposed to a sociological process, to contradictory forms of socialization, at the crucial stage of fundamental acquisitions: childhood."[30]

Beur Literature(s)

The 1980s literature produced by the children of immigrants coincided with the first march for racial equality, orchestrated in 1983.[31] The children of Maghrebis called themselves "Beurs." Consequently, the novels they wrote came under the category "Beur literature," and according to Hargreaves,

They are part of the so-called "Beur" generation. Beur is a name popularly applied to the sons and daughters of North African immigrants. A longer-established label is that of "second-generation immigrants," but as most of those concerned were born in France, this is something of a misnomer, for they have never migrated from one country to another. In their daily lives the Beurs have, however, been compelled to migrate constantly between the secular culture of France and the traditions carried with them with their Muslim parents from across the Mediterranean.[32]

From 1980 to 1989, mostly male Beur writers published twenty-seven novels.[33] Hargreaves and Michel Laronde were among the first academics to offer a useful taxonomy of Beur literature.[34] Hargreaves in particular argues that the Beur novels of the first wave usually involve the following themes: the violence of the urban landscape and living conditions; racial discrimination and racist violence; and cultural conflicts triggered by the generational conflicts between parents and children.[35] Through the characters in their novels, the Beur writers underline the living conditions the North African community in France has experienced, such as moving from shantytowns to the subsidized housing estates located (always) on the outskirts of Paris or other major French cities (such as Lyon, as seen in Azouz Begag's *Le gone du Chaâba* [Shantytown Kid]).[36]

Poverty, drugs, and the lack of soothing green spaces mark the daily lives of the characters in these novels. In addition, of course, clashes with representatives of French official power are usually highly traumatic. Police violence, racism at school, and daily humiliations are emphasized. "Arab"-looking youths are always under suspicion but, more than that, are in constant danger. An encounter with the police leads most of the time to a deadly resolution. Like the Algerian during French colonial rule, the typical Beur protagonist quickly learns that he is always to be seen as both guilty and disposable by the French police. The police do not protect him but have *au contraire* his worst interests in mind.[37]

The 1980s Beur novels understandably, and sometimes inevitably, always incorporate a brutal *death* (if not several, as in the case of Nacer Kettane's *Le sourire de Brahim* [Brahim's Smile]) caused/provoked by the French police or racist French citizens.[38] The French police use brutality in their daily encounters with the Beurs in a manner comparable to the colonial practices demonstrated during France's presence in Algeria. In *Point kilométrique 190* (Milestone 190), Ahmed Kalouaz uses a real incident, involving a young French Algerian and four French Legion recruits, which led to the brutal killing of the young man.[39] Kalouaz imagines the last moments of the young French Algerian before, during, and after—we are in the presence of a voice talking to the reader from beyond the grave—his murder while he is on the Bordeaux-Vintimille train. Kalouaz uses newspaper clippings as well as news broadcasts to give voice to a person whose life was absurdly taken away. As a consequence, as is underlined by Mireille Rosello, "novels written by contemporary authors of Algerian origin often seek to remember the lives of individuals either swallowed by the ideological presuppositions of the colonial archive or later dismissed by the logic of official postindependence national histories."[40] Beur writers crystallize the ambivalent position of Beurs, whose cultural memory is rejected as much by the French as it is by the new Algerian authorities.

In Search of Lost Kabyles in Mehdi Lallaoui's La colline aux oliviers 247

I now analyze the way these writers cope with this dual (French *and* Algerian) amnesia in their fictional writings. The idea of an "amputated memory" is central to Beur novels. The Beur writers connect the reason for the presence of Algerian workers in France to France's colonial past. Algerian workers did not come to France overnight.[41] They came to work *for* France after having fought *for* France during World War II; sometimes the Algerian effort in World War I is even mentioned in Beur literature, for instance, by Lallaoui in *La colline aux oliviers.*

The corpus of books published between 1980 and 1998 also incorporates the Algerian war and the backlash against Algerians to which it led.[42] For instance, in Nacer Kettane's *Le sourire de Brahim,* the eponymous character Brahim loses his childhood and joie de vivre after his younger brother Kader is killed during the FLN (Front de Libération Nationale) demonstration in Paris on October 17, 1961.[43] Algerian workers left shantytowns that had relegated them to a hypocritically invisible position in French society. They demonstrated—peacefully—against racist police curfews imposed on them and against intense racial profiling of which they were the regular targets. However, the French police met their demands with violence. Hundreds of unarmed Algerians, for whom the whole purpose of the demonstration was to be peaceful and dignified, were killed, thrown into the Seine, while hundreds of others disappeared. The French press gave hardly any coverage to the demonstration and its aftermath. Like the Algerian war, the demonstration was amputated from French official memory but remained in the collective memory of the Algerian workers living in France.[44]

Le sourire de Brahim begins with the preparations for the FLN demonstration. The hope of the Algerian workers' community contrasts markedly with the disproportionate and violent response of the French government. Brahim's seven-year-old brother, Kader, is killed, a victim of "collateral damage." By starting his novel with so much violence, Kettane reclaims part of the amputated memory of the clashing French/Algerian relationship. Many other novels written by Beur writers allude to the demonstration as well: for example, Akli Tadjer's *Les ANI du "Tassali"* (The "Tassali's" NIA/Non Identified Arabs) mentions the "incident" that follows the return from Algeria of a young Beur called Omar, who has been endeavoring to find his "Algerianness."[45] Traveling on the ship *Tassali* from Algiers to Marseilles, Omar meets a gallery of lively characters, among them some older Algerian factory workers who remember the October "events." Tadjer goes even further in his novel *Le porteur de cartable,* showing a little boy helping his Algerian parents in their involvement with the FLN.[46] Mehdi Charef's *Le harki de Meriem* (Meriem's Harki) portrays not only the demonstration but also the lack of unity in the Algerian community in France: the "harkis" were Algerian collaborators working for France during the Algerian war.[47]

Most of the Beur novels involve a desire on the part of the Beur protagonist to connect with the parents' homeland. An idealization occurs, in which the protagonist has a firm hope of escaping the racial discrimination and disillusionment that he must face on an everyday basis in France. A *tourisme des racines*, or roots tourism, emerges in the mind of the protagonist, who fantasizes about his ancestral land. Unfortunately, most returns to the ancestral land result in complete disillusionment, as on the other side of the Mediterranean, the "Beur" is considered "French."[48] His presence appears to be clearly unwanted in Algeria. This double exclusion, this double sense of nonbelonging, is illustrated in, for instance, Ketane's *Le sourire de Brahim* and Tadjer's *Les ANI du "Tassali."*

In the Name of Memory

Mehdi Lallaoui's works differ from the conventions of Beur literature in important ways. First of all, Lallaoui's works have not been published by any major mainstream French publishers. In 1990, Lallaoui created the association Au nom de la mémoire (In the Name of Memory), with journalist Samia Messaouid and historian Benjamin Stora, in order to promote the publication of books and documentaries on the Algerian presence in France and the conflictual encounters between the French government (and population) and Algerian immigrants.[49] Lallaoui then transformed some of these documentaries into novels by incorporating the main topics of the documentaries as the central historical elements in the novels. Also, Lallaoui's characters do not always necessarily live on the periphery of Paris or other major French cities.

In his first novel, *Les Beurs de Seine* (1986), Lallaoui does use some of the conventions of the Beur novel, since we are in the presence of disenfranchised young Beurs.[50] The protagonists fight discrimination by organizing a strike against their factory employers. Both the strike and the novel end tragically as one of the main characters is the victim of a racist crime. However, starting with his second novel, *La colline aux oliviers* (1998), Lallaoui derives his inspiration from forgotten historical events.[51] Lallaoui's most recent novel, *Une nuit d'octobre* (An October Night; 2001), echoes the book and documentary *Le silence du fleuve* (The River's Silence; 2001) of Anne Tristan and others on the 1961 October massacre of Algerian workers.[52]

The event at the core of *La colline aux oliviers* represents a deeper aspect of the amputated memory with regard to France and Algeria, since very few people know about the 1871 Kabyle insurrection and

> the initial impetus for the novel came from a visit which Lallaoui made to the French Pacific colony of New Caledonia in 1983. He was intrigued and deeply

moved to learn that more than a hundred years earlier, Algerians opposed to French rule had been deported to the island following an uprising in 1871.[53]

The main protagonist in Lallaoui's novel, Kamel, although Beur, does not live *outside* Paris. True, he lives in a roiling ethnic neighborhood, but it is still *in* Paris, with its vivacity and dynamism. The urban landscape is not one of desolation but of animation. No racist crime occurs and Kamel does not feel threatened, unlike the protagonists in other Beur novels. Finally, Kamel has an urban family of friends, but his *direct* family—father, mother, or siblings—play no role in the narrative. There is, indeed, no mention in the novel of Kamel's father's migration to France. The only time his father is mentioned is in relation to his grandfather's village, to which his father took Kamel as a young child.

The *tourisme des racines* in this novel, then, happens by accident. At the beginning of the novel, Kamel travels to Algeria to paint some of its landscapes. He does not yearn for an encounter with his roots. However, after seeing his grandfather again, Kamel must face the need to reconsider his priorities. Interestingly, the roots of Kamel's cultural heritage are lost in France, not in Algeria. Lallaoui develops a plot in which roots and memories of the French/Algerian encounter are visible only to those looking for them—in museums and archives, for instance. Moreover, the novel produces a series of Algerian characters who go to France to find the truth and not to escape the past or a bleak future. Kamel is a Parisian, a somewhat goofy and absent-minded artist like any other stereotypically Parisian artist. Algeria does not represent a lost homeland until Kamel goes there to visit a grandfather he has not seen since his early childhood.

Le tourisme des racines is therefore accidental, not wanted or idealized by Kamel. However, the tourism of roots is crucial for Lallaoui, as he states in an interview with Hargreaves:

> We were born here but it is as if there was nothing before us. There is [something] like a wall. You are over here and when you try to leave and look back, you see this wall. But precisely through the story of Baba Mous—at first subconsciously but since I finished writing it two months ago, I have had time to think about all this—immigrants and I can breach the wall. Behind this wall, there is indeed the Mediterranean. And behind the Mediterranean, there is a country, which means that there is a life, a history, and a legacy one should not forget. We are coming from the other side, we are coming from Africa. And with that comes a memory that we must cultivate and recover.[54]

Thus, Lallaoui—writer, film producer, and intellectual—sees the breaking down of dichotomies erected by amnesia as his mission. The importance of comprehending and accepting one's cultural heritage appears to be crucial in Lallaoui's work, not only for Lallaoui himself but for the Beurs and for France as well. Hence, we cannot conflate Lallaoui's protagonist's lack of interest in his roots with that of the author himself.

"The story of Baba Mous" in *La colline aux oliviers* portrays the fulfillment of a promise made and kept over the course of three, but not successive, generations, each bound to recover the fate of a lost relative: Baba Mous's father, Baba Ali; Baba Mous himself; and then Kamel. Kamel's father, Baba Mous's son, does not appear to have been involved in the quest, since the novel is silent about him. In 1989, in France, Kamel receives a letter from his grandfather Baba Mous, who asks his grandson to visit him in Algeria. For the first time since his early childhood, Kamel goes to the ancestral land of his family, the olive grove in Kabylia. Once the two men are reunited, it turns out that Baba Mous has a request to make of Kamel; he explains that the 1871 rebellion resulted in the deportation of major Algerian leaders and fighters—one of them being Baba Mous's uncle, Si Larbi. Si Larbi fought against the confiscation of the ancestral land, the olive grove. However, nothing was known of his whereabouts after he was arrested and deported by the French authorities. Baba Mous promised his father he would find out what had happened to Si Larbi. He spent his whole life trying to uncover the truth but could not keep his promise. In the evening of his life, he decides to ask his grandson to keep on searching for their lost ancestor.[55]

Kamel's quest opens forgotten pages of French history. Si Larbi was not only deported to a penal colony but he was also in the company of defeated Communards. Prison camps, penal institutions, and penal ships punctuate Kamel's quest. Each stage of the prisoner's travels can be traced in France by those prepared to undertake the quest. Through his journey in time, through readings of lost letters and discoveries of photographs from the past, Kamel meets, directly through conversations or indirectly through testimonies from the past, characters of various origins—French, African, and New Caledonian—who all played a role in his great-uncle's life. Kamel finally learns that Si Larbi had assumed another identity and called himself Slimane Chakkib when he was arrested by the French. Si Larbi later tried to communicate with his relatives using his new name but was unsuccessful. It was under the name of Slimane Chakkib that Si Larbi was deported to a penal colony in New Caledonia.

Theoretical Framework

To discuss the relevance of memory in *La colline aux oliviers*, I will use three concepts that I see as linked to each other in Lallaoui's novel: Maurice Halbwachs's collective memory and Pierre Nora's *devoir de mémoire* and *lieux de mémoire*. Each of these concepts speaks to the others in terms of how an oppressed community, like the community of the olive grove, cultivates, protects, and preserves memory.

French sociologist Maurice Halbwachs devotes his book *The Collective Memory* to arguing that individual memory is not constructed on its own.[56] Indeed, individual memory is most of the time shaped by what he calls "collective memory." In particular, in the case of communities that have been persecuted, collective memory represents a crucial element in conserving what the oppressors have been trying to erase, so that

> place and group have each received the imprint of the other. Therefore every phase of the group can be translated into spatial terms, and its residence is but the juncture of all these terms. Each aspect, each detail, of this place has a meaning [intelligible] only to members of the group, for each portion of its space corresponds to various and different aspects of the structure and life of their society, at least of what is most stable in it.[57]

The olive grove in Lallaoui's novel works in a similar fashion, as the nineteenth-century characters follow an ancestral tradition that consists of planting an olive tree to commemorate each community member connected to the olive grove. Each tree corresponds to, and bears as a symbol, the mark of the year when the particular member of the community was born. As Rosello points out, Lallaoui may also have been influenced by Moroccan author Abdelkebir Khatibi's *La mémoire tatouée* (The Tattooed Memory).[58] In Lallaoui's *La colline aux oliviers*, we are in the presence of a literally tattooed memory, since each male member of the community has a tattoo on his left shoulder that commemorates the olive grove:

> Just like all of those from the grove who were leaving for a long and uncertain journey, we had been tattooed with a caroubier [carob tree] branch on our left shoulder, three olive tree leaves, a sun, and our date of birth. Under each of the three leaves, there was a series of numbers.... These numbers corresponded to the group of trees, the alleys and the olive trees that represented each of us in the grove. We had thus been proceeding this way since immemorial times in order to permanently mark in our flesh our belonging to this land, to these stones, to this sky above the home of each of us.[59]

Men carry the memory of the olive grove on their bodies as a mark that also serves as an identity card in the colonial context.[60] During French colonialism, the colonized, Arab and Kabyle, were given second-class citizenship, acknowledged not as individuals but as a large anonymous group. The tattoo, then, has the dual importance of carrying ancestral memory as well as of creating a system of identification and recognition among the members of the community. Identification through the tattoo reaches beyond the olive grove: "From that day on, and until his disappearance, Si Larbi would be with Cheik el-Haddad's sons during battles. He would be wounded twice and left for dead in a ravine. But, thanks to his tattoo and to the old families that knew of our dynasty, he was always brought back to the grove."[61] The French either did not wish to understand or simply did not acknowledge the symbolism of the tattoo. Moreover, at the time of the insurrection, tattoos in French culture were associated with convicts, especially those sent to penal colonies. Those men and women were marked permanently with tattoos that linked them to their criminal past, thus preventing any possible return to a normal civilian life, since everyone could recognize and identify the mark of "shame."[62]

The responsibility of the collective memory in the novel manifests itself through the concept of the *devoir de mémoire*.[63] Indeed, Mireille Rosello shows that what French historian Pierre Nora calls *le devoir de mémoire* appears to be crucial in *La colline aux oliviers*.[64] According to Nora, each individual has become his or her own historian, looking for his or her own roots and identity and, by the same token, preserving them:

> Historicized memory comes to us from without. Because it is no longer a social practice, we internalize it as an individual constraint. The transition from memory to history requires every social group to redefine its identity by dredging up its past. The resulting obligation to remember makes every man his own historian. Thus the historical imperative has reached well beyond the limited circle of professional historians. . . . The commandment of the hour is thus "Thou shalt remember." It is the self that remembers, and what it remembers is itself.[65]

By introducing the idea of *devoir de mémoire*, Nora acknowledges the fact that memory stimulates reflection on realms forgotten by history, since *le devoir de mémoire* underscores the importance of keeping alive the memory of events, of cultures, and of sites that are crucial to a living community. However, as Derderian points out, Nora "devotes only one chapter to France's vast imperial holdings—and even this chapter is restricted to the 1931 colonial exhibition in Paris. As for the empire proper . . . *Realms of Memory* offers nothing but silence."[66]

I agree with Rosello that "it may seem paradoxical to invoke Nora's work in an essay on Algerian memory considering that [Nora] deliberately excludes Algeria from his very corpus."[67] Nevertheless, "Nora's historical gaze and type of historical research is remarkably similar to the approach chosen by Franco-Maghrebi novelists who seek to redefine the narrative tools used by different generations in order to rewrite and manage their history."[68] In the case of *La colline aux oliviers*, Nora's concept of the duty to remember well describes the character of Baba Mous, for whom it is inconceivable to relinquish his promise, even in the evening of his life. Si Larbi is part of the memory of the ancestral land represented by the olive grove; he is part of the land and thus part of the collective memory of the inhabitants of the olive grove. Baba Mous cannot forget either his promise or his uncle, as he, Baba Mous, respects the collective memory of which he is a part.

In addition to the *devoir de mémoire,* the novel also puts to work the concept of *lieux de mémoire,* or memory sites: to Baba Mous it is the land that possesses and represents the memory of his people. According to Nora, a "*lieu de mémoire* is any significant entity, whether material or nonmaterial in nature, which by dint of human will or the work of time has become a symbolic element of the memorial heritage of any community."[69] The land represents not only the memory of the Kabyles but also the precise reason why they fought to keep this memory free and alive. Land is memory, land is roots. However, Kamel does not see it as such.[70] For instance, when Baba Mous asks Kamel what the land represents for him, the young man is unable to give the expected answer. Baba Mous explains to Kamel that "What really matters is the roots. Our land represents the depths of our memory.... Memory, son, is the eyes of men from here. Without this light that unites them to their past, they are lost."[71] Baba Mous emphasizes the connection between the olive grove, that is, the land, and the people who were born on the land. Therefore, any event connected to the land is also connected to the people of the land.

A Detective Story

The collective memory of the people of the olive grove has been injured by the disappearance of Si Larbi. The healing of the collective memory takes the shape of a detective story that takes place over the course of four generations. Kamel is the third, and final, investigator of the collective memory, after his great-grandfather, Baba Ali, and, more importantly, his grandfather Baba Mous. Baba Mous was trained by his father to become the family detective in order to search for his uncle:

> Since my early childhood Baba Ali had been training me for something I was far from realizing then, that would actually take up my whole life. He chose me among all his sons because he detected in my eyes the expression in Si Larbi's, my uncle's. Finding out what had happened to his brother after the Great Revolt had been an obsession for Baba Ali for more than thirty winters.[72]

Baba Mous's whole education was devoted to learning how to observe, analyze, and acquire the knowledge necessary to help him in his search for Si Larbi. Baba Ali had hired Cheikh Iskandar—a learned man who one day came to the olive grove—to tutor Si Larbi and thus prepare him for his mission. Therefore, the collective memory and *le devoir de mémoire* take priority over Baba Mous's own personal ambitions. When World War I starts, Baba Mous is drafted to fight in the trenches in France. Even though the draft once again shatters the fragile olive grove community, Baba Mous decides to consider it an opportunity to go to France where he can start his research on Si Larbi's disappearance.

During the great butchery of World War I, Baba Mous meets a dying soldier from the colonies. The dying soldier, who is black, has the same tattoo that Si Larbi evidently had: "I realized that it was the exact same tattoo as Si Larbi's."[73] Baba Mous manages to obtain the name of the dying soldier, Diallo Songda. When Baba Mous asks Diallo where his tattoo was made, the dying soldier mumbles some sounds that resemble "Paris." Baba Mous goes to Paris after the end of the war to search for his uncle—without any success. Before returning to Algeria, Baba Mous's path takes him to Lyons, where a drunken sailor describes Si Larbi's tattoo; Baba Mous then follows the sailor to Avignon, where he is supposed to live. Called back to Algeria to take care of his community, Baba Mous leaves France without finding any more clues as to the existence of his uncle or the identity of the mysterious drunk. In Algeria, the olive grove community receives fragments of a letter that bears the writing of Si Larbi but is signed "Slimane Chakkib." Again, Baba Mous looks for Slimane Chakkib. It is only at the end of the novel that, thanks to Kamel's investigation, the identity of Chakkib is revealed. Chakkib is the name taken by Si Larbi to escape capital punishment when the French army arrested him.

Many decades after the mysterious letter signed by "Slimane Chakkib" reaches the family, Kamel takes over the investigation at the request of Baba Mous. The old man gives all his files, his notes, and the information he has gathered in notebooks to his grandson. The notebooks constitute a crucial *lieu de mémoire* that Baba Mous has written, not only for his investigation but also as a testimony to the whole community:

> One day, I decided to keep a travel journal. On notebook sheets, I would try to describe places I visited and people I met. This journal, where I would add daily entries, would go to my children. When I was with my children again, I would use the journal to teach them reading and to educate them on the history, the miseries, and the beauties of their country.... I wanted my descendants to understand fully where my search for Si Larbi was taking me.[74]

In his notebooks, Baba Mous writes everything that is relevant to his search for Si Larbi. However, very quickly the notebooks become a testimony to the situation of the colonized. Suffering dispossession, hunger, and multiple injustices, the colonized are victims and objects in the hands of the colonizers. The notebooks function as a *devoir de mémoire*, since they stand as a means of remembering those dreadful times and of understanding that the recovery of the memory of a lost relative leads to the excavation of the dark times of colonialism as well. Baba Mous takes on the role of a scribe who tells what the colonial power does not report. By describing the beauty and the misery he has seen during his journeys, Baba Mous voices the beauty and the misery that French colonialism has ignored and marginalized.

Nevertheless, Kamel does not automatically appreciate the notebooks and has no desire to understand fully where the search for Si Larbi has taken Baba Mous. At first, Kamel is indeed a reluctant "detective," who does not consider the quest a valuable or valid one. He does not even experience guilt about the possibility of not pursuing the quest to its conclusion; to him it seems to be nothing but an embarrassing hobby. Because he is so far away from Kabylia, from the olive grove—this living memory site of roots—Kamel does not at first realize the importance of uncovering the truth. Without immediate reminders of the insurrection but also of the reasons for the insurrection—the impending confiscation of the ancestral land and therefore of the ancestral memory—Kamel is at first unable to understand what he sees as his grandfather's obsession.

Kamel understands himself as being monoculturally French. Nowhere in the novel are we in the presence of citizenship euphemisms such as "integrated" or "second generation immigrants." Therefore, Kamel does not feel the need to search for his origins. He is truly comfortable in his Parisian life:

> At the end of my walk, when I arrived at the Ourcq Canal, I felt indeed relieved. And there, my eyes on the grayish ice, I made my decision. I was going to stop my research.... It is not a laughing matter anymore, I told myself. I am no detective.... Baba Mous's adventure might have been extraordinary but it does not concern me whatsoever. I had my own life, my own problems.[75]

Kamel is concerned with his own personal future, as "my own life" underlines, whereas Baba Mous, when he was Kamel's age, had devoted his life to his community and to finding out what had happened to Si Larbi, sacrificing even the love of his life, a young French woman called Marinette, whom he met in Avignon. Rosello argues that

> two significant narrative choices thus distinguish Lallaoui's text from other fictional historiographies that seek to displace official discourse. First of all, the events that the novel allows us to discover (the 1871 uprising in Kabylia) are even less well known by the general public than the War of Independence. Then the novel tells us that it takes two generations to finally arrive

at a complete narrative about the lost member of the community. In other words, this text also tells the story of a failure, of bad historiography.[76]

No doubt Lallaoui put into fiction what he himself had to go through in order to find out about the fate of the Kabyles and Arabs deported to New Caledonia. The novel illustrates the fact that it was literally impossible for a young Kabyle under French colonialism, such as Baba Mous, to rescue the memory of the olive grove through his search for Si Larbi. How could it have been otherwise? Kamel is able to solve the mystery because he is French and Algeria is no longer French. He is not a second-class citizen, as his father is/was. He is a city dweller, a Parisian, who has access to resources that were denied to his grandfather and his father. He accepts that he is indeed a "detective," whether he likes it or not. Like a classic detective hero, Kamel must sift through the evidence, find the truth, and serve justice, simply because of who and where he is.

To discover the truth about the past, Kamel learns to rely on *lieux de mémoire*. However, at the beginning of the novel, he cannot yet read the olive grove as such a site. For Kamel, *lieux de mémoire* are places such as archives or photographs that have somehow survived in contemporary France and still bear traces of the violence of the past. Kamel's work as a detective cannot succeed on its own. He needs the presence and assistance of the French, because their histories are connected. The story of the Kabyle insurrection can be told only through a process of reconciliation between Kamel's Algerian heritage and his present-day French life.

Kamel decides to read Baba Mous's notebooks and use them as a precious source of information to start his investigation. Like Baba Mous before him, he will go after the first clue to Si Larbi: the tattoo on the dying Senegalese soldier. In order to find out who this man was, Kamel goes to the Military Archives in the Invalides in Paris. The Military Archives constitute the first *lieu de mémoire* in France. Baba Mous's notebooks are also a *lieu de mémoire*, as is the olive grove, for recovering the truth. The trail of the soldier, who was from Senegal, turns out to be a dead end when Kamel realizes that the dying soldier could not have had the name of Diallo Songda—the real Diallo registered in the Military Archives had died well before he was supposed to have met Baba Mous—but Kamel nevertheless recovers a *lieu de mémoire* linked to the colonial experience. By researching the identity of the Senegalese soldier, the *faux* Songda Diallo, Kamel revives the memory of the soldiers from the French colonies who fought for France during World War I. Lallaoui pays tribute to these forgotten heroes, who died anonymously and without any reward from France.

The second clue left by Baba Mous proves to be more useful: the drunk from Lyons who knew about Si Larbi and his tattoo. After a patient and meticulous investigation, Kamel discovers the name of this mysterious man: Octave Masson. Masson was a sailor and, more importantly, the son of a prison guard, Emile Masson, whose life was saved by Si Larbi during a prison transfer. This part of the investigation brings back to life another key moment in the French-Algerian relationship: the first moments of Algerian immigration to France and the debt that France owes to the Algerians' underpaid labor.

As soon as Kamel starts finding memory sites that he can comprehend and observe—such as pictures of Octave and Emile Masson, who knew Si Larbi, or letters describing the Kabyles in New Caledonia—he finally begins to accept his quest. For instance, when he gains access to the archival list of the deported rebels, the fact that these people actually existed and that the great insurrection actually occurred becomes a matter of vital importance to him.

The Tattoo of Evidence

Significantly, Kamel pays attention to the memory in the olive grove, which is why he is able to decipher the mystery of Slimane Chakkib. I would argue that Si Larbi's tattoo and Kamel's ability to identify it articulate the collective memory that Kamel now acknowledges. Kamel reads the following description in the military archives: "Slimane Chakkib was among them. On a sheet of paper, across from his name, was written: 'Special Peculiarities: Arab, wears a tattoo on his left shoulder; condemned for insurrectional deeds.'"[77] Kamel realizes that the French were unable to comprehend the tattoo on Si Larbi's left shoulder—the intricate details of the tattoo are not even described. Moreover, the Chakkib clan did not have the same tradition of tattoos as the men from the olive grove, and thus no man bearing that tattoo could really be Chakkib; but this was not a matter of interest to the French and did not even arouse their curiosity. The tattoo operates as the main description of Si Larbi, as if we are present at a physical examination, comparable to an autopsy. Like a detective, Kamel observes and identifies the body of evidence, which here is Si Larbi's tattoo.

Kamel and his girlfriend Anne realize at the same time that Slimane Chakkib might very well be Si Larbi, since both had the same complex, unique tattoo with the same series of drawings and numbers. Anne is actually the one who declares: "I strongly believe that Slimane Chakkib and Si Larbi were one and the same person."[78] Kamel shows that the *lieu de mémoire*, the French archive he consulted, is crucial in this interpretation as well: "As for me, I was equally convinced ever since I had looked up the register at the National Archives."[79] The narrative positions Anne's hypothesis, that Chakkib and Si Larbi were the same person, before Kamel's, thus emphasizing that one does not need to be from or to be related to the olive grove to have an interest in solving the mystery of Si Larbi's disappearance. Of course, Lallaoui adds a romantic twist to the character of Anne, since the young woman turns out to be the granddaughter of Marinette, who was Baba Mous's first, lost, love. Anne and Kamel are not related and they meet by accident in Avignon. They represent the couple that Baba Mous and Marinette could never be. They need each other to heal the wounds of the past. Anne is also the one who realizes that Octave Masson's father, Emile, was a prison guard in the same prison as Si Larbi and that they had probably met.

A Communal Memory

Anne and Kamel visit the crucial *lieux de mémoire* together, in particular the Musée de la Commune in the town of Saint-Denis. This museum possesses extensive information on the Parisian Commune, especially testimonies, letters, and diaries written by Communards before, during, and after the Commune. These various pieces of writings constitute essential *lieux de mémoire* through which Kamel will finally put together the pieces of the puzzle. In this section, we will see how Lallaoui includes these alternative histories, narrated by marginalized French nationals, to create *lieux de mémoire* that function as testimonies in the detective story *La colline aux oliviers*.

The Communards' writings that Anne and Kamel find clearly provoke an epiphany for Kamel, as testimonies from eyewitnesses would. Indeed, the young man is able to reach beyond time to the memory of the olive grove, since through the Communards the presence of the colonized is witnessed and crystallized:

> We immersed ourselves... in the testimonies of the Parisian insurgents. Through them, we learnt the names of the islands where the communards as well as the vanquished of the great Algerian insurrection had been sent.... Those vanquished were disappearing as if by magic from the list of prisoners, only to become anonymous numbers.[80]

While the colonial power reduced the Algerian prisoners to mere numbers, the Communards' writings describe the particularities of some of the Algerians they met during the journey and after they arrived in the penal colony. Kamel reads a letter from an unnamed Communard, who mentions Si Larbi by his *real* name, which shows solidarity and trust between the two deported men:

> Dear father, there are three inmates from Africa with me. They help and support me as best as they can.... Si Larbi, also called Chakkib Slimane by his companions, was condemned for insurrectional acts by the Court of Algeria.

In Search of Lost Kabyles in Mehdi Lallaoui's La colline aux oliviers 259

Prisoner Number 2825. Has a tattoo on his left shoulder. Some sort of symbol of three olive tree leaves.[81]

The letter written by the deported Communard to his father underlines the courage and empathy that Si Larbi displayed toward other prisoners and in particular toward a Frenchman. Lallaoui includes this episode in order to develop the idea that Algerians, including Kabyles, used agency in differentiating between the colonial power's unfair policies and civilians who had nothing to do with these policies. Once again, Lallaoui disrupts colonial dichotomies: not all French people are depicted as merciless colonizers; and the Kabyles are not "savages" but men capable of empathy and bravery in dire times.

To engage with the memory of the real-life deported Kabyles, Lallaoui adds actual voices of marginalized French witnesses to the aftermath of the insurrection: the Communards who were deported alongside the Kabyles. For instance, Kamel discovers that Louise Michel, a very famous real-life Communard, was also deported to New Caledonia.[82] By reading her memoirs, he finds out that she saw and met Kabyles who had been deported to the same penal colony.

Lallaoui includes the following quotation from Louise Michel's memoirs: "These Orientals who are imprisoned far away from their tents and their herds, they were good and simple people with a great sense of justice. This is why they could not understand why they had been treated in such a way."[83] Louise Michel was one of the most famous women who took part in the Commune, but her fierce fight for social justice did not go unpunished, and it resulted in her deportation to New Caledonia. By including the voice of this remarkable woman in French history, but also by selecting her thoughts on the deported Algerians, Lallaoui demonstrates that *some* French people already had the human and humane capacity to understand and respect the colonized who were fighting against the usurper of their land.

Besides Louise Michel's writings, Lallaoui includes other famous (but forgotten) names from the French Commune. For instance, Kamel reads the memoirs of Henri Bauer, who was one of Alexandre Dumas's illegitimate sons. If the penal administration tried to silence the Algerian insurgents twice—first by deporting them to an island far away from their land and calling all of them Arabs, and then by registering them by their prisoner numbers and not by their names—Communards like Henri Bauer include them nevertheless:

> I skimmed through Henri Bauer's memoirs, [that is, the memoirs of] Alexandre Dumas's illegitimate son. And I read the articles of Louis Barron, secretary to the War Delegation under the Commune. Thanks to them, I finally learnt that Algerian insurgents had lived on Pines Island, which was

for simple deportees; and on Ducos Island in a fortified compound for convicted prisoners.[84]

Finally, when Kamel finishes reading and analyzing the writings of the Communards, he is able to feel for the olive grove, as much as Baba Mous and Si Larbi did:

> I had a knot in my throat. Almost a century and a half after these forgotten torments, and thanks to the characters we had been following, I was recuperating, in the most unlikely fashion, this concealed portion of our history. This history that was extending the memory of those of the olive grove by reminding men of their past.[85]

For the first time in the novel, Kamel uses "our" to refer to the collective memory represented by the olive grove. This pronoun positions Kamel in relation to his responsibility as a member of the olive grove memory. He could not do it before, precisely because he did not grow up surrounded by the physical markers of the olive grove. However, because he has used the memory sites present in France concerning the Great Insurrection, Kamel reclaims a crucial part in the collective memory he has been trying to ignore.

Moreover, as was seen earlier on, Kamel receives the help of characters who are also passionate about discovering the truth. None of them are of Kabyle origin as he is. Sylvia, his neighbor, Anne, his girlfriend, and Pol, his former high school teacher, are incredible sources of help in Kamel's quest. This network of friends is soon completed by "kind" strangers who agree to lend letters, diaries, and photographs that can contribute to uncovering the truth. Emile Masson's grandchildren give their grandfather's entire correspondence to Anne so that the young woman can discover the connection between the prison guard and the Algerian inmate, Si Larbi.

Lallaoui includes these French characters so that the history of the Great Insurrection and of one of its main protagonists may actually be rediscovered by *all* kinds of French citizens, whether they are of Kabyle origin or not. For instance, Pol Rochardon suggests he should follow the Communards' trail after Kamel finds out that the Parisian insurgents were probably deported to the same penal colonies as Si Larbi: "Then, we have to follow the path of the Parisian insurgents as well. The Communards' fate and that of the Algerian insurgents led them to the same prisons, and their final destination was almost certainly the same."[86] Anne accompanies Kamel to the Museum of the Commune. She reads with him the testimonial writings about the deportation to New Caledonia, testimonials written by the Communards. If Kamel resented starting his investigation on his own, by the end of the novel, the lonely "I" almost disappears, to be replaced by a collective "we," referring to Kamel and his non-Kabyle French companions.

Earrings of the Truth

Here I would like to bring back a character mentioned very briefly before: Cheikh Iskandar, who was Baba Mous's tutor in the olive grove. Rosello analyzes Iskandar as providing "a different type of identification," since he is a stranger to the village and therefore does not bear the tattoo on his shoulder.[87] Iskandar's teaching completes the oral memory of the olive grove received by Baba Mous. Because of his duty to educate Baba Mous, Iskandar is actually put in charge of preparing the young man to understand and comprehend the world beyond the olive grove that has snatched away his uncle. However, Baba Mous's education is interrupted when he is drafted to fight for France during World War I. Before parting with his student, Cheikh Iskandar offers Baba Mous a pair of gold earrings, telling him to give them to the woman he will fall in love with:

> At the end, he pulled out from his burnous a box within which was a pair of fine gold gazelle-head-shaped earrings.... "Take them, they are yours.... They are my most precious possession. They are for me what the olive grove is for all of you here, the proof of our existence. The earrings used to belong to my mother and before that to the mother of my mother. They were from a *sigaya* [goldsmith's shop] dating from the great lords of Africa at the far ends of the desert. Take care of them as preciously as your life and then give them to the one woman that will carry them to your children."[88]

After the end of World War I, Baba Mous remains in France, where he searches for Si Larbi. He stays in Avignon where he meets Marinette, who helps him in his quest. However, Baba Mous suddenly has to leave France and Marinette, and he returns to Algeria where his father is dying. Heartbroken at having to leave his love in Avignon, Baba Mous gives one of the earrings to Marinette as a token of his affection, while he keeps the other one. We find out about the connections between the two generations (Baba Mous/Marinette and Kamel/Anne) thanks to the gold earrings. Indeed, fifty years after Marinette receives one earring, Baba Mous gives the remaining earring to Kamel. When Anne comes to Paris to visit Kamel, she recognizes the earring as being the twin of her grandmother's and realizes there is more than a coincidence here.

Mireille Rosello interprets the earrings as a *lieu de mémoire* as follows: "Whereas olive trees keep the memory of a dynasty of men whose contingent birth attached them to a land, Iskandar's earrings preserve memory while authorizing exile and exogamous relationships. He gives Baba Mous the right to choose who will be the recipient of the story."[89] I would also say that the fact that Iskandar gives a piece of jewelry that comes as a pair (instead of a ring, a necklace, or a bracelet, for instance) provokes the idea that history and memory function as a dual process. In other words, the painful remembrance of the Kabyle insurrection and its aftermath needs to be achieved by *both* parties that have been involved in the insurrection: France and Algeria. Kamel *is* French but his Frenchness has a dual heritage because of his affiliation to *both* Algeria/Kabylia and France. And France needs to acknowledge its colonial past as well.

Consequently, because the olive grove's memory was shattered and traumatized by French colonialism, it becomes imperative that the healing of the olive grove should also involve the healing of France in relation to its colonial past. The amputation of memory happened in the olive grove physically and literally because Si Larbi, as well as the land, was snatched away from the community. However, this amputation became amnesia on the French side. Symbolically the two earrings cannot be together in Baba Mous's and Marinette's time but can be reunited in 1989 France where Kamel and Anne can love each other since there is no colonial barrier. When Baba Mous's and Marinette's earrings are reunited, the fate of Si Larbi is finally known and Baba Mous is at peace, having kept the ancestral promise. Moreover, gender is finally reinscribed in the story of the olive grove, thanks to Iskandar's earrings.

Rosello analyzes this reinscription of gender as crucial:

> That Anne should find the second earring at Kamel's and should suddenly recognize her grandmother's earring at the very moment when the two lovers can fit this last piece into the almost completely assembled puzzle is a fictional deus ex machina. At the same time, this narrative decision makes a point about the presence of women in this picture.... And yet Anne's discovery makes the point that her model of history, inherited from Iskandar, works perfectly. History as gift, history as transmitted by women and by people who do not necessarily belong to the *colline aux oliviers*, is just as successful as Baba Mous's stubborn determination.[90]

Hargreaves sees Lallaoui's novel as different from the rest of the corpus of contemporary Beur novels, since "no [other] Beur novel ends with an unequivocal sense of completion."[91] I would also add that the originality of Lallaoui's novel lies in the fact that at no moment in the course of his quest does Kamel encounter racism or primal animosity from French people or the French authorities. Moreover, his friends are sometimes even more passionate and less discouraged than he is when a trail reveals itself to be of no use.

The action of the novel begins in July 1989. Kamel has just left France after July 14, Bastille Day. That year, France's national holiday was no ordinary event, since the whole country was celebrating the bicentennial anniversary of the French Revolution. Nevertheless, some events, such as the consequences of the revolution, the revolutionary wars, and the spread of the French Empire were not commemorated. By setting the action of the novel in such a special year for French nationalism, Lallaoui reinscribes forgotten events in the canon of French history.

Conclusion: Remembering the Great Insurrection

It is only after he finishes his investigation into what happened to his great-great-uncle Si Larbi that Kamel is truly able to appreciate the significance of the land for his forefathers and for his grandfather. Kamel solves the mystery, through his investigation justice is restored, and the *devoir de mémoire* has therefore been fulfilled. In some way, the reader follows Kamel's efforts to uncover the truth and then, like the young protagonist, has to wait until the end of the novel to understand how it all began. Si Larbi represents more than a prison number. Indeed, it is only at the end of the novel that for the first time we hear words attributed to Si Larbi himself. Those words are remembered by Baba Mous, who recounts them when telling the history of the Great Insurrection to Kamel and other children of the olive grove.[92] Baba Mous credits Si Larbi for having said:

> We belong to this land as much as it owns us. We have cherished it and it has cherished us since the beginning of the world. Men, women, children, and elders have suffered for it. We must preserve it. What is better work of the human soul than to fight for this land that saw our birth?[93]

Si Larbi was once part of the ancestral community that lived by the olive grove for which he fought so fiercely. The use of "we" reinforces the idea of a community whose roots are merged in a land that should be protected against the usurper. Si Larbi's voice appears in the text only at the end of the novel because only then is Kamel able to understand and appreciate the words of his ancestor. The insurrection and Si Larbi's fate are now part of Kamel's own present-day identity and experience.

Therefore, just like Si Larbi's speech, the description of the Great Insurrection only appears at the end of the novel when Kamel once again visits his grandfather at the olive grove. During the same occasion on which he recounts Si Larbi's words in front of a gathering of village children and elders, Baba Mous also retells the unfolding of the events of the insurrection:

> For the thousandth time, Baba Mous was making us relive the Great Insurrection. Relentlessly, with the same words, as a Tuareg storyteller would do, he was passing the message to the village children who were eager for emotions and adventures. But the elders also enjoyed remembering these old events that had harvested their field with blood.[94]

Kamel must have heard this when he visited Baba Mous as a child, but the words presumably did not mean anything to him then. Baba Mous assumes the position of the community storyteller, and young and old listen, mesmerized by his retelling of the story of the Great Insurrection. Through his position as community storyteller, Baba Mous fulfills his *devoir de mémoire*, since he passes on to the next generation the story of the Great Insurrection that was fought to preserve the community of the olive grove and its *mémoire collective*.

The Great Insurrection was triggered by the fact that Algeria was undergoing a change of rule. Since its invasion in 1830, Algeria had been under French military control. However, in 1871, after the fall of the Second Empire, French settlers managed to obtain civil rule in Algeria. In other words, the settlers were going to take full possession of the land and encourage settler immigration since "as a result of a series of decrees passed in the autumn of 1870 and culminating in 1871 with the appointment of Governor-General Vice-Admiral de Gueydon, the colonial administration of Algeria passed out of military hands."[95] Civilian rule meant more settlers, and more settlers meant more confiscation of native land: "The transformation of the economy enriched the setters and accelerated the pauperization of the indigenous population in rural Algeria, driving it off the land into the cheap labour market, first in the colony and then in France."[96]

Lallaoui incorporates agency on the part of the Kabyles by showing how they understood what civil rule meant for them: full dispossession of their lands,

> In village assemblies, a single word kept on being muttered under the tone of fear and malediction, the word "dispossession." . . . A decree gave away the military rule to the settlers. "What is civilian rule, according to you?" a settler asked an Arab one day. "Well, it is very simple," answered the son of the land. "I have ten goats, you take eight of them. I have two thousand sheep. You only leave me eight to keep."[97]

This short dialogue is part of the history of the Great Insurrection that Baba Mous shares with the village people at the end of the novel. Positioning the Great Insurrection in the context of civilian rule not only demonstrates the importance of the land for the Kabyles but also emphasizes the fact that after the Great Insurrection there was no end to full colonization of Algeria by the French settlers.[98]

Ironically, the events are told on the Algerian side, but the evidence is found on the other side of the Mediterranean. Of the Great Insurrection, indeed, there is no visible physical trace, such as written accounts, in 1989 Algeria, whereas colonial archives in France have the minutes of the trials of the rebels as well as the names of the deportees. It seems that colonial memory has space only for the names of those that France, the colonial power, punished for having crossed its path. On the other side of the Mediterranean, however, the memory of the events is passed on from one generation to another. For the Kabyles of the olive grove, the land *is* memory. More importantly, any event linked to colonization takes the form of knowledge engraved in the land. Indeed, colonization aimed at dispossessing the tribes from their land; therefore, the Kabyles view time in relation to the land. The dispossession truly robs them of their history, for they tell time not by dates but in terms of the effects of events on the land itself. For example, the Great Insurrection is not remembered as having taken place in 1871, but as having taken place in the year when the land was taken away.

As already mentioned, Mehdi Lallaoui has created an association called Au nom de la mémoire (In the Name of Memory) to retrace tumultuous moments in the French-Algerian relationship. Passionate about the Great Insurrection and its terrible aftermath, including both the unilateral seizing of native land in Algeria and the deportation of the insurgents to New Caledonia, Lallaoui tries to reach a wider audience by creating an original and innovative novel that Hargreaves calls "the story of a positive quest for origins. The problematic nature of the relationship between the Beur protagonists and the historical past is emphasized by the constant deferral within the text of what, in chronological terms, precedes and conditions everything else."[99]

Having the reader learn about the events at the same time as the main protagonist provokes curiosity, knowledge, and empathy. The reader too becomes an actor in the positive quest for origins, since the rescue of Si Larbi's memory is an experience shared by people not necessarily of Kabyle origin. The novel is now out of print in France, which is unfortunate because Lallaoui brings a message of reconciliation, asking France to admit, acknowledge, and accept its colonial past. Lallaoui achieves reconciliation by deconstructing simplistic dichotomies and by valorizing intricate complexities.

Notes

1. Mehdi Lallaoui, *Kabyles du Pacifique* (Bezons, France: Au nom de la mémoire, 1994). This essay is based on the first chapter of my PhD dissertation, "Reconciliations: Memory and Mediation in Narratives of the Postimperial Second Generation," defended in spring 2010 at the University of Texas at Austin. My dissertation examines narratives of transplanted identity building and memory in European languages by second-generation non-European writers who choose to write their stories in European languages. It compares the ways in which colonial trauma is reclaimed by writers of Algerian, Iranian, and Caribbean descent, living, respectively, in France, the United States, and Great Britain.

2. Patricia M. E. Lorcin, *Imperial Identities: Stereotyping, Prejudice and Race in Colonial Algeria* (London: I. B. Tauris, 1995), 4.

3. Ibid.

4. See Tassadit Yacine, "Les ancêtres redoublent de vérité," in *Hommage à Kateb Yacine*, ed. Nabil Boudraa (Paris: L'Harmattan, 2006), 129–32. In her essay, Tassadit Yacine emphasizes how Kateb Yacine denounced the imposition of Arabic as the only national language for Algeria.

5. Kateb Yacine, *Nedjma* (Paris: Seuil, 1956), 90–91.

6. "Forefathers' souls" refers to the epigraph, taken from Yacine, *Nedjma*, 90–91.

7. Mehdi Lallaoui, *La colline aux oliviers* (Paris: Editions alternatives, 1998).

8. Richard L. Derderian, "Algeria as a *lieu de mémoire*: Ethnic Minority Memory and National Identity in Contemporary France," *Radical History Review* 83 (2002): 28–43.

9. Both *lieux de mémoire* and *devoir de mémoire* are concepts created and developed by Pierre Nora. See Pierre Nora, ed., *Realms of Memory: The Construction of the French Past; Conflicts and Divisions*, European Perspectives: A Series in Social Thought and Cultural Criticism, vol. 1, trans. Arthur Goldhammer (New York: Columbia University Press, 1996). All citations are to this edition.

10. See Charles Debbasch, J. Bourdon, Jean-Marie Pontier, and Jean-Claude Ricci, *La Ve République* (Paris: Economica, 1985).

11. For example, Le Pen developed the idea of national preference in order to promote racist politics and practices in his book *Les Français d'abord* (For the French First of All) (Paris: Carrere-Michel Lafon, 1984).

12. Gérard Noiriel, *Le creuset français: Histoire de l'immigration XIXème–XXème siècle* (Paris: Seuil, 1988). When citing Noiriel, I will use the English edition: Gérard Noiriel, *The French Melting Pot: Immigration, Citizenship, and National Identity*, trans. Geoffroy de Laforcade (Minneapolis: University of Minnesota Press, 1996).

13. Noiriel, *The French Melting Pot*, 189–226.

14. Recent accounts of this period in French history include Jonathan Marcus, *The National Front and French Politics: The Resistible Rise of Jean-Marie Le Pen* (Basingstoke, England: MacMillan, 1995); Harvey G. Simmons, *The French National Front: The Extremist Challenge to Democracy* (Boulder, CO: Westview, 1996).

15. The suppression of the peaceful demonstration of Algerian immigrants in Paris on October 17, 1961, is a crude example of the violent silencing of this community. I will dwell on this painful and traumatic event below.

16. See, for instance, Alec G. Hargreaves, *Voices from the North African Immigrant Community in France: Immigration and Identity in Beur Fiction* (New York: Berg 1991); Michel Laronde, *Autour du roman beur: Immigration et identité* (Paris: L'Harmattan, 1993). As Hargreaves and Laronde demonstrate, most of these writers were of Algerian descent, since the Algerian immigrants represented the core of North African immigration in France.

17. Hargreaves, *Voices*, 12.

18. See Yamina Benguigui, *Mémoires d'immigrés: L'héritage maghrébin* (Paris: Canal + Editions, 1997). Benguigui gathers oral testimonies from fathers, mothers, and children in this community.

19. Subsidized public housing or Habitations à Loyer Modéré (HLM). See John S. Ambler, ed., *The French Welfare State: Surviving Social and Ideological Change* (New York: New York University Press, 1993).

20. See Noiriel, *The French Melting Pot*, 119–21, 133.

21. See Carrie Tarr, *Reframing Difference:* Beur *and* Banlieue *Filmmaking in France* (Manchester, England: Manchester University Press, 2005).

22. French "pig" Latin for "Arabe." "Beur" became a way for the children of North Africans to claim a hybridity that France had so far refused to acknowledge.

23. Assia Djebar, *Children of the New World* (New York: Feminist Press at CUNY, 2005; originally published in French, 1962). This great novel is unfortunately out of print in French, but the Feminist Press published a wonderful new English translation in 2005.

24. Hargreaves, *Voices*, 4.

25. I do not idealize or offer a pessimistic image of immigration; there is, however, a belief central to any immigrant community that the parents, the first generation coming to France, will have to experience dire living circumstances so that their offspring, born and raised in France, will not. The children will be French and have advantages (civil and social) that their parents could not have claimed, since they were not French before the law.

26. Alec G. Hargreaves, *Multi-ethnic France: Immigration, Politics, Culture and Society*, 2nd ed. (New York: Routledge, 2007), 3.

27. Ibid.

28. Ibid., 9.

29. Noiriel, *The French Melting Pot*, 161.

30. Ibid., 162.

31. Major publishers all "had" a Beur novel during the decade of the 1980s. For instance, J. C. Lattès published Akli Tadjer; Denoël published Nacer Kettane; and Seuil published Azouz Begag.

32. Hargreaves, *Voices*, 1.

33. See, for instance, Laronde, *Autour du roman beur.* Female Beur writers would appear later on the French literary scene, especially at the beginning of the 1990s.

34. See Michel Laronde, ed., *L'Ecriture décentrée: La langue de l'Autre dans le roman contemporain* (Paris: L'Harmattan, 1996).

35. Hargreaves in particular offers a thorough examination of these elements in *Voices*, 36–57.

36. Azouz Begag, *Le gone du Chaâba* (Paris: Seuil, 1986).

37. See Hargreaves, *Voices*.

38. Nacer Kettane, *Le sourire de Brahim* (Paris: Denoël, 1985).

39. Ahmed Kalouaz, *Point kilométrique 190* (Paris: L'Harmattan, 1986).

40. Mireille Rosello, "Tattoos or Earrings: Two Models of Historical Writing in Mehdi Lallaoui's *La colline aux oliviers*," in *Algeria and France 1800–2000: Identity, Memory, Nostalgia*, ed. Patricia M. E. Lorcin, 201 (Syracuse, NY: Syracuse University Press, 2006).

41. See Noiriel, *The French Melting Pot*, 240–45.

42. The same is also true 1998. However, because I am situating Lallaoui's writing within a publishing timeframe, I am referring only to major novels published by Beur writers up to 1998.

43. Lallaoui himself wrote a novel on the demonstration. *Une nuit d'octobre* (An October Night; Paris: Editions alternatives, 2001) was published on the occasion of the fortieth anniversary of the demonstration.

44. I will discuss the collective memory of this incident for the Algerian community living in France later in this essay.

45. Akli Tadjer, *Les ANI du "Tassali"* (Paris: Editions du Seuil, 1984). The acronym ANI stands for Arabes Non Identifiés (Non Identified Arabs). By using this acronym, Tadjer pinpoints the fact that Arabs are deprived of any individuality.

46. Akli Tadjer, *Le porteur de cartable* (Paris: J. C. Lattès, 2002).

47. Mehdi Charef, *Le harki de Meriem* (Paris: Folio, 1989). "Le problème des harkis" (the problem of the harkis) constitutes a complex theme in Beur literature because, during and after the Algerian War, both the FLN sympathizers and the harkis had to learn to live together in the same French housing estates. Charef complicates the issue by showing how the Algerian revolution affected the national spirit of Algerians.

48. These novels portray disappointing pilgrimages to the characters' roots. Hargreaves mentions this disappointment in *Voices*, 53–54.

49. See Lallaoui's presentation of the association at http://www.africine.org/?menu=fichedist&no=3026. Also see Derderian, "Algeria as a *lieu de memoire*," 37.

50. Medhi Lallaoui, *Les Beurs de Seine* (Paris: L'Arcantère, 1986).

51. There are no English translations of Lallaoui's works. All the translations are mine. However, I borrow the translation of the title, *La colline aux oliviers*, from Mireille Rosello, who was the first to offer "the olive grove" as a translation. Rosello presents this translated title in her article "Tattoos or Earrings."

52. See Derderian, "Algeria as a *lieu de mémoire*," 37; Lallaoui, *Une nuit d'octobre*. Anne Tristan wrote the book *Le silence du fleuve: Octobre 1961* (Bezons, France: Au nom de la mémoire, 1991). Unfortunately (and not surprisingly, given the French reluctance to remember the horror of the demonstration's repression) the book is now out of print. Lallaoui codirected the documentary *Le silence du fleuve* with Agnès Denis in 1991. The documentary echoes Tristan's book.

53. Hargreaves, *Voices*, 65.

54. Interview conducted on April 17, 1988, and included in Hargreaves, *Voices*, 151–52. Hargreaves included the interview in French. The translation from French into English here is mine. At the time of the interview, in 1988, *La colline aux oliviers* had been completed, but it had not yet been published.

55. The novel does not offer any information concerning the rest of Baba Mous's direct descendants. Kamel seems to appear as his only hope to uncover the truth, even though logically Baba Mous should have asked his son, Kamel's father. However, as I mentioned earlier, Kamel's father is surprisingly absent from the novel. We do not even know the name of Kamel's father. At this point, I think the text does not present enough elements to build any hypothesis as to what happened to Kamel's father or between him, his father, and his son. One could nevertheless suggest that having only a grandfather and his grandson search for the truth might reflect a desire by Lallaoui to give more space to forgotten colonial memories from the nineteenth century in his novel than to the Algerian War (1954–62). It is also possible to argue that the generation of Kamel's father constitutes another generation of "lost Kabyles."

56. Maurice Halbwachs, *The Collective Memory*, trans. Francis J. Ditter Jr. and Vida Yazdi Ditter (New York: Harper & Row, 1980). All citations are to this translation.

57. Ibid., 130–31.

58. Abdelkebir Khatibi, *La mémoire tatouée: Autobiographie d'un décolonisé* (Paris: Les lettres nouvelles, 1971). Rosello makes the parallel between Lallaoui and Khatibi in "Tattoos or Earrings," 215.

59. Lallaoui, *La colline*, 48–49.

60. Interestingly we do not know if the women from the olive grove have and had such a marker. The women are hardly ever mentioned and not even named. The text does not tell us the name of Baba Mous's mother nor his wife's name. Rosello mentions the androcentrism of the olive grove in "Tattoos or Earrings," 208–9.

61. Lallaoui, *La colline*, 188.

62. For further information on the stigma associated with French penal colonies (*bagnes*) and tattoos, see Marc-Alain Descamps, *L'invention du corps* (Paris: PUF, 1986).

63. Nora, *Realms of Memory*, 10. The French expression *devoir de mémoire* is translated as "the obligation to remember" in Goldhammer's translation of Nora. Following Derderian and Rosello, I will use "duty to remember" instead.

64. Rosello, "Tattoos or Earrings," 201–2.

65. Nora, *Realms of Memory*, 10–11.

66. Derderian, "Algeria as *lieu de mémoire*," 28–29.

67. Rosello, "Tattoos or Earrings," 202.

68. Ibid.

69. Nora, *Realms of Memory*, xvii.

70. The text does not mention Kamel having a tattoo of the olive grove on his shoulder. We can interpret this omission as a sign that Kamel was not born and raised in the olive grove.

71. Lallaoui, *La colline*, 64.

72. Ibid., 12.

73. Ibid., 58.

74. Ibid., 96.

75. Ibid., 106.

76. Rosello, "Tattoos or Earrings," 205.

77. Lallaoui, *La colline*, 209.

78. Ibid., 218.

79. Ibid.

80. Ibid., 220–21.

81. Ibid., 223–24.

82. For further information on Louise Michel, see the biography by Françoise d'Eaubonne, *Louise Michel la Canaque, 1873–1880* (Paris: Encre, 1985).

83. Lallaoui, *La colline*, 228. This is my translation of the passage quoted by Lallaoui. For more information on Louise Michel's memoirs, see Louise Michel, *Souvenirs et aventures de ma vie* (Paris: Maspero, 1983).

84. Lalloui, *La colline*, 221.

85. Ibid., 225.

86. Ibid., 209.

87. Rosello, "Tattoos or Earrings," 213.

88. Lallaoui, *La colline*, 48–49. At the end of *La colline*, Lallaoui provides a lexicon of the Arab and Kabyle words used in the novel. He gives the following French translation for sigaya: *orfèvrerie*, which means goldsmith's art or goldsmith's shop. See *La colline*, 235.

89. Rosello, "Tattoos or Earrings," 213.
90. Ibid., 215.
91. Hargreaves, *Voices*, 165.
92. We may suppose that Baba Mous learnt Si Larbi's words as a child when he was trained by his father to find out what happened to his uncle. The novel does not mention when Baba Mous learnt Si Larbi's words, but as Baba Mous recounts his uncle's words in front of the village, he seems to imagine *how* Si Larbi would have spoken them.
93. Lallaoui, *La colline*, 185.
94. Ibid., 178.
95. Lorcin, *Imperial Identities*, 167.
96. Ibid.
97. Lallaoui, *La colline*, 180–81.
98. For detailed historical information on the consequences of civilian rule in French Algeria, see Charles-Robert Ageron, *Les Algériens musulmans et la France (1871–1919)*, vol. 1 (Paris: Presses universitaires de France, 1968).
99. Hargreaves, *Voices*, 151.

13

"Lament for the Casualties"

The Nigerian War of 1967–70 and the Poetry of John Pepper Clark-Bekederemo

Michael Sharp

Introduction

John Pepper Clark-Bekederemo's *Casualties* (1970), a classic literary account of the nation-rending years of the Biafran secession from the Federation of Nigeria, is a uniquely African book of poems in English. A noncombatant, Clark-Bekederemo was a committed federalist with good friends, like the novelist Chinua Achebe and the poet Christopher Okigbo, on the secessionist side. Of his lack of involvement in the hostilities, Clark-Bekederemo has written wistfully, "The pity is that I have had no part at any time in the drama still unfolding."[1] Yet, through the structure of *Casualties*, Clark-Bekederemo captures with prophetic insight the political events in Nigeria, which moved breathlessly from disturbance to massacre,[2] from civil war to uneasy peace. Clark-Bekederemo's quiet assault gains agonizing momentum as the collection builds toward "The Casualties" and "Night Song," the final poems of the war-sequence.

Clark-Bekederemo is an accomplished poet who has not received the critical attention outside his native Nigeria that he deserves. Despite the publication of Robert M. Wren's *J. P. Clark* (1984), which explores the politics and persons involved in the Nigerian crisis, Clark-Bekederemo's war poetry within the context of the English-language literary canon deserves further analysis.

While an undergraduate at University College, Ibadan,[3] during the 1950s, Clark-Bekederemo read widely in the canonical works of English modernism, including the World War I poetry of Edmund Blunden, Ivor Gurney, Wilfred Owen, Isaac Rosenberg, and Siegfried Sassoon. Of Edmund

Blunden's memoir, *Undertones of War* (1928), Paul Fussell has written, "every word, every rhythm, allusion, and droll personification, can be recognized as an assault on the war."[4] Blunden's magisterial account of his life as an infantry lieutenant during what he called "the slow amputation"[5] of trench warfare and Wilfred Owen's cautionary "Preface" to his posthumous *Poems* (1920), which announced that "All a poet can do today is warn,"[6] inform the poetry of Clark-Bekederemo's *Casualties,* which confronts with great sensitivity the disturbing nature of disorganized civil violence.

Despite the fact that earlier war poetry by noncombatants has enjoyed an indisputable position in the literary canon, this has not been true of more recent work. This can especially be seen in the scholarly criticism of the World War I poets, where it has been fashionable to privilege poetry by battle-hardened soldiers as opposed to responses by concerned civilians. This trend has, perhaps, been one of the reasons for the fact that there is only a small body of criticism focusing on Clark-Bekederemo's war poetry.[7]

Unlike the World War I poets whom he admired, Clark-Bekederemo writes of the effects of civil conflict and especially of a "republic of suffering,"[8] which ironically led—like Abraham Lincoln's United States of America—to the rebirth of Nigeria. That the war was brutally fought on home soil in Africa adds, in W. B. Yeats's words, a "terrible beauty"[9] to the poetry of *Casualties,* which broods meditatively on the unthinkable and unanticipated consequences of the Biafran secession. As a pastiche of "fragments given by friends directly affected," the poems in *Casualties* ruminate on battle, fratricide, disease, ethnic division, and the West African tradition of *ars moriendi.*[10]

Poems Reflecting the Course of the War

The chronological beginning of *Casualties* is the third poem in the sequence, "Vulture's Choice,"[11] which examines the dilemma, faced by Major Emmanuel Ifeajuna and the other coup leaders,[12] of how to govern Nigeria.[13] The poems that follow present by parable, debate, and witness the federation's gradual descent into civil war. In the note on "The Burden in Boxes," Clark-Bekederemo writes that "In the first flush of the coup, Nigerians saw it as a gift from the gods, but when the coffins began to be counted, the Pandora character of the gift became apparent."[14] Clark-Bekederemo complains bitterly that "a man of character other than General Ironsi[15] could still have rescued the situation for the country."[16] Aguiyi-Ironsi, who became head of state and supreme commander of the army on the day of the coup, is accused of being stone-deaf to the "ominous music" the coffins made as they were dragged away "Into cold storage."[17]

Emmanuel Ifeajuna, to whom Clark-Bekederemo remains fiercely loyal, is the one great Nigerian "who woke up the lion."[18] The poem "Conversations at

Accra," which is punctuated by three voices—"A" as Ifeajuna, "B" as Christopher Okigbo, and "C" as Clark-Bekederemo—states "the case he [Ifeajuna] would have put up at a court-martial."[19] At the end of the poem, Ifeajuna's defense delineates his personal vision for a new Nigeria in which he imagines "A new estate" presided over by "a man / Burnt clean by fires he had / Himself started."[20]

A last-ditch effort to head off civil war in Nigeria took place at Aburi, Ghana, on January 4 and 5, 1967, between the Federal Military Government under Lieutenant-Colonel Yakubu Gowon[21] and a delegation from the Eastern Region led by Governor Chukwuemeka Ojukwu.[22] Despite follow-up meetings in Benin and a national conciliatory mission to the Eastern Region, headed by Chief Obafemi Awolowo,[23] Gowon nevertheless went forward with a plan to create twelve states out of the existing four regions on May 27, 1967. Three days later, Ojukwu declared the independence of the Republic of Biafra.

In "Dirge," written after the conference at Aburi had failed to save the fragile union of the Nigerian Federation, Clark-Bekederemo writes with prophetic sadness that "Earth will turn a desert / A place of stone and bones."[24]

Poems That Recoil from the Violence

Edmund Blunden wrote in the "Preliminary" to *Undertones of War* that "it was impossible not to look again and to descry the ground, how thickly and innumerably yet it was strewn with the facts or notions of war experience."[25] Similarly, Wilfred Owen's poetry is a telling testament to the horrors of mindless slaughter. His poems are about neither "deeds, or lands, nor anything about glory, honour, might, majesty, dominion, or power, except War." "Above all," Owen wrote, "I am not concerned with Poetry. / My subject is War, and the pity of War. / The Poetry is in the pity."[26] W. B. Yeats, whose poetry, like Blunden's and Owen's, Clark-Bekederemo had discovered at Ibadan, ends "The Second Coming" (1919) with the question: "And what rough beast, its hour come round at last, / Slouches towards Bethlehem to be born?"[27] In Clark-Bekederemo's poem "The Beast," the "dragon" that Ifeajuna and his coconspirators have inadvertently released "out of mad love of the land" has finally slouched into Nigeria to "set the rivers on fire" and make "catacombs of cities and farms."[28]

During the Nigerian civil war, the images of death, the destruction of towns and villages, the indiscriminate bombing of civilians, the disruption of agriculture and industry, the endless lines of refugees, the public executions, the interference of foreign governments, and the starvation and death caused by kwashiorkor[29] that especially affected the children in the breakaway republic were, for a while, front-page news in the world's press.[30]

The first twenty-one poems of *Casualties* reflect some of these images as they spiral downward in jagged Yeatsian gyres into "The Beast." Each poem preceding "The Beast" presents a relentless assault on the unstoppable events that led inevitably to "blood [calcifying] into boulders / For brother to hurl against brother."[31]

The photographic images sent out of Biafra by international news organizations were predictably graphic. The stark photographs taken by Donald McCullin[32] of tiny children and nursing mothers suffering from malnutrition in Biafra are particularly harrowing.[33] The widely syndicated photograph taken by Romano Cagnoni[34] for the July 12, 1968, issue of *Life*, at a militia training center in Okigwi of volunteers for the Biafran army is the subject of Clark-Bekederemo's "A Photograph in *The Observer*." In the poem, terrifyingly reminiscent of Wilfred Owen's "Anthem for Doomed Youth,"[35] the dark night of war falls over young conscripts, "Statuettes of ebony ganged together / As ibeji[36] at an altar," a "cache certified fit / For hurling at the ogre / . . . in the dark."[37]

Poems about Friends

Like many literary noncombatants, Clark-Bekederemo absorbed vicariously not only the savagery of the battlefield but also the deep-rooted ramifications of a fraternal conflict that caused ethnic allegiances to break down, political differences to fester, academic suspicion to deepen,[38] and disaffected brotherhood to stagnate. For Clark-Bekederemo, the civil war brought with it both the death of friends and the cooling of friendships.[39]

The first two poems, "Song" and "Skull and Cups," act as a coda to the sequence. These are poems that may have been written after the final "Night Song" of the sequence. In "Song," the opening poem, Clark-Bekederemo can "look the sun in the face" but not "the friends" he has "lost."[40] In "Skulls and Cups," the lost friends are named: "Sam" [Agbam],[41] who was executed for profederalist activities; "Emman" [Ifeajuna], one of the so-called January Majors of the 1966 army coup, who was executed for planning a countercoup to return Biafra to the federation; and fellow-poet "Chris" [Okigbo], who was killed fighting for Biafra in August 1967.

When interviewing Clark-Bekederemo in Lagos in 1983, Robert M. Wren reported that when the conversation turned to Okigbo, "the strain of talking about friends and crisis was clear in his voice and anguished look."[42] Unlike many of the writers and intellectuals who flocked into the Eastern Region after May 1967, Okigbo enlisted in the Biafran army and was given the rank of a major. The journalist John de St. Jorre reports that the "passionate, idealistic, mercurial" Okigbo "simply picked up a gun, and with no military training whatsoever, recklessly put himself at the head of a group of Biafran soldiers" and "was killed early on in the battle" for the university town of Nsukka in August 1967.[43] This was in keeping, Clark-Bekederemo recalled, with the picture of an "energetic, restless man, fully charged with life."[44]

"Death of a Weaverbird" is a praise poem for Christopher Okigbo and is one of the elegiac masterpieces of Nigerian poetry. Like Ivor Gurney's "To His Love," published just after World War I, which praises "that red wet / Thing I must somehow forget,"[45] Clark-Bekederemo's poem is seminal to the literature of war, and reflects deeply and mysteriously on the strange beauty of death in battle. It also hints, in the italicized song that ends the poem, that Okigbo, who believed, like Shelley, in the power of the poet, also favored a peaceful return of Biafra to the federation. As "*the black-kite, / At the head of a flock*," the poetic voice asks,

How can I return to sing another song?
To help start a counter surge?[46]

The poem "The Casualties" is pointedly dedicated to the novelist Chinua Achebe, who traveled internationally to drum up support for the secessionist cause. It is a bitter poem, in which Clark-Bekederemo inveighs against Achebe and "the emissaries of rift," those "wandering minstrels who, beating on / The drums of the human heart, draw the world / Into a dance with rites it does not know."[47] The poem concludes that everyone is a casualty of the Nigerian war.

The poem "Night Song" brings Clark-Bekederemo's *Casualties* full circle. Previously, the poet has been unable to look into the faces of the friends he has lost; in the final poem, however, "the night" for him is haunted by familiar ghostly faces. As he contemplates the loss of those young men taken into "the siren arms of war," Clark-Bekederemo visualizes in the brutal half-light of the poem the symbolic gesture of Okigbo's sacrifice. Okigbo understood, Clark-Bekederemo suggests, that his death would have some consolatory effect on the outcome of the war. Similarly, the execution of Ifeajuna, who also dreamed of a united Nigeria, takes on an emblematic meaning. Both men and all the "Others" who "touched on / A chord resonant to the root" will follow "at the great crossroads, / A dance into the forest."[48] Just as the arrival of Shakespeare's Fortinbras may shore up the state of Denmark after Prince Hamlet's death, "another"—probably Yakubu Gowon—"ignored by all as dumb" will be responsible for building "The house / Of our dream, with a mansion / For them"—that is, for Okigbo and Ifeajuna and the other secessionists.[49]

The ending of *Casualties*, while seemingly optimistic, nevertheless sounds out the deep-down silences that persist "In pots their mouths make / In fields already forgotten / In the fight."[50] In "The Flood," written before the Aburi conference, Clark-Bekederemo, like Okigbo's *black-kite*, has already sown the seeds of uncertainty:

> I flounder in my nest, a kingfisher,
> Whose flockmates would play
> At eagles and hawks, but like
> Chickens, are swept away[51]

Even before secession, as a consequence of the ethnic violence in the Northern Region, the oracular voices of impending civil war had already uttered their unspeakable predictions: friends will die, friendships will disappear, places will be destroyed, ideas will flounder, and poetry will be "in no sense consolatory"[52] to the generation it was written for. Seeing Clark-Bekederemo as "the protagonist in his own play," Robert M. Wren, having found the dénouement "not so poetically effective," concludes his balanced discussion of *Casualties* with the Audenesque[53] remark that "art is useless, coming late only to look upon the debris."[54] While General Gowon may conveniently seem to be at center stage in the drama, his very presence, like that of Fortinbras, further strengthens Clark-Bekederemo's sense of uncertainty.

Conclusion

Some years after the publication of *Casualties*, Clark-Bekederemo added a twenty-ninth poem to the sequence: "Epilogue to *Casualties*."[55] The poem is dedicated to the poet Michael Echeruo[56] and involves a journey through the former Biafra, taken "four years / After the war."[57] Ifeajuna's dream of a united Nigeria, now in the capable hands of Gowon's military, seems well on the way to achievement; but, despite the oil boom of the 1970s, "the unnatural / Disaster that is war"[58] is everywhere to be seen.

In his memoir *Sunset in Biafra* (1973), for example, the novelist Elechi Amadi had written that "the earth had become a monster, a ubiquitous monster licking her fangs," and that "Life was a bitter, cruel dream arranged by a sadistic god!"[59] Similarly, the poet Gabriel Okara, writing in *The Fisherman's Invocation* (1978), remembers Port Harcourt "lumbering out of a bad dream." The "garden city" is now a nightmare place of "festering wounds" and "glowering Rat[s]."[60] For Clark-Bekederemo, the former Republic of Biafra is "scalped and scarred beyond surgery," and there are "amputated" bridges over the Niger River.[61] The domestic scene of a woman pounding yams on her balcony offers no consolation. The land has not been devastated only by civil war but also by what the Ogoni novelist Ken Saro-Wiwa in *The Singing Anthill* (1991) called "the harsh crudity of Nigerian politics."[62] Clark-Bekederemo is sadly aware that the "two cathedral spires"—Nigeria and Biafra—are "still in conflict / For eastern pastures, as they were before the war."[63]

Notes

I would like to thank Dr. Ann Albuyeh and Dr. Dannabang Kuwabong of the University of Puerto Rico and Dr. Toyin Falola of the University of Texas at Austin for their suggestions during the writing of this essay.

1. J. P. Clark-Bekederemo, *Casualties: Poems 1966–68* (New York: Africana, 1970), 54. Unless specified otherwise, all citations are to this edition. Despite Clark-Bekederemo's rejection of political involvement, the novelist and environmentalist Ken Saro-Wiwa has written that "J. P., an Ijaw of the Mid-Western State, was indeed very supportive and did a lot to espouse the cause of River States." *On a Darkling Plain: An Account of the Nigerian Civil War* (Port Harcourt: Saros International Publishers, 1989), 147.

2. Zdanek Červenka reports that "only the Ibos know the whole terrible story from the 600,000 or so refugees who have fled to the safety of the Eastern region—hacked, slashed, mangled, stripped naked and robbed of all their possessions, the orphans, the widows, the traumatized." *A History of the Nigerian War 1976–1970* (Ibadan, Nigeria: Onibonoje, 1972), 31. No less graphically, Ken Saro-Wiwa's naïve recruit in his novel *Sozaboy* says in his "rotten" English: "In the motor park, the returning people were saying many things. I heard plenty tory by that time. About how they are killing people in the train; cutting their hand or their leg or breaking their head with matchet or chooking them with spear and arrow. Fear begin catch me small. Soon, everybody begin to fear." *Sozaboy: A Novel in Rotten English* (London: Longman, 1994), 3.

3. In Clark-Bekederemo's praise-poem "Ibadan," the university city is described as "flung and scattered / . . . like broken / china in the sun." *Collected Poems 1958–1988* (Washington: Howard University Press, 1991), 14.

4. Paul Fussell, *The Great War and Modern Memory* (New York: Oxford University Press, 1977), 68.

5. Edmund Blunden, *Undertones of War* (London: Collins, 1965), 190. All citations are to this edition.

6. Wilfred Owen, *The Collected Poems*, ed. C. Day Lewis (London, Chatto & Windus, 1971), 31. All citations are to this edition.

7. See especially Bernard Bergonzi's *Heroes' Twilight: A Study of the Literature of the Great War* (London: Constable, 1965); and John Silkin, *Out of Battle: The Poetry of the Great War* (London: Oxford University Press, 1972).

8. The phrase is Frederick Law Olmsted's. See *Hospital Transports: A Memoir of the Embarkation of the Sick and Wounded from the Peninsula of Virginia in the Summer of 1862* (1863), 115, quoted in Drew Gilpin Faust, *This Republic of Suffering: Death and the American Civil War* (New York: Knopf, 2008), xiii.

9. This is from Yeats's poem "Easter in 1916," in *The Collected Poems of W. B. Yeats* (Toronto: Macmillan, 1956), 178.

10. Clark-Bekederemo, *Casualties*, 54.

11. Clark-Bekederemo, in the manner of praise poetry, uses a variety of animals to symbolize the characters of the major players in *Casualties*. There are at least forty animal references in all, to vultures, rabbits, monkeys, cows, crocodiles, snakes, lions, elephants, bulls, cockerels, leopards, pigeons, antelopes, jackals, sheep, hounds, boars, hyraxes, squirrels, dogs, rats, crickets, buffaloes, flies, donkeys, locusts, egrets,

grasshoppers, ticks, mastiffs, cats, parakeets, kingfishers, eagles, hawks, chickens; kites, swifts, swallows, and weaverbirds.

12. According to Červenka, "The chief plotters were Major C. K. Nzeogwu, Major E. Ifeajuna, Major D. Okafor and Capt. E. N. Nwobosi." *A History of the Nigerian War*, 11. Philip Efiong writes that "These young officers were looked upon as heroes by the generality of the Nigerian people and any move to arrest and discipline them openly was fraught with danger." *Nigeria and Biafra: My Story* (Astoria, NY: Seaburn Books, 2007), 21. Of Ifeajuna, Efiong writes, "From my experience of him in Biafra during the Civil War, he could come to plot, plead, pressurize, but be shifty and extremely dangerous. Yet, in spite of the alarm signals, the coup plotters still believed in him and even saw him as the linchpin for the success of the coup in the south." Ibid., 35.

13. Nigeria gained full independence from Britain on October 1, 1960. Until 1967, Nigerian Federation consisted of the Northern Region (largely Hausa and Fulani); the Western Region (Yoruba); the Midwest region (largely Edo); and the Eastern Region (largely Igbo).

14. Clark-Bekederemo, *Casualties*, 56.

15. Major General Johnson Aguiyi-Ironsi (1924–66) "became the first military head of state in 1966, but only for a few months." Toyin Falola, *The History of Nigeria* (Westport, CT: Greenwood, 1999), 233.

16. Clark-Bekeremo, *Casualties*, 56.

17. Ibid., 6

18. Ibid., 8.

19. Ibid., 58.

20. Ibid., 20.

21. Gowon was supreme commander of the army and head of state from 1966 to 1975. Falola has noted that "When he tried to come to power via the democratic process in the 1990's, Gowon lacked the money, astuteness, and network to compete in a treacherous political arena." *The History of Nigeria*, 238. Clark-Bekederemo remarks in the "Notes" (61) to *Casualties*: "I asked Major Ifeajuna in Accra what had happened to Lt. Col. Gowon, who I had not seen for years. His reply was that he had not thought enough of my friend to include him in his plans. Surely a case of the rejected stone becoming the head of the corner!"

22. Colonel Chukwuemeka Odumegwu Ojukwu joined the army in 1957 and was appointed the military of the Eastern Region in 1966. Ken Saro-Wiwa has written that Ojukwu was "a rebel leader whose masturbatory egoism, intransigence and political illiteracy [wreaked] . . . much horror on the peoples of Eastern Nigeria." *Genocide in Nigeria: The Ogoni Tragedy* (Port Harcourt, Nigeria: Saros International Publishers, 1992), 27. Since his presidential pardon and exile, Ojukwu has been "active in politics with disappointing results." Falola, *The History of Nigeria*, 243.

23. According to Falola, Obafemi Awolowo (1909–87) was "an enterprising politician, lawyer, author, businessman, nationalist, journalist, and Yoruba hero." *The History of Nigeria*, 233.

24. Clark-Bekederemo, *Casualties*, 28.

25. Blunden, *Undertones of War*, 11–12.

26. Owen, *The Collected Poems*, 31.

27. *The Collected Poems of W. B. Yeats*, 185. Abiola Irele argues that Yeats's influence "is so pervasive that it can be said to have been wholly absorbed into the texture of Clark-Bekederemo's personal idiom." *The African Imagination: Literature in Africa and the Black Diaspora* (New York: Oxford University Press, 2001), 190.

28. Clark-Bekederemo, *Casualties*, 31.

29. A Ga word for protein deficiency. Ga is spoken in southeast Ghana and is the principal language of the capital, Accra.

30. That is, until they were eclipsed by stories from America's war in Vietnam and acts of political dissidence in the former Soviet Union.

31. Clark-Bekederemo, *Casualties*, 31.

32. McCullin, a photojournalist with London's *Sunday Times Magazine*, went on to make his name in Vietnam and Northern Ireland.

33. According to John de St. Jorre, "The worst starvation in Biafra came in September/October 1968, an estimated five to ten thousand dying daily; adults, especially nursing mothers, joined the emaciated ranks of the very young and very old." *The Brothers' War: Biafra and Nigeria* (Boston: Houghton Mifflin, 1972), caption to photograph between 352 and 353.

34. In "Biafra: A War of Extinction and Starvation," *Life* 65, no. 2, July 12, 1968, 20–29. Cagnoni's work has taken him from the battlefields of Eastern Nigeria to the ongoing conflict in Chechnya.

35. Owen's poem, written in September 1917, begins: "What passing-bells for these who die as cattle?" "Anthem for Doomed Youth," in *The Collected Poems*, 44.

36. A Yoruba deity representing twins.

37. Clark-Bekederemo, *Casualties*, 34.

38. See the caustic poem "To my Academic Friends who sit tight on the Doctoral theses and have no Chair for Poet or Inventor," in Clark-Bekederemo, *Collected Poems*, 46.

39. Wole Soyinka has written that "The poet and playwright J. P. Clark and I had been quite close to Christopher Okigbo—all three of us having been based in Ibadan in the early 1960's—and now I experienced something close to the sadness of a family breakup." *You Must Set Forth at Dawn: A Memoir* (New York: Random House, 2006), 112. Later on in his memoir, Soyinka refers cryptically to his relationship with Clark-Bekederemo as having "Not lately been the best." Ibid., 244.

40. Clark-Bekederemo, *Casualties*, 3.

41. According to John de St. Jorre, Agbam was "a Foreign Service official" who "shared the 'One Nigeria' and radical beliefs of Ifeajuna." *The Brothers' War*, 171.

42. Robert M. Wren, *Those Magical Years: The Making of Nigerian Literature at Ibadan, 1948–1966* (Washington, DC: Three Continents, 1990), 110.

43. De St. Jorre, *The Brothers' War*, 149. Soyinka records that Okigbo died "with that chant from the Spanish Civil War issuing from his throat: *No pasarán*." Soyinka adds, "One person, at least, had given his life to the dreams of youth, but how sad that it should have been on a fratricidal field." *You Must Set Forth at Dawn*, 118.

44. Quoted by Adewale Maja-Pearce in the introduction to Christopher Okigbo, *Collected Poems* (London: Heinemann, 1986), xii.

45. Ivor Gurney, *Selected Poems* (Oxford: Oxford University Press, 1990), 7.

46. Clark-Bekederemo, *Casualties*, 32.

47. Ibid., 38.
48. Ibid., 41.
49. Ibid., 40.
50. Ibid., 39.
51. Ibid., 29.
52. Wilfred Owen's phrase, in "Preface," *Collected Poems*, 31.
53. In his poem "In Memory of W. B. Yeats" (1939), Auden wrote that "poetry makes nothing happen." W. H. Auden, *Collected Shorter Poems 1927–1957* (London: Faber, 1971), 142.
54. Robert M. Wren, *J. P. Clark* (Lagos, Nigeria: Lagos University Press, 1984), 154.
55. J. P. Clark-Bekederemo, *Collected Poems*, 61–62.
56. In "Ne Nos Inducas," Echeruo advocated "discriminating brotherliness" as a means of solving Nigeria's political problems. See *Mortality* (London: Longman, 1968), 7.
57. Clark-Bekederemo, *Collected Poems*, 61.
58. Ibid.
59. Elechi Amadi, *Sunset in Biafra: A Civil War Diary* (London: Heinemann, 1973), 63.
60. Gabriel Okara, *The Fisherman's Invocation* (London: Heinemann, 1978), 49.
61. Clark-Bekederemo, *Collected Poems*, 61.
62. Ken Saro-Wiwa, *The Singing Anthill: Ogoni Folk Tales* (Port Harcourt, Nigeria: Saros International Publishers, 1991), 10.
63. Clark-Bekederemo, *Collected Poems*, 62.

Bibliography

Achebe, Chinua. "New Songs of Ourselves." *New Statesman and Society*, February 9, 1990, 30–32.
———. *Collected Poems*. New York: Anchor Books, 2004.
ACQUIRE Project. *Traumatic Gynecologic Fistula: A Consequence of Sexual Violence in Conflict Settings*. New York: ACQUIRE Project/Engender Health, 2005. www.acquireproject.org/fileadmin/user_upload/ACQUIRE/Publications/TF_.
Adejunmobi, Moradewun. *Vernacular Palaver: Imaginations of the Local and Non-native Languages in West Africa*. Clevedon, England: Multilingual Matters, 2004.
Adi, Hakim, and Marika Sherwood. *Pan-African History: Political Figures from Africa and the Diaspora since 1787*. London: Routledge, 2003.
Adichie, Chimamanda Ngozi. *Half of a Yellow Sun*. New York: Anchor Books, 2006.
———. "The Story behind the Book." http://www.halfofayellowsun.com/content.php?page=further_reading&n=5&f=2.
Afolayan, Funso. "African Nationalism: 1914–1939." In Falola, *Africa*. Vol. 3, *Colonial Africa, 1885–1939*, 281–312.
African Women and Peace Support Group. *Liberian Women Peacemakers: Fighting for the Right to Be Seen, Heard and Counted*. Trenton, NJ: Africa World Press, 2004.
Ageron, Charles-Robert. *Les Algériens musulmans et la France (1871–1919)*. Vol. 1. Paris: Presses universitaires de France, 1968.
Ag Wacawalen, Akly. "Contribution à l'histoire des Kel Tamacheq de la conquête arabe à la veille des indépendances. Le cas des Kel Tamacheq de l'Adrar des Iforas." PhD diss., Ecole Normale Supérieure de Bamako, Mali (section Histoire et Géographie), 1988.
Agyeman, Opoku. "The African Publius." *Journal of Modern African Studies* 23, no. 3 (1985): 371–88.
Albuyeh, Ann. "A Linguistic Legacy of the Diaspora and the Empire: New Englishes in West Africa and the Caribbean." In *The Histories, Languages, and Cultures of West Africa: Interdisciplinary Essays*, edited by Akua Sarr, Edris Makward, Amadou T. Fofana, and C. Frederick, 29–42. Lewiston, NY: Edwin Mellen, 2006.
All about Darfur. DVD. Produced and directed by Taghreed El Sanhouri. San Francisco: California Newsreel, 2005.
Alleyne, Mervyn C. *Comparative Afro-American: An Historical-Comparative Study of English-based Afro-American Dialects of the New World*. Ann Arbor, MI: Karoma, 1980.
———. *The Construction of Race and Ethnicity in the Caribbean and the World*. Kingston, Jamaica: University of the West Indies Press, 2000.
Allman, Jean Marie. "The Youngmen and the Porcupine: Class, Nationalism and Asante's Struggle for Self-Determination, 1954–57." *Journal of African History* 31, no. 2 (1990): 263–79.
Altick, Richard D. *Victorian People and Ideas*. New York: Norton, 1973.
Amadi, Elechi. *Sunset in Biafra: A Civil War Diary*. London: Heinemann, 1973.

Amnesty International. *It's in Our Hands: Stop Violence against Women.* London: Amnesty International, 2004. http://www.amnesty.org/en/library/asset/ACT77/001/2004/en/dom-ACT770012004en.pdf.

———. *Liberia: No Impunity for Rape: A Crime against Humanity and a War Crime.* London: Amnesty International, 2004. http://www.amnesty.org/en/region/liberia.

Anastario, Mike P. "An Analysis of Violence, Victimization and Women's Mental and Reproductive Health in Two Internally Displaced Populations." PhD diss., Boston College, 2007.

Anderson, David. *Histories of the Hanged: The Dirty War in Kenya and the End of Empire.* New York: Norton, 2005.

Andwele, Adisa. *Don't Let Me Die.* St. Philip and St. Michael, Barbados: ÁJA Productions and Acute Vision, 2005.

Angola E A Nossa Terra. DVD. Directed by Jenny Morgan. New York: Women Make Movies, 1988.

Appiah, Kwame Anthony. *In My Father's House: Africa in the Philosophy of Culture.* New York: Oxford University Press, 1992.

———. "Benjamin Nnamdi Azikiwe." In Appiah and Gates, *Africana,* 154.

———. "Ethnicity and Identity in Africa: An Interpretation," in Appiah and Gates, *Africana,* 703–5.

———. "African Philosophy and African Literature." In Wiredu, *A Companion to African Philosophy* (2006), 538–48.

———, and Henry Louis Gates Jr., eds. *Africana: The Encylopedia of the African and African American Experience.* New York: Basic Civitas Books, 1999.

Arcel, Libby T. "Deliberate Sexual Torture of Women in War: The Case of Bosnia-Herzegovina." In *International Handbook of Human Response to Trauma,* edited by Arieh Y. Shalev, Rachel Yehuda, and Alexander C. McFarlane, 179–93. New York: Kluwer, 2000.

Arends, Jacques, Pieter Muysken, and Norval Smith, eds. *Pidgins and Creoles: An Introduction.* Amsterdam: Benjamins, 1995.

Arias, Arturo. "Conjunctions, Disjunctions: Similar Goals, Contradictory Strategies." *Modern Fiction Studies* 46, no. 4 (2000): 1017–24.

Armstrong, Andrew. "Speaking through the Wound: Irruption and Memory in the Writing of Ben Okri and Festus Iyayi." *Journal of African Cultural Studies* 13, no. 2 (2000): 173–83.

Arndt, Susan. "African Gender Trouble and African Womanism: An Interview with Chikwenye Ogunyemi and Wanjira Muthoni." *Signs: Journal of Women in Culture and Society* 25, no. 3 (2000): 709–26.

Arnoldi, Mary Jo. *Playing with Time: Art and Performance in Central Mali.* Washington, DC: Smithsonian Institution Press, 1995.

Asante, Samuel Kingsley Botwe. *Pan-African Protest: West Africa and the Italo-Ethiopian Crisis 1934–1941.* London: Longman, 1977.

Askin, Kelly D. *War Crimes against Women: Prosecution in International War Crimes Tribunals.* The Hague: Martinus Nijhoff, 1997.

Athey, Stephanie, and Daniel Cooper Alarcón. "Oroonoko's Gendered Economies of Honor/Horror: Reframing Colonial Discourse Studies in the Americas." *American Literature* 65, no. 3 (1993): 415–43.

Atton, Chris. "Alternative Media in Scotland: Problems, Positions and 'Product.'" *Critical Quarterly* 42, no. 4 (2003): 40–46.
———. "Reshaping Social Movement Media for a New Millennium." *Social Movement Studies* 2, no. 1 (2003): 3–15.
Aubrey, Lisa. *The Politics of Development Cooperation: NGOs, Gender and Partnership in Kenya*. New York: Routledge, 1997.
Auden, W. H. *Collected Shorter Poems 1927–1957*. London: Faber, 1971.
Autesserre, Séverine. "Local Violence, National Peace? Post-war 'Settlement' in the Eastern DR Congo." *African Studies Review* 49, no. 3 (2006): 1–29.
———. "DR Congo: Explaining Peace Building Failures: A Study of the Eastern DR Congo, 2003–2006." *Review of African Political Economy* 34, no. 113 (2007): 423–41.
Baker, Philip, and John Eversley, eds. *Multilingual Capital: The Languages of London's Schoolchildren and Their Relevance to Economic, Social, and Educational Policies*. London: Battlebridge, 2002.
Balandier, Georges. "Social Changes and Social Problems in Negro Africa." In *Africa in the Modern World*, edited by Calvin W. Stillman, 58–69. Chicago: University of Chicago Press, 1955.
Barber, Karen. "Popular Arts in Africa." *African Studies Review* 30 (1987): 1–78.
Barnes, Andrew E. "Western Education in Colonial Africa." In Falola, *Africa*. Vol. 3, *Colonial Africa, 1885–1939*, 139–56.
Bastian, Misty, and Jane Parpart. *Great Ideas for Teaching about Africa*. Boulder, CO: Lynne Rienner, 1999.
Beah, Ishmael. *A Long Way Gone: Memoirs of a Boy Soldier*. New York: Farrar, Straus and Giroux, 2007.
Begag, Azouz. *Le gone du Chaâba*. Paris: Seuil, 1986.
Beltz, Amanda. "Prosecuting Rape in International Criminal Tribunals: The Need to Balance Victim's Rights with the Due Process Rights of the Accused." *St John's Journal of Legal Commentary* 23, no. 1 (2008): 167–209.
Benguigui, Yamina. *Mémoires d'immigrés: L'héritage maghrébin*. Paris: Canal+ Editions, 1997.
Bénot, Yves. *Massacres coloniaux 1944–1950: La IVe République et la mise au pas des colonies françaises*. Paris: La Découverte, 1994.
Benthall, Jonathan. "The Disaster—Media—Relief Nexus." *Anthropology Today* 24 (2008): 4–5.
Ben-Zur, Hasida, and Moshe Zeidner. "Gender Differences in Coping Reactions under Community Crisis and Daily Routine Conditions." *Personality and Individual Differences* 20, no. 3 (1996): 331–40.
Bergonzi, Bernard. *Heroes' Twilight: A Study of the Literature of the Great War*. London: Constable, 1965.
Berkeley, Bill. *The Graves Are Not Yet Full: Race, Tribe and Power in the Heart of Africa*. New York: Basic Books, 2001.
Berman, Bruce, and John Lonsdale. *Unhappy Valley: Conflict in Kenya and Africa*. Book 2. London, James Currey, 1992.
Bernus, Edmond. *Touaregs nigériens: Unité culturelle et diversité régionale d'un peuple pasteur*. Paris: Editions de l'ORSTOM, 1981.

Beti, Mongo. *Dictionnaire de la négritude*. Paris: L'Harmattan, 1989.
"Biafra: A War of Extinction and Starvation." *Life* 65, no. 2, July 12, 1968, 20–29.
Birmingham, David. *Kwame Nkrumah: The Father of African Nationalism*. Rev. ed. Athens: Ohio University Press, 1998.
Blood Diamond. DVD. Directed by Edward Zwick. Burbank, CA: Warner Home Video, 2007.
Blunden, Edmund. *Undertones of War*. London: Collins, 1965.
Bogle, Donald. *Toms, Coons, Mulattoes, Mammies, and Bucks: An Interpretive History of Blacks in American Films*. New York: Continuum, 1995.
Boilley, Pierre. *Les Touaregs Kel Adagh; Dépendances et révoltes: Du Soudan français au Mali contemporain*. Paris: Khartala, 1999.
Bope, Eugène Bakama. "Comment: North Kivu's Fragile Peace." *Africa Report* 154. Institute for War and Peace Reporting (IWPR), February 4, 2008. http:www.iwpr.net/?p=acr&o=342445&apc_state=henh.
Borel, François. "Rythmes de passage chez les Touaregs de l'Azawagh." *Cahiers de musiques traditionnelles* 2 (1989): 28–38.
Bosire, Lydiah Kemunto. "The Limits and Possibilities of Transitional Justice." *Pambazuka News*, July 14, 2008. http://pambazuka.org/en/category/comment/49421.
Bouchareb, Rachid, director and writer. *L'Ami y'a bon* (The Colonial Friend). Produced by Jean Bréhat. Tessalit Production, 2004.
Bourgault, Louise M. *Playing for Life: Performance in Africa in the Age of AIDS*. Durham, NC: Carolina Academic Press, 2003.
Brennan, Richard J., Michael Despines, and Leslie F. Roberts. "Mortality Surveys in the Democratic Republic of Congo: Humanitarian Impact and Lessons Learned." *Humanitarian Exchange Magazine* 35 (2006). http://www.odihpn.org/report.asp?id=2838.
Breton, Roland J. L. "Sub-Saharan Africa." In *Languages in a Globalising World*, edited by Jacques Maurais and Michael A. Morris, 203–16. Cambridge: Cambridge University Press, 2003.
Brett, Rachel. "Girl Soldiers: Challenging the Assumptions." New York: Quaker United Nations Office, 2002.
———, and Irma Specht. *Young Soldiers: Why They Choose to Fight*. Boulder, CO: Lynne Rienner, 2004.
Bretton, Henry L. *The Rise and Fall of Kwame Nkrumah: A Study of Personal Rule in Africa*. London: Pall Mall, 1966.
Briggs, Jimmie. *Innocents Lost: When Child Soldiers Go to War*. New York: Basic Books, 2005.
Bromber, Katrin, and Birgit Smieha, eds. *Globalisation and African Languages: Risks and Benefits*. Berlin: Mouton de Gruyter, 2004.
Brownmiller, Susan. *Against Our Will: Men, Women, and Rape*. New York: Simon and Schuster, 1975.
Burke, Colleen. "Women and Militarism." Women's International League for Peace and Freedom. http://www.wilfp.int.ch/publications/womenmilitarism.htm.
Busia, Abena. "Silencing Sycorax: On African Colonial Discourse and the Unvoiced Female." *Cultural Critique* 14 (1989–90): 81–104.

Buss, Doris. "Prosecuting Mass Rape: Prosecutor v. Dragoljub Kunarac, Radomir Kovac and Zoran Vukovic." *Feminist Legal Studies* 10, no. 1 (2002): 91–99.
Byron, Lord. *Don Juan*. London: Penguin Books, 1977.
Campbell, James T. *Middle Passages: African American Journeys to Africa, 1787–2005*. New York: Penguin Books, 2006.
Cannon, Garland. *The Life and Mind of Oriental Jones: Sir William Jones, the Father of Modern Linguistics*. Cambridge: Cambridge University Press, 1991.
Card, Caroline. "Music and Social Identity in Tuareg Society." PhD diss., Indiana University, 1978.
Card, Claudia. "Rape as a Terrorist Institution." In *Violence, Terrorism, and Justice*, edited by Raymond G. Frey and Christopher W. Morris, 296–319. New York: Cambridge University Press, 1991.
———. "Rape as a Weapon of War." *Hypatia* 11 (1996): 5–18. www.iupress.indiana.edu/journals/hypatia/hyp11-4.html.
Casajus, Dominique. *Gens de parole: Langage, poésie et politique en pays touareg*. Paris: Editions La Découverte, 2000.
Cato Institute. "Can We Export Democracy?" *Cato Policy Report* 30, no. 1 (2008): 11–13. http://www.cato.org/pubs/policy_report/v30n1/cpr30n1.pdf.
CBS News. "War against Women: The Use of Rape as a Weapon in Congo's Civil War." *60 Minutes*, January 11, 2008, updated August 14, 2008. http://www.cbsnews.com/stories/2008/01/11/60minutes/main3701249_page3.shtml.
Centre d'Espoir pour Filles et Femmes (CEFF-ONG). http://www.centrefillefemme.org.tripod.com.
Červenka, Zdanek. *A History of the Nigerian War 1967–1970*. Ibadan, Nigeria: Onibonoje, 1972.
Chabal, Patrick, and Jean-Pascal Daloz. *Africa Works: Disorder as Political Instrument*. Oxford: James Currey, 1999.
Charef, Mehdi. *Le harki de Meriem*. Paris: Folio, 1989.
Charles, Jeff, Larry Shore, and Rusty Todd. "The *New York Times* Coverage of Equatorial and Lower Africa." *Journal of Communication* 29, no. 2 (1979): 148–55.
Chick, John D. "The Ashanti Times: A Footnote to Ghanaian Press History." *African Affairs* 76, no. 302 (1977): 80–94.
Childs, G. Tucker. *An Introduction to African Languages*. Amsterdam: John Benjamins, 2003.
Chinkin, Christine. "Rape and Sexual Abuse of Women in International Law." *European Journal of International Law* 5 (1994): 326–41.
Chuku, Gloria I. "Women and Nationalist Movements." In Falola, *Africa*. Vol. 4, *The End of Colonial Rule: Nationalism and Decolonization*, 109–30.
Clark-Bekederemo, J. P. *Casualties: Poems 1966–68*. New York: Africana, 1970.
———. *Collected Poems 1958–1988*. Washington, DC: Howard University Press, 1991.
Claudot-Hawad, Hélène. *Les Touaregs: Portrait en fragments*. Aix-en-Provence, France: Edisud, 1993.
———. *Voyager d'un point de vue nomade*. Paris: IREMAM, Editions Paris-Méditerranée, 2002.
———, and Hawad, eds. *Touaregs: Voix solitaires sous l'horizon confisqué*. Paris: Ethnies, Documents 20–21, 1996.

Clifford, Lisa. "Ituri's Fragile Peace." *Africa Report* 194. Institute for War and Peace Reporting (IWPR), December 3, 2008. http://www.iwpr.net/?p=acr&o=342445&apc_state=henh.
Clough, Marshall S. *Mau Mau Memoirs: History, Memory, and Politics.* Boulder, CO: Lynne Rienner, 1998.
Coburn, Kathleen, ed. *Inquiring Spirit: A Coleridge Reader.* London: Minerva, 1951.
Cock, Jacklyn. "Keeping the Fires Burning: Militarization and the Politics of Gender in South Africa." *Review of African Political Economy* 45/46 (1989): 50–64.
Cockburn, Cynthia. "The Gendered Dynamics of Armed Conflict and Political Violence." In Moser and Clark, *Victims, Perpetrators or Actors?* 13–29.
———. "The Continuum of Violence: A Gender Perspective on War and Peace." In Giles and Hyndman, *Sites of Violence: Gender and Conflict Zones,* 24–44.
Cohen, Rhonda, and Francis M. Deng, eds. *Masses in Flight: The Global Crisis of Internal Displacement.* Washington, DC: Brookings Institution Press, 1998.
Cole, Catherine M. *Ghana's Concert Party Theatre.* Bloomington: Indiana University Press, 2001.
Coleridge, Samuel Taylor. *Biographia Literaria XVI.* Vol. 2. In *Inquiring Spirit: A Coleridge Reader,* edited by Kathleen Coburn. London: Minerva, 1951.
Colson, Elizabeth. "Gendering Those Uprooted by 'Development.'" In Indra, *Engendering Forced Migration,* 23–39.
Comas-Diaz, Lillian, M. Brinton Lykes, and Renato D Alarcón. "Ethnic Conflict and the Psychology of Liberation in Guatemala, Peru, and Puerto Rico: International Perspectives." *American Psychologist* 53, no 7 (1998): 778–92.
Comrie, Bernard, Stephen Matthews, and Maria Polinsky, eds. *The Atlas of Languages: The Origin and Development of Languages throughout the World.* New York: Quarto, 1996.
Congo Global Action. http://www.congoglobalaction.org/.
CongoWarResource. http://www.congowarresource.org.
Coomaraswamy, Radhika, UN Secretary-General's Special Representative for Children and Armed Conflict. "Statement in the Security Council on the Occasion of the Open Debate on Children and Armed Conflict." New York: United Nations Security Council. February 12, 2008. http://www.un.org/children/conflict/english/12-feb-2008-open-debate-security-council.html.
Cooper, Frederick. "Decolonization in Africa: An Interpretation." In Appiah and Gates, *Africana,* 571–82.
Cooper, Robert L. *Language Planning and Social Change.* Cambridge: Cambridge University Press, 1989.
Corne, Chris. *From French to Creole: The Development of New Vernaculars in the French Colonial World.* London: Battlebridge, 1999.
Cornwall, Andrea. "Introduction: Perspectives on Gender in Africa." In *Readings in Gender in Africa,* edited by Andrea Cornwall, 1–19. Bloomington: Indiana University Press, 2005.
Cosgrove, Lisa, and Maureen C. McHugh. "Speaking for Ourselves: Feminist Methods and Community Psychology." *American Journal of Community Psychology* 28, no. 6 (2000): 815–38.
Crowley, Tony. *Standard English and the Politics of Language.* Urbana: University of Illinois Press, 1989.

Crystal, David. *The Cambridge Encyclopedia of Language*. Cambridge: Cambridge University Press, 1987.
Daiute, Colette, and Cynthia Lightfoot, eds. *Narrative Analysis: Studying the Development of Individuals in Society*. Thousand Oaks, CA: Sage, 2004.
D'Amico, Francine. "Feminist Perspectives on Women Warriors." In Lorentzen and Turpin, *The Women and War Reader*, 119–25.
Daniel, E. Valentine. *Charred Lullabies: Chapters in an Anthropography of Violence*. Princeton, NJ: Princeton University Press, 1996.
Davidson, Basil. *Africa in History*. 4th ed. New York: MacMillan, 1991.
Davies, Carole Boyce. "Motherhood in the Works of Male and Female Igbo Writers: Achebe, Emecheta, Nwapa and Nzekwu." In *Ngambika: Studies of Women in African Literature*, edited by Carole Boyce Davies and Anne Adams Graves, 241–56. Trenton, NJ: Africa World Press, 1990. Originally published 1986.
Davis, Mary. "Sylvia Pankhurst Memorial Lecture: Race, Class and Gender." Sylvia Pankhurst Memorial Committee, 2003. http://sylviapankhurst.gn.apc.org/SPML%202003.pdf.
Dayak, Mano. *Touareg: La tragédie*. Paris: Editions J. C. Lattès, 1992.
de Abreu, Alcinda A. "Mozambican Women Experiencing Violence." In *What Women Do in Wartime: Gender and Conflict in Africa*, edited by Meredeth Turshen and Clotilde Twagiramariya, 73–84. New York: Zed Books, 1998.
Deacon, Zermarie, and Cris Sullivan. "An Ecological Examination of Rural Mozambican Women's Attainment of Postwar Wellbeing." *Journal of Community Psychology* 38, no. 1 (2010): 115–30. http://dx.doi.org/10.1002/jcop.20355.
d'Eaubonne, Françoise. *Louise Michel la Canaque, 1873–1880*. Paris: Encre, 1985.
Debbasch, Charles, J. Bourdon, Jean-Marie Pontier, and Jean-Claude Ricci. *La Ve République*. Paris: Economica, 1985.
de Beauvoir, Simone. *The Second Sex*. Translated and edited by H. M. Parshley. Harmondsworth, England: Penguin Books, 1979. Originally published in French, 1949.
Decalo, Samuel. *Historical Dictionary of Niger*. London: Scarecrow, 1989.
de Certeau, Michel. *The Practice of Everyday Life*. Translated by Steven Rendall. Berkeley: University of California Press, 1988.
Defoe, Daniel. *Robinson Crusoe*. New York: Penguin Books, 2003. Originally published 1719.
Derderian, Richard L. "Algeria as a *lieu de memoire:* Ethnic Minority Memory and National Identity in Contemporary France." *Radical History Review* 83 (2002): 28–43.
Descamps, Marc-Alain. *L'invention du corps*. Paris: PUF, 1986.
de St. Jorre, John. *The Brothers' War: Biafra and Nigeria*. Boston: Houghton Mifflin, 1972.
De Temmerman, Els. *Aboke Girls: Children Abducted in Northern Uganda*. Kampala, Uganda: Fountain, 2001.
Diawara, Manthia. *African Cinema: Politics and Culture*. Bloomington: Indiana University Press, 1992.
Dibua, J. I. "Pan-Africanism." In Falola, *Africa*. Vol. 4, *The End of Colonial Rule: Nationalism and Decolonization*, 29–48.

Diken, Bülent, and Carsten Bagge Laustsen. "Becoming Abject: Rape as a Weapon of War." *Body and Society* 11, no. 1 (2005): 111–28.
Diop, Boubacar Boris. *Le temps de Tamango*, followed by *Thiaroye terre rouge*. Paris: L'Harmattan, 1981.
Djebar, Assia. *Children of the New World*. New York: Feminist Press at CUNY, 2005. Originally published in French, 1962.
Dominicy, Marc. "Prolégomènes à une théorie générale de l'évocation." In *Sémantique textuelle et évocation*, edited by M. Vanhelleputte, 9–37. Leuven, Belgium: Peeters, 1990.
Donham, Donald. "Staring at Suffering: Violence as a Subject." In *States of Violence: Politics, Youth, and Memory in Contemporary Africa*, edited by Edna G. Bay and Donald L. Donham, 16–33. Charlottesville: University of Virginia Press, 2006.
Downing, John D. H. *Radical Media: The Political Experience of Alternative Communication*. Boston: South End Press, 1984.
———. *Radical Media: Rebellious Communication and Social Movements*. Thousand Oaks, CA: Sage, 2001.
The Dream Becomes a Reality. DVD. Directed by Eva Beth Egensteiner. Berkeley: University of California Extension Center for Media and Independent Learning, 1995.
Drewal, Margaret Thompson. "The State of Research on Performance in Africa." *African Studies Review* 34 (1991): 1–64.
Duara, Prasenjit. *Decolonization: Perspectives from Now and Then*. London: Routledge, 2004.
Dugan, James, and Laurence Lafore. *Days of Emperor and Clown: The Italo-Ethiopian War 1935–1936*. Garden City, NJ: Doubleday, 1973.
Ebo, Bosah. "American Media and African Culture." In Hawk, *Africa's Media Image*, 15–25.
Eboh, Marie Pauline. "The Woman Question: African and Western Perspectives." In *African Philosophy: An Anthology*, edited by Emmanuel Chukwudi Eze, 333–37. Oxford: Blackwell, 1997.
Echenberg, Myron J. "Tragedy at Thiaroye: The Senegalese Soldiers' Uprising of 1944." In *African Labor History*, edited by Peter C. W. Gutkind, Robin Cohen, and Jean Copans, 109–28. Beverly Hills, CA: Sage, 1978.
Echeruo, Michael. *Mortality*. London: Longman, 1968.
Edwards, John. *Language, Society and Identity*. Oxford, Blackwell, 1985.
Efiong, Philip. *Nigeria and Biafra: My Story*. Astoria, NY: Seaburn Books, 2007.
Eisele, John C. "The Wild East: Deconstructing the Language of Genre in the Hollywood Eastern." *Cinema Journal* 41, no. 4 (2002): 68–94.
Ekwensi, Cyprian. *Survive the Peace*. London: Heinemann, 1976.
Eliasoph, Nina. "Routines and the Making of Oppositional News." *Critical Studies in Mass Communication* 5 (1988): 313–34.
Emecheta, Buchi. *Destination Biafra*. New York: Allison & Busby, 1982.
Enloe, Cynthia. *Does Khaki Become You? The Militarization of Women's Lives*. Boston: South End Press, 1983.
———. *Maneuvers: The International Politics of Militarizing Women's Lives*. Berkeley: University of California Press, 2000.

Ertürk, Yakin. *Promotion and Protection of All Human Rights, Civil, Political, Economic, Social and Cultural, Including the Right to Development. Report of the Special Rapporteur on Violence against Women, Its Causes and Consequences.* New York: United Nations General Assembly, 2008.

Etchart, Linda, and Rawwida Baksh. "Applying a Gender Lens to Armed Conflict, Violence and Conflict Transformation." In *Gender Mainstreaming in Conflict Transformation: Building Sustainable Peace*, edited by Elsie Onubogu, Linda Etchart, Rawwida Baksh, and Tina Johnson, 14–33. London: Commonwealth Secretariat, 2005.

Evenson, Elizabeth M. "Truth and Justice in Sierra Leone: Coordination between Commission and Court." *Columbia Law Review* 104, no. 3 (2004): 730–67.

Ezra. DVD. Directed by Newton Aduaka. San Francisco: California Newsreel, 2007.

Fairclough, Norman. *Critical Discourse Analysis: The Critical Study of Language.* London: Longman, 1995.

———. *Media Discourse.* New York: Hodder Arnold, 1995.

Falola, Toyin. *Violence in Nigeria: The Crisis of Religious Politics and Secular Ideologies.* Rochester, NY: University of Rochester Press, 1998.

———. *The History of Nigeria.* Westport, CT: Greenwood, 1999.

———. *Key Events in African History: A Reference Guide.* Westport, CT: Greenwood, 2002.

———. *Nationalism and African Intellectuals.* Rochester, NY: University of Rochester Press, 2004. Originally published 2001.

———, ed. *Africa.* Vol. 3, *Colonial Africa, 1885–1939.* Durham, NC: Carolina Academic Press, 2002.

———, ed. *Africa.* Vol. 4, *The End of Colonial Rule: Nationalism and Decolonization.* Durham, NC: Carolina Academic Press, 2002.

Fanon, Frantz. *The Wretched of the Earth.* Translated by Constance Farrington. New York: Grove, 1991; London: Penguin Books, 2001. Originally published in French, 1961.

Faraclas, Nicholas. *Nigerian Pidgin.* London: Routledge, 1996.

Farwell, Nancy. "War Rape: New Conceptualizations and Responses." *Affilia* 19, no. 4 (2004): 389–403.

Faust, Drew Gilpin. *This Republic of Suffering: Death and the American Civil War.* New York: Knopf, 2008.

Faye, Cheikh Faty. *Aube de sang.* Paris: L'Harmattan, 2005.

Feeley, Rebecca, and Colin Thomas-Jensen. *Getting Serious about Ending Conflict and Sexual Violence in Congo.* ENOUGH Strategy Paper 15, March 2008. http://www.enoughproject.org/reports.congoserious.

———. *Past Due: Remove the FDLR from Eastern Congo.* ENOUGH Strategy Paper 22, 2008. http://www.enoughproject.org/publications/past-due-remove-fdlr-eastern-congo.

Feminist Majority Foundation. "Senate Committee Hearing on Rape as a Weapon of War." *Feminist Daily News Wire*, April 3, 2008. http://feminist.org/news/newsbyte/uswirestory.asp?id=10919.

Fernandez, James W. *Persuasions and Performances: The Play of Tropes in Culture.* Bloomington: Indiana University Press, 1986.

Ferreira, Eduardo de Sousa. *Portuguese Colonization in Africa: The End of an Era*. Paris: UNESCO, 1974.
Fistula Foundation. http://www.fistulafoundation.org/.
Flame. DVD. Directed by Ingrid Sinclair. San Francisco: California Newsreel, 1996.
Foa, Edna B., Terence Martin Keane, and Matthew J. Friedman., eds. *Effective Treatments for PTSD: Practice Guidelines from the International Society for Traumatic Stress Studies*. London: Guilford Press, 2000.
Fontaine, Nasio. *Living in the Positive*. Sanctuary/RAS compact disc B0002XMF12.
Foss, Sonja K. "Ideological Criticism." In *Rhetorical Criticism: Exploration and Practice*, edited by Sonja K. Foss, 239–71. Long Grove, IL: Waveland, 2004.
Foucault, Michel. *Discipline and Punish*. New York: Vintage, 1979.
Forsyth, Frederick. *The Biafra Story: The Making of an African Legend*. Barnsley, England: Pen & Sword, 2007.
Fraser, Robert. *Ben Okri: Towards the Invisible City*. London: Northcote House, 2002.
Fussell, Paul. *The Great War and Modern Memory*. New York: Oxford University Press, 1977.
Gast, Marceau. "Relations amoureuses chez les Kel Ahaggar." In *Amour, phantasmes et sociétés en Afrique du Nord et au Sahara*, edited by Tassadit Yacine, 151–73. Paris: L'Harmattan-Awal, 1993.
Genova, James E. "Conflicted Missionaries: Power and Identity in French West Africa during the 1930s." *The Historian* 66, no. 1 (2004): 45–59.
Gershoni, Yekutiel. "War without End and an End to a War: The Prolonged Wars in Liberia and Sierra Leone." *African Studies Review* 40, no. 3 (1997): 55–76.
Giles, Wenona, and Jennifer Hyndman, eds. *Sites of Violence: Gender and Conflict Zones*. Berkeley: University of California Press, 2004.
Gioseffi, Daniela, ed. *Women on War: An International Anthology of Writings from Antiquity to the Present*. New York: Feminist Press at CUNY, 2003.
Glassborow, Katy, and Peter Eichstaedt. "Paralysis over Deepening Goma Crisis." *Africa Report* 192. Institute for War and Peace Reporting (IWPR), November 2008. http://www.ipr.net/?=acr&s=f&o&apc_state=henh.
Glover, Jonathan. *Humanity: A Moral History of the Twentieth Century*. London: Pimlico, 2001. Originally published 1999.
Going Home. DVD. Directed by Emily Marlow. Produced by Jenny Richards. Oley, PA: Bullfrog Films, 1999.
Goldstone, Richard J. "Prosecuting Rape as a War Crime." *Case Western Reserve Journal of International Law* 34, no. 3 (2002): 277–86.
Gordon, Raymond G., ed. *Ethnologue: Languages of the World*. 15th ed. Dallas, TX: SIL International, 2005. Online version at http://www.ethnologue.com.
Graham-Douglas, Nabo B. *Ojukwu's Rebellion and World Opinion*. London: Galitzine, Chant, Russell, and Partners, 1968.
Grant, Iain Hamilton. "Postmodernism and Politics." In *The Routledge Companion to Postmodernism*, edited by Stuart Sim, 23–32. 2nd ed. London: Routledge, 2001.
The Greatest Silence: Rape in the Congo. Produced and directed by Lisa F. Jackson. New York: Jackson Films, 2007. http://www.thegreatestsilence.org/.
Green, Edward C., and Alcinda Honwana. "Indigenous Healing of War-affected Children in Africa." *Africa Policy E-Journal* 10 (1999). http://www.africaaction.org/docs99/vio19907.htm.

Griffin, Susan. *Rape: The Power of Consciousness.* New York: Harper & Row, 1979.
Gurney, Ivor. *Selected Poems.* Oxford: Oxford University Press, 1990.
Halbwachs, Maurice. *The Collective Memory.* Translated by Francis J. Ditter Jr. and Vida Yazdi Ditter. New York: Harper & Row, 1980. Originally published in French, 1950.
Hale, Sondra. "The Soldier and the State; Post-liberation Women: The Case of Eritrea." In Waller and Rycenga, *Frontline Feminisms: Women, War, and Resistance,* 349–70.
Halim, Asma Abdel. "Attack with a Friendly Weapon." In *What Women Do in Wartime,* edited by Meredeth Turshen and Clotilde Twagiramariya, 85–100. London: Zed Books, 1998.
Hall, Stuart. "The Whites of Their Eyes: Racist Ideologies and the Media." In *Silver Linings: Some Strategies for the Eighties,* edited by Georges Bridges and Rosalind Brundt, 28–52. London: Lawrence & Wishart, 1981.
Hamilton, James, and Chris Atton. "Theorizing Anglo-American Alternative Media: Toward a Contextual History and Analysis of US and UK Scholarship." *Media History* 7, no. 2 (2001): 119–35.
Handelman, Don. *Models and Mirrors: Towards an Anthropology of Public Events.* Oxford: Berghahn Books, 1998.
Hansen, Lene. "Gender, Nation and Rape: Bosnia and the Construction of Security." *International Feminist Journal of Politics* 3, no. 1 (2001): 55–75.
Hargreaves, Alec G. *Voices from the North African Immigrant Community in France: Immigration and Identity in Beur Fiction.* New York: Berg, 1991.
———. *Multi-ethnic France: Immigration, Politics, Culture and Society.* 2nd ed. New York: Routledge, 2007.
Hargreaves, John D. *Decolonization in Africa.* 2nd ed. London: Longman, 1996.
Harris, Roxy, and Ben Rampton. "Creole Metaphors in Cultural Analysis." In *Deconstructing Creole,* edited by Umberto Ansaldo, Stephen Matthews, and Lisa Lim, 265–85. Amsterdam: John Benjamins, 2007.
Harvey, Penelope, and Peter Gow, eds. *Sex and Violence: Issues in Representation and Experience.* London: Routledge, 1994.
Hawk, Beverly G., ed. *Africa's Media Image.* New York: Praeger, 1992.
———. "Introduction: Metaphors of African Coverage," in *Africa's Media Image,* 3–14.
———. "African Politics and American Reporting." In *Media and Democracy in Africa,* edited by Goran Hyden, Michael Leslie, and Folu F. Ogundimu, 157–76. New Brunswick, NJ: Transaction Publishers, 2002.
Heal Africa. "Global Call for Action: Demand End to War-rapes in Goma DRC." October 30, 2008. healafrica.org/cms/files/media/Goma%20Global%20Action%20Petition.doc.
Hegel, Georg Wilhelm Friedrich. *Hegel's Phenomenology of Spirit: Selections.* Translated by Howard P. Kainz. University Park: Pennsylvania State University Press, 1994. Originally published in German, 1807.
———. *The Philosophy of History.* Translated by J. Sibree. New York: Dover, 1956; Amherst, NY: Prometheus Books, 1991. Originally published in German, 1837.
Heine, Bernd, and Derek Nurse, eds. *African Languages: An Introduction.* Cambridge: Cambridge University Press, 2000.

Héritiers de la Justice. *Congo, terre d'impunité et d'arbitraire*. Bukavu, DRC: Héritiers de la Justice, 2003.
Herman, Judith. L. *Trauma and Recovery*. New York: Basic Books, 1992.
Hernández, Pilar. "Trauma in War and Political Persecution: Expanding the Concept." *American Journal of Orthopsychiatry* 72, no. 1 (2002): 16–25.
Herzfeld, Michael. *The Poetics of Manhood: Contest and Identity in a Cretan Mountain Village*. Princeton, NJ: Princeton University Press, 1985.
———. *Anthropology: Theoretical Practice in Culture and Society*. Malden, MA: Blackwell and UNESCO, 2001.
Hesford, Wendy S. "Documenting Violations: Rhetorical Witnessing and the Spectacle of Distant Suffering." *Biography* 27, no. 1 (2004): 104–44.
Higgins, Maryellen. "Human Rights in Hollywood's Africa: *Blood Diamond* and *The Last King of Scotland*." Paper presented at the annual African Studies Association Conference, New York, October 18–21, 2007.
Himmelstrand, Ulf. "The Problem of Cultural Translation in the Reporting of African Social Realities." In *Reporting Africa*, edited by Olav Stokke, 117–33. New York: Africana, 1971.
Hobsbawm, Eric. *The Age of Empire 1875–1914*. New York: Random House, 1989.
Hochschild, Adam. *King Leopold's Ghost: A Story of Greed, Terror, and Heroism in Colonial Africa*. New York: Houghton Mifflin, 1999.
Hock, Hans Henrich, and Brian D. Joseph. *Language History, Language Change, and Language Relationship: An Introduction to Historical and Comparative Linguistics*. Berlin: Mouton de Gruyter, 1996.
Holm, John A. *Languages in Contact: The Partial Restructuring of Vernaculars*. Cambridge: Cambridge University Press, 2003.
Honwana, Alcinda. "Sealing the Past, Facing the Future: Trauma Healing in Rural Mozambique." *Accord* 3 (1998): 75–81.
———. *Child Soldiers in Africa*. Philadelphia: University of Pennsylvania Press, 2006.
hooks, bell. *Talking Back: Thinking Feminist, Thinking Black*. Boston: South End Press, 1989.
———. *Salvation: Black People and Love*. New York: HarperCollins, 2001.
———. *Child Soldiers in Africa*. Philadelphia: University of Pennsylvania Press, 2006.
Howe, Russell Warren. "Gold Coast into Ghana." *Phylon Quarterly* 18, no. 2 (1957): 155–61.
Human Rights Watch. *Seeking Protection: Addressing Sexual and Domestic Violence in Tanzania's Refugee Camps*. New York: Human Rights Watch, 2000.
———. *Reluctant Recruits: Children and Adults Forcibly Recruited for Military Service in North Kivu*. New York: Human Rights Watch, 2001/2005.
———. *The War within the War: Sexual Violence against Women and Girls in Eastern Congo*. New York: Human Rights Watch, 2002.
———. *Stolen Children: Abduction and Recruitment in Northern Uganda*. New York: Human Rights Watch, 2003.
———. *Renewed Crisis in North Kivu*. New York: Human Rights Watch, October 2007. http://hrw.org/reports/2007/drc/007/.
———. Briefing to the UN Security Council on the Situation in the Democratic Republic of the Congo, November 25, 2008. http://www.hrw.org/en/news/2008/11/25/briefing-un-security-council-situation-democratic-republic-congo.

Human Rights Watch/Africa, Human Rights Watch Women's Rights Project, Fédération Internationale des Ligues des Droits de l'Homme. *Shattered Lives: Sexual Violence during the Rwandan Genocide and Its Aftermath*. New York: Human Rights Watch, 1996.
Hume, David. *Essays, Moral, Political, and Literary*. Edited by Eugene F. Miller. Library of Economics and Liberty, 1987. http://www.econlib.org/library/LFBooks/Hume/hmMPL.html. Originally published 1742.
Hunt, Swanee, and Cristina Posa. "Women Waging Peace." *Foreign Policy* 124 (2001): 38–47.
Igreja, Victor. "'Why Are There So Many Drums Playing until Dawn?' Exploring the Role of Gamba Spirits and Healers in the Post-war Recovery Period in Gorongosa, Central Mozambique." *Transcultural Psychiatry* 40, no. 4 (2003): 460–87.
———, Bas Schreuder, and Wim Kleijn. "The Cultural Dimension of War Traumas in Central Mozambique: The Case of Gorongosa." *International Forum for Psychiatry* (2004). http://www.priory.com/psych/traumacult.htm.
———, Wim Kleijn, and Annemiek Richters. "When the War Was Over, Little Changed: Women's Posttraumatic Suffering after the War in Mozambique." *Journal of Nervous and Mental Disease* 194, no. 7 (2006): 502–9.
Ike, Vincent Chukwuemeka. *Sunset at Dawn: A Novel about Biafra*. London: Collins & Harvill, 1976.
Indra, Doreen, ed. *Engendering Forced Migration: Theory and Practice*. New York: Berghahn Books, 1999.
———. "Not a 'Room of One's Own': Engendering Forced Migration Knowledge and Practice." In Indra, *Engendering Forced Migration*, 1–22.
Institute for War and Peace Reporting (IWPR). *Special Report: Sexual Violence in the Democratic Republic of Congo*. Edited by Caroline Tosh and Yigal Chazan. The Hague: Institute for War and Peace Reporting, 2008. http://www.iwpr.net/pdf/IWPR_NL_DRC_special_102008.pdf.
Integrated Regional Information Network (IRIN). "Our Bodies—Their Battle Ground: Gender-based Violence in Conflict Zones." United Nations Office for the Coordination of Humanitarian Affairs (UNOCHA), 2004. http://www.irinnews.org/InDepthMain.aspx?InDepthID=20&ReportID=62817.
———. "Congo-Kinshasa: Campaign against Sexual Violence in South Kivu." United Nations Office for the Coordination of Humanitarian Affairs (UNOCHA), November 29, 2007. http://www.irinnews.org/report.aspx?ReportID=75580.
———. Congo-Kinshasa: "Sexual Abuse of Minors Doubles in Kasai Occidental Town," December 5, 2008. http://www.irinnews.org/Report.aspx?ReportId=81836.
Internal Displacement Monitoring Center. *Focus on North Kivu Province: IDPs on the Move Face Grave Human Rights Violations*. IDMC Report, November 21, 2008. http://www.internaldisplacement.org/idmc/website/countries.nsf/(httpCountries)/554559DA500C858880257OA7004A96C7?OpenDocument&count=1000.
International Crisis Group. *Congo Crisis: Military Intervention in Ituri*. ICG Africa Report 64, 2003. http://www.crisisgroup.org/home/index.cfm?1=1&id=1626.
———. *The Kivus: The Forgotten Crucible of the Congo Conflict*. ICG Africa Report 56, 2003. http://www.crisisgroup.org/home/index.cfm?id=1630&1=1.
———. *Congo: Bringing Peace to North Kivu*. ICG Africa Report 133, 2007. http://www.crisisgroup.org/home/index.cfm?id=5134.

In the Wake of War. DVD. Directed by James Heer. Produced by Brenda Kelly. Oley, PA: Bullfrog Films, 2004.
Invisible Children. DVD. Directed by Jason Russell, Bobby Bailey, and Laren Poole. Spring Valley, CA: Invisible Children, 2006.
Irele, Abiola F. *The African Imagination: Literature in Africa and the Black Diaspora.* New York: Oxford University Press, 2001.
Isichei, Elizabeth. *A History of Nigeria.* New York: Longman, 1984.
Israel, Adrienne M. "The Afrocentric Perspective in African Journalism: A Case Study of the Ashanti Pioneer, 1939–1957." *Journal of Black Studies* 22, no. 3 (1992): 411–28.
Itote, Waruhiu. *"Mau Mau" General.* Nairobi, Kenya: East African Publishing House, 1967.
Iyayi, Festus. *Heroes.* Harlow, England: Longman, 1986.
James, Winston. *Holding Aloft the Banner of Ethiopia: Caribbean Radicalism in Early Twentieth-century America.* New York: Verso, 1998.
Jefferson, Thomas. *Notes on the State of Virginia.* Chapel Hill: University of North Carolina Press, 1995. Originally published 1787.
Johns Hopkins Bloomberg School of Public Health. "Obstetric Fistula: Ending the Silence, Easing the Suffering." *Info Reports* 2, 2004. http://www.info.k4health.org/inforeports/fistula/index.shtml.
Johnson Jr., David P. "Léopold Sédar Senghor." In Appiah and Gates, *Africana*, 1691–92.
Jok, Jok Madut. "Militarization and Gender Violence in South Sudan." *Journal of African and Asian Studies* 34, no. 4 (1999): 427–42.
Joseph, Brian D., and Richard D. Janda, eds. *The Handbook of Historical Linguistics.* London: Blackwell, 2005.
July, Robert W. "Toward Cultural Independence in Africa: Some Illustrations from Nigeria and Ghana." *African Studies Review* 26, nos. 3/4 (1983): 119–31.
Kalouaz, Ahmed. *Point kilométrique 190.* Paris: L'Harmattan, 1986.
Kant, Immanuel. *Observations on the Feeling of the Beautiful and Sublime.* Translated by John T. Goldthwait. Berkeley: University of California Press, 1960. Originally published in German, 1764.
Karani, Florida. "The Situation and Roles of Women in Kenya: An Overview." *Journal of Negro Education* 56, no. 3 (1987): 422–34.
Kariuki, Josiah Mwangi. *"Mau Mau" Detainee: The Account of a Kenyan African of His Experiences in Detention Camps, 1953–1960.* Foreword by Margery Perham. London: Oxford University Press, 1963.
Keck, Margaret E., and Kathryn Sikkink. *Activists beyond Borders: Advocacy Networks in International Politics.* Ithaca, NY: Cornell University Press, 1998.
Keenan, Jeremy. *The Tuareg: People of Ahaggar.* London: Allen Lane, 1976.
Keim, Curtis. *Mistaking Africa: Curiosities and Inventions of the American Mind.* Boulder, CO: Westview, 1999.
Keitetsi, China. *Child Soldier: Fighting for My Life.* Johannesburg: Jacana Media, 2005.
Kettane, Nacer. *Le sourire de Brahim.* Paris: Denoël, 1985.
Khatibi, Abdelkebir. *La mémoire tatouée: Autobiographie d'un décolonisé.* Paris: Les lettres nouvelles, 1971.

Killam, Douglas, and Ruth Rowe, eds. *The Companion to African Literatures.* Oxford: James Currey, 2000.
Kilson, Martin L., Jr. "Nationalism and Social Classes in British West Africa." *Journal of Politics* 20, no. 2 (1958): 368–87.
Kinoti, Kathambi. "What Are the Challenges in Using Transitional Justice Structures to Address Sexual Violence in Situations of Conflict?" Association of Women's Rights in Development (AWID), July 25, 2008. http://www.awid.org/eng/Issues-and-Analysis/Library/Transitional-Justice-and-Rape-in-Conflict.
Kinyatti, Maina wa, ed. *Thunder from the Mountains: Mau Mau Patriotic Songs.* London: Zed Books, 1980.
Kipling, Rudyard. "The White Man's Burden." *McClure's Magazine* 12 (1899).
Kourouma, Ahmadou. *Allah Is Not Obliged.* New York: Anchor Books, 2006.
Krause, Charles. "Conflict in Congo." *Online NewsHour.* PBS, October 22, 1998. http://www.pbs.org/newshour/bb/africa/july-dec98/congo_10-22.html.
Kubai, Ann Nkirote. "Living in the Shadow of Genocide: Women and HIV/AIDS in Rwanda." In *Women, Religion and HIV/AIDS in Africa: Responding to Ethical and Theological Challenges,* edited by T. M. Hinga, A. N. Kubai, P. Mwaura, and H. Ayanga, 51–74. Pietermaritzburg, South Africa: Cluster Publications, 2008.
Laitin, David D. "The Tower of Babel as a Coordination Game: Political Linguistics in Ghana." *American Political Science Review* 88, no. 3 (1994): 622–34.
———, Robert H. Bates, Peter Lange, eds. *Language Repertoires and State Construction in Africa.* Cambridge: Cambridge University Press, 2007.
Lallaoui, Mehdi. *Les Beurs de Seine.* Paris: L'Arcantère, 1986.
———. *Kabyles du Pacifique.* Bezons, France: Au nom de la mémoire, 1994.
———. *La colline aux oliviers.* Paris: Editions alternatives, 1998.
———. *Une nuit d'octobre.* Paris: Editions alternatives, 2001.
———, and Agnès Denis. *Le silence du fleuve.* Documentary. Directed by Mehdi Lalloui and Agnès Denis. Bezons, France: Au nom de la mémoire, 1991.
Laronde, Michel. *Autour du roman beur: Immigration et identité.* Paris: L'Harmattan, 1993.
———, ed. *L'Ecriture décentrée: La langue de l'Autre dans le roman contemporain.* Paris: L'Harmattan, 1996.
Last, Murray. "Healing the Social Wounds of War." *Medicine, Conflict and Survival* 16, no. 4 (2000): 370–82.
Le Page, Robert, and Andrée Tabouret-Keller. *Acts of Identity: Creole-based Approaches to Language and Ethnicity.* Cambridge: Cambridge University Press, 1985.
———. *Acts of Identity: Creole-based Approaches to Language and Ethnicity.* 2nd ed., with additional comments. Fernelmont, Belgium: InterCommunications & EME, 2006.
Le Pen, Jean-Marie. *Les Français d'abord.* Paris: Carrere-Michel Lafon, 1984.
Levine, Donald N. *Greater Ethiopia: The Evolution of a Multiethnic Society.* Chicago: University of Chicago Press, 1974.
Liberia: A Fragile Peace. DVD. Produced and directed by Steven W. Ross. San Francisco: California Newsreel, 2006.
Liberia: An Uncivil War. DVD. Produced and directed by Jonathan Stack. San Francisco: California Newsreel, 2005.

London, Charles. *One Day the Soldiers Came: Voices of Children in War.* New York: Harper Perennial, 2007.
Lonsdale, John. "Ethnicité morale et tribalisme politique." *Politique Africaine* 61 (March 1996): 98–115.
Loomba, Ania. "Seizing the Book." In Ania Loomba, *Gender, Race, Renaissance Drama,* 142–58. New York: Manchester University Press, 1989.
Lorcin, Patricia M. E. *Imperial Identities: Stereotyping, Prejudice and Race in Colonial Algeria.* London: I. B. Tauris, 1995.
Lorentzen, Lois Ann, and Jennifer Turpin, eds. *The Women and War Reader.* New York: New York University Press, 1998.
Loughran, Kristyne, and Thomas Seligman, eds. *Art of Being Tuareg: Sahara Nomads in a Modern World.* Los Angeles and Stanford, CA: Fowler Museum and Cantor Arts Center, 2006.
Lowell, A. Lawrence. "Alternatives before the League." *Foreign Affairs* 15, no. 1 (1936): 102–11.
Lubkemann, Stephen C. *Culture in Chaos: An Anthropology of the Social Condition in War.* Chicago: University of Chicago Press, 2008.
Lyons, Tanya. "The Forgotten Soldiers: Women in Zimbabwe's Liberation War." *Southern Africa Report* 12, no. 2 (1997): 12.
———. "Guerrilla Girls and Women in the Zimbabwean National Liberation Struggle." In *Women in African Colonial Histories,* edited by Jean Allman, Susan Geiger, and Nakanyike Musisi, 305–26. Bloomington: Indiana University Press, 2002.
———. *Guns and Guerrilla Girls: Women in the Zimbabwean Liberation Struggle.* Trenton, NJ: Africa World Press, 2004.
Mabon, Armelle. "La tragédie de Thiaroye, symbole du déni d'égalité." *Hommes et migrations* 1235 (2002): 86–95.
MacAloon, John J. *This Great Symbol: Pierre de Coubertin and the Origins of the Modern Olympic Games.* Chicago: University of Chicago Press, 1981.
———, ed. *Rite, Drama, Festival, Spectacle: Rehearsals toward a Theory of Cultural Performance.* Philadelphia: Institute for the Study of Human Issues, 1984.
Macey, David. *Frantz Fanon: A Life.* London: Granta Books, 2000.
MacKinnon, Catharine A. *Are Women Human? And Other International Dialogues.* Cambridge, MA: Belknap Press of Harvard University Press, 2006.
Macklin, Audrey. "Like Oil and Water, with a Match: Militarized Commerce, Armed Conflict, and Human Security in Sudan." In Giles and Hyndman, *Sites of Violence: Gender and Conflict Zones,* 75–107.
Magaia, Lina. *Dumba Nengue: Run for Your Life; Peasant Tales of Tragedy in Mozambique.* London: Karnak House, 1989.
Makoni, Sinfree, Geneva Smitherman, Arnetha F. Ball, and Arthur K. Spears, eds. *Black Linguistics: Language, Society, and Politics in Africa and the Americas.* London: Routledge, 2003.
Maloba, Wunyabari O. "The Media and Mau Mau: Kenyan Nationalism and Colonial Propaganda." In Hawk, *Africa's Media Image,* 51–61.
———. *Mau Mau and Kenya: An Analysis of a Peasant Revolt.* Bloomington: Indiana University Press, 1993.
———. *African Women in Revolution.* Trenton, NJ: Africa World Press, 2007.
Maraire, J. Nozipo. *Zenzele: A Letter for My Daughter.* New York: Dell, 1996.

Marchal, Jules. *E. D. Morel contre Léopold II: L'histoire du Congo 1900–1910.* Vols. 1 and 2. Paris: L'Harmattan, 1996.

———. *L'Etat libre du Congo: Paradis perdu; L'Histoire du Congo 1876–1900.* Vols. 1 and 2. Borgloon, Belgium: Editions Paula Bellings, 1996.

Marcus, Jonathan. *The National Front and French Politics: The Resistible Rise of Jean-Marie Le Pen.* Basingstoke, England: MacMillan, 1995.

Marshall, Judith. "Structural Adjustment and Social Policy in Mozambique." *Review of African Political Economy* 17, no. 47 (1990): 28–43.

Martínez, Samuel. "Making Violence Visible: An Activist Anthropological Approach to Women's Rights Investigation," in *Engaging Contradictions: Theory, Politics, and Methods of Activist Scholarship*, edited by Charles R. Hale, 183–209. Berkeley, CA: University of California Press, 2008.

Marysse, Stefaan, and Filip Reyntjens. *Political Economy of the Great Lakes Region of Africa: The Pitfalls of Enforced Democracy and Globalization.* London: Palgrave Macmillan, 2006.

Maughan-Brown, David. *Land, Freedom and Fiction: History and Ideology in Kenya.* London: Zed Books, 1985.

The Mau Mau in Kenya. With foreword by Granville Roberts. London: Hutchinson, 1954.

Mazrui, Alamin M. *English in Africa: After the Cold War.* Clevedon, England: Multilingual Matters, 2004.

Mazrui, Ali A. "Nkrumah: the Leninist Czar." *Transition* 26 (1966): 9–17.

———. "Nationalism, Ethnicity, and Violence." In Wiredu, *A Companion to African Philosophy*, 472–82.

———, and Alamin M. Mazrui. *The Power of Babel: Language and Governance in the African Experience.* Oxford: James Currey, 1998.

Mbaluka, Rosemary Mueni. In Pursuit of Justice: A Research Report on Service Providers' Response to Cases of Violence against Women in Nairobi Province. Nairobi: Coalition on Violence against Women, 2002.

Mbembe, Achille. *On the Postcolony.* Berkeley: University of California Press, 2001.

McCarthy, Michael. *Dark Continent: Africa as Seen by Americans.* Westport, CT: Greenwood, 1983.

McChesney, Robert W. *Rich Media, Poor Democracy: Communication Politics in Dubious Times.* Chicago: University of Illinois Press, 1999.

McCrum, Robert, William Cran, and Robert MacNeil. *The Story of English.* 2nd ed. New York: Penguin Books, 1992.

McDonnell, Faith J. H., and Grace Akallo. *Girl Soldier: A Story of Hope for Northern Uganda's Children.* Grand Rapids, MI: Chosen Books, 2007.

McEvedy, Colin. *The Penguin Atlas of African History.* Rev. ed. London: Penguin Books, 1995.

McKay, Susan. "The Effects of Armed Conflict on Girls and Women." *Peace and Conflict: Journal of Peace Psychology* 4, no. 4 (1998): 381–92.

McWhorter, John H. *Defining Creole.* Oxford: Oxford University Press, 2005.

Médecins Sans Frontières. *Ituri: "Civilians Still the First Victims." Permanence of Sexual Violence and Impact of Military Operations.* Geneva: Médecins Sans Frontières, 2007.

Mendoza-Denton, Norma. "Language and Identity." In *The Handbook of Language Variation and Change*, edited by J. K. Chambers, Peter Trudgill, and Natalie Schilling-Estes, 475–99. London: Blackwell, 2004.

Meredith, Martin. *The Fate of Africa from the Hopes of Freedom to the Heart of Despair: A History of 50 Years of Independence.* New York: Public Affairs, 2005.
Meyer, Karl E. *The Dust of Empire: The Race for Mastery in the Asian Heartland.* New York: Public Affairs/A Century Foundation Book, 2004.
Michel, Louise. *Souvenirs et aventures de ma vie.* Paris: Maspero, 1983.
Michel, Marc. "*Hosties noires* entre mémoire et reconnaissance." In *Léopold Sédar Senghor: Africanité-universalité.* Edited by Jacques Girault and Bernard Lecherbonnier, 101–10. Paris: L'Harmattan, 2002.
Michelman, Fredric. "From Tamango to Thiaroye: The Revolution Back on Course?" *Research in African Literatures* 21 (1990): 59–65.
Millward, C. M. *A Biography of the English Language.* 2nd ed. Fort Worth, TX: Harcourt Brace College, 1996.
Milne, June. *Kwame Nkrumah: A Biography.* London: Panaf, 1999.
Ministry of State for Planning and National Development and Vision 2030. *Kenya Vision 2030.* Nairobi, Kenya: National Economic and Social Council of Kenya, 2007.
Monfils, Barbara S. "A Multifaceted Image: Kwame Nkrumah's Extrinsic Rhetorical Strategies." *Journal of Black Studies* 7, no. 3 (1977): 313–30.
Moore, Gerald, and Ulli Beier. *The Penguin Book of Modern African Poetry:* London: Penguin Books, 1998.
Morgan, Philip D., and Sean Hawkins. *Black Experience and the Empire.* Oxford: Oxford University Press, 2004.
Morrison, Toni. "Unspeakable Things Unspoken: The Afro-American Presence in American Literature." In *Within the Circle: An Anthology of African American Literary Criticism from the Harlem Renaissance to the Present,* edited by Angelyn Mitchell, 368–98. Durham, NC: Duke University Press, 1994.
Mortu Nega (Those Whom Death Refused). DVD. Directed by Flora Gomes. San Francisco: California Newsreel, 1997.
Moser, Caroline O. N. "The Gendered Continuum of Violence and Conflict: An Operational Framework," In Moser and Clark, *Victims, Perpetrators or Actors?* 13–51.
Moser, Caroline O. N., and Fiona C. Clark, eds. *Victims, Perpetrators or Actors? Gender, Armed Conflict and Political Violence.* New York: Zed Books, 2001.
Mouralis, Bernard. *République et colonies. Entre mémoire et histoire: la République française et l'Afrique.* Paris: Présence africaine, 1999.
Mueni Mbaluka, Rosemary. *In Pursuit of Justice: A Research Report on Service Providers' Response to Cases of Violence against Women in Nairobi Province.* Nairobi: Coalition on Violence against Women—Kenya, 2002.
Mufwene, Salikoko S. *The Ecology of Language Evolution.* Cambridge: Cambridge University Press, 2001.
Murphy, William P. "Military Patrimonialism and Child Soldier Clientism in the Liberian and Sierra Leonean Civil War." *African Studies Review* 46, no. 2 (2003): 61–87.
Mwaura, Njoroge, et al. "Kenya: Celebrating Power Deal." Kenya Television Network, February 28, 2008.
———. "Swearing In of Kenyan Cabinet." Kenya Television Network, April 17, 2008. http://www.Africast.tv.

Myers-Scotton, Carol. *Duelling Languages: Grammatical Structures in Codeswitching.* Oxford: Clarendon, 1993.
Nance, Kimberly. "Disarming Testimony: Speakers' Resistance to Readers' Defenses in Latin American *Testimonio.*" *Biography* 24, no. 3 (2001): 570–88.
Ndumbe, J. Anyu. "Diamonds, Ethnicity, and Power: The Case of Sierra Leone." *Mediterranean Quarterly* 12, no. 4 (2001): 90–105.
NGO Working Group on Women Peace and Security. *Resolution 1325: Two Years On.* October 31, 2002. http:www.peacewomen.org/un/ngo/ngopub/NGOWGTwoYearsOn.pdf.
Ngugi wa Thiong'o. *Decolonising the Mind: The Politics of Language in African Literature.* Nairobi: Heinemann, 1988. Originally published 1986.
———. "A Statement." In Ngugi wa Thiong'o, *Decolonising the Mind*, xiv.
———, and Micere Githae Mugo. *The Trial of Dedan Kimathi.* Oxford: Heinemann, 1977.
Nicol, Davidson. "Politics, Nationalism and Universities in Africa." *African Affairs* 62, no. 246 (1963): 20–28.
Nicolaisen, Ida, and Johannes Nicolaisen. *The Pastoral Tuareg: Ecology, Culture and Society.* Copenhagen: Rhodos, 1997.
Nikolić-Ristanović, Vesna. "War and Violence against Women." In *The Gendered New World Order: Militarism, Development and the Environment*, edited by Jennifer Turpin and Lois Ann Lorentzen, 195–210. London: Routledge, 1996.
Nkrumah, Kwame. *Ghana: The Autobiography of Kwame Nkrumah.* Edinburgh: Thomas Nelson, 1957.
Noddings, Nel. *Philosophy of Education.* 2nd ed. Boulder, CO: Westview, 2007.
Noiriel, Gérard. *Le creuset français: Histoire de l'immigration XIXè–XXème siècle.* Paris: Seuil, 1988.
———. *The French Melting Pot: Immigration, Citizenship, and National Identity.* Translated by Geoffroy de Laforcade. Minneapolis: University of Minnesota Press, 1996.
Nora, Pierre, ed. *Realms of Memory: The Construction of the French Past; Conflicts and Divisions.* European Perspectives: A Series in Social Thought and Cultural Criticism. Vol. 1. Translated by Arthur Goldhammer. New York: Columbia University Press, 1996.
———. *Les lieux de mémoire.* Paris: Gallimard, 1997.
Nordstrom, Carolyn. *A Different Kind of War Story.* Philadelphia: University of Pennsylvania Press, 1997.
———. "Girls and War Zones: Troubling Questions." In Indra, *Engendering Forced Migration: Theory and Practice*, 63–82.
———. "(Gendered) War." *Studies in Conflict and Terrorism* 28, no. 5 (2005): 399–411.
Norwegian Refugee Council. *Profile of Internal Displacement: Democratic Republic of the Congo.* Geneva, Switzerland: Norwegian Refugee Council/Global IDP Project, 2001. http://www.nrc.no/?aid=9167171.
Nwahunanya, Chinyere. *A Harvest from Tragedy: Critical Perspectives on Nigerian Civil War Literature.* Owerri, Imo State, Nigeria: Springfield, 2002.
Nwapa, Flora. *Never Again.* Trenton, NJ, Africa World Press, 2002. Originally published 1975.
Nwauwa, Apollos O. "Educational Policies and Reforms." In Falola, *Africa.* Vol. 4, *The End of Colonial Rule: Nationalism and Decolonization*, 167–83.

Nzegwu, Nkiru. "Feminism and Africa: Impact and Limits of the Metaphysics of Gender." In Wiredu, *A Companion to African Philosophy*, 560–69.
Nzimiro, Ikenna. *The Nigerian Civil War: A Study in Class Conflict*. Enugu, Nigeria: Frontline, 1982.
Obama, Barack. "Remarks by the President on a New Beginning." The White House: Office of the Press Secretary (Cairo, Egypt), June 4, 2009. http://www.whitehouse.gov/the_press_office/Remarks-by-the-President-at-Cairo-University-6-04-09/.
Obasanjo, Olesegun. *My Command*. London: Heinemann, 1981.
Ochieng', Harun. "Resettlement Operation for the Displaced Kenyans Starts." Nation Television, May 4. 2008, http://www.ntv.co.ke.
Okara, Gabriel. *The Fisherman's Invocation*. London: Heinemann, 1978.
Okazawa-Rey, Margo. "Warring on Women: Understanding Complex Inequalities of Gender, Race, Class, and Nation." *Affilia* 17, no. 3 (2002): 371–83.
Okigbo, Christopher. *Collected Poems*. London: Heinemann, 1986.
Okri, Ben. *Incidents at the Shrine*. London: Vintage, 1993. Originally published 1986.
———. *Stars of the New Curfew*. London: Vintage, 1999. Originally published 1988.
———. *Songs of Enchantment*. London: Jonathan Cape, 1993.
———. *Astonishing the Gods*. London: Phoenix, 1995.
———. *Dangerous Love*. London: Phoenix, 1996.
———. *Infinite Riches*. London: Phoenix, 1998.
Oliver, Roland. *The African Experience: Major Themes in African History from Earliest Times to the Present*. New York: HarperCollins, 1992.
Omanyondo Ohambe, Marie Claire, Jean Berckmans Bahananga Muhigwa, and Barnabé Mulyumba Wa Mamba. *Women's Bodies as a Battleground: Sexual Violence against Women and Girls during the War in the Democratic Republic of Congo, South Kivu (1996–2003)*. Edited by Martine René Calloy, Ndeye Sow, and Catherine Hall. Paris: International Alert, 2005.
Omari, T. Peter. *Kwame Nkrumah: The Anatomy of an African Dictatorship*. New York: Africana, 1972.
Omolewa, Michael. "Educating the 'Native': A Study of the Education Adaptation Strategy in British Colonial Africa, 1910–1936." *Journal of Afro-American History* 91, no. 3 (2006): 267–85.
Onana, Charles. *La France et ses tirailleurs: Enquête sur les combattants de la République 1939–2003*. Paris: Duboiris, 2003.
On the Frontlines: Child Soldiers in the DRC. DVD. Directed by Ajedi-Ka. Brooklyn, NY: Witness, 2000.
Operation Fine Girl. DVD. Produced and directed by Lilibet Foster and Binta Mansaray. Brooklyn: Witness, 2001.
Osadolor, Osarhieme Benson. "Contested History in Colonial Historiography." In *The Foundations of Nigeria: Essays in Honor of Toyin Falola*, edited by Adebayo Oyebade, 57–77. Trenton, NJ: Africa World Press, 2003.
Osaghae, Eghosa E., and Ebere Onwudiwe. "General Introduction: The Relevance of the Nigerian Civil War." In *The Nigerian Civil War and Its Aftermath*, edited by Eghosa E. Osaghae, Ebere Onwudiwe, and Rotimi T. Suberu, 3–7. Ibadan, Nigeria: John Archers, 2002.

Ostler, Nicholas. *Empires of the Word: A Language History of the World.* New York: HarperCollins, 2005.
Osundare, Niyi. *Thread in the Loom: Essays on African Literature and Culture.* Trenton, NJ: Africa World Press, 2002.
Otieno, Wambui Waiyaki. *Mau Mau's Daughter: A Life History.* Introduction by Cora Ann Presley. Boulder, CO: Lynne Rienner, 1998.
Owen, Wilfred. *The Collected Poems.* Edited by C. Day Lewis. London, Chatto & Windus, 1971.
Oyebade, Adebayo. "Radical Nationalism and Wars of Liberation." In Falola, *Africa.* Vol. 4, *The End of Colonial Rule: Nationalism and Decolonization*, 63–87.
Pakenham, Thomas. *The Scramble for Africa: White Man's Conquest of the Dark Continent from 1876 to 1912.* New York: Avon Books, 1991.
Pankhurst, Richard. *Sylvia Pankhurst: Counsel for Ethiopia.* Hollywood, CA: Tsehai Publishers, 2003.
Parent, Sabrina. "West African Prepresentations of World War II: (Re)Writing the Massacre of Thiaroye." PhD diss., University of Texas at Austin, 2008.
Parpart, Jane L. "Masculinities, Race and Violence in the Making of Zimbabwe." In *Manning the Nation: Father Figures in Zimbabwean Literature and Society*, edited by Kizito Muchemwa and Robert Muponde, 102–14. Harare, Zimbabwe: Weaver, 2004.
Patrick, Erin. "Surrounded: Women and Girls in Northern Uganda." Washington, DC: Migration Policy Institute, 2005. http://www.migrationinformation.org/Feature/display.cfm?id=310.
Patton, Michael Quinn. *Qualitative Research and Evaluation Methods.* 3rd ed. Thousand Oaks, CA: Sage, 2002.
Pedersen, Morten Bonde. "Women Hold the Key to Peace." MS ActionAid (Denmark), November 22, 2007. http://www.ms.dk/sw87249.asp.
Pen, Michael L., and Rahel Nardos. *Overcoming Violence against Women and Girls: An International Campaign to Eradicate a Worldwide Problem.* Lanham, MD: Rowman & Littlefield, 2003.
Pennycook, Alastair. *The Cultural Politics of English as an International Language.* London: Longman, 1994.
Perlmutt, Bent-Jorgen, and Nelson Walker III. *Lumo: One Woman's Struggle to Heal in a Country Beset by War.* Goma, DRC: The Goma Film Project, 2007.
Physicians for Human Rights. U.S. Senate Committee on the Judiciary, Human Rights and the Law Subcommittee. *Rape as a Weapon of War: Accountability for Sexual Violence in Conflict.* U.S. Senate Hearing on Rape in the DRC, Washington, DC, April, 2008. http://physiciansforhumanrights.org/library/documents/testimony/rape-as-a-weapon-of-war.pdf.
Pieterse, Jan Nederveen. *White on Black: Images of Africa and Blacks in Western Popular Culture.* Translated by Jan Nederveen Pieterse. Repr. paperback ed. New Haven, CT: Yale University Press, 1998. Originally published in Dutch, 1990.
Pordzik, Ralph. "An African Utopographer: Ben Okri's *Astonishing the Gods* and the Quest for Postcolonial Utopia." *ZAA: A Quarterly of Language, Literature and Culture* 48, no. 1 (2000): 44–56.
Pouilly, Cecile. "Can Congo Turn the Page?" *Refugees* 145, no. 1 (2007): 4–14.

Pratt, Marion, and Leah Werchick et al. *Sexual Terrorism: Rape as a Weapon of War in Eastern Democratic Republic of Congo: An Assessment of Programmatic Responses to Sexual Violence in North Kivu, South Kivu, Maniema and Orientale Provinces, January 9–16, 2004.* Washington, DC: USAID/DCHA, 2004.

Prendergast, John, and Colin Thomas-Jensen. *Averting the Nightmare Scenario in Eastern Congo.* ENOUGH Strategy Paper 7, September 2007. http://www.enoughproject.org/files/reports/congonightmare.pdf.

Protocol on the Rights of Women in Africa. http://www.equalitynow.org/english/campaigns/african-protocol/african-protocol_en.html.

Puechguirbal, Nadine. "Gender Training for Peacekeepers: Lessons from the DRC." *International Peacekeeping* 10, no. 4 (2003): 113–28.

———. "Women and War in the Democratic Republic of Congo." *Signs* 28, no. 4 (2003): 1271–81.

Raise Hope for Congo: Protect and Empower Congo's Women (ENOUGH campaign). "New! Ten Reasons Why Eastern Congo Is the Most Dangerous Place on Earth for Women." October 21, 2008. http://www.raisehopeforcongo.org/tenreasons.

Ranchod-Nilsson, Sita. "'This, Too, Is a Way of Fighting': Rural Women's Participation in Zimbabwe's Liberation War." In *Women and Revolution in Africa, Asia, and the New World*, edited by Mary Ann Tétreault, 62–88. Columbia: University of South Carolina Press, 1994.

Rashid, Ronald. "Kisumu Election Violence." Nation Television. December 29, 2007. http://www.ntv.co.ke.

Rasmussen, Susan. *Spirit Possession and Personhood among the Kel Ewey Tuareg.* Cambridge: Cambridge University Press, 1995.

———. *The Poetics and Politics of Tuareg Aging: Life Course and Personal Destiny in Niger.* DeKalb: Northern Illinois University Press, 1997.

———. "Between Several Worlds: Images of Youth and Age in Tuareg Popular Performances." *Anthropological Quarterly* 73 (2000): 133–44.

———. *Healing in Community: Medicine, Contested Terrains, and Cultural Encounters among the Tuareg.* Westport, CT: Bergin & Garvey, 2001.

———. "Gendered Discourses and Mediated Modernities: Urban and Rural Performances of Tuareg Smith Women." *Journal of Anthropological Research* 59, no. 4 (2003): 487–509.

———. *Those Who Touch: Tuareg Medicine Women in Anthropological Perspective.* DeKalb: Northern Illinois University Press, 2006.

Ratemo, Lenah B., Alice Ondigi, and John Kebaso, "Is There Time for Family: Working Men in Nairobi–Kenya," February 12, 2007. www.womenofthemountains.org.

Ray, Benjamin C. *African Religions: Symbol, Ritual, and Community.* Englewood Cliffs, NJ: Prentice-Hall, 1976.

Reader, John. *Africa: A Biography of the Continent.* London: Penguin Books, 1998.

Reed, Daniel B. *Dan Ge Performance: Masks and Music in Contemporary Côte d'Ivoire.* Bloomington: Indiana University Press, 2007.

Rehn, Elisabeth, and Ellen Johnson Sirleaf. *Women, War and Peace: The Independent Experts' Assessment on the Impact of Armed Conflict on Women and Women's Role in Peace-Building.* New York: UNIFEM, 2002.

Rice, Edward. *Captain Sir Richard Francis Burton*. New York: Charles Scribner's Sons, 1990.
Richards, Paul. "War as Smoke and Mirrors: Sierra Leone 1991–2, 1994–5, 1995–6." *Anthropological Quarterly* 78, no. 2 (2005): 377–402.
Robinson, Lisa Clayton, "Lincoln University (Pennsylvania)," in Appiah and Gates, *Africana*, 1168–69.
Rodd, Francis James Rennell, 2nd Baron Rennell of Rodd. *People of the Veil*. London: MacMillan Anthropological Publications, 1926.
Rodney, Walter. *How Europe Underdeveloped Africa*. Washington, DC: Howard University Press, 1972.
Roesch, Otto. "The Politics of the Aftermath: Peasant Options in Mozambique." *Southern Africa Report* 9, no. 3 (1994): 16–30.
Rollins, Leslie. "Ethiopia, African Americans, and African-Consciousness: The Effect of Ethiopia and Africa-Consciousness in Twentieth-century America." *Journal of Religious Thought* 54/55, no. 2/1 (1998): 1–25.
Romero, Patricia W. *E. Sylvia Pankhurst: Portrait of a Radical*. New Haven, CT: Yale University Press, 1987.
Rosello, Mireille. "Tattoos or Earrings: Two Models of Historical Writing in Mehdi Lallaoui's *La colline aux oliviers*." In *Algeria and France 1800–2000: Identity, Memory, Nostalgia*, edited by Patricia M. E. Lorcin, 199–216. Syracuse, NY: Syracuse University Press, 2006.
Rosen, David. *Armies of the Young: Child Soldiers in War and Terrorism*. New Brunswick, NJ: Rutgers University Press, 2005.
Rozée, Patricia. "Forbidden or Forgiven? Rape in Cross-cultural Perspective." *Psychology of Women Quarterly* 17 (1993): 499–514.
Ruddick, Sara. *Maternal Thinking: Toward a Politics of Peace*. Boston: Beacon, 1989.
———. "'Woman of Peace': A Feminist Construction." In Lorentzen and Turpin, *The Women and War Reader*, 213–26.
Ruhlen, Merritt. *A Guide to the World's Languages*. Vol. 1, *Classification*. Stanford, CA: Stanford University Press, 1991.
Said, Edward W. *Orientalism: Western Conceptions of the Orient*. New York: Vintage, 1978, 1979; New York: Penguin Books, 1991.
Sala-Molinas, Louis. *Dark Side of the Light: Slavery and the French Enlightenment*. Translated by John Conteh-Morgan. Minneapolis: University of Minnesota Press, 2006.
Salopek, Paul. "Who Rules the Forest?" *National Geographic: Special Africa Issue; Africa: Whatever You Thought, Think Again*, September 2005, 74–93.
Salwen, Michael B. "Evelyn Waugh in Ethiopia: The Novelist as War Correspondent and Journalism Critic." *Journalism Studies* 2, no. 1 (2001): 5–25.
Saro-Wiwa, Ken. *Sozaboy: A Novel in Rotten English*. London: Longman, 1994. Originally published 1985.
———. *Songs in a Time of War*. Port Harcourt, Nigeria: Saros International Publishers, 1985.
———. *On a Darkling Plain: An Account of the Nigerian Civil War*. Port Harcourt, Nigeria: Saros International Publishers, 1989.
———. *The Singing Anthill: Ogoni Folk Tales*. Port Harcourt, Nigeria: Saros International Publishers, 1991.

———. *Genocide in Nigeria: The Ogoni Tragedy*. Port Harcourt, Nigeria: Saros International Publishers, 1992.
Sbacchi, Alberto. *Legacy of Bitterness: Ethiopia and Fascist Italy, 1935–1941*. Lawrenceville, NJ: Red Sea Press, 1997.
Schabas, William A. *An Introduction to the International Criminal Court*. 2nd ed. Cambridge: Cambridge University Press, 2005.
Schach, Paul, ed., *Languages in Conflict*. Lincoln: University of Nebraska Press, 1981.
Schechner, Richard. *Between Theater and Anthropology*. Philadelphia: University of Pennsylvania Press, 1985.
———, and Willa Appel, eds. *By Means of Performance: Intercultural Studies of Theatre and Ritual*. Cambridge: Cambridge University Press, 1990.
Schmied, Josef. *English in Africa: An Introduction*. London: Longman, 1991.
Scott, James C. *Domination and the Arts of Resistance: Hidden Transcripts*. New Haven, CT: Yale University Press, 1990.
Sembene, Ousmane, and Thierno Faty Sow, writers and directors. *Camp de Thiaroye*. Performed by Ibrahim Sane, Sigiri Bakara, Hamed Camara, Ismaila Cisse, and Ababacar Sy. Enaproc and Société nouvelle de promotion cinématographique, 1987.
Sen, Amartya, *Identity and Violence: The Illusion of Destiny*. New York: Norton, 2006.
Senghor, Léopold Sédar. *Hosties noires*. Paris: Seuil, 1948.
———. *Ethiopiques: Poèmes*. Paris: Seuil, 1964.
———. *The Collected Poetry*. Translated by Melvin Dixon. Charlottesville: University of Virginia Press, 1991.
Sharp, Jeb. "Congo Rape: Part 2—Responding to the Crisis." *BBC News*, January 9, 2008. http://www.theworld.org/?q=node/15207.
———. "Interview with Sarah Mosely of the International Rescue Committee." *BBC News*, January 9, 2008. http://www.theworld.org/?q=node/15227.
Shaw, Carolyn Martin. *Colonial Inscriptions: Race, Sex, and Class in Kenya*. Minneapolis: University of Minnesota Press, 1995.
Sheldon, Kathleen. E. *Pounders of Grain: A History of Women, Work, and Politics in Mozambique*. Portsmouth, NH: Heinemann, 2002.
Sherwood, Marika. *Kwame Nkrumah: The Years Abroad, 1935–1947*. Legon, Ghana: Freedom Publications, 1996.
Shohat, Ella, and Robert Stam. *Unthinking Eurocentrism: Multiculturalism and the Media*. New York: Routledge, 1994.
Sideris, Tina. "War, Gender and Culture: Mozambican Women Refugees." *Social Science and Medicine* 56, no. 4 (2003): 713–24.
Silkin, Jon. *Out of Battle: The Poetry of the Great War*. London: Oxford University Press, 1972.
Simmons, Harvey G. *The French National Front: The Extremist Challenge to Democracy*. Boulder, CO: Westview, 1996.
Simpson, David. *Romanticism, Nationalism, and the Revolt against Theory*. Chicago: University of Chicago Press, 1993.
Singer, P. W. *Children at War*. New York: Pantheon Books, 2005.
Smertin, Yuri. *Kwame Nkrumah*. New York: International Publishers, 1987.
Smith, Cory. "Bring Peace to Eastern Congo: End Violence against Women and Girls." *ENOUGH News*, July 11, 2008. http://www.enoughproject.org/news/bring-peace-eastern-congo-faith-action.

Smith-Spark, Laura. "How Did Rape Become a Weapon of War?" *BBC News*, December 8, 2004. http://www.news.bbc.co.uk/1/hi/in_depth/40788677.stm.
Sorenson, John. *Imagining Ethiopia: Struggles for History and Identity in the Horn of Africa*. New Brunswick, NJ: Rutgers University Press, 1993.
Soyinka, Wole. *Idanre and Other Poems*. London: Methuen, 1967.
———. *Poems of Black Africa*. Oxford: Heinemann, 1975.
———. *Myth, Literature and the African World*. Repr. paperback ed. Cambridge: Cambridge University Press/Canto, 1999. Originally published 1976.
———. *You Must Set Forth at Dawn: A Memoir*. New York: Random House, 2006.
Spivak, Gayatri. "Can the Subaltern Speak?" In *Colonial Discourse and Post-colonial Theory: A Reader*, edited by Patrick Williams and Laura Chrisman, 66–111. New York: Columbia University Press, 1994.
Staunton, Irene. *Mothers of the Revolution: The War Experiences of Thirty Zimbabwean Women*. Bloomington: Indiana University Press, 1990.
Stiglmayer, Alexandra. "The Rapes in Bosnia-Herzegovina." In *Mass Rape: The War against Women in Bosnia-Herzegovina*, edited by Alexandra Stiglmayer and translated by Marion Faber, 82–169. Lincoln: University of Nebraska Press, 1994.
Stilwell, Sean. "The Imposition of Colonial Rule." In Falola, *Africa*. Vol. 3, *Colonial Africa, 1885–1939*, 3–26.
Stoller, Paul. *Sensuous Scholarship*. Philadelphia: University of Pennsylvania Press, 1997.
Stromberg, Roland N. *European Intellectual History since 1789*. Englewood Cliffs, NJ: Simon and Schuster, 1990.
Sutherland, Bill, and Matt Meyer. *Guns and Gandhi in Africa: Pan-African Insights on Nonviolence, Armed Struggle and Liberation in Africa*. Trenton, NJ: Africa World Press, 2000.
Swiss, Shana. "Rape as a Crime of War: A Medical Perspective." *Journal of the American Medical Association* 270, no. 5 (2001): 612–15.
Tabouret-Keller, Andrée. "Language and Identity." In *The Handbook of Sociolinguistics*, edited by Florian Coulmas, 315–26. Oxford: Blackwell, 1997.
Tadjer, Akli. *Les ANI du "Tassali."* Paris: Seuil, 1984.
———. *Le porteur de cartable*. Paris: J. C. Lattès, 2002.
Tankard, James W. "The Empirical Approach to the Study of Media Framing." In *Framing Public Life*, edited by Stephen D. Reese, Oscar H. Gandy Jr., and August E. Grant, 95–106. Mahwah, NJ: Lawrence Erlbaum Associates, 2001.
Tarr, Carrie. *Reframing Difference:* Beur *and* Banlieue *Filmmaking in France*. Manchester, England: Manchester University Press, 2005.
Tatulli, John R. "Resolving Africa's Longest Civil War: Updates on the Case concerning Armed Activities in the DRC." *New York Law School Journal of Human Rights* 9, no. 3 (2003): 903–12.
Taussig, Michael. *Shamanism, Colonialism, and the Wild Man: A Study in Terror and Healing*. Chicago: University of Chicago Press, 1987.
Tegla Loroupe Peace Foundation. http://www.tegla.org/TDec/Tegla_Loroupe_Peace_Foundation/Home.html.
Thomason, Sarah G. *Language Contact: An Introduction*. Washington, DC: Georgetown University Press, 2001.
Thomas-Slayter, Barbara, and Dianne Rocheleau. *Gender, Environment, and Development in Kenya: A Grassroots Perspective*. Boulder, CO: Lynne Rienner, 1995.

Thumboo, Edwin. *Ulysses by the Merlion.* Singapore: Heinemann Educational Books, 1979.
Time. "Man of the Year." January 6, 1936.
Trench, Richard Chenevix. *English Past and Present.* Edited with emendations by A. Smythe Palmer. London: Routledge, 1905.
Tristan, Anne, *Le silence du fleuve: Octobre 1961.* Bezons, France: Au nom de la mémoire, 1991.
Tshefu Bibiane, Aningina, and the Peace Women Project. "Women Advocating for Resolution 1325 in the Democratic Republic of Congo." *Project for the 1325 Peace Women E-News*, no 10, 4 October 2002. http://www.peacewomen.org/1325inaction/Africa/DRC1325 1ist.html.
Tshiyembe, Mwayila. "La science politique africaniste et le statut théorique de l'Etat africain: un bilan negative." *Politique Africaine* 71 (October 1998): 109–32.
Tuchman, Gaye. *Making News: A Study in the Construction of Reality.* New York: Free Press, 1978.
Turner, Thomas. *The Congo Wars: Conflict, Myth and Reality.* London: Zed Books, 2007.
Turner, Victor. *Dramas, Fields, and Metaphors: Symbolic Action in Human Society.* Symbol, Myth, and Ritual Series. Ithaca, NY: Cornell University Press, 1974.
Turshen, Meredeth. "The Political Economy of Violence against Women during Armed Conflict in Uganda." *Social Research* 67, no. 3 (2000): 803–24.
———. "The Political Economy of Rape: An Analysis of Systematic Rape and Sexual Abuse of Women during Armed Conflict in Africa." In Moser and Clark, *Victims, Perpetrators or Actors?* 55–68.
Undiyaundeye, Udida A. "Issues and Causes of the Nigerian Civil War." In *The Nigerian Civil War Forty Years After: What Lessons?* edited by Armstrong Matiu Adejo, 3–27. Makurdi, Nigeria: Aboki, 2008.
United Nations Economic Commission for Africa. *Post-conflict Reconstruction in Africa: A Gender Perspective.* Addis Ababa: United Nations Economic Commission for Africa, 1999.
United Nations High Commissioner for Refugees, Office of the UNHCR. *UNHCR Handbook for the Protection of Women and Girls.* Geneva, Switzerland: UNHCR, 2008. http://www.unhcr.org/protect/PROTECTION/47cfae612.html.
United Nations Security Council. *Press Release.* Z /9246. New York: United Nations Department of Public Information, February 12, 2008. http://www.un.org/News/Press/docs/2008/sc9246.doc.html.
United States Department of State. *Country Reports on Human Rights Practices 2006.* Washington, DC: Bureau of Democracy, Human Rights, and Labor, 2007. http://www.state.gov/g/drl/rls/hrrpt/2006/.
USAID/OTI. *Democratic Republic of Congo Field Report.* Field Report no. 19. Washington, DC: USAID, 2003. http://www.usaid.gov/our_work/cross-cutting_programs/transition_initiatives/country/congo/rpt1103.html.
Vaillant, Janet. *Black, French and African: A Life of Léopold Sédar Senghor.* Cambridge, MA: Harvard University Press, 1990.
Van der Kolk, Bessel A., Lars Weisaeth, and Onno van der Hart. "History of Trauma in Psychiatry. In *Traumatic Stress: The Effects of Overwhelming Experience on Mind, Body, and Society*, edited by Bessel A. van der Kolk, Alexander C. McFarlane, and Lars Weisaeth, 47–74. New York: Guilford Press, 1996.

Van Dijk, Teun. *News as Discourse*. Hillsdale, NJ: Lawrence Erlbaum Associates, 1988.
V-Day website. www.vday.org/contents/vday/vcampaigns/amea/congo.
Vlassenroot, Koen. "Violence et constitution des milices dans l'Est du Congo: Le cas des Mayi Mayi." In *L'Afrique des Grands Lacs. Annuaire 1999–2000*, edited by Stefaan Marysse and Filip Reyntjens, 115–52. Paris: L'Harmattan, 2003.
———, and Timothy Raeymaekers, eds. *Conflict and Social Transformation in Eastern DR Congo*. Ghent, Belgium: Academia Press Scientific Publishers, 2004.
Wakerley, Veronique. "The Status of European Languages in Sub-Saharan Africa." *Journal of European Studies* 24, no. 94. (1994): 97–105.
Walker, Alice. *In Search of Our Mothers' Garden: Womanist Prose*. San Diego: Harcourt Brace Jovanovich, 1983.
A Walk to Beautiful. Produced by Steven Engel. Directed by Mary Olive Smith. New York: Engel Entertainment, 2007. http://www.walktobeautiful.com/.
Wall, Melissa. "The Rwanda Crisis: An Analysis of News Magazine Coverage." *International Communication Gazette* 59, no. 2 (1997): 121–34.
Waller, Marguerite R., and Jennifer Rycenga, eds. *Frontline Feminisms: Women, War, and Resistance*. New York: Garland, 2000.
Ward, Jeanne. *If Not Now, When? Addressing Gender-based Violence in Refugee, Internally Displaced, and Post-conflict Settings: A Global Overview*. The Reproductive Health for Refugees Consortium, 2002. http://www.womenscommission.org/pdf/ifnotnow.pdf.
Wardhaugh, Ronald. *Languages in Competition: Dominance, Diversity, and Decline*. London: Blackwell, 1987.
Webb, Vic, and Kembo-Sure, eds. *African Voices: An Introduction to the Languages and Linguistics of Africa*. Oxford: Oxford University Press, 2001.
Weber, Robert Philip. *Basic Content Analysis*. 2nd ed. Sage University Paper Series on Quantitative Applications in the Social Sciences. Newbury Park, CA: Sage, 1990.
Weiss, Herbert. *War and Peace in the Democratic Republic of the Congo*. Uppsala, Sweden: Nordiska Afrikainstitutet, 2000.
Weissman, Fabrice, ed. *In the Shadow of "Just Wars": Violence, Politics and Humanitarian Action*. Ithaca, NY: Cornell University Press.
West, Michael O. "Like a River: The Million Man March and the Black Nationalist Tradition in the United States." *Journal of Historical Sociology* 12, no. 1 (1999): 81–101.
Williams, Michael W. "Nkrumahism as an Ideological Embodiment of Leftist Thought within the African World." *Journal of Black Studies* 15, no. 1 (September 1984): 117–34.
Wilson, Amrit. *The Challenge Road: Women and the Eritrean Revolution*. Trenton, NJ: Red Sea Press, 1991.
Wilson, Kathleen. *A New Imperial History: Culture, Identity and Modernity in Britain and the Empire 1660–1840*. Cambridge: Cambridge University Press, 2004.
Wilson, Richard. "Children and War in Sierra Leone: A West African Diary." *Anthropology* 17, no. 5 (2001): 20–22.
Wiredu, Kwasi, ed. *A Companion to African Philosophy*. Oxford: Blackwell, 2006.
Woldemariam, Metasebia. "Lessons on Writing from the Margins: Sylvia Pankhurst and the *New Times and Ethiopia News*." *Feminist Media Studies* 5, no. 3 (2005): 362–65.

Wolf, Eric R. *Europe and the People without History.* Berkeley: University of California Press, 1982.
Women and War. DVD. Directed by Robyn Hofmeyr and Minky Schlesinger. Produced by Robyn Hofmeyr, Mark Newman, and the Centre for the Study for Violence and Reconciliation. Hamilton, NJ: Films for the Humanities and Sciences, 2001.
Women's Commission for Refugee Women and Children. *No Safe Place to Call Home: Child and Adolescent Night Commuters in Northern Uganda.* New York: Women's Commission for Refugee Women and Children, 2004.
Women's Dignity Project. *Faces of Dignity: Seven Stories of Girls and Women with Fistula.* Edited by Kristina Graff and Maggie Banser. Dar es Salaam, Tanzania: Women's Dignity Project, 2003. http://www.womensdignity.org/Face_of_Dignity.pdf.
Wren, Robert M. *J. P. Clark.* Lagos, Nigeria: Lagos University Press, 1984.
———. *Those Magical Years: The Making of Nigerian Literature at Ibadan, 1948–1966.* Washington, DC: Three Continents, 1990.
Wubneh, Mulatu, and Yohannis Abate. *Ethiopia: Transition and Development in the Horn of Africa.* Boulder, CO: Westview, 1988.
Yacine, Kateb. *Nedjma.* Paris: Seuil, 1956.
Yacine, Tassadit. "Les ancêtres redoublent de vérité." In *Hommage à Kateb Yacine*, edited by Nabil Boudraa, 129–32. Paris: L'Harmattan, 2006.
Yeats, W. B. *The Collected Poems of W. B. Yeats.* Toronto: Macmillan, 1969.
Young, Lola. *Fear of the Dark: "Race," Gender and Sexuality in the Cinema.* New York: Routledge, 1996.
Young, Robert J. C. *Colonial Desire: Hybridity in Theory, Culture and Race.* New York: Routledge, 1996.
———. *Postcolonialism: An Historical Introduction.* Oxford: Blackwell, 2001.

Contributors

ANN ALBUYEH is professor of English linguistics at the University of Puerto Rico. She received her PhD from the University of Wisconsin–Madison. She has taught in Tehran, Iran, and Jalingo, Nigeria, as well as at Harvard University and the University of Wisconsin–Madison. Professor Albuyeh has also been a teaching fellow at the International School of Theory at the University of Santiago de Compostela in Spain. In addition to teaching, Dr. Albuyeh writes and has worked as a magazine and newspaper reporter and editor for English-language publications in the Middle East. Although her academic research has included the exploration of theoretical issues in language acquisition, her linguistics publications have most often focused on the evolution of English from Old English to the current varieties of English pidgins, creoles, and standard dialects worldwide, with a particular emphasis on Africa and the Caribbean.

ZERMARIE DEACON, is assistant professor in the Department of Human Relations at the University of Oklahoma in Norman. She is also adjunct professor in women's and gender studies and an affiliate faculty member with the School of International and Area Studies. Dr. Deacon received her PhD in ecological-community psychology from Michigan State University. Her research focuses on cross-cultural definitions of health and well-being as well as factors that facilitate thriving. In 2005, she received a U.S. Department of State Fulbright Award in order to investigate factors that facilitated Mozambican women's recovery from the impact of warfare. Her other work has focused on factors that facilitate refugee women's adjustment to resettlement in the United States and definitions of health and well-being in Native American communities.

ALICIA C. DECKER is assistant professor of history and women's studies at Purdue University. She received her PhD in women's studies from Emory University in 2007. She also holds an MA in gender studies from Makerere University (Uganda) and a BA in anthropology from the University of Minnesota. Her research and teaching interests include postcolonial African history, gender and militarization, armed conflict and forced migration, oral history, and global feminisms. She is currently working on a book manuscript entitled "Beyond the Barrel: Gender, Power, and Militarism in Idi Amin's Uganda, 1971–1979."

TOYIN FALOLA obtained his BA and PhD from the University of Ife, Nigeria. He worked at the University of Ife till 1989. He was a Smuts Fellow at the University of Cambridge in 1988, a visiting professor at York University, Toronto, Ontario, Canada, in 1990, and he moved to the University of Texas at Austin in 1991 as a professor. He has held visiting appointments at Smith College in the United States and at the Australian National University. A former editor of *Odu: A Journal of West African Studies*, and a current coeditor of *African Economic History*, Falola serves on the board of twelve scholarly journals. In addition, he is the series editor for Greenwood's Culture and Customs of Africa series; the series editor of Classic Authors and Texts on Africa, Africa World Press; and the series editor for the University of Rochester's Studies in African History and the Diaspora. He has contributed to professional associations, serving, for example, as the general secretary of the Historical Society of Nigeria and as a member of the Board of the Association of African Studies. For his contributions to the study of Nigeria, he has been presented with three Festschriften: Adebayo Oyebade, ed., *The Transformation of Nigeria: Essays in Honor of Toyin Falola* (Africa World Press, 2002); Adebayo Oyebade, ed., *The Foundations of Nigeria: Essays in Honor of Toyin Falola* (Africa World Press, 2003), and Akin Ogundiran, ed., *Precolonial Nigeria: Essays in Honor of Toyin Falola* (Africa World Press, 2005).

HETTY TER HAAR holds her BA in history from the London School of Economics and is an independent researcher. Her essay "Out of Africa: Theory and the Displacement of African Literature" was published in *Migrations and Creative Expressions in Africa and the African Diaspora*, ed. Toyin Falola, Niyi Afolabi, and Adérónké Adésolá Adésànyà (2008).

AMÉNA MOÏNFAR earned her PhD in the Program of Comparative Literature at the University of Texas at Austin. Her dissertation, "Reconciliations: Memory and Mediation in Narratives of the Postimperial Second Generation," examines narratives of transplanted identity building and memory in European languages by second-generation writers of non-European origins who choose to write their stories in European languages.

KAYODE OMONIYI OGUNFOLABI is assistant professor in the Department of English, West Virginia University. He focuses on African, Caribbean, Latin American, and South Indian literatures, through which he explores the intersections of history, memory, and the marvelous.

SABRINA PARENT obtained a joint "doctorat" from the Université de Toulouse–Le Mirail and the Université Libre de Bruxelles in French and Belgian literature in 2006. She completed a PhD in Francophone literature and culture at the University of Texas at Austin in November 2008. Her dissertation deals with African representations of World War II, especially with the representations of the mutiny/massacre of Thiaroye (Senegal), which occurred in 1944. She is currently teaching French and Belgian poetry at the Facultés Universitaires Notre-Dame de la Paix in Namur (Belgium).

SUSAN RASMUSSEN is professor of anthropology at the University of Houston. Her interests include religion, healing, gender, aging and the life course, and verbal art performance; and she has conducted research in Tuareg (Kel Tamajaq) communities of northern Niger and Mali and, more briefly, with Tamajaq-speaking expatriates in France and the United States. Her publications include a number of articles and four books, the most recent entitled *Those Who Touch: Tuareg Medicine Women in Anthropological Perspective* (2006).

MICHAEL SHARP was educated at universities in Britain and the United States. His PhD is from the University of Wisconsin–Madison. Professor Sharp has taught in Scotland, Greece, Portugal, and Nigeria, and at Binghamton University (SUNY), Harvard University, and the University of Wisconsin–Madison. He has been a teaching fellow in the International School of Theory in the Humanities at the University of Santiago de Compostela in Spain. Trained as a Romanticist and in the literature and ideas of the nineteenth century, Michael Sharp now teaches in the University of Puerto Rico's Department of English, where he is active in both the English MA and the Caribbean PhD programs. His research focuses on the poetry of Anglophone Africa and the Caribbean diaspora. Michael Sharp's poetry has been published on both sides of the Atlantic.

CHERYL STERLING teaches African and African diaspora studies in the Global Liberal Arts Program at New York University. She has published critical essays, including "Finding Africa in the Dances of the Gods" and "Future Conditionality as a Visionary Imperative in Ayi Kwei Armah's *Two Thousand Seasons*," among others. She is currently finishing a book project based on Yoruba traditions in Brazil, entitled "African Roots, Brazilian Routes: Africa in the Formation of Afro-Brazilian Identity." She is the cofounder and coeditor of the online arts journal, *Afro-Beat Journal*.

MELISSA TULLY is a doctoral student in mass communication at the University of Wisconsin–Madison. Her research focuses on communication, conflict, and resolution in Africa. Melissa is particularly interested in the role new media play in conflict situations and how media technologies are used to report and record human rights violations. She is also interested in how people use journalistic and literary accounts to express, complicate, and understand conflict situations. Melissa has presented her work at several national conferences including the African Studies Association annual meeting and the Association for Education in Journalism and Mass Communication convention. She is coauthor of a forthcoming article in *Newspaper Research Journal*.

PAMELA WADENDE is a doctoral student in the Education and Psychological Services Department of Texas State University–San Marcos, specializing in adult, professional, and community education. Her research interests include Kenyan women's social history, women's social action, and the enhancement of Kenyan adult education services as a basis for community development and the creation of peace. She has presented a number of research papers in national and state conferences on topics involving women and development.

METASEBIA WOLDEMARIAM is associate professor in communication and media studies at Plymouth State University in New Hampshire. Her research interests include African media and cultural studies, feminist media scholarship, and international/developmental communication.

JONATHAN ZILBERG is an affiliate research scholar in the Program for African Studies at the University of Illinois at Urbana–Champaign. A cultural anthropologist with field experience in Africa, Latin America, and Asia, he specializes in combining anthropological and archival research, particularly as it relates to Zimbabwean art history. Zilberg is interested in the intersections of media and civil society. Currently he is concentrating on museum ethnography in Indonesia and completing a manuscript entitled "From Bloodstains to Brancusi: A History of Zimbabwean Modernism."

Index

Abate, Yohannis, 47
Aburi conference, 275
Accra, 278n21, 279n29
Accra Evening News, 33
Accra Government Training College, 34
Accra Herald, 32
Achebe, Chinua, 15, 35, 271, 275
Achimota, 34
actors, 10, 11, 156, 157, 160, 161, 162, 163, 164–76, 197, 224n34. See also *ibaraden*
acts of identity, 23, 37
Addis Ababa, 44, 51–52; Fistula Hospital, 120
Adejunmobi, Moradewun, 22–23, 35; *Vernacular Palaver*, 22
Adichie, Chimamanda Ngozi, *Half of a Yellow Sun*, 183
adolescents, 120, 123, 158–59, 160. See also children; youths
Aduaka, Newton, 198–99, 209, 217, 225n44, 225n54
aesthetics, 10, 11, 155, 156, 157, 166, 168, 176, 177, 195, 198, 209, 214
Afghanistan, 80
Afolayan, Funso, 41n51
Africa Works, 12, 189
African, 53
African Morning Post, 34
African National Congress (ANC), 142
African Studies Association conference, 197
African Times, 32
African Women and Peace Support Group: *Liberian Women Peacemakers*, 84
agency, 51, 176, 207, 210, 217, 221 259, 264; tactical versus strategic, 84, 213–14

Aggrey, Kwegyir, 34
Agnes Scott College, 79–80
Aguiyi-Ironsi, Johnson, 182, 272, 278n15
AIDS, 116, 168, 217. See also HIV
ÁJA, 227mn78–80; *Don't Let Me Die*, 12, 196, 209, 217–21, 222; "Legacy of Poverty," 219–20; "Poor People Dead," 220; "Victim of Heritage," 219
Akan, 30, 33, 35
Akede Eko, 32
Alarcón, Daniel, 205
Alarcón, Renato, 150
Albuyeh, Ann, 4, 5
Alexander VI (pope), 39n21
Algeria, 14, 38n1, 157, 162, 241–65, 266n4, 266n15–16, 268n44, 268n47, 268n55
All about Darfur, 83, 89
All Peoples Congress, 222n12
Allah Is Not Obliged, 84
Al-Liwa, 32
alternative media, 5, 6, 44–45, 46, 49–50, 81. See also *New Times and Ethiopia News*
Amadi, Elechi, *Sunset in Biafra*, 173, 276
America. See United States of America
Amharic, 53
Amnesty International, 113, 114
Anderson, David, 58, 59
Angola, 17n34, 38n1, 84, 89–90, 203, 209
Angola E A Nossa Terra, 89
Anguish of War in the Congo, 115
Andwele, Adisa. See ÁJA
anticolonialism, 2, 4, 5, 8, 21, 34, 37, 38, 82, 83, 86, 98. See also colonialism; neocolonialism; postcolonialism
antifascism, 6, 44, 46, 49, 50–51, 54. See also fascism

anti-imperialism, 6. *See also* imperialism
anti-Semitism, 242
Appiah, Kwame Anthony, 5, 30, 52
Arabic (language), 24, 28, 31, 32, 241, 266n4, 269n88
Arabs, 14, 31, 41n45, 157, 159, 241, 246, 247, 251, 256, 257, 259, 264, 268n45
Arguin Bay, 39n21
Armed Forces Revolutionary Council (AFRC), 204
ars moriendi, 272
Asante, 30
Asante, Samuel, 52, 53
Association of Women's Rights in Development (AWID), 135n23
Athey, Stephanie, 205
Atton, Chris, 6, 45, 49–51
Au nom de la mémoire, 248, 265
Aube de sang (Faye), 13, 232–33, 236–37, 238
Aubrey, Lisa, 103
Auden, W. H., 276; "In Memory of W. B. Yeats," 280n53
Australia, 41n46
Autesserre, Séverine, 117
Awolowo, Obafemi, 273, 278n23
Azikiwe, Benjamin Nnamdi, 34, 37, 42n60, 53

Balandier, Georges, "Social Changes and Social Problems in Negro Africa," 32
Bambara, 158, 159, 160, 165
Banda, Kamuzu, 34, 37
Barbazon, James, 92
Baring, Evelyn, 59
Barron, Louis, 259
Bauer, Henri, 259
BBC World Service, 81
Beah, Ishmael, *Long Way Gone*, 12, 84, 196, 202, 204, 209, 212–13, 214–15, 216, 219
Begag, Azouz, *Le gone du Chaâba*, 246
Belgium, 137n36, 163, 164, 199, 223n24
Beltz, Amanda, 125
Benin, 273
Bénot, Yves, 232
Berbers, 157, 241

Berlin Conference, 29, 199
Beurs, 14, 242, 243–44, 245–48, 249, 250, 262, 265, 267n31, 267n33, 267n42, 268n47
Biafra, 15, 182, 184, 192n23, 271–76, 279n33–34
Bible, the, 2, 29
Blood Diamond, 12, 196, 197–98, 199–208, 209, 212, 213, 221
Blunden, Edmund, *Undertones of War*, 271–72
Bobo, 160, 165
Bogle, Donald, 224n34
Borana, 105
Bosire, Lydiah Kemunto, 116–17, 126; "Limits and Possibilities of Transitional Justice," 116
Bosnia, 93, 129
Bouchareb, Rachid; *L'Ami y'a bon*, 232
Bourgault, Louise, 163
Boyce Davies, Carole, 3
Branson, Joan, 118
Break the Silence Speakers Tour, 115
Britain. *See* Great Britain
British East India Company, 28
British Empire. *See* Great Britain
Bukavu, 116, 118, 121, 124
bureaucracy, 11, 156, 162, 176–77
Burgi, 105
Burkina Faso, 17n34, 157, 223n24
Burton, Sir Richard, 28, 40n31
Burundi, 1, 83–84, 91, 125
Bush, George W., 92, 161
Busia, Kofi Abena, 32, 205

Cabral, Amilcar, 92
Cagnoni, Romano, 274, 279n34
Campbell, James, 2, 7, 12
capitalism, 1, 101, 143, 182, 201
Card, Claudia, "Rape as a Weapon of War," 123–24
Casualties (Clark-Bekederemo), 15, 271–76; "The Beast," 273, 274; "The Burden in Boxes," 272; "The Casualties," 15, 271, 275; "Conversations at Accra," 272–73; "Death of a Weaverbird," 15, 275; "Dirge," 273; "Epi-

logue to *Casualties*," 15, 276; "The Flood," 275; "Night Song," 15, 271, 275; "A Photograph in *The Observer*," 274; "Skull and Cups," 274; "Song," 274; "Vulture's Choice," 15, 272. *See also* Clark-Bekederemo, John Pepper
Červenka, Zdanek, 277n2, 278n12
Césaire, Aimé, 32, 233
Chabal, Patrick, 12, 188, 189–90
Chad, 1
chama, 9, 102, 107, 108
Chaouia, 241
Charef, Medhi, *Le harki de Meriem*, 247, 268n47
child soldiers, 84, 88, 90, 92–93, 96n29, 96n31, 123, 129, 196, 198, 203, 204, 208–15, 215, 219, 225n40, 225n54, 226n70
childhood, 210, 245
children, 4, 8, 81, 84, 86, 91, 100, 101, 103–4, 106, 107, 119, 120, 121, 122, 123, 124, 125, 127, 138n49, 141, 142, 161, 164–65, 166, 169, 170, 172, 175, 187, 189, 199, 205, 216–19, 226n64, 227n80, 243, 244–45, 246, 267n22, 267n25, 273–74. *See also* adolescents; child soldiers; youths
Children's Parliament, 172
China, 50
Christ, 233
Christianity, 28, 29
Christians, 47, 58, 182. *See also* missionaries
Chuku, Gloria, 3–4, 98
City of Hope, Bukavu, 118
civil disobedience, 34
civil war, 1, 3, 7; in Burundi, 91; in Guinea Bissau, 92; in Liberia, 91–92; in Nigeria, 11, 15, 180–83, 271, 272–74, 276, 278n12; in Sierra Leone, 10, 12, 90, 195–222; in Spain, 279n43
Clark-Bekederemo, John Pepper, 14–15, 271–76, 277n1, 277n3, 277–78n11, 278n21, 279n27, 279n39. See also *Casualties*
class, 5, 32, 41n49, 45, 49, 101, 182, 188, 189, 191, 217

classism, 82
clientelism, 210, 212
Coalition on Violence against Women (COVAW), 109
Cockburn, Cynthia, 82
Cold War, 45, 129
Coleridge, Samuel Taylor, 38
collective memory, 14, 232, 233, 242, 251, 252, 253, 254, 257, 260
colline aux oliviers, La (Lallaoui), 14, 241–70
Collins, Stephen, 199, 200, 208, 223n13
colonial languages, 4–5, 22, 23–24, 26
colonialism, 1–7, 14, 33n1, 52, 56, 61, 71, 73, 82, 98, 103, 128, 156, 158, 177–78n7, 195, 197, 201, 207, 226n73, 232, 235, 236–38, 240n35, 242, 246–47, 251, 252, 255–56, 258–59, 262, 264–65, 265n1, 268n55. *See also* anticolonialism; colonial languages; neocolonialism; postcolonialism
Columbia, 119
Comas-Diaz, Lillian, 150
comedians, 162, 166, 167
Communards, 250, 258, 259, 260
communism, 35
communists, 34, 57, 98
Conflict Coltan and Cassiterite Act, 130
Congo, Democratic Republic of the, 1, 9–10, 15, 17–18n34, 34, 83, 84, 86, 88, 92–93, 113–31, 138n64, 138n67, 140n95
Congo Global Action; group, 127; Project, 9, 114
Congo Reform Association, 9, 128
Congo Week 2008, 115
Connelly, Jennifer, 204
Convention People's Party, 33
Coomaraswamy, Radhika, 125
coping mechanisms, 7, 9, 108
Cornwall, Andrea, 98
Côte d'Ivoire, 32, 33
Council on African Affairs, 53
creole, 23, 24, 39n11, 39n13
cross-dressing, 171
curandeiros, 145, 146–47

Cyprus, 2

Dagnan, General, 232
Dakar, 231, 232
Daloz, Jean-Pascal, 12, 188, 189–90
Damas, Léon-Gontran, 233
D'Amico, Francine, 82
Danquah, J. B., 53
Darfur, 83, 89, 114, 116, 120
"dark continent," 2, 215
Davis, Mary, 49
Deacon, Zermarie, 4, 9–10
de Beauvoir, Simone, 7
De Beers Corporation, 201
de Certeau, Michel
Decker, Alicia C., 7–8
decolonization, 7, 57, 70, 72
Decree no. 34, 182
de Gaulle, Charles, 231
democracy, 1, 129, 175; in Mali, 169; in Mozambique, 147; in Nigeria, 185, 278n21; in Sierra Leone, 208, 216, 223n14
Denmark, 39n20, 275
Derderian, Richard, 252, 269n63; "Algeria as a *lieu de mémoire*," 242
de St. Jorre, John, 274, 279n33, 279n41
De Temmerman, Els, *Aboke Girls*, 84
devoir de mémoire, 14, 240n38, 242, 250, 252–55, 263, 264, 266n9, 269n63
diamonds, 83, 197–98, 199, 200, 201, 202, 207, 208, 212, 223n14, 224n35. See also *Blood Diamond*
diaspora, 9, 46, 52, 107
Diawara, Manthia, 199
DiCaprio, Leonardo, 197
Diop, Boubacar Boris, 237; *Le Temps de Tamango*, 235; *Thiaroye terre rouge*, 13, 232–33, 235–36, 238
direct rule, 29. See also indirect rule
discourse analysis, 63
discrimination, 52, 243, 244, 246, 248
Dixon, Melville, 233
Djebar, Assia, *Les enfants du nouveau monde*, 244
Dominicy, Marc, 234

Don't Let Me Die (ÁJA), 12, 196, 209, 217–22
Doumbi-Fakoly, *Morts pour la France*, 232
Downing, John, 6, 45
DRC. See Congo, Democratic Republic of
Dream Becomes a Reality, 83, 90
Dreyfus Affair, 242
drought, 156, 157, 160, 162, 169
drugs, 174, 203, 213, 214–15, 216, 217, 246
DuBois, W. E. B., 34, 53
Dugan, James, 48

East Africa, 30, 40n31, 68, 110n14
East African Association (EAA), 59
Eboh, Marie Pauline, 101
Echenberg, Myron, 231
Echeruo, Michael, 15, 276
Eclaireur de la Côte d'Ivoire, L', 32
ECOMOG (Economic Community of West African States Monitoring Group), 226n66
ECOWAS (Economic Community of West African States), 226n66
Edo, 278n13
education, 5, 30, 59, 129, 143, 147–48, 150, 156, 162, 163, 164, 165, 169, 172, 173, 181, 187, 189, 208, 211, 253, 261. See also Western Education
Efiong, Philip, 278n12
Eisele, John, 201, 202
Ekwensi, Cyprian, *Survive the Peace*, 183
Eldoret, 106, 107
Eliasoph, Nina, 6, 45
Eliot, Sir Charles, 58
Emecheta, Buchi, *Destination Biafra*, 183
England. See Great Britain
English (language), 4, 5, 22–26, 28, 29, 31, 32, 33, 34, 35, 38, 41n46, 42n59, 53, 205, 271, 277n2
Enlightenment, the, 28, 190, 207, 217, 226–27n73
Enloe, Cynthia, 82, 94n5, 95n9
ENOUGH; campaign, 9, 114, 116; project's *Past Due: Remove the FDLR from Eastern Congo*, 130; report, 124, 125
Ensler, Eve, 115; *Vagina Monologues*, 118

Eritrea, 22, 35, 82, 83, 86, 88, 90, 95n13, 95n18
Eritrean Liberation Front, 95n18
Eritrean People's Liberation Front, 95n18
Ertürk, Yakin, 124
Eshete, Warqenah, 50
essentialism, 45–46, 188
Ethiopia, 4, 6, 44–54, 83, 90, 95n18, 120. *See also* Italian–Ethiopian War
ethnicity, 2–3, 7, 11–12, 15, 23–24, 30, 89, 102, 104, 159–60, 175, 180–91, 210, 217, 242–44, 272, 274, 276
Etudiant Noir, L', 32
Europe, 2, 4, 5, 6, 21, 22, 24–25, 28–30, 31, 51, 56, 59, 70, 71, 83, 168, 173, 175, 197, 200, 236, 265n1
Evangelical Christianity, 28, 96n31
Executive Outcomes, 202–3
Ezra (Aduaka), 12, 196, 198–99, 203, 204, 208–12, 213, 216–17, 221, 225n54–55

Fanon, Frantz, 2, 212
FARDC, 122
fascism, 5, 44, 47, 48, 50, 51, 242. *See also* antifascism
"Father of African Independence." *See* Nkrumah, Kwame
Faye, Cheikh Faty, *Aube de sang*, 13, 232–33, 236–37, 238
FDLR (Forces Démocratiques de Libération du Rwanda), 130, 138n64
female genital mutilation, 109, 120
feminism, 3, 8, 82, 98, 100, 101, 105, 109; and resistance to military intervention, 80, 94n4
Fernandez, James, 173
Figgis, J. N., 27
film, 10, 80, 83; about women and war in Africa, 89–93. *See also* Hollywood
fistula, 118–20. *See also* obstetric fistula; rape-related fistula
Fistula Foundation at the Hamlin Fistula Hospitals, 120
Flame, 83, 90

Fontaine, Nasio, *Living in the Positive*, 213
food, 82, 102, 103, 104, 131, 145, 148, 160, 165, 188, 227n79. *See also* hunger
Fox News, 81
France, 13–14, 25–26, 28, 29–31, 32, 38n1, 39n22, 41n45, 156, 158, 159, 160, 161, 175, 177n7, 231–35, 237, 240n35, 241, 242–52, 254, 256, 257, 260, 262, 264, 265, 266n15, 267n25, 267n33, 268n47, 268n52, 269n62
Fraser, Robert, 180–81, 183, 187–89
Freetown, 200, 202, 203, 204, 214, 218
French (language), 4, 24, 25, 26, 29, 31, 33, 155, 159, 162, 166, 267n22, 269n63, 269n88
French Revolution, 262
French West Africa, 158
French-Algerian War, 243
Frente de Libertação de Moçambique (FRELIMO), 10, 142, 144
Friends of the Congo, 9, 114, 115
Front de Libération Nationale (FLN), 247, 268n47
Front National, 242, 243
Fulani, 182, 278n13
Fussell, Paul, 272

G8, 224n35
Ga, 279n29
Gabbras, 105
Gao, Mali, 157, 158, 161
Garvey, Marcus, 34
gender, 3, 4, 7, 9–10, 12, 82–86, 90, 128–29, 141–42, 147, 150, 165, 171, 188–89, 191, 217, 262. *See also* women; gender-based violence
gender-based violence, 83, 116–17, 125, 127. *See also* genital mutilation; rape
Geneva Convention, 51, 96n27, 136n31
genital mutilation. *See* female genital mutilation
genocide, 114, 116, 124, 125, 128, 130, 160, 222n4
Germany, 25–26, 231
Gershoni, Yekutiel, 203, 226n66
Gettleman, Jeffrey, 105–6, 118

Ghana, 30, 31, 32, 33, 36, 53, 273, 279n29
Gikuyu, 4–5
girls, 83, 84, 93, 94n4, 96n31, 104, 109, 114, 116, 120–21, 126, 128, 129, 130, 145, 148, 160, 162, 165, 170, 172, 175, 219, 220
Global Witness, 199
Glover, Jonathan, 2–3
Going Home, 84, 90
Gold Coast Independent, 32
Gold Coast Leader, 41n51
Gold Coast Weekly Review, 33
Goma, 125, 130, 131
Gomes, Flora, 92
Gowon, Yakubu, 273, 275, 276, 278n21
Graham-Douglas, Nabo B., 192n23
Great Britain, 5, 6, 7, 23, 25, 26, 28, 29, 30, 31, 34, 38, 38n1, 39n20, 40n35, 41n46, 44, 47, 49, 50, 53, 56–73, 102, 103, 203, 265n1, 278n13
Great Depression, 48
Great Insurrection, 257, 260, 263–65
"Greatest Generation," 22, 37
Greek (language), 25
Green, Edward, 143
Gueckedou refugee camp, 90
Guest, Edwin, 29
Guéye, Lamine, 233
Guide de Dahomey, Le, 32
Guinea, 90
Guinea Bissau, 38n1
Gumede, William, "Africa Remains Shrouded in Myth," 15–16
Gurney, Ivor, 271; "To His Love," 275

Hague, The, 126
Haiti, 39n13, 227n78–79
Halbwachs, Maurice, 250; *The Collective Memory*, 251
Half Assini, 33–34
Hall, Stuart, 12, 201
Hamilton, James, 6, 45
Handelman, Don, 176
Harewood, David, 200
Hargreaves, Alec G., 242–46, 249, 262, 265; *Multi–ethnic France*, 244; *Voices from the North African Immigrant Community in France*, 243
Hari, Johann, "Congo's Tragedy: The War the World Forgot," 116
Harris, Roxy, 23, 39n11
Harvard Humanitarian Initiative, 9, 114
Hausa, 158, 182, 278n13
HEAL Africa campaign, 9, 114, 130; hospital, 118
health, 119, 145, 156, 161, 163, 175, 209; care, 129, 143, 144, 146, 211
Hegel, Georg Wilhelm Friedrich, 1, 207, 224n32, 226n73
Herbert, Bob; "Invisible War," 133n7
Hernández, Pilar, 150
Hesford, Wendy, 200, 217, 219
Higgins, Maryellen, 197, 208
HIV, 121, 217. *See also* AIDS
Hochschild, Adam, *King Leopold's Ghost*, 128
Holland, 39n20
Hollywood, 10, 12, 196–97, 199, 204, 208, 224n34
homosexuality, 16, 80, 94, 242
Honwana, Alcinda, 143, 149, 209, 211, 213, 214; *Child Soldiers in Africa*, 84
hooks, bell, 101; *Talking Back: Thinking Feminist, Thinking Black*, 100
Hotel Rwanda, 197
Hounsou, Djimon, 197
Hu Chow Yuan, 50; "Chinese Opinion," 50
human rights, 12, 84, 113, 115, 121, 126, 147, 150, 196, 198, 199, 200, 205, 209, 210, 215, 217, 219, 220, 221, 226n67
Human Rights Watch, 9, 83, 114, 116, 126
humanism, 13, 195, 217, 221
Hume, David, 224n33, 226n73
hunger, 103, 148, 213, 254
Hutus, 91, 188, 197, 222n4

Ibadan, 31, 271, 273, 277n3, 279n39
ibaraden, 10, 155, 156, 157, 161, 162, 163, 166, 170, 172, 174, 175
Ibo, 277n2. *See also* Igbo

identity, 2, 4, 5, 11, 12, 21–22, 24, 29–31, 33, 37, 41n46, 52, 95n10, 142, 176, 180, 181, 184, 188, 189–90, 191, 244, 250, 251, 252, 254, 256, 263
Ifeajuna, Emmanuel, 272–74, 275, 276, 278n12, 278n21
Ifoghas, 155, 156, 158, 159, 160, 162, 164, 166, 167, 169
Igbo, 11, 182–84, 278n13; language, 183. *See also* Ibo
Igreja, Victor, 143, 149
Ijaw, 184, 277n1
Ike, Chukwuemeka, *Sunset at Dawn*, 183
Ikwerre, 184
Imbruglia, Natalie, 118; Campaign to End Fistula, 118
Imesli-n-Tenere (Voices of the Desert), 163, 168, 171, 175
immigration, 242, 257, 264, 266n16, 267n25
imperialism, 5, 49. *See also* anti-imperialism
In the Wake of War, 91
independence, 1–7, 95n10. 236; Algerian, 243; Biafran, 182, 273; Eritrean, 90, 95n18; Ethiopian, 44–54; Eritrean, 90, 98–99, 102–4, 108; Guinea-Bissauan, 92; Kenyan, 56–73, 98; and language, 21–38, 38n1, 42n60, 42–43n66; Malian, 160; Nigerian, 278n13; Rhodesian, 142; Senegalese, 232, 235, 237
Independent, 16, 116
India, 30, 31, 34, 40n27, 120
indirect rule, 29, 30, 41n51. *See also* direct rule
Indymedia network, 50–51
Integrated Regional Information Network (IRIN), 9, 120
International African Friends of Abyssinia, 53
International Criminal Court (ICC), 117, 130; Rome Statute of the, 114, 126, 134–35n18
International Crisis Group (ICG), 9
International Relief Committee, 122, 127
International Rescue Committee, 116; Aid in Congo, 133n9

International Voices of Women Festival, 164
International Women's Day Vigil, 115
Internet, 9, 16, 114, 115, 121, 127, 129, 225n63
Invisible Children, 84, 91
Invisible Children Movement, 84
Iraq, 80
Ireland, 2
Islam, 3, 157–58, 167, 177–78n7. *See also* Muslims
isolationism, 48
Italy, 5, 6, 26, 46–54
Italian-Ethiopian War, 4, 5, 6, 44–54
Itote, Waruhiu, *"Mau Mau" General*, 71, 99
Itsekiris, 184
Ituri, 120, 138n49
Iyayi, Festus, *Heroes*183

Jackson, Lisa, 113
Jayawardena, Kumari, *Feminism and Nationalism in the Third World*, 98
Jefferson, Thomas, 31, 226n73
Johns Hopkins Bloomberg School of Public Health, "Obstetric Fistula: Ending the Silence, Easing the Suffering," 119
Johnson, Hilde, 119
Johnson, Samuel, 25
Johnson Sirleaf, Ellen, 85
Jones, Sir William, 28, 40n27
Jos, 120

Kabyles, 14, 241–65, 268n55
Kabyles du Pacijque (Lallaoui), 14, 241
Kabylia, 241, 242, 250, 255, 262
Kalabaris, 184
Kallon, Mamusum, 213
Kalouaz, Ahmed, *Point kilométrique* 190, 246
Kamajoh, 206
Kamanyola, 128
Kamara, Mamodou Turay, 213
Kant, Immanuel, 224n33, 226n73
Kariuki, Josiah Mwangi, *"Mau Mau" Detainee*, 71
Karua, Martha, 109

Kayingeli, Fatima, 128
Keita, Fodeba, "Aube africaine," 232
Keita, Modiba, 160
Kel Adagh, 156, 158
Kel Essuk, 164, 169, 170
Kel Isuha, 162, 164, 166, 167
Kel Tamajaq. *See* Tuareg
Kennedy, John F., 129
Kenya, 1, 5, 34, 38n1, 53; African Union, 59; and cattle-raiding conflicts, 98, 100, 104, 108; presidential election of 2007, 98, 100, 106–8; Vision 2030, 109. *See also* Mau Mau movement
Kenyatta, Jomo, 34, 37, 53, 55n40
Kericho, 105
Kettane, Nacer, *Le sourire de Brahim*, 246, 247
Khadaffi, 161. *See also* Qaddafi, Muammar
Khatibi, Abdelkebir, *La mémoire tatouée*, 251, 269n58
Kidal, 10, 11, 155, 156, 158–65, 167, 168, 169, 172, 175
Kikuyu, 5, 56, 58–62, 64–65, 70–71, 104, 106
Kikuyu Association (KA), 58–59
Kikuyu Central Association (KCA), 59
Kilson, Martin L., Jr., 41n49
Kimathi, Dedan, 60, 99
King's African Rifles, 60
Kipling, Rudyard, 82, 195
Kipsigis, 100, 104, 105
Kisii, 106
Kleijn, Wim, 149
Kourouma, Ahmadou, 84
Krio, 39
Kristof, Nicholas, "Alone and Ashamed," 118, 120
Kroobay, 218
Kungu, Chief Waruhiu wa, 59
kwashiorkor, 273

Lafore, Laurence, 48
Lagos Weekly Record, 32
Laitin, David, 30
Lallaoui, Medhi, 241–70, 267n42, 267n43, 268n55, 269n58, 269n88; *Les Beurs de Seine*, 248; *Kabyles du Pacifique*, 14, 241; *Une nuit d'octobre*, 248
Lamu, 103, 104
Lancashire Fusiliers, 60
land, 5, 14, 30, 57–58, 59, 61, 71, 149, 178n12, 200, 248–53, 255, 259, 261, 262, 263, 264, 265, 276
language, 4–5, 11, 22, 23–25, 28, 29–31, 37–38, 40n27, 105, 166, 180–85, 189, 190, 241, 265n1. *See also* colonial languages; naming
Laronde, Michel, 246, 266n16
Latin, 25, 34
League of Nations, 5, 6, 46–48; Covenant, 44, 48
Lebanon, 2
Lenin, Vladimir I., 34
Leopold, King, 128
Le Page, Robert, 24, 37; *Acts of Identity*, 23
Le Pen, Jean-Marie, 242, 266n11
Levine, Donald, 47
Lewis, Stephen, 116
Liberia, 52, 84–85, 90, 91–92; rape in, 119, 132n2, 135n21; war in, 222–23n12, 223n14, 223n24, 225n54, 226n66
Liberia: A Fragile Peace, 91
Liberia: An Uncivil War, 91–92
Liberians United for Reconciliation and Democracy (LURD), 92
Libya, 17–18n34, 157, 161, 168, 175, 222–23n12
lieux de mémoire, 14, 240n39, 242, 250, 253, 254, 256, 257, 258, 261, 266n9
Lincoln University, 34, 42n60
"linguistic betrayal," 37–38
linguistic community, 23, 31
linguistics, 3, 5, 11, 21–38, 39n11, 189, 245
Literary Road to Empowerment, 109
literature, 13, 14, 29, 98, 109, 183, 209, 237, 242, 243, 245–48, 268n47, 275
Lomé Peace Accord, 226n67
London School of Economics, 34
Long Way Gone (Beah), 12, 84, 196, 201–2, 204, 208, 209, 212–17, 221

Lonsdale, John, 190–91
Loomba, Ania, 12, 205
Lorcin, Patricia M. E., 241
Lord's Resistance Army, 84
Loroupe, Tegla, 105–6. *See also* Tegla Loroupe Peace Foundation
Lubkemann, Stephen, 142
Lumo: One Woman's Struggle to Heal in a Country Beset by War, 118
Lumumba, Patrice, 34, 37
Luo, 100, 104
Lykes, M. Brinton, 150
Lyons, Tanya, 83

Maasai, 104
Mabon, Armelle, 231
MacKinnon, Catharine, 7
Macklin, Audrey, "Like Oil and Water, with a Match," 83
Macua: language, 144; communities, 146
Maendeleo ya Wanawake (MYWO), 103
Mai Mai, 119, 124
malaria, 103
Malawi, Lake, 40n21
Maleki, 241
Mali, 10, 155–77
Mali Empire, 24
Maloba, Wunyabari, 60, 62
Mande, 24
marabouts, 162, 164, 170, 171, 177–78n7
Maraire, J. Nozipo, *Zenzele: A Letter for My Daughter*, 83
Marker, Chris, 92
Marley, Bob, *Exodus*, 214
marriage, 105, 120, 144, 159, 163, 172, 174
Marsabit Women Advocacy and Development Organization of Northern Kenya (MWADO), 100, 105
Martin, Charles. *See* Eshete, Warqenah
Martinique, 32
Marx, Karl, 34, 200, 223n14
Marxism, 200, 223n14
masculinity, 84, 122, 201, 207
Mau Mau in Kenya, 61
Mau Mau movement, 4–5, 6–7, 8, 9, 56–73; British depiction of, 56–57, 61; and British government responses, 60–62; depiction as terrorist movement, 62, 65, 66; emergence of, 57–60; and land, 57–58, 61, 71; news coverage of, 62–72; women and the, 99, 102–4, 108
Mazrui, Alamin M., 24, 26, 30–31, 37, 41n45–46
Mazrui, Ali A., 2, 24, 26, 30–31, 35, 37, 41n45–46
Mbembe, Achille, 12, 196, 216, 218
McChesney, Robert, 6, 45
McCrum, Robert, 41n46
McCrummen, Stephanie, 106
McCullin, Donald, 274, 279n32
McGreal, Chris, 116
Meconta District, 143–44
Médecins Sans Frontières, 116, 138n49
media, 1, 2, 5–6, 12, 15–16, 81, 100, 156, 161, 243; efforts to end rape in the DRC, 9, 113, 114–16, 117–23, 127; and the Italo-Ethiopian War, 44–54; and the Kenyan presidential elections of 2007, 106, 107; and the Mau Mau movement, 56–73; and the Nigerian civil war, 273–74. *See also* alternative media; Western media
Mediterranean, the, 245, 248, 249, 264
Mendoza-Denton, Norma, 37
Mérimée, Prosper, 236
Messaouid, Samia, 248
Meyer, Karl, *Dust of Empire*, 129
Michel, Marc, 233
Michelman, Fredric, 235–36
Middle East, 2, 30, 93
migration, 157, 158, 159, 161, 175, 210
missionaries, 2, 3, 28–29, 30, 32, 34
Mitterrand, François, 242
Mobutu era, 129
modernism, 271
Moïnfar, Aména, 14
Momoh, Joseph, 222n12
Monrovia, 92
MONUC (Mission de l'Organisation des Nations Unies en République Démocratique du Congo), 130–31, 140n95

Morrison, Toni, 217
Mortu Nega, 92
Mosely, Sarah, 116, 117, 122, 127
Mouralis, Bernard, 238n4
Mozabites, 241
Mozambique, 1, 9–10, 17–18n34, 38n1, 40n35, 84, 141–50, 203, 209
Mpingwe, 28, 40n31
Mugo, Beth, 109
Mugo, Micere, 99
multilingualism, 23, 24, 30, 33
Murphy, William, 210, 211, 212
Mushikiwabo, Louise, 15–16
music, 158, 159, 163, 165–67, 188, 203–4, 213, 243, 272
Muslims, 182, 241, 243–45. *See also* Islam
Mussolini, Benito, 48; "Sylvia e Tafari," 51
Mvuyekure, Philippe, 91

Namibia, 17–18n34, 38n1, 42n60
naming, 95n10, 105, 180–81, 186–87
Nampula Province, 143
Nance, Kimberly, 215
narratology, 99
National Children's Week, 172
National Geographic Special Issue: Africa: Whatever You Thought, Think Again, 120
National Negro Congress, 53
nationalism, 30, 31, 32, 34, 35, 37, 41n49, 52–53, 211, 263. *See also* Mau Mau movement; nationalist movements; Nigerian civil war; Pan-Africanism; Western education
nationalist movements, 3–4, 5, 98, 178n12. *See also* nationalism
nation-state, 1, 2, 156, 157, 176, 178n10, 191
Nazis, 50, 232
Nderi, Senior Chief, 60, 64
N'Diaye, Mariame, 214
Ndumbe, Anyu, 203
Nedjma (Yacine), 241, 242, 243, 244
Négritude, 32, 233
Negro World, 32

neocolonialism, 14, 31, 187, 200, 208, 210, 235, 238. *See also* anticolonialism; colonialism; postcolonialism
neoimperialism, 94n4
New Caledonia, 14, 248, 250, 256, 257, 259, 260, 265
New Times and Ethiopian News, 6, 44, 53
New World, 25, 39n21
New York Times, 6, 7, 9, 48, 57, 62–63, 64, 65, 69–72, 105, 118, 120, 133n7
news. *See* alternative media; media; newspapers
newspapers, 5, 6, 16, 32–34, 42, 44–54, 63, 70, 74n37, 246
NGOs, 11, 113, 115, 117, 118, 131, 139n78, 143, 144, 147, 157, 158, 159, 167, 173, 175
Ngugi wa Thiong'o, 5, 22, 99
Niger, 157, 169, 178n12
Niger River, 276
Nigeria, 1, 10, 180–91, 271–76, 278n12–13, 278n22, 279n34; eastern region of, 181–82, 184, 273, 274, 277n2, 278n13, 278n22; Federal Military Government of, 273; fistula in, 120; midwestern state of, 182, 277n1; northern region of, 181–82, 184, 276, 278n13; River States of, 277n1
Nigerian civil war, 11, 14–15, 180–85, 271–76, 278n12
night commuters, 84
Nkrumah, Kwame, 5, 22, 33–35, 36, 37, 42n59, 44n66, 44n61, 44n66, 223n14
Nkunda, General, 130
Noddings, Nel, 100
Noiriel, Gérard, 245; *Le creuset français*, 242
Nolte, Nick, 197
nomads, 71, 156, 157, 158, 162, 164, 170, 175
nontraumatic fistula. *See* obstetric fistula
Nora, Pierre, 14, 242, 250, 253, 266n9; *Realms of Memory*, 252, 269n63
Nordstrom, Carolyn, 143
North Africa, 14, 24, 157, 159, 242–46, 266n16, 267n22
North Kivu, 125, 128, 130–31

Northern Ireland, 2, 279n32
Nsukka, 275
NT&EN. See *New Times and Ethiopia News*
Nwakanma, Obi, 183
Nwauwa, Apollos, 31
Nwapa, Flora, *Never Again*, 183
Nyanza Province, 104–5
Nyasa, Lake, 40n21
Nzegwu, Nkiru, 3
Nzima (language), 33, 42n59
Nzimiro, Ikenna, 182–83

OAU. *See* Organization of African Unity
Obama, Barack, 3
obstetric fistula, 113; causes of, 119; medical consequences of, 120; estimates of, 120. *See also* fistula; rape-related fistula
Ogoni, 184, 276
Ogun, 4
Ogunfalobi, Kayode Omoniyi, 11–12
Ogunyemi, Chikwenye, 102
Ojukwu, Chukwuemeka Odumegwu, 182, 278n22
Okara, Gabriel, *The Fisherman's Invocation*, 276
Okigbo, Christopher, 15, 271, 273, 274–75, 279n39, 279n43
Okri, Ben, 11, 180–81, 183–91; *Astonishing the Gods*, 11, 180–81, 185–88, 190–91; *Dangerous Love*, 181; "In the Shadow of War," 181; *Incidents at the Shrine*, 11, 180, 186; *Infinite Riches*, 188–89; "Laughter beneath the Bridge," 11, 12, 180–81, 183–85, 187, 189–91; *Stars of the New Curfew*, 181, 186; "Worlds that Flourish," 181
Olmsted, Frederick Law, 277n8
On the Frontlines: Child Soldiers in DRC, 84, 92–93
Onwudiwe, Ebere, 182
Operation Cowboy, 64
Operation Fine Girl, 93
Operation Jock Scott, 60
"Operation No Living Thing," 204
Oprah Winfrey Show, 118

Orange Democratic Movement (ODM), 106
Ordinance of Villers-Cotterêts, 39n22
Organization of African Unity (OAU), 5, 34, 225n66, 226n66; Convention, 90
Organization of Angolan Women (OMA), 90
Orient, 28, 40n28, 47, 201, 259
Orient Review, 32
Orientalism, 28, 47, 201
orphans, 101, 161, 226, 241, 277n2
Osaghae, Eghosa, E., 182
Ostler, Nicholas, *Empires of the Word*, 24
Osundare, Niyi, 12–13
Otieno, Wambui Waiyaki, 9, 101, 102–3, 104; *Mau Mau's Daughter*, 99
Ousmane, Sembene, *Camp de Thiaroye*, 232
Owen, Wilfred, 271–72, 273, 274, 279n35; "Anthem for Doomed Youth," 274

Pakistan, 120
Pambazuka News, 135n23
Pan-Africanism, 5, 6, 34, 44, 46, 50, 52–54, 223n14
Pan-Africanist Conference, 1900, 52
Pankhurst, Sylvia, 6, 49–50, 53. See also *New Times and Ethiopia News*
Panzi Hospital, 122, 124
Parent, Sabrina, 13–14
Paris, France, 246, 247, 248, 249, 252, 254, 255, 256, 258, 260, 261, 266n15
Parisian Commune, 258, 259, 260
paternalism, 12, 31, 196
patriarchy, 83, 205, 211
peace building, 7, 8, 81, 82, 84, 117, 127–28, 131, 170. *See also* Tegla Loroupe Peace Foundation
peacekeeping, 87, 91–92, 128, 133n7, 226n66
performance, 10, 11, 155–73, 175–76, 177–78n7, 187, 204
Perlmutt, Bent-Jorgen, 118
photography, 10, 50, 51, 165, 209, 217, 218, 220, 221, 250, 256, 260, 274

pidgin, 24, 39n13
Pieterse, Jan Nederveen, 12
plays, 10–11, 13–14, 99, 156, 157, 158, 161–76, 232–33, 235–38. *See also* theater
poetry, 12, 13–15, 38, 82, 156, 158, 161, 162, 163, 164, 166–68, 195, 209, 217–21, 226n72, 227n79, 232–35, 238, 240n40, 241, 242; war, 271–26, 277n11, 279n38–39, 280n53
police, 60, 64–70, 90, 107, 119, 126, 129, 246, 247
Popolo d'Italia, 51
Pordzik, Ralph, 185–86
Port Harcourt, 276
Portugal, 21, 24–25, 38n1, 39n21, 40n35
Portuguese (language), 144
postcolonialism, 1, 2, 12, 13, 86, 156, 180, 187, 209; and the DRC, 128. *See also* anticolonialism; colonialism; neocolonialism
postmodernism, 180, 190
poverty, 119–23, 129, 161, 172, 217, 218, 219, 246
Pratt, Marion, 126
Prince of Wales College, 34
propaganda, 49, 51, 57, 60–61
Protocol on the Rights of Women in Africa, 7
Purdue University, 85

Qaddafi, Muammar, 223n14. *See also* Khadaffi
Queen of Sheba, 47

race, 30, 48, 51, 52, 71, 80, 102, 104, 148, 189, 205, 217, 218, 226n73, 234, 235, 242, 245. *See also* racism
Race Nègre, 32
racism, 28, 31, 32, 47, 48, 49, 58, 82, 101, 201, 202, 232, 235, 242, 243, 244, 245, 246, 247, 248, 249, 262, 266n11. *See also* race
radio, 160, 161, 164, 174
Radio Tisdas, 159, 162, 163, 165
Raise Hope for Congo campaign, 129
Rambo, 173, 201–2, 214

Rampton, Ben, 23, 39
rape, 4, 82, 83, 93, 184, 189, 220; in the Eastern DRC, 9–10, 113–31; of elderly women, 120, 124; and effects on communities, 122–23, 124; and effects on men, 122, 123; efforts to end, 113, 114–16, 117–23, 125, 127, 130–31; efforts at healing after, 127; and fistula, 113, 118; and genocide, 125, 130; in literature, 184; and male domination, 123, 129; motivations for, 123–24, 141; in Mozambique, 142, 143, 145–46; prosecution of, 125–26, 129, 139n73; and war, 113–31, 142, 143, 145–46
"Rape as a Weapon of War in the Congo": Part 2: The Savagery, 116, 117, 120; Part 3: The Healing and What You Can Do to Help, 117–18
rape-related fistula, 113, 118; causes of, 120; medical consequences of, 121–22; social consequences of, 121–22; surgical challenges surrounding, 120. *See also* fistula; obstetric fistula
Rasmussen, Susan, 10
realism, 185, 201
reconstruction, 7, 81, 90, 142, 143. *See also* recovery
recovery, 5, 10, 14, 108, 128, 141–50, 216, 255
Red Cross, 50, 51; International, 51; Norwegian, 51
refugees, 50, 84, 89, 90, 91, 96n26, 156, 159, 169, 198, 208, 212; internal, 90, 129, 208, 212; Nigerian, 273, 277n2
reggae, 204, 213–14
regionalism, 2, 182. *See also* Decree no. 34
Registre, Judithe, 121
Rehn, Elizabeth, 84
religion, 3, 6, 24, 29, 60, 61, 102, 143, 161, 168, 170, 218
Rendille, 105
representational dilemma, 6, 7, 46–48, 54. *See also* Western media
representational myths, 12, 196. *See also* Western media

Resistência Nacional Moçcambicana (RENAMO), 10, 142, 144
Réveil, 32
Revolutionary United Front. *See* RUF
Rhodesia, 38n1, 142
Rice, Edward, 40n31
Richards, Paul, 203, 210, 225n40, 226n64
Richards Constitution, 181
Richelieu, Cardinal, 25
Richters, Annemiek, 149
Rift Valley Province, 104–5
rites of passage, 186–87
Roberts, Granville, 61
Robinson Crusoe, 197
Rollins, Leslie, 53
romantic movement, 28
Rosello, Mireille, 246, 251, 252, 255, 261, 262, 268n51, 269n58, 269n63
Rosenberg, Isaac, 271
Royal Africa Company, 40n35
Ruddick, Sara, 82, 94n8
RUF (Revolutionary United Front), 199–205, 222n12, 223n14, 223n24, 225n40, 225n44
Rusesabagina, Paul, 222n4
Russia, 223n24. *See also* Union of Soviet Socialist Republics
Rwanda, 1, 2, 16, 17–18n34, 114, 116, 119, 128, 136n32, 188, 197, 222n4

Sahara, 24, 30, 156, 158, 159, 162, 241
Said, Edward, 28, 47, 197
Salwen, Michael, 46
San Soleil, 92
Sangari, Kumkum, *Recasting Women: Essays in Colonial History*, 98
Sankoh, Foday, 223n14
Saro-Wiwa, Ken, 277n1, 278n22; *The Singing Anthill*, 276; *Sozaboy: A Novel in Rotten English*, 183, 277n2
Sassoon, Siegfried, 271
Satyagraha, 34
Schuler Deschryver, Christine, 121
Scotland, 45
Scramble for Africa, 25, 29, 30
Second Congress of Negro Writers and Artists, 22

segregation, 6, 47, 52
Selassie, Haile, 42–43n66, 47–48, 50, 95n18
semistructured interviews, 9, 141, 143
Sen, Amartya, 11–12, 188–90
Senegal, 13–14, 231–38
Senghor, Léopold Sédar, 32–33, 37, 232–35, 238; *Hosties noires*, 233; "Tyaroye," 13–14, 232–35
sexism, 3, 82, 101
Shakespeare, William, 275
Sharp, Michael, 14–15
Shaw, Carolyn Martin, 60
Shaw, George Bernard, 41n46
Sheikh Ali, 103
Shohat, Ella, 199, 200, 203, 206
Sideris, Tina, 143
Sierra Leone, 1, 10, 12, 39n13, 53, 83, 84, 90, 195–222, 222–23n1, 225n54, 226n64, 226n66–67, 226n70, 226n72, 227n78
Sierra Leone Weekly, 32
Sinai, Lumo, 118
Singer, P. W., 84
Sirleaf, Ellen Johnson. *See* Johnson Sirleaf, Ellen.
60 Minutes, 122
sketches, des, 10, 156
slavery, 47, 120, 165, 166, 177n7, 226–27n73
slave trade, 24, 39n20, 40n35, 236
socialism, 34, 49, 242
Solomon, King, 47
Somalia, 1
song, 162, 163, 164, 165, 166, 167, 178, 204, 74n37. *See also* music
Songhai, 155, 158, 165
Sons of Azawagh, 168, 169, 174
Sorenson, John, 47
South Africa, 1, 10, 17–18n34, 25, 26, 38n1, 89–90, 93, 202, 203, 206, 208, 224n35, 227n78, 227n80; support for RENAMO, 142
South African Defence Force, 203
South Kivu, 93, 124, 131
Southern Rhodesia, 38n1. *See also* Zimbabwe
Sow, Thierno Faty, *Camp de Thiaroye*, 232

Soyinka, Wole, 279n39
Spain, 25, 26, 39n21, 279n43
Spanish Civil War, 279n43
Spivak, Gayatri, 208
St. Lucia, 24
Stack, Jonathan, 92
Stam, Robert, 199, 200, 203, 206
STAND campaign, 9, 114
Stapleton, Tim, 202
Stephen Lewis Foundation, 133n9
Sterling, Cheryl, 4, 12
stereotypes, 1, 3, 4, 8, 10, 12, 16, 63, 80, 81, 162, 204, 206, 207, 224n34, 235
Stevens, Siaka, 222n12
Stoller, Paul, 155
Stora, Benjamin, 248
Sudan, 1, 119, 120
suffragists, 6, 49, 50
Sunday Times Magazine, 279n32
Swahili, 9, 30

Tabouret-Keller, Andrée, 24, 37; *Acts of Identity*, 23
Tadjer, Akli, 268n45; *Les ANI de "Tassali,"* 247, 248; *Le porteur de cartable*, 247
Talk Future Petition's "Global Call for Action: Demand End to War Rapes in Goma," 130
Tamajaq (language), 10, 155, 159–61, 162, 164, 166, 167, 168, 176
Tanzania, 17–18n34, 84, 91
Taoudeine salt mines, 160, 161
Taylor, Charles, 91, 92, 222–23n12, 223n14, 226n66
Tegla Loroupe Peace Foundation, 100, 106, 110n14. *See also* Loroupe, Tegla
terrorism, 7, 57, 62, 63, 64, 65–66, 69–71, 72, 114, 123, 161
textual strategies, 13, 233, 234, 235
theater, 10, 243
Thiaroye, massacre of, 13–14
Thiaroye terre rouge (Diop), 13, 232–33, 235–36, 238
Thumboo, Edwin, 21, 23, 32
Those Whom Death Refused. See *Mortu Nega*
Tilwat Jeunesse, 163, 164, 167, 172, 173

Time, 48
Times, 57, 62, 63, 64, 65, 67–69, 72
tirailleurs, 13, 231, 233, 234, 236, 237, 238
Tordesillas, treaty of, 39n21
Toxamen, 172
trade, 24, 33, 50, 158, 177–78n7, 201, 223n14. *See also* slave trade
Traore, Moussa, 160
traumatic fistula. *See* rape-related fistula
Travelers of the Desert, 168, 170, 172, 175
Trench, Archbishop Richard Chenevix, 35–37
Trevor-Roper, Hugh, 1
Tristan, Anne, *Le silence du fleuve*, 248
truth and reconciliation commissions (TRCs), 126, 208, 209, 216–17, 226n67, 226n70
Tshiyembe, Mwayila, 190–91
Tuareg, 10–11, 155–77, 177n7, 178n10, 178n12, 241, 263
Tully, Melissa, 5–7
Turner, Victor, 176
Turshen, Meredeth, 143
Tutsis, 91, 188, 222n4
"Tyaroye" (Senghor), 13–14, 232–35

Uganda, 1, 31, 84, 91, 93, 96n31
Undiyaundeye, Udida, 182
UNICEF, 119
Union of Soviet Socialist Republics, 279n30. *See also* Russia
United Nations, 92, 95n18, 113, 116, 197, 216, 226n66, 226n72; efforts against rape in the DRC, 9, 114, 117, 125, 127, 129, 130; Population Fund's Campaign to End Fistula, 118, 126; rape estimates, 124; Resolution 1804; Resolution 1820, 130; Resolution SC/9246; Security Council Resolution 1325, 96n27, 114, 126, 130; Security Council resolutions, 118. *See also* MONUC
United Nations Children's Agency, 119
United Nations Development Program, 226n72

United Nations First International Children's Parliament, 216
United Nations High Commissioner for Refugees, 84, 90, 129; *Handbook for the Protection of Women and Girls*, 96n26
United Nations Office for the Coordination of Human Affairs (UNOCHA), 120
United States of America, 2, 3, 6, 8, 34, 37, 41n46, 42n66, 44, 46, 47, 48, 50, 51, 52, 53, 56, 57, 62, 72, 81, 91, 92, 113, 114, 118, 119, 120, 127, 130–31, 156, 176, 197, 221, 223n13, 223n24, 225n66, 226n66, 265n1, 272, 279n30
United States Holocaust Memorial Museum, 127
United States House Resolution 1227, Condemning Sexual Violence in the DRC, 130
United States Pan-Sahel Initiative, 161
United States State Department African Affairs, 131
University College of East Africa at Makerere, 31
University College of the Gold Coast at Legon, 31, 32
University College of Ibadan, 31, 271
Urhobo (language), 183–84
utilitarians, 28
utopianism, 11, 181, 185

Vaid, Sudesh, *Recasting Women: Essays in Colonial History*, 98
Van Dijk, Teun, 63
Van Woudenberg, Anneke, 126
Vasey, E. A., 64
V-Day campaign, 115, 118
Vichy Regime, 242
Vietnam, 279n30, 279n32
Virgin Atlantic, 118
Virgin Unite, 118
Vlassenroot, Koen, 117
Voice of America, 81
Voices of the Desert. *See* Imesli-n-Tenere
Voice of Ethiopia, 53
Vosloo, Arnold, 202

Wadende, Pamela, 8
Walk to Beautiful, 120
Walker, Alice, 101
Walker, Nelson, III, 118
Wall, Lewis, 126–27
Wanjira, Muthoni, 109
War within the War: Sexual Violence against Women and Girls in the Congo, 83, 114, 116
Washington Post, 106
Waugh, Evelyn, 46
Werchick, Leah, 126
West, Michael, 53
West Africa, 13, 15, 39n20, 40n31, 52–53, 158, 161, 231–32, 272
West African Pilot, 42n60, 53
Western education, 29; and African independence, 31–33, 34
Western media, 2, 5, 6, 15–16, 46–48, 56, 196–98, 199, 200, 201, 204, 206, 221, 247. *See also* alternative media; Hollywood; media
"white man's burden," 12, 195, 196, 205
"White Man's Burden," 82, 195
Williams, Henry Sylvester, 52
Wilson, Amrit, *The Challenge Road*, 83
Wilson, Richard, 226n70
Woldemariam, Metasebia, 5–6
womanism, 8, 100, 101, 102, 105
women, 3–4, 7–10, 12, 51, 79–86, 98–108, 113–31, 141–50, 157, 165, 167, 169, 170–72, 173, 175, 187, 189, 269n60
Women and War, 93
Women for Women, 121
Women, War, and Peace, 84
Women's Bodies as a Battleground, 124
Women's Dignity Project, 120
World Food Program, 131
World Trade Organization Summit, 1999, 50
World War I, 15, 25, 247, 254, 256, 261; poetry, 271–72, 275
World War II, 25, 27, 30, 31, 37, 59, 231, 233, 237, 247
Wren, Robert M., 271
Wubneh, Mulatu, 47

xenophobia, 94n4, 242–43

Yacine, Kateb, 266n4; *Nedjma*, 241, 242, 243, 244
Yacine, Tassadit, 266n4
Yamarin, 11, 184
Yeats, W. B, 274, 277n9, 279n27, 280n53; "Easter in 1916," 272, 277n9; "The Second Coming," 273
Yoruba, 4, 32, 278n13, 278n23, 279n36
Young, Lola, 220
Young, Robert, 98

Youth Week, 172
youths, 5, 34, 109, 156, 158–70, 172, 174, 175, 204, 210, 212, 215, 241, 246. *See also* adolescents; children
Yugoslavia, 2, 119

Zaire, 1. *See also* Congo, Democratic Republic of
Zilberg, Jonathan, 9
Zimbabwe, 1, 38n1, 42, 82–83
Zimbabwean National Liberation War Veterans Association, 83

Rochester Studies in African History and the Diaspora

Toyin Falola, Senior Editor
The Frances Higginbotham Nalle Centennial Professor in History
University of Texas at Austin

(ISSN: 1092-5228)

Power Relations in Nigeria: Ilorin Slaves and their Successors
Ann O'Hear

Dilemmas of Democracy in Nigeria
Edited by Paul Beckett and Crawford Young

Science and Power in Colonial Mauritius
William Kelleher Storey

Namibia's Post-Apartheid Regional Institutions: The Founding Year
Joshua B. Forrest

A Saro Community in the Niger Delta, 1912–1984: The Potts-Johnsons of Port Harcourt and Their Heirs
Mac Dixon-Fyle

Contested Power in Angola, 1840s to the Present
Linda Heywood

Nigerian Chiefs: Traditional Power in Modern Politics, 1890s–1990s
Olufẹmi Vaughan

West Indians in West Africa, 1808–1880: The African Diaspora in Reverse
Nemata Blyden

The United States and Decolonization in West Africa, 1950–1960
Ebere Nwaubani

Health, State, and Society in Kenya
George Oduor Ndege

Black Business and Economic Power
Edited by Alusine Jalloh and Toyin Falola

Voices of the Poor in Africa
Elizabeth Isichei

Colonial Rule and Crisis in Equatorial Africa: Southern Gabon ca. 1850–1940
Christopher J. Gray

The Politics of Frenchness in Colonial Algeria, 1930–1954
Jonathan K. Gosnell

Sources and Methods in African History: Spoken, Written, Unearthed
Edited by Toyin Falola and Christian Jennings

Sudan's Blood Memory: The Legacy of War, Ethnicity, and Slavery in Early South Sudan
Stephanie Beswick

Writing Ghana, Imagining Africa: Nation and African Modernity
Kwaku Larbi Korang

Labour, Land and Capital in Ghana: From Slavery to Free Labour in Asante, 1807–1956
Gareth Austin

Not So Plain as Black and White: Afro-German Culture and History, 1890–2000
Edited by Patricia Mazón and Reinhild Steingröver

Writing African History
Edited by John Edward Philips

African Urban Spaces in Historical Perspective
Edited by Steven J. Salm and Toyin Falola

Yorùbá Identity and Power Politics
Edited by Toyin Falola and Ann Genova

Constructions of Belonging: Igbo Communities and the Nigerian State in the Twentieth Century
Axel Harneit-Sievers

Sufi City: Urban Design and Archetypes in Touba
Eric Ross

A Political History of The Gambia, 1816–1994
Arnold Hughes and David Perfect

The Abolition of the Slave Trade in Southeastern Nigeria, 1885–1950
A. E. Afigbo

HIV/AIDS, Illness, and African Well-Being
Edited by Toyin Falola and Matthew M. Heaton

Ira Aldridge: The African Roscius
Edited by Bernth Lindfors

Natural Resources and Conflict in Africa: The Tragedy of Endowment
Abiodun Alao

Crafting Identity in Zimbabwe and Mozambique
Elizabeth MacGonagle

Locality, Mobility, and "Nation": Periurban Colonialism in Togo's Eweland, 1900–1960
Benjamin N. Lawrance

Sufism and Jihad in Modern Senegal: The Murid Order
John Glover

Indirect Rule in South Africa: Tradition, Modernity, and the Costuming of Political Power
J. C. Myers

The Urban Roots of Democracy and Political Violence in Zimbabwe: Harare and Highfield, 1940–1964
Timothy Scarnecchia

Radicalism and Cultural Dislocation in Ethiopia, 1960–1974
Messay Kebede

The United States and West Africa: Interactions and Relations
Edited by Alusine Jalloh and Toyin Falola

Ben Enwonwu:
The Making of an African Modernist
Sylvester Okwunodu Ogbechie

Representing Bushmen:
South Africa and the Origin of
Language
Shane Moran

Afro-Brazilians: Cultural Production
in a Racial Democracy
Niyi Afolabi

Movements, Borders, and Identities
in Africa
Edited by Toyin Falola and
Aribidesi Usman

Africans and the Politics of
Popular Culture
Edited by Toyin Falola and
Augustine Agwuele

Political Culture and Nationalism in
Malawi: Building Kwacha
Joey Power

Women's Authority and Society in
Early East-Central Africa
Christine Saidi

Afro-Cuban Diasporas in the
Atlantic World
Solimar Otero

Narrating War and Peace in Africa
Edited by Toyin Falola and
Hetty ter Haar

Narrating War and Peace in Africa interrogates conventional representations of Africa and African culture—mainly in the twentieth and early twenty-first centuries—with an emphasis on portrayals of conflict and peace. While Africa has experienced political and social turbulence throughout its history, more recent conflicts seem to reinforce the myth of barbarism across the continent: in Nigeria, Rwanda, Somalia, Sierra Leone, Uganda, Kenya, Mozambique, Chad, South Africa, Zimbabwe, and Sudan. The essays in this volume address reductive and stereotypical assumptions of postcolonial violence as "tribal" in nature, and offer instead various perspectives—across disciplinary boundaries—that foster a less fetishized, more contextualized understanding of African war, peace, and memory. Through their geographical, historical, and cultural scope and diversity, the chapters in *Narrating War and Peace in Africa* aim to challenge negative stereotypes that abound in relation to Africa in general and to its wars and conflicts in particular, encouraging a shift to more balanced and nuanced representations of the continent and its political and social climates.

Contributors: Ann Albuyeh, Zermarie Deacon, Alicia C. Decker, Aména Moïnfar, Kayode Omoniyi Ogunfolabi, Sabrina Parent, Susan Rasmussen, Michael Sharp, Cheryl Sterling, Hetty ter Haar, Melissa Tully, Pamela Wadende, Metasebia Woldemariam, Jonathan Zilberg.

Toyin Falola is the Jacob and Frances Sanger Mossiker Chair in the Humanities and University Distinguished Teaching Professor at the University of Texas at Austin. Hetty ter Haar is an independent researcher in England.

www.ingramcontent.com/pod-product-compliance
Lightning Source LLC
Chambersburg PA
CBHW031705230426
43668CB00006B/111